THE BEST OF CALIFORNIA

The Best of
California

Some people, places and
institutions of the most
exciting state in the
nation, as featured in
California magazine,
1976-86

Capra Press
SANTA BARBARA

TO THE MEMORY OF ADRIENNE GOULD

The editors of *California* wish to thank their colleagues, Victoria Cebalo Irwin and Lisa Blansett, for their special care and concern with the preparation of this book.

Permission to use the following copyrighted material is gratefully acknowledged: "*California's* California and Vice Versa" by Kevin Starr first appeared in *New West/California** January 1986; "California Rising" by Wallace Stegner, October 1981; "Letter Home" by Mickey Kaus, June 1984; "Best Roads" by Jon Carroll, April 1981; "Welcome to the L.A. Freeway" by Tom Huth, August 1985; "Thunder Road" by David Barry, July 31, 1978; "Inside the Pink Palace" by Jon Bradshaw, May 10, 1976; "The World's Biggest Newspaper" by Rian Malan, appeared as "Paper Giant," October 1982; "Operation Wigwam" by Dan Noyes, Maureen O'Neill, and David Weir, December 1, 1980; "Almost 86'ed" by Anne Lamott, September 1985; "The Ontology of the Pitch" by Lynda Obst, October 1985; "How Success Almost Spoiled Chez Panisse" by Merrill Shindler, May 9, 1977; "The California Defense Establishment" by Ehud Yonay, appeared as "The Anatomy of U.S. Defense," October 1985; "The Founding Mother" by Reyner Banham, March 1985; "Your Browns and Reagans May Come and Go, But Jesse Endures..." by Gladwin Hill, July 1984; "Look, Then, at Harry Bridges" by James Hamilton, October 1984; "Garrett Hardin Is the Original Thinker's Original Thinker" by David Ehrenfeld, November 1984; "Gene Scott: A View From the Pew" by Neela Campbell, November 7, 1977; "Portrait of the Surfer as Middle-Aged Man" by Michael Parrish, May 1981; "Good Wine, Bad Blood" by Anthony Cook, November 8, 1976; "Sissy Het" by Charlie Haas, March 1985; "The Science of Edward Teller" by David Ehrenfeld, August 1985; "When Fame Puts Its Feathery Crowbar Under Your Rock" by Keith Abbott, April 1985; "A Poisoned Pen" by Page Stegner, August 1983; "The Long Goodbye" by Neil Morgan, June 1982; "Confronting the Sea Gods of the Northern Coast" by Tracy Johnston, April 1983; "Adventures in Paradise" by Steve Oney, November 1983; "The Politics of Big Sur" by Ehud Yonay, December 22, 1980; "My Neighborhood" by Ishmael Reed, March 1983; "The Uncity of the Future" by Tom Huth, May 1984; "Getting Away with Murder" by Peter Collier and David Horowitz, April 1982; "Letter From a Man in Jail" by Michael Hardy, December 1985; "God Rest Ye Merry Aaron and John" by John Sack, December 1985; "Best Books (1976-86)" by Digby Diehl, January 1986; "Best Movies (1976-86)" by Kenneth Turan, January 1986; "On Sophistication" by Cristina Clapp, May 1985.

*New West became *California* in October 1981.

Cover design by Marilyn Babcock
Painting: *View of the Bay, Pacific Palisades, 1985*
by Larry Cohen (courtesy of Hunsaker/Schlesinger Gallery)
Design and typography by Jim Cook

LIBRARY OF CONGRESS CATALOGUING IN PUBLICATION DATA
THE BEST OF CALIFORNIA
1. California—Social life and customs—Addresses, essays, lectures.
I. California magazine (Los Angeles, Calif.)
F866.2.B47   1986   979.4   85-29120
ISBN 0-88496-245-8 (pbk.)

Published by
CAPRA PRESS
Post Office Box 2068, Santa Barbara, California 93120

Table of Contents

V. NECROLOGY

VI. HOMETOWNS

VII. LAW AND ORDER

VIII. ARTS AND LETTERS

IX. FUTURE PROSPECTS

LIKE MOST PEOPLE in California, my wife and I came from someplace else. Looking around, we traveled one day from a sixteenth-century British inn, true to its time in every detail (except that it was built seven years ago), to a lighthouse overlooking a rolling sward that might have been the coast of Wales, to a Mediterranean villa hidden in the hills of Sonoma. We had bangers for breakfast before a walk-in fireplace, oysters of the region looking out on Tomales Bay, and that night, in a room made radiant by freshly cut flowers, wine from the proprietor's grapes and quail from the olive grove in back. Another time we had beer in a bar beside the Salton Sea (solace for the surrounding desolation) and drove home across the moonscape of Joshua Tree. In Death Valley we rode at sea level alongside a dry soda lake that stretched twenty-nine miles, and next day, seven thousand feet high in the Sierra, watched cameramen from a network crew swinging from the end of tethered cable, trying to close in on two men scaling a mountain wall by fingertip. Out of Ferndale, one of us took the narrow logging road winding through undisturbed hills to find on the other side, dropping sharply and under constant surveillance by eagles and hawks, the Pacific Ocean.

It is like that out here. California has more of most things than you would ever expect to see, and despite its great size—running lengthwise rather than horizontally—they are surprisingly accessible. Our new mail boy, who is one of the few natives on the staff, says he can ski the San Bernardino mountains in the morning and surf at Malibu in the afternoons, without speeding. Soon enough, there comes a sense of urgency about it all. You want to see what there is to be seen and get on with it—go other places. But too much more of California lies ahead, as anyone will tell you, places you *must* see if you haven't: the open mountain meadows of the northeast; the Saline Valley of the southeast, where there is a hot springs oasis, with thirty permanent residents; the trails at the top of Yosemite, where you can walk in a day from one cabin to the next, a hot meal awaiting your arrival; that little bed and breakfast just south of Mendocino, overlooking the ocean (but you'll need to book six months in advance)....

California, as has been said before and will be again further on in this book, is more a nation than a state. Hard to generalize about such things, but to the newly arrived resident, the people of this nation seem friendlier, too, than one these days has the right to expect, more courteous; in a distinctly visible way, more content with themselves and their place. They drive like stock-car racers, but considerately: if you're waiting at a crosstown street, they stop and wave you in, and they don't blow their horns. "Have a good day," the all-California salutation, which is received elsewhere like the sound of a fingernail scraping a windowpane, is genuine and well-intended out here. An old friend of mine back east said she was so pleased with the place where she lived she would find herself on a beautiful day singing the doxology. It's like that here. Called away, people who come from California, no matter how recently arrived, can't wait to get back.

As nations go, however, this one has no recognizable center. No Paris here, no London, or New York City. Certainly neither Los Angeles nor San Francisco, her most prominent cities, where residents make a great show of having little interest in (or even knowledge) of the other, will so serve. Nor Sacramento, the state capital of a near-invisible government. Nor San Diego, which is larger than San Francisco, but close-mouthed about it. A veteran newspaperman told me, when I first arrived, don't expect anybody to pay close attention to what you want them to hear. If they pick it up in L.A., they probably won't in Orange County. Anywhere you look there is little interest in what goes on only twenty-five miles away. In the state of California, there are 119 daily newspapers, more dailies than in any other state, with one of them (as will also be seen further on), the largest and most successful in the world. More than its share of television stations. And in a land where the car is a birthright, God knows how many radio stations. From this battery of information pounding away day and night on the eye and the ear, it may be assumed Californians know as much as anybody else about what is going on in the rest of the world. But for all their enthusiasm about their native state, and however elusive the reason to account for the fact, not much is available about the state of themselves.

Which is where, in 1976, we came in. Our territory is here—the people who live here, their ideas, traditions, institutions, their fears and desires. What we have sought to be from the first is for Californians, a *magazine,* in Kevin Starr's etymylogical sense: "a storehouse," as he writes in our January 1986 issue, "providing ammunition for the battle of identity, isolating and dramatizing the building blocks of personal and social self-knowledge while providing guidance for those in the emerging stages of their taste." A formal way of saying that *California* is about California.

As we mark now the tenth year of our preoccupation with such objectives, we offer you herewith some of the best of what we've been able to find out.

—HAROLD HAYES

I.
Prologue

KEVIN STARR

California's California and Vice Versa

TEN YEARS AGO, at a dinner party at novelist Paul Erdman's home in Northern California, I met Clay Felker. Born and raised in the Midwest, Felker had made journalistic history in the late-1960s as the editor who had helped the new New York define itself in the pages of *New York* magazine. Felker was now in the process of discovering California via a new magazine he was calling *New West*.

Something in Clay Felker's midwestern sensibility craved such acts of coastal definition. The Midwest—so massive, so solidly anchored, so fundamentally secure—does not engender the need for definition as a primary response in its inhabitants. One may celebrate the Midwest or wish to escape it; but the need to define it, endlessly to distinguish the subtleties of its composition, is not high on the list of midwestern priorities. Ask Harry Truman.

But Clay Felker was a midwesterner who had gone to New York. He was also a magazine editor of unerring instincts. He understood intuitively that the magazine came into history as a vehicle of definition for those—the new bourgeoisie of the eighteenth century—who were suffering what we would today call an identity problem. The word magazine has for its primary meaning "an arsenal, a storehouse for weaponry"; and this is what magazines have been doing since the eighteenth century: providing ammunition for the battle of identity, isolating and dramatizing the building blocks of personal and social self-knowledge while providing guidance for those in the emerging stages of their taste.

New York magazine helped the first back-to-the-city generation of young New Yorkers define for themselves the special promise, the magic even, of a New York that had not been intensely mythologized since the 1930s. It also provided a survival manual of basic information: about food, clothing, rentals, restaurants, entertainment and all those other areas of urban experience that call for taste, discernment and a rapidly expanding information base.

Having gone east and assisted the first generation of yuppies in defining the genre of urban living they were pioneering in their restored townhouses and reconverted lofts, Clay Felker, with a true magazine editor's instincts, was feeling by the mid-1970s that California was ready for a comparable act of definition.

Two generations of young people were converging in California, Felker believed: a local product, natives, born in the 1940s, highly educated, affluent, and Californian to the core; and an equally Californian group that had chosen to come to California because California—as a place, a dream, a myth—had bespoken itself to them in their twenties, promising, among other things, personal liberation, a more enjoyable lifestyle and, more subtly, a way of not surrendering completely to the rat race, of discovering a more exuberant, expansive round of days.

To return, as I have recently done, to those bound volumes of *New West*, beginning with the first issue, April 26, 1976, is to reexperience, in part, Clay Felker's process of definition. *New West* begins its career as a magazine laying down what Felker and crew considered the significant elements of the Californian identity.

A historian of California such as myself notes instantly that these early issues were in no way energized by what might be called nativist strains. *New West* was not, in other words, a thinking person's *Sunset*, nor the *Los Angeles Times* with color pictures, nor a middlebrow *Evergreen Review*, nor any other style or cluster of attitudes that might be traced to twentieth-century California: the aestheticizing Mediterraneanism of the turn-of-the-century genteel tradition, the arroyo culture of the Spanish Southwest with its passion for mission revival and arts and crafts, the Sierra Club backpacking syndrome, the pacifist/Beat sensibility of the Bay Area, the Zen of the central coast, the Baghdad-by-the-Bay fixation, whatever.

New West staked out a new sector, California Glitz, which, ten years later, impresses me as essentially an outsider's view of California, with a strong emphasis on the New York perspective. This is why, very soon, show biz began to dominate the magazine. Show biz was at once intelligible to the East Coast sensibility and at the same time Californian. In that first year, under the editorship of Dick Adler, *New West* came very close to becoming predominantly a show-biz magazine. We read about Barbra Streisand and her hairdresser boyfriend, about a new star by the name of Sylvester Stallone, about life at the top with Robert Evans and company (how sad that all turned out to be), about the suicide of Freddie Prinze, and we were challenged to ask such profound questions as: "Is Kunta Kinte the Next Fonzie?" The high point of this initial show-biz glitz phase, I suppose, was the cover of the December 20, 1976, issue, which featured those two great Californians, Dino De Laurentiis and King Kong.

At the same time it must be said that show-biz glitz, even in those early issues, never took over *New West* completely. It was just that the non-show-biz material had not yet achieved the autonomy of perspective that would later characterize the magazine under editor Jon Carroll. But Jerry Brown was, after all, on the cover of the premier *New West*. Governor Brown was described as the leader par excellence of those who were shaping the future of California. Neil Morgan, San Diego's superb columnist, wrote a piece on his generation of Californians, those who had chosen California after the Second World War, and their native-born offspring. Gail Sheehy profiled Helen Copley, publisher of the Copley newspapers, in an article that also managed to be a capsule history of power in the San Diego area since the 1940s. These and other articles—Jonathan Kirsch's insightful treatment of busing and the public schools in big-city California, a cover article on the Chowchilla kidnappings, Aaron Latham's report on the efforts of Reg Murphy to revitalize the *San Francisco Examiner* (Will Hearst III is currently pursuing this same noble task)—all underscored that *New West* was also carving out for itself a role as a newsmagazine capable of covering California straight, accurately, to the point and without the gee-whiz-this-is-California perspective that is always the danger when outsiders talk about the life and times of the Golden State. This investigative dimension would flourish under *New West's* second editor, Frank Lalli, whose instincts were primarily reportorial, and it would reach its climax in his regime with *New West's* investigation of the Peoples Temple in San Francisco.

This incident stands at the tragic center of the decade in terms of its final result, the most massive group suicide since Masada. An aura of ambiguity, however, still hovers about the entire affair. *New West's* investigation of the Peoples Temple had its intended result, I suppose, the bringing to light of a species of nasty fascism that could hold in its thrall innocent churchgoing folk, white and black alike. But the investigative articles, far from diminishing the Reverend Jim Jones's power, seemed perversely to increase that power by increments of paranoia, which Jones took with him into the heart of darkness in Guyana, with all-too-well-known results.

Looking back at these early issues, we also encounter an almost baroque exuberance in matters pertaining to lifestyle. The writers of *New West* sallied forth heroically in search of the best pasta, the best sushi, the ten best places to get pâté while marching with César Chávez. A food revolution was under way, and *New West* caught it enthusiastically: caught and described the lightening of American cuisine, the emergence of an indigenous approach to cookery, the concern for the healthfulness of food and drink, and the dawning golden age of California wine that Moira Johnston began to cover with such élan, commencing with her August 2, 1976, article on the Californian sweep of wine prizes at an important Paris tasting. Wine—its production, the feuding and flourishing of the state's wine families, the growth of new vineyards, connoisseurship and the exquisite interaction of wine and food—asserts itself in all ten volumes of *New West/California* as a primary, recurring concern. Whatever it is to be a Californian, wine somehow points the way.

Bound volumes of any good magazine await the historian's future use. In this regard, it must be said that, as of yet, *New West/California* still has much important work to do in covering and defining its territory. The great Valley of the San Joaquin remains largely un-represented in the harvest of the first decade. There is minimal coverage of agriculture, of Fresno, Sacramento, Chico, Bakersfield, Stockton, the Tejon Ranch and the peoples and traditions of this vast region. Not until the debut of Richard Rodriguez in September 1981 had the magazine published an authentically Hispanic voice. It took five years for there to be a major article on contemporary California art.

During Jon Carroll's editorship, the environment became a major concern of the magazine. Carroll brought an essentially 1960s-inspired Northern California vision to *New West*. Such a vision had its strengths. The environmental reporting of *New West* in the late 1970s and early 1980s is magnificent. The Center for Investigative Reporting, headquartered in San Francisco, revealed in the December 1, 1980, *New West* that the navy conducted underwater testing of nuclear weapons off the coast of San Diego and that certain personnel associated with that testing had later died of cancer. *New West* followed this article up in January 1981 with an expose of nuclear fuels used in foreign vessels just offshore of California. While lacking the sovereignty of New Zealanders, Californians reading these two articles might very well have asked serious questions, as New Zealand has now done, about the nuclear pollution of the Pacific.

The environmental focus of *New West* during these years was informed, celebratory and strongly preservationist. Ehud Yonay, writing in the December 22, 1980, *New West*, for instance, raised the issue, for the first time on a statewide basis in a popular forum, of the serious environmental stress being experienced by the Big Sur coast. There were also groundbreaking articles on urban toxic waste (*New West* also ran one of America's first major articles, on April 21, 1980, on the Star Wars space defense strategy), on Yosemite (writer Tom DeVries was the first to alert Californians to the ongoing destruction of California's primary environmental symbol), on water, flora and fauna, backpacking and other aspects of the outdoors.

Ironically, it was the absentee ownership of Rupert Murdoch that enabled Carroll and his staff to exercise the autonomy they enjoyed. Or was it just absentee landlordship on Murdoch's part? It might have been a very shrewd judgment by Murdoch that California constituted for him terra incognita and it would be best to allow the locals to run his newly acquired enterprise.

But just as California was for Dick Adler Hollywood, and for Frank Lalli an Aeolian cave of secret deals, Carroll's California, which was in great measure the California of *New West*, likewise involved a restricted definition: the embattled outlook of Northern California, Berkeley specifically, nurtured in the protest environment of the late 1960s. Sensing that a more hard-edged, bottom-line era was dawning with the 1980s, the outlook turned, somewhat defensively, to lifestyle—most dramatically, the connoisseurship of cuisine—as a way of solacing itself.

As valuable as the Carroll vision was, the problem remained: was it Californian, or was it, in its essential dynamics, Northern Californian? The question was more than merely academic. It struck at the core of the editorial and circulation future of the enterprise. *Los Angeles* magazine, by contrast, had the question instantly answered by geographical limits; but as every editor and every editorial orientation *New West* was discovering, California as geography, as place, at once promised a definition, then snatched it away by means of an astonishing diversity that defied any encompassing understanding beyond geography, the place on the map. In an effort to create a unifying force field between the polarities of Berkeley suspicion of the new order and the sensibility of Los Angeles County, which in a year or two would have under way more development than thirty-five other American states, *New West* began in the late 1970s and early 1980s to open up a previously restricted sector—namely, the arts and, more specifically, the arts as they related to the heritage of California and to its unfolding identity.

The founding generation of *New West* editors had rejected this alternative almost completely. It seemed to them too stuffy, too academic. But in the heritage and art articles that began to appear in *New West* at the end of the decade—especially the articles that featured the work of California photographers—a successful campaign was launched to define California, not by what was wrong with it, but by how its painters, photographers and writers captured some of its basic building blocks. By January 1981, art, woefully neglected in the early years, was worthy of cover treatment.

There was, it was apparent, a new change of direction, a new commitment to intellectual inquiry and the written word, a concern for the deeper resonances of the California experience that were underrepresented in the magazine as it strove to capture what was hip, what was with-it. The new editor, William Broyles Jr., who took over in December 1980, came from the thoughtful tradition of *Texas Monthly*, a magazine that has functioned—in celebration, analysis and, when necessary, condemnation—as the cutting edge of Texas self-awareness for nearly two decades. Broyles took California seriously in every dimension of its existence: as a present-tense place of astonishing diversity, but also as a fully mature example of the larger

American experience, localized in regional terms, energized by a rising economy and of significance to the national experience. That philosophy of editorship remains intact.

It was at this point, October 1981, that *New West* became *California*. Changing itself from *New West* to *California*, the magazine formalized a process that was already under way as early as 1980: an editorial approach to California, not as the new or the exceptional, the *New West*, but as an American environment that was worth covering, not because it was new, unique or eccentric, but because it was a challenging case study, geographically strategic, of how American civilization was progressing in the later decades of the twentieth century. In his statement of purpose regarding the name change (Behind the Lines), Broyles announced that it would now become the explicit goal of the magazine to evoke the diversity of the state while insisting that it is, somehow, one place and one culture. What unified it? Its optimism, said Broyles, and its future orientation. "Most cultures are united by their pasts," Broyles insisted. "Californians have in common a belief in the future, a sense that anything is possible, an openness to new ideas in religion, politics, business, and living. The great thing about California is that it isn't finished—we are still building it." *California*, Broyles promised, had as its special mission the assembly and dramatization of California's component parts.

This work of identity building is a classic function of magazines. In 1980, 1981, 1982, *New West/California* broadened its range of interest through a series of major articles that, while not ponderous, represented serious-minded journalism at its best. Jonathan Kirsch (one of the best journalists the magazine developed) investigated the question of "California Kids: Are We Giving Them Too Much Too Soon?" in July 1981. That previous February he had asked, "Is Anyone Safe Anymore?"—in a cover article that was chillingly illustrated with photographs of everyone murdered in California in one week's time. Kirsch's investigations of spoiled kids and a soaring homicide rate certainly suggested that the *New West* was more than Eden and that the magazine had more important work to do than suggest the ten best places to get pâté while marching with César Chávez.

As a historian, I consider many articles of the early 1980s classics: rich evocations of California's component parts. Whereas Dick Adler had rejected a story on the Jews of San Francisco in 1977 as being "too parochial," the magazine now ran Nancy Friedman's celebratory portrait of Rabbi Edgar F. Magnin of the Wilshire Boulevard Temple, which distilled and personified the pioneer Jewish heritage of Southern California. Mard Naman, a little later, profiled the Sikh community of the San Francisco Bay Area. As a frustrated senior editor of *New West* in its first year, I had watched in horror as an article I commissioned on the monastic establishments of California—Christian, Buddhist, Zen and other—was scotched as being inappropriate to what I was told was an essentially secular society. But religion, it turned out, was emerging as more than a matter of the Peoples Temple when it came to assessing what forces were motivating California and shaping its imagination.

No historian of California in the twenty-first century will be able to ignore such articles as Moira Johnston's on California's last rancho-owning families (August 1982), Armistead Maupin's cover article on senatorial candidate Gore Vidal (May 1982), or Ishmael Reed's "My Neighborhood" (March 1983) when attempting to assess the texture of California in the early eighties as it began to balance heritage and innovation, a sense of the past and a sense of new beginnings. Neil Morgan's evocation of his friend Raymond Chandler (June 1982) displayed for the first time, in my opinion, the magazine's capacity for literary journalism in the classic *Esquire* sense of that term. When Michael Parrish and Jonathan Kirsch explored surfing in Southern California, including a wonderful portrait of a middle-aged surfer, they created a document that will attract future historians wishing to chronicle the emergence of stylized self-consciousness—a conviction that a major regional American culture had been effected in Southern California.

With Californian Ronald Reagan in the White House, the politics of the state shifted with that of the nation; or rather, California was showing itself in a major way as a political bellwether. Just recently the Republican registration of the state outstripped Democratic registration for the first time in decades; but an astute reader of the magazine, encountering William Murray's approving portrait of Mayor Pete Wilson in San Diego (March 1981) or Jamie Wolf's iconoclastic psychological portrait of Jerry Brown ("Looking for Jerry," April 1981) or Jonathan Kirsch's profile of California's chief crime fighter, attorney general George Deukmejian (February 1981), could easily tell that the times they were a-changing. Jerry Brown may have been profiled with awe and approval in that first *New West* ever, but now, five years later, Jamie Wolf was suggesting that Californians, and even the governor's immediate staff, were growing tired of the enigma within the enigma within the enigma. And down in San Diego Pete Wilson had emerged as one of the most successful mayors in the country. Not that *California* went right; it was, however, allowing the centrist conservative elements of the state to find a place in the magazine, just as they were finding their place in the politics of the state.

The magazine that in its early years had orchidaceously celebrated the good life, Hollywood-style, now told the story, in December 1982, of how

Norman Garey, one of Hollywood's most powerful and respected lawyers, put a gun to his head and pulled the trigger.

All this is to suggest that by the mid-1980s, as Harold Hayes took over from Scott Kaufer, who had taken over from Bill Broyles in May 1982, *California* was fully capable of looking California squarely in the face, for better or for worse, with assured recognition that California had come of age. This maturity was more than a mere matter of firsts, the fact that California led the nation in wine production, Nobel Prize winners, defense contracts, scientific research, alcoholism, golf courses, commercial biotech firms, egg and avocado production, numbers of daily newspapers, private high schools. It was more than a matter of California being the seventh largest economy in the world, surpassed only by the United States (minus California), the U.S.S.R., Japan, West Germany, France and the United Kingdom. Or, as startling as the numbers might be, that it led the nation in resident American Indians, Chinese, Filipinos, Japanese, Koreans, Vietnamese, Samoans and Guamanians. No, it was something else: something exemplified in the 1984 Summer Olympics, in which California, considered separately, far surpassed the gold medals won by any other commonwealth; something about major American energies having consolidated themselves in this place called California.

As *California* enters the mid- and late-1980s ten years after its founding, it is covering a region unambiguously of national importance. Accusations of kookiness and epidemic eccentricity may linger, and in certain cases may be justified; but at the core of California's current identity is a conviction that in the last years of the twentieth century, this is the American region where, not just a new Californian identity, but a new American identity, is being forged. Here, where the Sunbelt and the Asian/Pacific Basin collide in a burst of energy, is being synthesized the American identity of the future: an amalgam of European, Hispanic, Asian and other elements that can, in a negative scenario, result in the polyglot malevolence of *Blade Runner,* a goulash of cultures to no purpose, or that can, more positively, achieve an interactive pluralism between East and West, Mesoamerica, the Sunbelt, high European culture and the achievements of the Atlantic eastern states (civility, orthodoxy, tradition) that will at long last bring about a culture at once American, nurturing itself from the strength and force of the continent, and cosmopolitan, drawing unto itself, into eclectic harmony, the diversified peoples and cultures of the world.

It just may be that what it is to be an American in the twenty-first century is having an early run-through, a dress rehearsal, in California. We Americans have refused to melt into the melting pot. On the other hand, we have also refused to remain isolated in our own traditions and points of view. Whether pluralism can work—pluralism between left and right, most dramatically, but also pluralisms of religion, tastes, values—is in my opinion also the major American question confronting us. California may not have the answer, but pluralism is working here; diversity and unity are playing off each other with gratifying results.

The 1984 Summer Olympics showed America and the rest of the world that not only was California working, it was working joyously, exuberantly. This joy, this frank and naive delight in who we are and the wonderful place we find ourselves in, is one of the few continuities of the California experience, historically considered. Combine this with the tragic sense—an awareness of evil and limitations, of mistakes made and opportunities missed—and you have the beginnings of a truly vital human culture. This is why *California* can now cover California unburdened by any need to come up with a definition of the slate that plays it off the East Coast. We are no longer out here on the coast. America has joined us.

WALLACE STEGNER

California Rising

ONE OUT OF EVERY ten Americans is a Californian. There are many more Californians in the world than there are Australians and New Zealanders combined, more Californians than all the Norwegians, Swedes, Danes, Finns, and Icelanders in Scandinavia, more than twice as many Californians as Hungarians, Portuguese, or Greeks. Nations that have shaken the world, and some that still trouble it, look puny by comparison with this single state. The California economy exceeds that of all but a handful of nations. The state has a fantastic variety of topographies, climates, products, natural beauties. It has the biggest congressional delegation, and it has produced—though not everyone brags about this—two out of the last four presidents, and become the adopted home of a third.

Ask a Hungarian, a Norwegian, or a Greek who he is, and he can tell you, probably with pride. He is bonded to his fellow countrymen by blood, language, history, folkways, evolved arts, shared triumphs and shared defeats, even by the degree of inbreeding and adaptation that produces a recognizable physical type. And he is as definable to others as to himself; outsiders have an image of him that may be wrong in detail but is broadly accurate.

But ask a Californian who he is and you may get any of two dozen answers, in two dozen languages. Native sons and daughters will identify themselves as Californians without hesitation—indeed, with the same sort of patriotic pride that a Greek or Norwegian might show. But immigrants, and we are many, may not. I tried it on the luncheon table the other day and found that the people seated at it, though they have all lived in California since at least the 1940s, still think of themselves as Iowans, Kansans, or Scotsmen. Identification with a place, they agreed, has much to do with growing up in it, and may not be fully achieved short of a couple of generations. But they agreed on something else, too: non-Californians though they were, they didn't want to live anywhere else, including the places where they grew up.

A generation ago, writing on this same subject, I concluded that California was "America only more so...the national culture at its most energetic end....In a prosperous country we are more prosperous than most; in an urban country more urban than most; in a gadget-happy country more addicted to gadgets; in a mobile country more mobile: in a taste-less country more tasteless; in a creative country more energetically creative; in an optimistic society more optimistic; in an anxious society more anxious."

It did not seem to me then that California could be called a cultural region. It didn't have the isolation, the homogeneity, or the humility to be called a region. It didn't feel like any spur track, it felt like the main line, and it was likely to assert that if Columbus had landed on the West Coast instead of the West Indies, Manhattan Island would still belong to the Indians.

That was in 1959, at the height of the postwar boom. With the aid of hindsight I would not really change that judgment, but I would temper it. For it seems clear now that in 1959, and before it, and after it, California has not only been America only more so, it has sometimes been America in the worst sense of the word. It has plundered itself, it has permitted the worst excesses of wide-open opportunism and uncontrollable growth. Mainly over water, it has split it-self politically in two.

Now things have changed and grown tighter. We are making real estate millionaires in smaller numbers. We are tearing down and selling off the schools that for a while we were completing at the rate of two or three a week. We live at a different point on the population curve than during those years when more than fifty percent of the population was under twenty-five. We have seen the influx of millions of immigrants, many of whom will not make it to full citizenship for two or three generations, if ever. The movement of Pacific and mesoamerican peoples into the state has postponed for a long time the development of a recognizable California type—either that, or it has guaranteed the continuation and widening of the gap between haves and have-nots that has ominous economic and racial possibilities for the future.

A full generation after 1959 we are further than ever from being able to define a Californian or California culture. We are probably further from a unifying California pride, though by the evidence of our luncheon table not many of us want to move. Maturing pains turn out to be as bad as growing pains. By and large, the less a Californian reads and thinks, the more satisfied he is. Even with the boat ramps overcrowded on Shasta Lake, even with far-ahead reservations necessary in most state parks and on the Muir Trail, it is still a life that few would trade for any available alternative. Children reared in California find it hard to live anywhere else. College football players used to the California climate grieve when they are drafted by Green Bay or Buffalo.

Curiously, as the boom slows and we near the limits of available water, as we have to fight for the open space we once took for granted, as we feel the competition of the energy-rich mountain states and the Sunbelt Southwest, we show more regional stigmata than we did in 1959. We reveal a provincial self-consciousness and touchiness, we make tacit admissions of cultural inferiority. In their relations with the East, California writers, painters, musicians, and publications display the attitudes, alternately apologetic and defiant, that mark the colonial complex, as when some Bay Area writers expressed in a recent issue of the *San Francisco Examiner* their distress at being ignored by New York reviewers. Quaintly, some of the complainers had recently moved out here from the East. By becoming Californians, they complained, they had lost status.

They should not have wasted their breath. I suggest that, in matters of cultural evaluation, the colonial complex arises from first granting some other place the authority to make judgments about us, and then believing the judgments they make.

The colonial complex is nothing new. Early American writers and critics were infuriated by (because they half accepted) condescending British opinions of them. American patriots smarted under the scorn of British travelers, and tried to make up in brag what they lacked in cathedrals. Later, the regions deferred in the same way to New York opinion, and were angered for the same reasons.

American writing is done everywhere; a lot of it, and some of the best, is done in California. But American publishing is done pretty much between Broadway and Third Avenue and between Thirty-third and Sixtieth streets, and American literary opinion, though its territory may extend south to take in the Village, is generated on essentially the same ground. The book reviews that every bookstore in the country accepts as the highest authorities are *The*

New York Times Book Review and the *New York Review of Books*, both admirable journals that express New York superbly and either do not know or do not much care about the rest of the country. Seeing itself occasionally in those pages, California as often as not is embarrassed to find itself pictured as grotesque or trivial. But since the judgment comes from headquarters, half of us believe it.

The case of the review media is especially irritating to some Californians because those periodicals make judgments, presume to sift the important from the unimportant, and they do so from premises that often seem uninformed, biased, or condescending. But the editorial assumptions of other media are not too different. And that, it seems to me, is a change. In 1959 I think we did not feel that Gotham was against us, or indifferent to us, or affiliated with a culture that repudiated ours. Big times were afoot then, and we felt the interest in them from beyond our borders. By 1981 that interest, often amused, but interest, seems to have hardened into resistance.

Well, we have produced a lot of screwballs since 1959, and all Californians may be tainted by association. In a notably free and exuberant society, nearly anything goes, and sometimes it goes sour. But I think it is not California's failures land excesses that have bred antagonism in the East. Success has more to do with it. Emotions simple, direct, and understandable are at work. Envy and fear.

"American history is history in transition from an Atlantic to a Pacific phase," said historian Garrett Mattingly thirty-five years or so ago. What was apparent to a historian then is apparent to almost anybody now. The East wanes, the West waxes. It is no longer unthinkable that a distinguished scholar should leave Harvard for Berkeley or Stanford. Growth, energy, opportunity, shift westward. Our most populous and powerful state fronts the Pacific, our foremost trading partner is not Great Britain but Japan. And the garrison mentality often charged against regional patriots can affect rear-guard positions as well as outposts. It cannot be entirely coincidental that the condescension and antagonism of the Atlantic states toward California grows shriller and less charitable at the precise time when population, money, and political power are bleeding out of the Atlantic states toward the South, the Southwest, and the West.

But rivalry, even when acknowledged, doesn't have to be pursued. By resenting and resisting eastern prejudice and distaste, we would only reduce ourselves to the shrillness of regional scolds. The eastern stranglehold on the publication-and-opinion industry, though it has proved hard to break, will not last indefinitely.

West Coast journals, if they are smart, will not become simply regional retorts to eastern journals. They will not be regional at all in the limiting sense. They will base themselves firmly on their own territory and shoot for an audience as wide as the English-speaking world. To do that they will need confidence. They will also need a wider view of California and the California culture than that provided by Hollywood or even by the contemporary Hollywood variety of politics. There is every sort or richness, every sort of quality in California, to counteract a fairly pervasive vulgarity. No richness and no quality should go unreported, and the merely sensational doesn't need to be hyped.

In 1959 I said that California, if it is a region at all, is a region with a view. I meant a *wide* view. And I see no reason in 1981 to revise that description.

MICKEY KAUS

Letter Home

V ICTOR VASARELY, the "Father of Op Art," was in New York the other day in an expansive mood. "The general interest in Op Art has diminished," the seventy-six-year-old Hungarian noted, with some understatement. Still, Vasarely was feted at four birthday parties, attended by Andy Warhol, Yoko Ono, John Cage, and various other New York civic leaders. At his gallery on Madison Avenue he said his work "is a beauty that does not demand specific culture, only the necessity to love life." (Mr. Vasarely, Mr. Vasarely, please return to your car. Your fifteen minutes are up.) Vasarely was also made an honorary New Yorker in a ceremony at the Guggenheim Museum, and given a ruby pin in the shape of an apple. He announced he was delighted with New York, which gave *The New York Times* the angle it needed.

FATHER OF OP ART FINDS CITY EXCEPTIONAL, ran the headline on *The Times* story. "It is an exceptional city," Vasarely was quoted as saying. "On every block there is a surprise." Vasarely liked the Pan Am building ("It looks pasted on"). He added, "Look at all these dogs. I think they're good for the city. They break the monotony of the yellow cabs."

Civic self-congratulation has become one of The Times' favorite activities, but it has a brittle, tense quality that distinguishes it from ordinary robust Chamber-of-Commerce boosterism in a town like San Diego or Dallas. That sort of boosterism reflects aspirations for future growth, or at least future prosperity. New York's reflects an unspoken intimation of decline.

At first glance, this city appears to have made tremendous progress in the years following the humiliating bankruptcy of 1974 to 1976. Its debt is now being paid off on schedule—the budget has even showed a small surplus the past few years. Fiscal responsibility was accompanied in the the late seventies by a boom of prestige and celebrity. The symbolic event was the moving of *Rolling Stone's* offices from San Francisco to Fifth Avenue in 1977. Linda Ronstadt soon followed, leaving Los Angeles because, she said, New York was where all the action was. Jerry Rubin, surely a bellwether in this sort of thing, soon turned up in Manhattan as a Wall Street trader.

For New Yorkers, however, a more painful reality is beginning to sink in. The effects of the bankruptcy—and the pattern of municipal decline that produced it—are turning out to be deeper and longer-lived than they once seemed. New York has not "come back," if by coming back you mean that its citizens enjoy the same quality of life they once enjoyed. Services cut during the fiscal crisis have not been restored. Instead, more of the city's dollars now go to pay fewer workers. New York City employed 2,500 street sweepers in 1975. Last year there were 1,250, and the streets are visibly filthier. In many of the city's public high schools, a teacher must handle forty or forty-five students in a class. The dropout rate has remained high, at about forty percent.

The precipitous decline of the New York subways has been arrested, thanks to a $6.5 billion capital expenditure plan—but every year brings new evidence of the long-range costs of the maintenance that was deferred during the crisis years. Just when things had supposedly been patched up last summer, a rash of derailments revealed still more track work to be done, and forced trains to slow to a crawl. The latest MTA chairman now says that despite the billions already spent, significant improvements might not be seen for a decade. Three years ago, in a challenge to graffiti artists, the Transit Authority put guard dogs in the rail yards and repainted many subway cars a virginal white. It is currently planning to repaint the cars—now dusty, defaced, and depressing—a deep red, the better to hide the signs of decisive defeat.

People sense a deterioration, but they are unsure whether the world outside New York has deteriorated as well. They need to be grabbed by the lapels every few hours and told—Hey! This is still New York, the Big Apple! They need to be told that they are right to pay incredible rents and private school tuitions to live in a town where bums with festering sores crowd the seats in the public library, where young punks suck subway tokens right out of the turnstiles in front of startled commuters, where there are welded metal locks on basketball hoops, where the Mayor cheerfully forks over 52.3 percent of his income in federal, state, and city taxes, and where the leading newspaper saw the need to editorialize—calmly, as if the citizenry of any other American town needed the same public chastising—against its readers' practice of defecating in building foyers, subway tunnels, or the middle of the street. They need to be told they are indeed privileged to live in a Center of Culture, a town where they can go to a nighttime concert in Central Park and hear everything but Tchaikovsky's cannons drowned out by the burbling of the white wine and the babbling of the audience.

So we have *The Times*, the Newspaper of Record, the authoritative voice of reassurance, tirelessly attempting to counteract the unmistakable signs of urban collapse that appear daily in its own pages. Early in 1983 *The Times* published a series of articles titled "New York, New York; The City As Leader." A little box accompanying each article proclaimed: "Despite New York City's high crime rate, fiscal troubles, and other problems, it has managed to retain and strengthen its pre-eminence in a number of fields."

CITY'S POSITION SECURE AS FOCUS OF ART WORLD was the first in-depth probe. "New York City's position as the Capital of the art world seems, at the moment, even more invincible today than it has been in the last twenty-five years. . . . There is no other city, in America or abroad, where the structure of the art world is as solid, from top to bottom, as it is in New York." A curator from Minnesota said, "New York is still the beacon, and indisputably so. . . . I don't see any challenge." Succeeding installments in the seven-part series followed the same pattern: FOR PUBLISHING, CITY REMAINS 'THE MECCA'; NEW YORK: WORLD FINANCIAL MAGNET AND MARKET WHERE THE DEALS ARE MADE. "I couldn't conceive of running the business I run anywhere but in New York," said an author's agent.

Did New York used to have to brag like this? If the city really were "secure" and "invincible" one suspects it wouldn't have to tell itself so often that it was. Instead, there is always the nervous looking back over the shoulder for the someone Satchel Paige warned us about.

Indeed, these days New York boosters increasingly seem to rely not on building up the city's virtues so much as hoping that knowledge of the alternatives will be suppressed. Last September, when a part of the city's decrepit water system burst and blacked out the Seventh Avenue garment district at the height of the sales season, *The Times* featured ominous front-page accounts of the buyers who had detoured to a competing apparel mart in Atlanta. The fear was unmentioned but palpable. Give all those buyers a taste of the Sunbelt. It was a bad break. They might like it and never come back. When New Jersey got a $40 million federal grant this year to help with a $2 billion housing and office development in Jersey City across the Hudson River from Wall Street, New York Mayor Ed Koch reacted with characteristic confidence in his city's economic future. After all, New Jersey was cheaper. It had lower taxes and better roads. People might like it there. New York immediately moved to block the federal loan, claiming that the project represented a major threat to its millions of "back office" clerical jobs.

Even in the "New York, New York" series you could hear the muffled sound of drums from beyond the Hudson. New York was, of course, "unparalleled" in the art world—but *The Times* noted an ominous growth of "regional collectors and museums" like the rich, rich Getty collection in Malibu. Major exhibitions on Braque, El Greco, and the de Stijl movement had in fact bypassed New York. (The Museum of Modern Art didn't have space for many of them because it was too busy remodeling, adding a banal new façade by Cesar Pelli, and turning itself into a living exhibit of the death of modern architecture.) In publishing, Harcourt Brace Jovanovich, sixth largest in the field, had moved its trade book division to San Diego. Attempting to recreate the heady days of sassy Manhattan magazines, Condé Nast had reintroduced *Vanity Fair,* and New York's best and brightest produced a pretentious, empty failure (until a new editor was imported from England). And while CITY IS STILL NO. 1 IN PERFORMING ARTS, it had to be noted that "the Broadway theater is troubled at the moment, beset by skyrocketing costs, shrinking ticket sales, and a season's worth of offerings that, for the most part, have failed to ignite critical or public enthusiasm." But "Broadway is still Broadway." Hey! This is the Big Apple!

BROADWAY MAY NOT be Broadway for very long if, as is likely, the latest plan for redeveloping Times Square is carried out. The famous theater district is now a seamy combat zone—but the theaters enjoy a symbiotic relationship with the pimps, whores, pushers, thieves, punks and junkies who work the Square. The theaters provide the criminals their best victims; in exchange, the criminals help keep the rents down.

But now Times Square is to be made respectable. The city and state governments, and *The Times* itself (which owns a nice chunk of property in the area), have lined up behind a plan to plunk down four chockablock office buildings designed by Philip Johnson and John Burgee on the north side of the square. In theory, stockbrokers and lawyers will flock to the area and the stench of quiche will be enough to drive the pimps away. According to the city, the $1.6 billion plan will thus "eliminate blight on Forty-second Street." Of course, the pimps won't really be "eliminated"; they will just go somewhere else (along with those legitimate, if déclassé, businesses that can't pay law firm rents).

This is one of the lessons liberals supposedly learned from the disastrous efforts of the Department of Housing and Urban Development in the sixties and seventies. But in New York, where they would rather debate the Rosenbergs' guilt than Japanese management styles, old arguments die hard.

The Times Square plan might be quite desirable (if Johnson and Burgee's buildings, with their pompous, costive archways and silly mansard roofs, weren't so god-awful ugly). The plan will create some new offices and add to the city's general wealth. It will not end blight or have anything but a marginal impact on the burgeoning "underclass."

And the possible side effects of the plan are quite perverse. The idea is to save the theater district, but the plan will drive up rents, so the theaters will either have to pay those rents, sell out to developers, or become permanently dependent on government subsidies and fragile zoning restrictions. Even *The Times* might become the victim of these "unintended consequences"— once the value of its own building is driven up, will *The Times'* stockholders be able to afford not to sell it, and move their operations to cheaper quarters? Perhaps reporters wouldn't mind commuting to Jersey City?

IN TIMES SQUARE, New Yorkers are once again displaying their penchant for struggling vainly against the basic tides of capitalism (as if you could eliminate poverty and "blight" by building a building). This tendency has gotten the city in trouble before, when New Yorkers tried to offer the nation's most generous social benefits and impose high taxes to pay for those benefits, while pretending that businesses would not react by moving to less expensive jurisdictions, taking the city's tax base with them. The result was the 1976 bankruptcy.

If the city has learned that painful, basic fiscal lesson, the spirit of '76 lives on in New York's byzantine rent-stabilization scheme, which attempts, in one of the most expensive locales on earth, to maintain housing costs that approximate those in Peoria, Illinois.

I don't want to dwell on the unfortunate economic side effects of rent controls—how they subsidize the middle class, discriminate against the newcomers, and generally screw up the housing market. Those of you who live near Santa Monica already know about that. More interesting are the psychological side effects—how they reinforce the collective insecurity that underlies all the This-is-the-Big-Apple talk of New Yorkers.

I'm as good a case study as any. I pay $471 a month for a one-and-a-half bedroom place in the East Village. The place is not exactly comfortable— you never know what will crawl out of the walls. But thanks to people like me, the area is rapidly gentrifying. (And unless New Yorkers really do stop the tides of capitalism, all of Manhattan will eventually be gentrified. Already Manhattan landlords are lobbying to move the bums from the nearby Bowery to Queens.)

As a result, my cruddy little apartment is now a Great Deal. A vacant, unstabilized apartment would now go for almost $1,000 a month. And that's what it would cost me, too, if I tried to move to another neighborhood (without evading the law by becoming somebody's illegal subtenant). If I actually left New York, who knows what it would cost me to get back in?

It's the Rent Control Trap. Every time I think of moving, I think how crazy I would be to give up my cheap apartment. Millions of New Yorkers are in my position. Should we stay in Manhattan? Is it really so great here? Maybe we'd like San Diego better. But we don't dare experiment. Unlike those fashion buyers detoured to Atlanta, we don't know what we're missing. This makes us very insecure. Like Calvinists searching for signs of election, we hunt desprately for signs that we have made the right choice. We *need* those stories in *The Times,* the little Vasarely hype jobs, the seasonal odes (CITY BE-JEWELED FOR SPARKLING CHRISTMAS), the smug seven-part series (A RICH DIVERSITY IS THE KEY INGREDIENT IN NEW YORK'S ABUNDANT FOOD SCENE), the charming vignettes of New York spunk and savvy in the "Metropolitan Report" (where the menacing teenagers who extort quarters by "washing" the windows of cars immobilized at stoplights were recently described as a SIGN OF THE CITY'S SPRING and "part of New York's great street theater").

Another reassuring sign of election, of course, is the hundreds of thousands of people who still want "in" to Manhattan. This explains the subtle pleasure with which New Yorkers tell each other about their cousin who just moved to town and paid $1,200 a month for a tiny, sterile, high-rise studio apartment, or their friend who put an ad in *The Village Voice* and found a dozen wretched yuppies, tipped off by friends in *The Voice* composing room, camped out on his doorstep the night before the paper went on sale—all desperate to pay him $6,000 in illegal "key money" for a one-year sublet.

The Germans have a word for it—*schadenfreude,* which means joy at the suffering of others. New York runs on *schadenfreude*—the same kind that fuels college hazing, the survivors sneering at the newcomers. I can enjoy my $471 apartment, not because I like it, but because the poor bugger down the street is paying $800. Never mind that I might enjoy even more living in Milwaukee for $250. Are the newcomers scared of all the crime? Are they frustrated when they go to the library and wait an hour in line for the two still-functioning microfilm machines? That makes me feel good. I know which streets are safest to walk down, and I know to bring a novel and a roll of quarters when I go to the library. This is called "learning to appreciate the city." It is, I suspect, the real reason I am always told, "Be patient. It takes three years to learn to like New York."

But I am not patient. I have been here three years. *Schadenfreude* is not enough. I want to be in a place where people make things other than bad plays and weird clothes, where they lobby for something other than a federal arts policy. I don't care about the Rosenbergs, and I don't like having to join a seven-story health club to get exercise. I want to do sports, not just talk about them. I want to drive a car again. The song says, "If I can make it here, I'd make it anywhere." Right. I'll take anywhere.

II.
Getting Around

Best Roads

T HE MOST OBVIOUS and least noticed man-made marvel in California is
its highway system. It is an engineering event on the scale of the
transcontinental railroad, over 15,000 miles long and fifty years in the
making. By a long measure, it is the best highway system in the country,
which means that it is the best highway system in the world. California, its
various departments and agencies, has taught numberless nations how to
build modern roads, and if the world is now less convinced about the
necessity of superhighways than it used to be, that has more to do with
geology and geography than with design and engineering.

The California highway system is also where many of us learned the
pleasures of motoring. Much has been written about California's love affair
with the automobile, and much of it is wrong. To be sure, a few citizens
lavish an inordinate amount of attention on their sedans, but for most of us
routine maintenance and a sporty little ironclad warranty are all that are
necessary. The real pleasures of the road have to do with driving, the
experience rather than the vehicle, the verb rather than the noun. The
pleasures of driving are an obvious extension of the pleasures of the trail, the
progressive revelation of natural wonders and cultural information. Driving
is an aesthetic experience so commonplace that it is frequently ignored, yet a
bad drive is as painful as a bad painting and requires much more stamina to
endure. For Americans, driving is also nearly universal; more people have
reveled in a good drive than have, say, attended a baseball game or gotten
divorced.

So it is the good drives that we celebrate here. The following list is
arbitrary and personal—and incomplete. I have not driven every road in
California. I have heard, for instance, that 299 from Redding to Alturas is
worth a detour, but I have not included it because I've never done it. Call this
list, rather, a talking paper, a work in progress, a set of nominations (there are
only seven drives on it, which suggests that the California top ten has three
slots open). My criteria were mostly predictable—scenic beauty, surprise,
transformation, ease of driving, traffic flow, plus a leavening of whim. They
are listed in a vague order of preference, as follows:

Highway 1 from Morro Bay to Carmel Valley Road: The champ. Obvious, but obligatory. If it's not the most spectacular seaside road in the world, it's close. From the wholly improbable Morro Rock to the quiet mysteries of Point Lobos, this drive never fails to put the bloom back in the cheeks. There's San Simeon and Nepenthe (think of the years when Orson Welles and William Randolph Hearst lived just up the street from each other), the geometry of erosion at the Pfeiffer state beaches, the elvish huts of the Big Sur Inn, the delicate engineering of Bixby Creek Bridge, on and on. Take all strangers and children on this drive: fossil fuel on this stretch of pavement is never wasted.

Highway 195 from Interstate 10 to Joshua Tree: Runs right through the heart of Joshua Tree National Monument; starts in the low desert east of Indio and, in forty miles, climbs 3,000 feet to the high Mojave, with the local ecology changing several times along the way. By the time you get into the high reaches of the park, in the spacious Joshua tree forests near Hidden Valley, it becomes otherworldly, a supernaturally pleasing and disorienting landscape. Like all desert drives, this is best taken in the spring. From mid-April to mid-June the wild flowers are certain to be out somewhere along this route; the higher the altitude, the later the wild flower blush. Look for white desert lilies and desert primroses, purple asters, pink monkey flowers, brilliant barrel and beavertail cactus blooms. Honorable mention in this neck of the woods should go to Highway 195 between Interstate 10 and Mecca, essentially a continuation of the Joshua Tree road, little known except to natives, quite remarkable. I won't spoil it; its surprises are best left surprising.

Pierce Point Road between Sir Francis Drake Boulevard and McClure's Beach: Those lips, those eyes! Those vistas, those horizons! Those cows, those pigs! From the giant sand dune at Abbotts Lagoon to the pastoral hillsides sprinkled with musing bovines to the steep drop just south or Upper Pierce Point Ranch, this short stretch or overabundant spectacle—Tomales Bay on one side, the wild Caledonian ocean on the other—is a feast for the senses. Honorable mention here to Limantour Road, on Point Reyes, the best opportunity the car-bound traveler will have to see the ghostly fallow deer, found nowhere else in the western Hemisphere, and Limantour Spit itself, a windy fingernail of land scratching the soft underbelly of Drakes Bay.

Ramona to Borrego Springs via Highways 78, 79, and S22: This route has always seemed to me like some sort of paradigm of western diversity. It starts in rolling horse-farm country, very tony in an exurban sort of way, moves higher into an apple-growing landscape where frost is frequent (the semidiscovered town of Julian, about a third of the way along this road, looks very much like a small Mammoth), more rolling hills and verdant vistas, then, absolutely without warning, the sudden desert two thousand feet below, the grassland giving way to yucca and ocotillo and mesquite, the road snaking down the side of an impossible cliff, and you are in the irrevocable glowing heart of the Anza Borrego, the desert that makes the Mojave look like Wisconsin. Astonishing. There are those who would vote for the better-known 74 from Lake Hemet to Rancho Mirage, which offers the same kind of contrast, but let them write their own articles.

Tioga Pass Road (Highway 120) from the 41 Junction to Lee Vining: Any trans-Sierra route is a jewel on the pillow of motoring; I just picked my childhood favorite. As the southernmost route (the next navigable road is 175 out of Bakersfield, hardly your purple-mountains'-majesty experience), Tioga Pass is closest to the big peaks. The drive itself is a pleasing and logical narrative: a meander up the moderate western slope of the Sierra, a lurch over the hump of the Cathedral Range at Polly Dome, a parade through the plushy grasslands of Tuolumne Meadows, then a plunge over the eastern escarpment with Mono Lake sweeping into view like a duchess on a staircase. If you have a cassette player in your car, and if you have tapes of the *Emperor Concerto* and the *Pastoral*...Also, in Lee Vining you can eat at Nicely's. Everybody does.

From Highway 395 to Horseshoe Meadow Trailhead via Lubken Canyon Road: I get one eccentric choice; this is it. This is that thing you see from 395 south of Lone Pine switch-backing precariously up the mountain. Scary. The road is broad but unpaved, there is little margin for error and no chance for speed, but the emerging views of the Owens Valley and the Inyo Mountains are worth the price of admission. Goes from 4,000 feet at the highway to 9,880 at the trail head in thirteen miles (!)—not for the easily overheated. At the end of the journey there's a short level hike to Horseshoe Meadow itself, a huge, semicircular symphony of rivulets and tundra spread like a tablecloth before Cottonwoods Pass. It's like going from the Gobi to the Alps in forty-five minutes.

Highway 1 from Jenner to Elk: I liked this road better twenty years ago, when it went right through the middle of Fort Ross, but I suppose constant traffic is not conducive to the maintenance of eighteenth-century Russian architecture. Still, it is a total delight—coastal meadows, sweeping vistas, the lot. Be sure not to miss Salt Point, near Fort Ross, unmarked on the roadway but findable with the right maps, a splendid and little-known treasure of wind and waves and mineral oxidation. Amusing passenger cabin conversation can be initiated around the topic "Sea Ranch: Noble Experiment or Blot on the Landscape?" I ended this route at Elk rather than Mendocino because the traffic gets heavier as soon as 128 kicks in south of Albion, but hell, I'll go up to MacKerricher if it'll settle any arguments.

TOM HUTH

Welcome to the L.A. Freeway

I T IS LATE in the afternoon (any afternoon, it could have been) and I am flying out the Ventura Freeway in tight configuration with a Catholic nun. Her Toyota is holding steady in the right lane and I'm alongside in the number three, doing an effortless sixty-five. Then suddenly, inexplicably, the semi ahead of us throws a rear tire. It pops off, whole, in a yellowish cloud of dust...arcs tantalizingly through the air...hangs suspended over the white line before our eyes. For a moment, that lifetime, the nun and I are joined in horrified communion, watching the tire falling back to earth. If it bounces left it will probably crash through my windshield; if right, then the nun will be chosen. There is no time to react, to think, to pray. But the good Lord is with us today, because the tire bounces neither left nor right, but true—straight into the air—and flies between our two capsules like a meteoroid. The drama is over in a couple of seconds, and we hurtle on (the trucker included) toward our destinations, catching just a glimpse in our rearview mirrors of the fresh panic behind.

This is the freeway: life as we know it, every lane the fast lane.

The Los Angeles freeway system is built upon an extraordinary set of assumptions upon which depend the lives of approximately five million people every day. A driver must take for granted that the brake lights of the cars in front of him are in good working order; that the driver behind him has nimble reflexes; that the vehicles on either side will not bust a kingpin or a steering rod; that the truck up ahead will not drop an i-beam in his path; that all parties to this scheme are awake, attentive, fairly sober and reasonably desirous of going on living. In fact, the driver's belief must be so absolute that he cannot allow himself to think about these things at all, or he'll have to pull over, drop out.

A highway patrolman recalls: "This lady she stopped in the number one [the left] lane on the northbound Hollywood at Mulholland, so they called me for a traffic hazard. I got there and, sure enough, all these cars are coming up and screeching their tires and moving around her. So I go up and say, 'What's the matter with your car?' and she goes, 'Nothing.' She's all shaking and everything. She says, 'I can't drive.' I say, 'What do you mean you can't drive?' She says, 'Because I'm scared.' So I made a traffic break and got her over to the right shoulder, and I says, 'You okay now?' and she goes, 'No.' And I says, 'Okay, I'll follow you off…and we'll call for help."

That lady wasn't crazy, she merely was seeing through the illusion.

Freeway aficionado Paul (Panther) Pierce, in his book *Take an Alternate Route*, remembers a man he found one afternoon cowering on the center divider alongside his disabled car. He was a farmer who'd never taken the freeways before, and this was his sorry tale: he had entered into traffic in the left lane that morning with a full tank of gas—had been swept up helplessly into the race, been boxed in place by the other drivers, been afraid even to change lanes—had driven on in terror like this, always keeping to the left, being shuttled from freeway to freeway, for six hours—until finally he ran out of gas and coasted to a merciful stop against the fence.

A psychiatrist in Houston has studied this phenomenon and duly classified it as a new type of phobia, and yet what's more interesting, actually, is how few drivers fall victim to it. The illusion of well-being at sixty miles an hour (the cars close enough that their occupants could reach out and shake hands) is so convincing that Angelenos can log a cumulative eighty-six million miles each day on their freeways—with less than one accident of any kind for every million miles driven. And in the process they have made an engrossing sport out of the ordinary act of commuting.

Picture it as a Parker Brothers board game, the players deftly shuttling their tokens between lanes, from one freeway to another, trying to find the quickest route to the buried treasure and back home again. If a player lives in Azusa and has to meet his agent in Westwood and then make a lunch date in Costa Mesa, it's easy—he just grabs the Foothill to the 605 to the westbound San Bernardino to the Santa Monica, then he jumps on the southbound San Diego down to the Newport, then he catches the Santa Ana up to the Orange to the westbound Foothill again and he's back at Go. If he's a heads-up player, he'll stay tuned into the radio traffic alerts—the Chance cards of the L.A. Freeway Game—and plan his strategies accordingly.

Of course, this same spirit might apply to negotiating any modern urban road network. But if you'll look at the divided-highway maps of other cities, you'll see only the most anemic of skeletons—a few east-west and north-south arteries, a scenic low-tech parkway, perhaps a tidy little beltway running around the perimeter—the routes named after the unremembered dead: Dan Ryan, Wilbur Cross, John C. Lodge, Henry Watterson. There's no grandeur at all to the chase, no complexity, no ingenuity required. Only L.A., with its twenty-six freeways covering some 700 miles between Ventura, San Bernardino and Laguna—freeways fabled in movie and song—provides an arena, a challenge to body and mind, worthy of the serious metropolitan driver. It was just a few years ago that everybody was babbling about the amazing dexterity that teenagers exhibited at the controls of video games. We kept exclaiming: "Why, their eye-to-hand coordination is simply out of this world!" But, all along, Angelenos by the millions have been out there on the freeways playing the game for keeps. It's not as brazenly heroic as hang gliding or skydiving or scaling El Capitan by the tips of one's fingers, but a sport for the masses, instead: Everyman taking his life into his own hands, as it should be.

At ten minutes past midnight the world's busiest roadway, the Ventura as it approaches the San Diego, is at peace with its city. A three-quarter moon is rising over the Valley Federal Savings sign and only a few taillights stretch out ahead of me to pinpoints in the backlit sky. The city looks extremely kind at night from the freeway, its detail softened by fog. I swing south on the Hollywood toward downtown and then north through the four-level to the Pasadena, the grandfather of them all, finished in '41.

Running with the freeways at night encourages dreaming, and I remember now when I was a boy, sitting in the backseat of the family Buick and watching over my dad's shoulder as he piloted us through the streets of Detroit, both hands clamped firmly on the wheel, always making tiny corrections in our course, apparently keeping us alive from one moment to the next. The city traffic seemed to annoy him, the stupidity of other drivers, and he'd snap at me if, in my eagerness to get his view of the road, I'd kick the back of his seat.

At 1:30 A.M. the Foothhill is an abadoned airport runway, as empty as the playgound in *West Side Story* in the lull before violence. The freeways are so smooth that one can lose all sense of motion, the curves so graceful that the steering wheel seems to move of its own accord. My father, I'm sure, would have enjoyed this sort of driving if he'd lived to know it—cruising alone through the concrete canyons, letting his mind drift away to the strains of Vivaldi, the cellos swooning along with the sweeps of the great interchanges—the Glendale to the Golden State to the eastbound 101 then peeling off to the Long Beach and looping around to the Pomona—trumpets heralding a power plant blazing past on the right, a woodwind quartet trilling in at the Paramount on-ramp.

The people who created our freeways certainly never intended them to be driven by motorists using only ten percent of their brain cells, with the other ninety percent off in space. But this is the result of such peerless design—raceways stripped of all activity but the performance of nonstop driving, whole hillsides blasted away to ensure uneventful passage—a total autopian environment in which monotony leads ineluctably to hallucination. Only the raised Botts dots between each lane (named after the Caltrans engineer who invented them) keep the voyager's consciousness from straying too far.

At 4:30 on the Riverside the smell of orange blossoms mingles with the aroma of yesterday's exhaust, and at five the dawn begins to show through a stand of eucalyptus trees in the outside world. A happy yellow Denny's sign looms to the east like the sun itself. Even now, an hour before the morning rush officially begins at monitoring stations throughout the metropolis, the inbound traffic on the San Bernardino is getting thick.

At 5:45 the first slowdown, brake lights flashing on. The radio chimes in:

> *On the Harbor Freeway northbound at the Artesia they've rolled an ambulance...on the Pomona northbound at Wilcox a couple of cars got together—they're prying them apart right now...on the southbound Glendale at Fletcher there's a workbench in the fast lane...and on the southbound Hollywood a quarter of a mile north of the four-level, a dead dog in the number one lane....*

Drivers dance from lane to lane, settling into their favorite slots. A VW dives into traffic from the right and skips across three lanes in one Nureyevian flourish. At 5:55 the traffic jams up and I kick off the San Bernardino onto the Foothill, but they're still chasing me—the pack, bearing down from behind.

AT ABOUT THIS time, Michael Mathias is arriving for work at the California Highway Patrol's central L.A. station, which squats in the shadows beneath one gargantuan arm of the Harbor-Santa Monica interchange. He runs through an equipment check on his cruiser—the siren, the flashers, the Remington shotgun loaded and mounted at arm's reach—and as the radio dispatcher calls "Move 'em out!" he rolls onto the streets and heads for his beat—those six miles of the Hollywood Freeway between Alameda and Lankershim.

"So far as procedures," he advises me casually enough, "whenever I make a stop, all I ask is that you get out of the car and stand behind the door and watch traffic. If you see a car coming, just yell at me and jump—that's the best I can tell you. It's safer outside the car than inside. If I get run over or something, all you have to do is turn on the radio...push this button down...just tell'em. 'Officer down,' or something like that, and give 'em the location."

Mathias is young and bouncy, square jawed, enthusiastic about being a highway patrolman—has been doing it for a year, goes strictly by the book, and the fun hasn't begun to wear off. "I just get on the Hollywood and go up and down," he says of his eight-hour day. "Basically, what we try to do is just keep a high visual horizon and look for violators and people doing things out of the ordinary. Just scan everything. . . . And if there's nothin' going on—if everybody's pretty much following the program—we catch up to the next bunch of traffic. . .check that out."

He notices a woman driver pulled over on the right shoulder and stops to offer help. I stand outside, as I'm told, the traffic roaring in my ears, the jet stream whipping at my hair, seeming to singe my eyebrows. Back in the car a few minutes later Mathias explains that if the driver had been a man, he wouldn't have stopped. "If they're close to a call box a man can usually handle himself," he says. "Females, we've found, you know, they get frightened easily. People try to molest 'em, things like that. So I just go up and tell her to lock all the doors and windows and not let anybody in except AAA."

Mathias issues his share of tickets, but for the most part he keeps order on the freeways in subtler ways—by merely making his enlightened presence known to people who aren't following the program. "Like that Monte Carlo in the number two lane," he says now, "he's following too close. I'll go up there, get alongside him, let him see me. . .like this. He'll back off and slow down." A moment later something amuses him. "That guy in the number one lane knows I can't get to him right now," he explains, "so he's speeding. People play games with me. See? He's up there in the number two lane now, going in and out of traffic." The cop laughs. He enjoys this hide-and-seek, playing with his power, relieving the boredom. "If I wanted him," he assures me, "I could get him."

WHILE THE FREEWAY patrolman is on the lookout for reckless drivers, his wide-angle vision is taking in much more than that—more than we civilians realize. As I sit there staring at the head of the driver in front of us, Mathias is noticing out-of-date registration stickers, illegally tinted windows, babies without car seats, outlawed axle modifications, open beer containers, drivers wearing stereo headsets ("That's a no-no, too"). Now he spies a green van without a rear license. He slides past it and reads the number off the front plate, calls it in to the dispatcher to check for outstanding warrants, and then falls back in traffic unobtrusively, keeping the suspect under observation until the dispatcher returns with a negative.

So the freeway driver, often unbeknownst, is continually being watched, followed, scrutinized by a higher consciousness. "It takes awhile," says Mathias, "but pretty soon your eyes are scanning everything. . .your eyes constantly going back and forth." There's a robotic quality to it, those eyes searching only for the x factors.

Still, the human element works its way into the game. He spots a Mustang with a year-old registration sticker and he knows this deserves a citation, but he hesitates. "This is a hard one," he admits. "I don't like stopping girls like that because when she went by I looked at her and she looked at me—and smiled real big. And if I stop her right now she'll think I'm trying to make her or something—and that's one of our big no-nos." While the young cop ponders such interdisciplinary delicacies, another violator catches his eye, and the pretty lady gets off free today.

On the Orange Freeway southbound approaching Lambert, a vehicle has gone off the roadway and over the side...on the Golden State southbound transition to the Pasadena, a vehicle fire reported...

The occasional foul-ups claim the attention of Skywatch Control, but in fact the morning rush hour is known in the freeway business as the easy one. The drivers are rested, refreshed, on their toes. In the words of Stan Buckmaster, supervisor of the Caltrans L.A. Traffic Operations Center, "The A.M. traffic is ninety percent regulars. These are the commuters—they're pros. They're familiar with the roadway, and they probably recognize the vehicles in their proximity because they all go in at the same time." They know where they're getting on, where they're exiting, when to make their moves—the pros.

At 7:25 this morning back on the eastbound Ventura the roadbed is a mass of shimmering sheet metal and yet the cars, locked into fighter-plane formation, still rocket ahead at fifty miles an hour. This is the time on the freeways—just one brake light short of congestion, one car length short of sanity—when we're taken to the edge. It requires acute concentration, a pianist's touch on the foot pedals, a sixth sense—"a strange and exhilarating mixture," says Reyner Banham, "of long-range confidence and close-range wariness." If a driver leaves too much space in front of him, the pack will jump in and destroy his momentum; if he leaves too little, he might end up with his head through the windshield. He has scant time to use his turn signals—if he sees an opening, he just goes for it. He forgets about his horn—that's a defensive measure. This sport is all offense, guts. And yet somehow the new players surging in from the right always find enough room to join in.

Gary Bork, chief of Caltrans's Traffic Operations Branch, refers to the attitude of the L.A. driver as "aggressive but polite." He says, "Recently I was in Oregon and we flew over in a helicopter...and their problem was that

nobody on that freeway let anybody in from the ramps. And another thing—
the people on the ramps were not aggressive. But, you know, you come up to
a ramp *here*, and those guys are going to get *on!* And the people *let* 'em on."
Not because they're just wonderful human beings, but because "they want
the system to work!" Whatever legends have been handed down about the
looniness of Los Angeles motorists, they don't describe the overwhelming
reality. Only when this morning's traffic finally slows to a creep around
Tarzana do the commuters snap out of their supercharged trances and begin
to look around at their neighbors, take out their newspapers, their hair-
brushes, their battery-powered shavers, their knitting, their famous little
distractions.

On the San Diego southbound at 8:15 our progress is herky—jerky over
Sepulveda Pass. A daredevil motorcyclist (wearing a camouflage jacket)
tears by between lanes, nearly amputating my left arm. We speed up around
Wilshire and now a semi is on my tail, fifty tons of brute intimidation
grinning in the mirror, its air horn bellowing, *"Move over, jackass!"*

Los Angeles, the city stuck on fast forward, is a miracle of synchronicity.
Even the casual stroller on the boardwalk gets used to hearing urgent voices
over his shoulder—demon bicyclists warning *"On your left!"* as they fly past,
or simply *"Left!"* or *"Right!"* or *"Behind you!"* We have taken to wheels and
developed out of daily habit the culture of the near-miss, which has been
elevated to its purest form on the freeways.

> *On the eastbound 210 west of Lake, a chemical spill...on the*
> *Pasadena in the vicinity of the Golden State, a solo spin out....*

For many people, commuting is the only chance they have to be alone, a
time to reflect (even while maneuvering to stay alive) on great and devilish
schemes. The patterns of movement lend themselves to reenacting the
morning's domestic squabble or rehearsing a confrontation with the boss.
David Brodsly writes, "Perhaps no aspect of the freeway experience is more
characteristic than the sudden realization that you have no memory of the
past ten minutes of your trip." It's a situation, says John Lilly, having "all the
characteristics of the most esoteric and far-out discipline that you could find
in the Far East"—a place, says Banham where many Angelenos "spend the
two calmest and most rewarding hours of their daily lives." It would not even
be an exaggeration to say that some people enjoy playing the freeway game
because, after all, it's the best thing they're able to do on this planet.

The San Diego to the Laguna to the Santa Ana, the Orange to the Artesia
to the Newport to the Garden Grove—we're doing Orange County now,
eating up the mileage like Pac-Man, doubling back to catch the northbound

Harbor, checking them off on the map one by one, more than 550 miles covered by noon.

When I get off for gas, the surface world is not a welcome relief but an aggravation. The interruptions to train of thought are less predictable—cars jerking out from the curb, trucks double parked, pedestrians darting through traffic with paper sacks in their arms. No rhythm, no hum, no flow. We have to stop at red lights, wait our turn, go where the arrows tell us to go. We have to obey a visible higher authority, whereas motion is all we want and need— motion, or at least the promise of motion any second now.

ACCORDING TO THE latest (1984) figures, there are seventy-four accidents a day on the urban freeways of Los Angeles, Orange, and Ventura counties. There are 29.5 people injured each day in those collisions, and for every three days that pass two people are killed. A carnage, you might say, and yet the odds for any one gambler are very, very attractive:

- The average motorist, if he commuted ten miles in each direction five days a week, would have an accident of some sort only once in approximately one hundred years.
- A company with one thousand employees, each commuting twenty miles a day, would go about twenty-three years before it lost even one of them to a fatality.

At Caltrans's downtown headquarters, engineers study traffic behavior and come up with new technologies such as ramp meters and message boards to try to accommodate the freeway animal—safely—in ever-larger numbers. The design standard is 1,800 vehicles per lane per hour—one every two seconds—but the engineers know that downgrades, for example, will carry more traffic than upgrades because drivers can see farther. Curves can reduce a road's capacity (although expert landscaping can diminish the effect). The weather, the angle of the sun, the width of the lanes—all play their roles. Friday brings the heaviest traffic and the most accidents. The engineers know that in the summer the morning load is lighter because students are out of school, the afternoon load heavier because hundreds of thousands of tourists are in the area. The weekend recreational driver is less mindful amd more accident prone than the same person commuting on weekdays. The right lane, according to one study, has more accidents than the left; the afternoons considerably more than the mornings.

Caltrans knows—because it has counted—the number of emergency call boxes on its system (3,335), the number of Botts dots (5,752,810), the precise number of trees (170,048.83). Caltrans has a traffic monitoring and strategy center—"the war room," one official calls it—to which highway planners come and gawk from all over the free and unfree worlds.

Nevertheless, no one at Caltrans seems willing to predict how much longer the system can work the way it does. The freeway grid is nearly completed, and yet every month more drivers enter the competition. It helps that industries keep spreading out over the Southland so that traffic increasingly flows in all directions at all times. It would help if more companies staggered their working hours, as they did during the Olympics. So perhaps the ultimate limit, theorizes senior transportation engineer Don Juge, is "1,800 vehicles per lane per hour for twenty-four hours."

However, it's just possible that imagination is the only constraint. Maybe the L.A. motorist will continue to sharpen his skills, intensify his focus, condition his synapses, deepen his belief, learn the program better and better. Maybe a new evolutionary species is emerging—a driver becoming one with his machine and its mission: a bionic pilot with the high-rise scanning capabilities of a highway patrolman, the reaction time of a Caltech computer, and the psychic preawareness of a Jedi saint—your basic twenty-first-century internal-combustion yogi, a Californian if ever there was one.

THE RUSH HOUR never ends. The thundering herd keeps charging up from behind (like those younger men at the office), and all a driver can do is snap off his rearview mirror. And keep driving. At one in the afternoon—two, three, it's all the same—unswervingly it's a men's game we're playing here, perpetual motion passing for relationship.

After fourteen hours on the freeways, the body begins faltering, the brain misfiring. The eyes burn from unblinking concentration; the heel of the accelerator foot goes numb. The mind reads danger on all sides now, a photochemical wasteland, and after 688 miles I finally abandon true faith, hypothetical as it was, and buckle the seat belt.

The afternoon rush hour is the sloppy one. People are tired from working, sluggish from lunchtime indulgences, hot, cranky, impatient to get home. Thrown in with the regular commuters now are the shoppers, the museum goers, the beach and ballpark and early theater crowds, the visiting cousins from Iowa, the luckless pensioners trying to fight their way back from the Social Security office.

> *Plenty of action out here...a collision involving a school bus and a tanker truck...a vehicle fire with a tie-up all the way back to the East L.A. interchange...a pedestrian stranded up on the center divider....*

On the Long Beach outbound, the last leg, 6:30 P.M., there are billboards for Smirnoff Vodka, Cuervo Tequila, Haagen-Dazs Cream Liqueur, Las Vegas, 93 on Your Dial—Traffic Reports Every Ten Minutes, and Peace in

Ireland. The afternoon's blinding metallic haze has given way to evening again and the first intimations of fog. Finally, at 6:40, after 855 miles and almost nineteen hours of headlong pursuit, I am able to report that it's possible to drive the entire Los Angeles freeway network in one day without getting killed or caught. But barely. The hard-charging night has a million eyes now—the retreating red taillights of the homebound warriors, the onrushing headlights of the counterinsurgents—and a big harvest Shell sign is coming up full over the South Compton offramp.

DAVID BARRY

Thunder Road

O LD CHARLEY DOESN'T come up on the hill to race anymore, but he's the fastest legend on Mulholland Drive because nobody ever conclusively beat him before he retired. The kids racing Mulholland now fancy themselves championship drivers and they'll tell you Charley was king of the hill more because of his car than his driving. Charley raced a hellacious 427 Corvette with rear tires as wide as the business end of a steamroller and enough horsepower to haul a freight train. They talk as if all he had to do in that car was put his foot down and steer.

Legend has Charley blasting through turns with the tires smoking and the rear end dancing and grabbing for pavement so hard it practically ripped up the asphalt. Old Charley, they say, drove with one hand on the wheel and the other around a beer can, a real gee-haw leadfoot cowboy arm-wrestling his car around the circuit and tossing empties behind him.

Charley began racing Mulholland about 1960 in a modified '51 GMC pickup. The fun then was running Sunset Boulevard sports in their Jaguars, MGs, Corvettes and Porsches, and rubbing their noses in the shame of losing to a maniac in a truck. Charley moved to more sophisticated racing equipment—a '55 Ford station wagon, a Hillman Minx, another truck and several other unlikely racers before the Corvette.

Mulholland racing is so dangerous one might compare it to a children's game of cowboys and Indians played with real guns and live ammo. For reasons nobody understands, none of the serious racers have been killed and few have been badly hurt, despite dozens of horrendous crashes over the years. Charley wears a scar from an end-over in his pickup truck and came close to passing away after a head-on collision in a blind turn.

Charley wouldn't want to race most of the kids up there now, because they drive minor-league stuff like Capris, trick Volkswagens, Datsuns, and Toyotas. He'd want to run Chris, the current king of the hill.

Chris is a serious, intellectual type who lives near Mulholland and built his own racer after deciding that the fastest production Porsche wasn't fast enough to make him king of Mulholland. With advice and consultation from the Porsche Works in Weissach, Germany, where he laid out about $25,000 for competition parts, Chris turned a '73 Porsche Carrera into a 165 m.p.h. race car.

If Chris and Charley drove a match with eleven sets of turns and a pit area called Grandstands. That 1.8-mile stretch has been a Gaza Strip in a continuing skirmish between street racers and the forces of law and order since about 1960. In the daytime and early evening it's just another segment of Mulholland Drive, a luxuriously scenic hilltop road that winds from Hollywood through West Los Angeles to the Santa Monica Mountains. On certain nights in racing season it becomes occupied territory for all-out racing from around 11 P.M. to 1 or 2 A.M. The turns are numbered and named after legends from past eras and the course is visible from Grandstands, the staging and parking area for racers, spectators and friends.

Chris is twenty-three, older than most of the current regulars, who are ordinary-looking middle-class boys loitering between the end of high school and the beginning of a career. Most of them live with their parents and the ones with jobs work mainly to buy presents for their cars—presents like fender flares, front air dams, quartz-iodine headlight conversions, wide-rim alloy wheels, nitrogen-damped shock absorbers, racing tires and competition seats.

The racing follows its own peculiar calendar, usually heating up in the fall, cooling off in the winter, coming back in the spring and shutting down for most of the summer. Race nights have traditionally been Wednesday and Friday, but on almost any night a few drivers are likely to gather at a coffee-and-pie shop on Laurel Canyon Boulevard until it's time to take their cars up the hill.

Mulholland racing dates back at least to 1960, but it's several social light years from the *American Graffiti* teenage rebel cruising in a Detroit muscle car with the rear end jacked up like a mating display. The game on Mulholland is driving flat-out on the short, bumpy straights and cutting lines through turns with no guardrails 600 feet above the city lights. It's played at night on sections of road where headlights of oncoming cars show up half a mile away and traffic is light enough for serious racing. The favored cars are Camaro Z-28s with modified suspensions, Corvettes, Porsche 911s, built-up Volkswagens with bored-out engines and oversize tires like giant rubber donuts, or Capris, Datsuns, Mazdas and Toyotas.

Besides being dangerous, Mulholland racing is totally illegal and blatantly unfair to the unsuspecting driver who happens into a race on the way home from a party and gets several years scared off the far end of his life. Breaking traffic laws for recreation makes delinquents out of the racers, but the road is at least partly to blame. Mulholland winds and snakes along so sensuously that it brings out the closet racer in almost anyone.

A typical scenario between your average Porsche driver and a Mulholland racer would go like this: You're rolling up Coldwater in your Porsche 911S and heading east on Mulholland at about 11 P.M. on a Friday night, basking in your $20,000 ego-blanket decked out in forged magnesium wheels, Koni shocks, Pirelli steel radials, five-speed gearbox and all that. You've always wanted to see what you and the car could do in a road contest and you skate up the hill from Coldwater through the Corkscrew (the first of the eleven turns on the circuit) with enough revs and tire squeal to lure a car out of the pack at Grandstands. You run a line through the Grandstands' turns, cutting across the yellow with a car on your tail, and head downhill into the Sweeper, a fast left-hander. The car closes fast behind you, quartz-iodine headlights and driving lamps cutting wild arcs through the night and stabbing your rearview mirror like drunken laser beams. The car is a $4,000 Japanese sedan and you gloat with the anticipation of a $16,000 put-down. You downshift, then punch it, holding as tight against the curve as you dare. The import stays close, but you hadn't really been going for it.

You push harder and shoot into the next turn over your head, tires shrieking as you hang on, the Porsche's rear end flirting with breakaway and a possible spinout. The import sticks behind you like a curse, with no apparent effort and absolutely no respect for your superior car. You fling the Porsche into the last set of curves at the outer limit of your skill, which suddenly occupies a much smaller space than you'd thought. Your sense of survival is begging your ego to back off, lose the race and live.

"Most drivers blow it up here by braking when they don't need to," says Mark Ralph, a twenty-year-old unemployed Brentwood resident. "If you know how to drive you can go much farther into a turn without braking than most people think, even in a sedan."

That's how hill racers in Capris or Sciroccos shame drivers of Corvettes, Jaguars and Porsche 911s, but it's more than knowing how to brake. It's more like the difference between walking down a hillside and running a downhill slalom. Charley, Chris and Chris's friend John Hall take Mulholland at speeds that grind a nonracing passenger into a whimpering casualty of total fear. The turns hurtle at you like screaming nightmares and G-forces pin you to the rail as the car drifts close to a sheer drop over the edge while the driver saws more lock on the wheel.

The tires slip, then bite, the engine rages and slams you back in the seat before the next hairpin rockets at you at least forty miles an hour faster than you know anything can get through it. It's like riding a roller coaster into the right-angle turn at the bottom of a skijump going fifty miles an hour over the limit.

None of this leisure-time activity goes unnoticed by the police, who come out in response to complaints they get from nonracing citizens. When the complaints get heavy—which is usually about twice a year—the police set up a sweep to nab a bunch of racers for aiding and abetting an illegal contest of speed. The charge doesn't last very long in court but many of the racers have spent enough time in jail before being acquitted to think twice about going back. A sweep in April 1977 that netted thirty-two people cut regular attendance to a handful and stopped most of the racing. A letter to the *Los Angeles Times* several months later complained about the hazard and asked why the police couldn't keep Mulholland safe from the racers. Most of the racers come from households on the *Times's* home delivery list. They knew about the letter.

"They've really been bugging us lately," said a nineteen-year-old Capri driver. "It's gotten so it's hardly fun up here anymore." He read the letter.

"That's bullshit," he said with anger. "For every race we have, we get blamed for twenty other people making noise and trying to go fast up here because they've heard about us."

Nobody felt like racing. The talk turned to accidents, police chases, tickets, court appearances, fines, license suspensions and jail sentences. The hill racers are familiar with the ins and outs of traffic law enforcement. Some of them know judges by name and a few have tickets by the dozen. Running the police and winning is part of Mulholland racing, not because it's fun but because stopping means getting a ticket and possibly going to jail. The heroes of the hill are drivers like Chris and John, who consistently outrun the police.

John studied the eleven curves of the racing section on foot to learn the optimum line through each degree of radius, camber change, apex and brake point. Like Chris, he lives close to Mulholland and has been driving it since he first got a license. John can run Mulholland at night without lights in heavy fog and legend has it that he's outrun the police more than twenty times and never been caught. He says he doesn't keep count.

"I don't stick around," John says. He's a clean-cut, UCLA dropout who drives like A.J. Foyt. "If you stop when you see the cops, you get a ticket; so I keep going." He has a disarmingly sheepish grin and a self-effacing way of talking, but there's a case-hardened steel edge of confidence underneath.

"I wouldn't run them anywhere but up here." John says. "I know these

roads too well for them to catch me, but I wouldn't run them anywhere else."
A teenager pulls up in a Chevy Nova with wide-rim wheels and racing tires.
The car has a four-speaker stereo system with a power booster playing a
punching rock tape at high volume.

"Mark," John says, half-turning to talk over his shoulder. "Turn it off."
Mark hesitates, gestures as if to say, isn't it bitchin'?

"Turn it off," John says with total authority. Mark walks back to his car and
dutifully turns it off. "People have been complaining about noisy radios."
John explains.

Despite the letters to the *Times*, most of the hours on the hill are spent
talking, hands in pockets, hunched against the cold. There's no drinking, no
dope and very few girls. Chris and John are constant subjects of conversation.

"Chris came by two nights ago," says a driver parked up the street from
Grandstands, at the end of another week of no racing.

"He took off from here with the rear end smoking and dancing like a fuel
dragster, still fishtailing halfway down into the corkscrew.

"That car has so much power it's hard to believe it can go in a straight line,
but it handles like a Formula-One car."

Talk like that makes it all worthwhile for Chris—the money spent on
parts, the year of designing and building a high-capacity dry sump oil
cooling system with sensors to open or close external radiators to maintain
constant oil temperature under all conditions, the fabrication of a full roll
cage and chassis stiffener of space-age aluminum compound, the installation
of brakes from the legendary 917 race car, and nine-inch wheels in front and
eleven-inch wheels in back. The tires are made of racing rubber that wears
out after three or four runs on the street.

"My dream was to build the fastest car on Mulholland," says Chris, whose
father started a lucrative chain of home furnishing stores and built a spacious
hilltop house with a panoramic view.

"I looked over the Porsche racing catalogue carefully, then consulted with
the performance representative of the factory racing division in Germany
and chose the components for my car."

Chris keeps the car on jacks under a fleece-lined cover when he's not in it.
He only drives in dry weather because the tires don't grip damp pavement.
If he's had a drink or a smoke within twenty-four hours, the Porsche stays
under the fleece-lined cover.

"I don't even think about that car if I've been drinking," Chris says
seriously. "You can't make a mistake in a car like that. I only drive it when
everything feels absolutely right." Chris avoids racing John. Chris says he has
the same confidence in his car as John has in his driving skill and will to win,
which racers usually call balls.

"I don't have to push as close to the limit as John does," Chris says. "because my car is faster at seven-tenths than John's car at nine-tenths. If John ever raced me in my car, he'd kill himself trying to beat me."

"I'll take on anybody in anything on Mulholland with this car," Chris says with the pride of a father of newborn twins. "There are cars that can go faster on race courses but nothing that could go faster on Mulholland than this. I designed and calibrated the suspension—the shocks, the torsion bars, the stabilizer bars, everything—for this road. I don't use it for anything else. It's really just a toy." A $40,000 toy to play with two or three times a month. Chris is said to have hit 140 m.p.h. on Mulholland and it can be reported that his speedometer passed 155 one afternoon along Sepulveda Boulevard near the intersection of Mulholland and the San Diego Freeway.

"I'll never stop for the police in my car," Chris says. "Not if they're after me with the militia. There are people out there who work for the city who want to get me, but there's no way anybody can catch me in this car. I wouldn't stop if they set up a barricade. If they caught me, they'd impound my car and mess it up. I'd kill myself if anything happened to this car. I love it more than anything."

The police don't talk about individual targets on Mulholland but they're very serious about stopping the racing. They call the racers the MRA (for the Mulholland Racing Association), initials used in the late 1960s when the racing was so heavy on Wednesday and Friday nights that several dozen cars would run in a single evening. The MRA split up after a major police bust in the late sixties. Other groups with different sets of initials came and went, drawing police sweeps when the action got heavy.

"We were using stock equipment against racing machinery," said Officer Jim Thompson. "They had modified suspensions, wheels, brakes and engines, which gave our cars a pretty hard time in the turns. Beyond that, they use both lanes of road in the curves [what the racers call 'cutting a line'], which gives them more speed. We're not going to endanger life and property by driving both sides of the yellow."

THE *Times* account of the April 1977 raid described an elaborate system of staging races involving CB radios, headlight signals to spotter cars, lookouts and police-band radio scanners.

"They'd use their cars to block off the road at each end of the race circuit," Thompson said, "then send a spotter car to give an all-clear signal with headlight flashes."

The police had their own tricks, including special radio frequencies, codes and CB radios, backed up by helicopters with high-powered binoculars.

Though the 1977 raid, like earlier sweeps, stopped most of the racing, chasing racers remained a dangerous game.

"I almost got taken out up there," Thompson said of a night when he slipped through the race warning system and met a pair of racers running two abreast flat out in a turn. In one of those instants where one's life supposedly flashes by on high-speed video tape, the racers parted, snicked past Thompson's car on either side and kept going. Thompson made a fast u-turn and went after them.

"I lost them," Thompson said. "They all have switches to kill their taillights in a chase. And they know all the side roads to use as getaway routes."

Thompson drove his Mulholland patrols without crashing but the search-and-pursue missions were halted after several cars were written off in wrecks.

"We were afraid they'd knock themselves off up there," said Sergeant Ronald Roarke of West L.A. "I don't mind losing a chase or two, if that's what they want to do, but I don't want to lose any officers."

The racers call the police story a fantasy, saying the discovery of a police scanner in one of the more than twenty cars involved in the bust, plus an uninstalled CB unit in another, gave rise to the story of a warning system and CB and scanners.

"It was never organized like that," John Hall said. "The police think we go up there and plan who's going to race and run them off against each other like drag racers. We go up there to talk and hang out and when people feel like racing, they do." Hall added that taillight cut-off switches are considered unnecessary because the police can't write speeding tickets against license numbers without positive identification of the driver—an almost impossible task in a night chase.

If the police can't catch the fast drivers on the hill, they've taken most of the fun out of it for drivers unwilling to run for it. The ones who keep up the vigil on the hill, waiting for the racing to pick up to pre-April 1977 levels, complain of police harassment. They say officers order them off Mulholland, unlawfully stop, question and persecute them for no reason. The reason, of course, is that the police are determined to keep the racing turned off.

"We'd pull into their pit area and talk to them, to let them know we were there," Officer Thompson said. "Let them know our position and that we weren't going to allow them to race. But at the same time we were there to show that we weren't completely the bad guys. It was never really a hostile situation."

The real gripe of the drivers who still stand vigil on Mulholland from the end of prime-time programming through the "Johnny Carson Show" is that the racing has tapered off to a trickle. Not like the days of the MRA in the late 1960s, when drivers in souped-up Mini-Coopers were the terror of Mulholland.

"I've heard stories about Minis running three abreast, flat out through the Sweeper in those days," one of the racers said wistfully. "It would have been something to see Old Charley running Minis in that battleship of his. I wonder if he can still drive?"

Another racer volunteers that Charley, who has been racing since the early sixties, maybe even the late fifties, is old—thirty or forty.

"He's getting kinda old to drive fast up here."

The legend of Mulholland Charley has been passed down through the various racing cliques that made Mulholland their private turf until they grew up, moved on, got drafted or married. A veteran of the pre-MRA era in the early sixties, now a successful race-car engineer and professional driver, remembers Charley as a menace.

"Crazy Charley. He raced a pick-up that terrified everybody. Nobody wanted to get near him 'cause you were likely to get run over a cliff. At the very least, you'd get hit by the flying beer cans in his slipstream."

Mark Ralph has never actually seen Charley drive, but he's heard the stories. "He hasn't been up here for a long time," Mark says.

Old or not, Chris wants to race him; otherwise, his $40,000 Mulholland racer will languish without ever meeting the big challenge.

"If I don't race him and beat him," Chris says, "it'll be like winning the heavyweight title after Ali retires. If you didn't fight him, you could never really feel like the champion."

Charley stopped running the hill when the MRA split up around 1965. There's never been much love lost between different groups of racers on the hill, and when Charley's racing friends moved on, he retired. He works at a Hollywood garage.

"I don't like to go up there much anymore," Charley says of the hill. He's an animated talker, with a hint of craziness in his eyes and smile. In a movie he'd be played by Al Pacino. He is thirty-two.

"There's too much traffic up there, too many racers who don't know what they're doing." Charley still has the Corvette and his eyes gleam at the suggestion of a match race with Chris.

"Might be fun," Charley says. "I haven't run the Corvette in a while." His mother is standing a few feet away, waiting for Charley to finish work and give her a ride home.

"Oh, Charley," she says, "you promised you weren't going back up there." Charley smiles at her and wipes his hands clean with a rag. His mother sat by his hospital bed for eleven days and nights waiting for him to come out of a coma after his head-on collision on the hill. The coma lasted thirty days.

"I've heard of that car," Charley says of Chris's Porsche. "I just don't go up there anymore. I raced my Corvette at an old-timer's race at Willow Springs a while back. Turned 150 on the straight. That was a hell of a kick. If I were up there in my car and he came by," Charley says, "I guess we'd have a race. If it happens, it happens."

III.
Institutions

Inside the Pink Palace

W HAT? WHAT WAZZAT? What wazzat? Instinctively, one of the diners, a Canadian, ducks behind his bowl of soup. And again, this high and hideous wail pierces the Polo Lounge like a cry for help, like the swan song of a parakeet that has spotted a cat in the parlor. "Mistafeelds... tellafuncahlfah Mistafeelds, pleese." It cuts through the room like a plastic whistle. "Jezus," says the Canadian, "whatwazzat?" The insistent squeaks seem to emanate from a tiny costumed man, a midget person, mousing tentatively among the tables like an actor who has wandered into the wrong play. He is just over four feet tall. He wears a red jacket embroidered with black welted seams, brass buttons, and black trousers with a red stripe down the sides. He is the hotel's official page. He must be sixty-five. He wears spectacles and, as he gads through the Polo Lounge, he clasps his hands behind him in the manner of the Prince of Wales. "Mistafeelds," comes the plaintive pipe again. "Tellafuncahl fah Mistafeelds."

Mister Freddie Fields is sitting in the premier booth of the Polo Lounge and, affecting a little look of irritation, he takes the call on a pink telephone at his elbow. He is having lunch with me and with Charlie Joffe, who produces Woody Allen's films. We have waited thirty minutes for Fields to arrive, and after his first drink he announces that he will have to leave within the hour— for Paramount. Formerly an agent, Fields has recently produced his first film. As he rattles into the telephone, I look distractedly around the room.

There is pandemonium in the Polo Lounge. Already, at 1:30, all the booths and the tables in the Lounge, the Loggia, and the Patio have been taken. It is not quite spring and the temperature is eighty-two degrees. There is a confusion of the seasons in Beverly Hills that creates confusion in the local dress. Here, at lunch, the men dress much alike; occasionally, one sees a man in a suit and tie, but more often than not they appear to have purchased their clothes from the same shop—the trousers in various violent colors, open-neck shirts, and woolen pullovers thrown carelessly round the shoulders and loosely tied in front. The men with tans, transplanted Easterners, wear Gucci shoes without socks. The women favor long white dresses, T-shirts and French jeans, or slacks and Missoni tops. Most of the younger women wear their hair long and straight with dark glasses thrown to the tops of their heads. It is the look of studied nonchalance.

Perhaps it is the assorted sun tans and long blond hair, but everyone in the room seems familiar. It seems that if you are not someone in Beverly Hills, it is more than passingly important to look like someone. But the Polo Lounge has always been famous for its faces—Charlie Chaplin, W.C. Fields, Errol Flynn. In booth number two, one recalls, Ehrlichman, Haldeman, and Mitchell were taking lunch when the call came through that Watergate had broken. Even in these bland times, in the less conspicuous booths or at corner tables, it is just possible to make out Raymond Massey, Petula Clark, Peter Ustinov, Donald Pleasence, and Doris Day. Sitting in booth number three with two young blondes is Eli Robbins, known as "the patriarch of the Polo Lounge." Now ninety-four, he has been dining here regularly for nearly forty years. He is dressed—as he always is—in a dark suit and bow tie, a white boutonniere in his lapel, and an emerald-and-diamond ring given to him by Marion Davies. It is not entirely clear what Eli Robbins does, or has ever done, but he tells me he lived with one of Bela Lugosi's ex-wives for thirty-two years.

After some minutes, Freddie Fields replaces the telephone and sips merrily at his drink. As he has so little time, I am rather anxious to get to the point of our lunch, but my opening sally is promptly turned aside. Easing out of the booth, Fields smiles and says: "Excuse me, uh, while I do some cheek-kissing." He shrugs, as if to say there are some duties a man cannot evade. "Do you see that blonde over there?" he says. "She is my absolute fantasy lady." She looks perfectly ordinary to me, but Joffe appears to understand and Fields walks across the room smiling easily at people en route. In the corner booth there are three girls, presumably starlets, each of them blond and pretty; they look almost precisely alike. As Fields approaches, they begin to effuse, to percolate; their preening and simpering is exquisite—and excessive. They have probably not seen Freddie since yesterday. Freddie, as he has promised to do, kisses each of them perfunctorily on the cheek. It is like a Beverly Hills benediction.

It is like a scene in an old movie. But scenes of this kind are as common in the new Hollywood as they were in the old—particularly in Beverly Hills. The mighty studios may have been chopped into parking lots and shopping malls, the film stars may have been replaced with music moguls and television chiefs, whole worlds may have shifted out there in the rest of the city, but the Beverly Hills Hotel keeps up appearances. It remains intact and insular, fashionable, yet old-fashioned, a kind of duchy, a preposterous little raj cocooned in the hills of Beverly. Nearly a third of its clients are regulars; they fly out from New York, from Chicago and Washington, check in, conduct their labyrinthine business at the pool or the Polo Lounge, and rarely leave the premises. They take up residence like émigrés in their favorite foreign country.

The Beverly Hills Hotel was built in 1912, at a cost of $500,000, on fifteen acres of land then known as the Rancho Rodeo de las Aguas. The surrounding area was farmland, producing lima beans. Sunset Boulevard was an obscure bridle path. There were only 550 people living in Beverly Hills when it was incorporated as a city in 1914, but as the film business became an industry, actors and actresses began to move in. In 1919, Douglas Fairbanks and Mary Pickford built "Pickfair" in the hills behind the hotel and it became known as the "White House of Hollywood." Between 1925 and 1930 Buster Keaton, Marion Davies, Harold Lloyd, John Barrymore, Charlie Chaplin, Will Rogers, Gloria Swanson, Hoot Gibson, Buck Jones, and Tom Mix constructed extravagant mansions within blocks of the hotel.

Over the years, the hotel changed hands frequently. In the early forties, it had a two-year period of bankruptcy, but in 1943 it was purchased by Hernando Courtright and soon entered its most prosperous time. Ten years later, Courtright (who subsequently bought the Beverly Wilshire) sold out to Ben Silberstein, the current owner, for $5.5 million. Under Silberstein's aegis, the hotel continued to flourish. With 325 rooms, the hotel now maintains a staff of 403. Given its prices, ranging from $35 for a small single room to $546 for a five-room bungalow, and an occupancy rate of ninety-five percent, the Beverly Hills is one of the country's most profitable hotels.

But for a new wing added in 1949, the hotel has remained relatively unchanged; its day-to-day life, though accelerated and more sumptuous, resembles the humdrum life of a country town. During the last sixty-four years, people have been born here, have been schooled and nursed and doctored, have been engaged, married, honeymooned, cuckolded, and have waited out divorces. Its guests have conducted business and love affairs, written books and screenplays, composed scores, and painted pictures. They have gone into hiding, been burglarized (there are two or three reported thefts a month), played tennis and swum and partied. They have grown old and died. The hotel itself has often been filmed, most recently in *Funny Lady* and *Once Is Not Enough*. The action of Neil Simon's current play, *California Suite*, is set in the hotel. It has had, in fact, an unusual (if predictable) history, and though Dorothy Parker liked to say that the Beverly Hills is the place where the elephants go to die, the owners continue to feel it is one of the world's great addresses.

For guests, the day begins at dawn at the Beverly Hills. By seven, one hears the waiters pushing their breakfast trollies along the paved paths between the bungalows and the gardeners hosing down the flower beds and the lawns. A part of the Polo Lounge called the Loggia is one of the few public places to eat breakfast in the predominantly residential area. Many people come from outside the hotel, eating here regularly two or three times a week. Breakfast is served between seven and eleven and by 7:30 the room is loud with travelers who will take the 9:30 flight to New York.

Because of the three-hour time difference between Los Angeles and New York, there is much business conducted over breakfast in the Loggia. Many transatlantic calls come in before 9 A.M. and the local brokers shout down the phones to the New York Stock Exchange.

Meanwhile, the rest of the hotel has come awake. Breakfast is being served in the coffee shop, where some guests prefer to eat since it is smaller and more secluded. Bill Gussman, the head gardener, and his staff of seven have been watering the extensive gardens, planted with coconut, banana and royal palms, orange trees, gardenias, oleanders, azaleas, jacarandas, magnolias, and Australian ferns. Madeline Waugh, the flower decorator, has arranged the flowers for incoming guests, and filled vases with one red rose for the room-service trays. The drugstore-newsstand has opened at eight and sells, among other items, fifty copies of *The New York Times* each day at sixty-five cents apiece and eighty copies of the Sunday *Times* at two dollars. On most days, Eastern businessmen occupy nearly eighty percent of the rooms and suites in the hotel.

Up in the lobby, a gas-lighted fire blazes in the hearth; it is never extinguished. Above the fireplace is a gaudy map depicting the king of Spain's original land grants in Los Angeles, on one of which the hotel now stands. The lobby is decorated in the same style as the rest of the hotel—a wallpaper of appliqued banana leaves, designed by the late Don Loper. The hotel interior is decorated to look as much as possible like the out-of-doors. Outside, the flags have been raised above the roof—the American, Californian, and Mexican.

Guests are checking in and out at the front desk. A list of new arrivals has been sent to all departments the day before and special VIP cards have been dispatched. Green-uniformed bellmen are everywhere; their tasks are endless, pedestrian, but occasionally unexpected. A few years ago, a Texas oilman sent one of them to Houston and Las Vegas with letters he preferred delivered by hand.

Guests spend an average of three days at the hotel. Permanency is not encouraged; that is, there are no special rates for long-term tenancy. But George Barrie, the president of Fabergé, and David Tebet, a senior vice-president of NBC, maintain permanent suites, as does a certain Miss Ruth Prell, who has lived here in seclusion for nearly forty years. There have been permanent guests in the past. Norton Simon kept a bungalow for nearly a year while waiting to marry Jennifer Jones, and Howard Hughes maintained bungalows and a series of suites for nearly thirty years before leaving in 1966. During his last four years, Hughes kept six bungalows year-round, one of which he lived in, one of which his wife lived in, three of which he had lived in, and one of which was for his occasional evening meetings with his wife, or starlets.

Out in front of the hotel, Leon Smith, the six-foot, four-inch head doorman, is busy by 9 A.M. A thirty-seven-year veteran of the hotel, he now owns the parking concession. Smitty, as he is known, is a key status figure at the hotel. Regulars tip him lavishly, since, if they are unfortunate enough to leave the hotel at the conclusion of a bar mitzvah or a wedding reception, they could wait up to forty minutes for their cars. Smith has four full-time assistants and twenty-one students helping him part time. Some 500 cars drive in and out each day, many of them Mercedes-Benzes, which Smith calls "the Beverly Hills Chevrolet." It is a frantic operation and Smith admits to taking four Valiums every day. He is almost certainly one of the most successful doormen in the country, but becomes wonderfully silent when asked to what extent.

Joseph Jacques Toulet, head chef, arrives in the kitchen at 8 A.M.; he has a staff of thirty. Toulet is not only responsible for breakfast, lunch, and dinner, but for the five to fifteen weekly banquets held in the hotel. There are also weekly lunches of the Rotary and Kiwanis clubs, numerous weddings, bar mitzvahs, social and political parties ranging from fifty to five hundred guests apiece. Such functions, usually held in the Crystal Room, have included Mark Spitz's wedding, Dean Martin's lavish wedding reception, and Harold Robbins's 1976 New Year's party, which is said to have cost some $40,000.

In the telephone room down on the promenade, there has been an operator on duty throughout the night. Another arrives at six, and by 8 A.M. the full complement of seven is at work. The guests' names are listed numerically and alphabetically, and the operators are expected to greet each new guest by name and to welcome back the regulars. This is complicated by the two thousand messages the operators take each day. The messages range from simple "ring back" calls to long stock reports from New York and detailed studio make-up calls. The operators must also screen calls for those guests under pseudonyms and other celebrities who will only speak to chosen intimates.

Each of the hotel's 325 rooms is decorated differently and, on certain occasions, will be redecorated to suit the tastes of its clientele. Some guests import their own paintings. Bungalow nine, at $546 a day the most expensive of the twenty-one bungalows, has been redecorated frequently and is the favorite of such guests as Tony Bennett, Perry Como, and Adnan Kashoggi. Elizabeth Taylor has stayed in one or another of the bungalows with each of her husbands, excepting Nicky Hilton. Once, when separated from Richard Burton, she took one suite for herself and another for her clothes.

The hotel is secluded and self-sufficient. One need not actually leave it for any reason or spend cash while one is there; everything can be charged. In the promenade, there is a travel agency, a beauty salon, a barber shop, men's and women's clothing shops, a drugstore, coffee shop, and private screening room. The screening room contains fifteen leather armchairs and may be hired, with projectionist, for $150 an evening. There is also a jade store and a flower shop on the main floor. For the rest, any real or eccentric whim can be ordered from the outside world.

The Beverly Hills is not considered to be one of the world's great hotels. It is not in the class of the Connaught or the Plaza Athenée or the Gritti Palace, but it is a luxurious little inn and, given the occupancy rate, often as difficult to enter as a private club. And, as in any private club, there are few irrevocable rules. Conventions are not permitted, nor men with name cards on their lapels. Until two years ago, pets were registered at five dollars a night. But it made for difficulties. The fourteen-year-old son of Ali Ipar of Turkey smuggled a bear cub into his room. The Duke and Duchess of Windsor always traveled with their pugs. Each evening, an order was placed with room service for three sirloin-carrot-and-pea burgers, cooked *saignant*. It was not for some time that the kitchen discovered they were for the pugs. Pets are not permitted now.

Idiosyncracies of this nature are noted scrupulously by the hotel management. Anyone who has ever stayed at the hotel has a "guest history card" on file. The hotel claims to have 100,000 of them. The cards note all guest preferences. Elizabeth Taylor demands little bowls of pistachio nuts waiting in her bungalow. One entrepreneur requires facilities for laundering his Rolls, a task he prefers to perform himself each morning. Van Johnson will only use red napkins, and a certain Mrs. Ziv refuses to have a rose on her room-service tray as it upsets her when it dies.

A Texas oilman once ordered bear steaks. There were none. Now, when he arrives, bear steaks are flown in from Alaska. And because General Sarnoff preferred suite 486 in a wing of the hotel that was not air-conditioned at the time, special 220-volt lines were run up to the room and an air conditioner installed. Some celebrities insist on anonymity and "no information" is noted, while other celebrities prefer the world be made aware of their arrivals and "notify press" is written down. For all that, there are those perfectly ordinary people who prefer the shield of anonymity, who are repelled by what seems to be an implied familiarity. On arrival, they become discomfited, suspecting their references have been checked: they develop the sorts of ugly insecurities that spring from straying into someone else's party. For the rest, however, the Beverly Hills is approximate bliss, a place in which their merest whim is, as it should be, gratified.

By three o'clock, lunch in the Polo Lounge is nearly over. Freddie Fields has left for Paramount, and most of the hotel clientele have retreated to their rooms or returned to the tennis court and the pool. The pool, in fact, has been the hotel's principal center of activity since two o'clock.

For the past sixteen years, the pool has been managed by Svend Petersen. During summer weekends, some 250 people a day crowd round the pool, though it is unusual to see more than five people actually in it at any one time. The pool at the Beverly Hills is a place in which to lie in the sun, to see and to be seen. From across the undisturbed waters comes a distinct aroma of coconut tanning oil.

Set back from the hotel and concealed by Australian ferns and royal palms, the pool is a separate entity, a place in which any excess, provided it is gracefully effected, is condoned, encouraged even. The pool is flanked by a series of cabanas—eleven on one side, eight on the other. Complete with changing-rooms and telephones, they can be hired by guests for $15 a day. At the northern end of the pool during the summer months, there is a snack bar. It is not, one is told, what it used to be. Once, some years ago, the tuna sandwich was the best in the universe, better even than the numbered duck at Tour D'Argent. Today, it is just another snack bar.

And the pool itself is not what it was. Other than the sound of the constant public paging, it is curiously quiet these days. Ten years ago, to sit around the pool and listen to the names on the public address system was like hearing a major studio call list. "Telephone call for Miss Hepburn," the public page would announce. "Telephone call for Miss Gabor, for Miss Novak, for Miss Welch," and all the old gray executive heads would jerk up and pivot round to watch the actresses take the call. Raquel Welch, it is pointed out, was discovered here. Today the shining girls strut round the pool with high, if misbegotten, hopes.

Some years ago the starlet's favorite scam was to be paged and, when the call came, to be as far from the telephone as possible. Many a minor part was won in this fashion. But times have changed and Svend claims not to have seen a real starlet in years. Even so, the occasional girl still saunters in, usually as someone's guest, and pretends she is there for the sun. One of these, a remarkable girl in a string bikini, lounges even now by the pool. She has been coming to the pool for several days, and we had struck up a loose though fruitful liaison. She had once had a minor role in a minor film and her heart was set on stardom. Her stratagems were wonderfully naive, and she had turned the old phone dodge into a bravura role. "One day, out there," she confided, waving vaguely toward the pool, "some old fart will catch my act and demand an immediate test." She saw it all quite clearly. "I know it's bullshit, darling, but what else can you do?" I had no easy answers, and now

as her name was paged and paged again, she slowly rose from the chaise
longue. Lifting the sunglasses to the top of her blond head and adjusting her
bikini bottom with thumb and index finger, she sashayed round the edge of
the pool to the telephone. And again, the old gray men jerked up from
Billboard, Variety, and the *Hollywood Reporter* and fixed lickerish eyes on
her ambulation. But that is all, a leer, a drool, and they returned to their
magazines. Her walk, perfect in its way, had come to nothing. Pearls before
swine. There is a different crowd in Hollywood today.

Around ten in the morning, the Eastern moguls begin to gather at the
sunny side of the pool. Their tycoonery is conducted in bathing suits, dark
glasses, and Cartier timers. Nat Cohen, the British film producer, is on the
telephone to London and next to him Mark Goodson talks sharply to New
York. Between them, Goodson's secretary waits, presumably for directions.
Two chaise longues away, three pallid men speak solemnly of stocks and
shares. Mark Goodson spends nearly six months a year at the Beverly Hills
Hotel and the remainder of his time in New York. California is for the body,
he likes to say; New York is for the mind. He has been coming to the hotel for
more than twenty years; he has probably spent enough money here to have
bought three houses in Malibu and a couple of sailing ships. But there are no
regrets; it is an old-fashioned hotel, an old-fashioned habit. "In twenty years,
the only things that have changed," he says, "are the prices and the Polo
Lounge."

Ten years ago these businessmen would have been in films; today they are
mainly in music. One sees just as many copies of *Billboard* as *Variety* at the
pool. At ten in the morning on this particular day the upper cabanas are
occupied with the likes of Ahmet Ertegun (Atlantic) and Clive Davis
(Arista). And curiously in their midst, like a piece of pork in a marmalade
spread, is Bob Guccione, the publisher of *Penthouse* magazine. For reasons
best known to himself, he has registered in the hotel under a pseudonym.
Standing now at the railing of his cabana overlooking the pool, he wears
swimming trunks; his dark matted chest is aswarm with golden chains.
"Wearing all those chains," says Svend "he'll be a hunchback in a year or
two."

And so it continues throughout the afternoon. Depending on the weather,
Svend will close the pool around six. But by then the action has moved
elsewhere—back, in fact, to the Polo Lounge and the tumultuous cocktail
hour.

During the twenties and thirties, Le Jardin, the bar at the Beverly Hills
Hotel, was frequented by a little group of nobs and polo players. Having
galloped through their Sunday chukkers, they would drive over from what is
now Will Rogers Park in Pacific Palisades to drink and reminisce. Toward six

o'clock, Le Jardin was crowded with such players as Darryl Zanuck, Will Rogers, Tommy Hitchcock, Walter Wagner, Robert Stack, and, though he was not one of the better horsemen, Spencer Tracy. It was not until 1941 that Hernando Courtright decided to change the name of the bar to the Polo Lounge; and by then, polo was rarely played in Los Angeles and a new group of drinkers had taken to roistering there.

Willie ("Pancho") Holguin, a Polo Lounge waiter for thirty-eight years, remembers the period well. In the Palm Terrace, before it was renamed the Persian Room, there was live music, and when the band had finished its gig and the customers had gone, Howard Hughes slipped in and paid the band for another session. Hughes liked to sit in the empty room and listen as Pancho poured him champagne. In the Polo Lounge, Charlie Chaplin and Paulette Goddard always lunched in booth number one. Errol Flynn was a regular, usually in the company of his friend, Freddie McAvoy. McAvoy, a playboy, rarely traveled without his butler, George. In the Polo Lounge it was George's job to pour his master Russian vodka. Irene Dunne and Loretta Young, who owned stock in the hotel, were early patrons. And Gene Fowler, W.C. Fields, Wilson Mizner, John Barrymore, Sadakichi Hartman, and George McManus, the creator of "Maggie and Jiggs," formed the nucleus of an eccentric group of drinkers. McManus once crashed a Polo Lounge party, posing as a newspaperman, with a button marked PRESS, which he had torn from one of the men's room urinals. In the thirties and the forties, the Polo Lounge was fun—filled nightly with the stars and their hangers-on. Those were the good times.

During the forties the Polo Lounge was enlarged several times to include the Loggia and the Patio, which is why today it has the feel of an exotic warren. To discourage oglers, the mirror behind the bar was replaced with a mural depicting an early Persian game of polo. But for that, the green-and-white Lounge, filled with fake ferns and potted plants, remains much as it was. During the fifties and sixties, a dress code continued to be enforced. No exceptions were made. Brigitte Bardot came for lunch in bare feet and was promptly dispatched; Anita Ekberg appeared in leopard-skin trousers and was given a white wraparound skirt to wear. "We used to have standards," Pancho Holguin recalls. But in 1970 the dress code was relaxed and the rock-and-roll crowd began to trickle in. "We had no choice," says Pancho, "we had to bow to the times."

It is all a darkness now. Dino Borelli, the Polo Lounge's evening host for eighteen years, died last year. It is said that there was no longing known to man that he could not sense in twenty minutes and gratify in twenty-five. He was replaced by Antoine Lupi, a Frenchman, who runs the Polo Lounge like a lion tamer who has lost his nerve. There is in Antoine's eyes what can only be described as a wild surmise.

The Polo Lounge is the Mecca of the Beverly Hills Hotel, but between five and nine it is as though someone had poured weed killer on the shrine. Dark, and filled with smoke and noise, it is populated with an unspeakable motley—what appear to be poachers and painted women, lamsters, fad-mongers, wetbacks, and penny-ante pinochle players. The place creates an instant and malign impression on the mind and one turns away as from a lazaretto. Even so, if the Polo Lounge has lost its style, it has lost none of its popularity.

At cocktail time, the great brown-and-silver tanks pull up before the porte-cochere and herds of little weasels disembark, strut through the doors, pass the front desk and the public telephones and, pausing only momentarily, leap into the murky pit. There, affecting a loose familiarity with Antoine in dodgy French, they disappear into the din. At eight o'clock, there must be two hundred revelers in the Polo Lounge—drinking, eating the free guacamole dip, jammed up against the tiny bar or trucking freely around the room. One enthusiast calls it "a cocktailery for the cognoscenti," but it is more in keeping with a bathhouse in Atlantic City. In the booths, at the bar, and at the tables, the drinkers shift constantly in their seats and look furtively round the darkened room, looking, looking, one is told, for movie stars. One can drink white wine elsewhere, of course, but white wine in the approximate company of Raquel Welch is the finest taste in Beverly Hills. Here the myth of celebrity persists, but Raquel Welch remains at home.

Despite the crush, the chapfallen Antoine and Buddy Douglas, the diminutive page, succeed in worming their way through the room. Douglas is crying, "Tellafuncahl, tellafunchal fah Mista Mogul." Originally the West Coast voice for Phillip Morris cigarettes, Douglas works as an actor in his spare time. There is little he does not know about the Polo Lounge, but he refuses to talk to me or to pose for photographs, as he does not wish to draw attention to himself.

The story is told of the evening several members of the New York Knicks came into the Polo Lounge. One of them looked down and said to Douglas: "And what might your position be?" Douglas became indignant. "I'm the bouncer," he shrieked, "and if you don't behave yourself, I'll get on a chair and kick you in the shins!"

Wherever pleasure is to be found, one can be sure that business will not be far behind. Scattered here and there among the motley are the jades, or actresses as they often call themselves, sitting two by two—looking hopefully, but discreetly, around the room. Despite the gloom, they are not difficult to isolate. As a local sage pointed out to me, "They're better dressed than the rest of the girls and they act more ladylike." Unaccompanied women are not permitted at the bar, but Antoine permits it, providing they are guests of the hotel and insist on sitting there. He will even allow suspected hookers in "if they behave discreetly and don't make a nuisance of themselves." The hotel management, of course, is horrified, but because it is difficult, if not impossible, to control, the trollops range at will.

Toward the end of my stay at the Beverly Hills, I was leaving the hotel for a six o'clock appointment. Walking down beneath the porte-cochere, I saw a beautiful girl with long dark hair and a mink coat coming toward me. She smiled, I smiled, and I continued on my way. Some two hours later, I returned. Leaving my car with the doorman, I saw her again coming out of the hotel. She smiled, I smiled, and she said: "Surely, we've met before?"

Introductions were hastily effected and we retired to drink in the Polo Lounge. Her name was Penelope and she liked to drink margaritas. She had been having a drink with a friend, she said, and had been going home when we met. Other than requesting minor details concerning my marital state and occupation, she seemed curiously unconcerned about the really outrageous portions of my life. Many margaritas later, I learned she had had a brief but bawdy history, which, as one might expect, was a variation on the same sad tale. Penelope was twenty-six, and following a tiresome marriage had come to California two years before. She had worked at many trades, she said with a smile, and was currently employed as a sales representative for a pharmaceuticals firm. In order to make ends meet, she modeled occasionally and moonlighted in such elegant groggeries as the Polo Lounge. She rarely worked more than two evenings a week, charging $50 an hour and $150 for the entire night. Given my purely professional interest in her activities, Penelope said, she might be persuaded to give me a token rate. She worked for herself, and though she recognized the regular girls in the Polo Lounge, she had never tried to talk to them. "Baby, there's a lot of truckin' going on in here," she said. But when it came to business, Penelope minded her own affairs.

She wasn't hungry, she said, and shortly after ten o'clock, we adjourned to my room to continue the interview in seclusion. I ordered six margaritas from room service and searched through my clutter for a notebook. When I turned around, Penelope had undone her blouse. She wasn't wearing a bra. "Penelope," I cautioned, "we haven't finished yet. I have a few more questions."

"How many?"

"Maybe three or four," I said. "The subject isn't particularly complex."

Penelope seemed satisfied, but did not rebutton her blouse. She sat on the sofa, pulled her skirt across her knees, and began to eat an apple. To begin with, she seemed hesitant and did not have much to say, but shortly after the margaritas arrived, she became quite voluble.

"Baby, everybody knows there are truckers in the Polo Lounge," she said. "Everybody knows that. It's been going on forever. It's changed a lot in the last few years though. I have a girlfriend who worked the Lounge a lot eight, nine years ago. It was a different gig then. My girlfriend called it 'playing polo.' There were a lot of starlets. Yeah, one more beautiful than the other. The place was packed with them, I guess, and who do you see now? Beauticians, nobodies. The place is jammed with beauticians and cheap swingers." She took a bite of her apple. "Still, it's a place to get your kicks," she said. "I go into the Lounge 'cause it's easier to find the live ones there. You know? I mean, you can find them at Scandia or at the Luau on Rodeo, but they're a different class. Cheap and sweaty. You get a lot of lonelies in the Polo Lounge, a lot of out-of-towners with time on their hands. But you've got to be discreet, baby. I mean, knowing the maitre d' helps a lot.

"The Polo Lounge has turned into a singles bar at night," she said. "That's one of the hang-ups. The women's movement and this whole sexual liberation thing have fucked the apple cart. I mean, it's warped the trade. These days, girls are giving it away for nothing. Giving it away for nothing is just screwing around. Listen, I'm no different from any other girl. I don't want one-night stands. I'm looking for the big score, too. But I'm choosy and I like to play. And sex is the only thing that doesn't give you a hangover. Nowadays, sex is a toy that everybody seems to have discovered yesterday. They can't leave it alone. That's what the Polo Lounge is all about. It's out in the open now. You can smell it."

Penelope took another bite of the apple. "Okay, baby? Is that it?" she said. Crawling across the sofa, she began to undo my shirt. "Penelope," I said, gently pushing her away, "there are only one or two more questions."

"Jesus," she said, "if I didn't know you were a bonafide writer, I'd think you had a fetish." Pouting, Penelope withdrew to the end of the sofa and finished her margarita.

"What about pimps?" I asked.

"Pimps?" she snapped. "I've got a good mind to take a hike. What do you think I am? A prostitute? Only prostitutes have pimps. You don't know *anything* do you? Jesus, they're the lowest. Listen, you got prostitutes, right? Then you got call girls. A call girl is more of a businesswoman. She really digs the dollars and cents. Then you got the courtesans, you know? The mistresses. They're in for the long haul, they're lifers."

"And what are you, Penelope?"

"Me?" She laughed. "Well, I guess some would call me a call girl, and I was more of a mistress when I was married. But now, I guess you'd call me a sex counselor."

"A sex counselor?"

"Yeah. I mean, men have a sexual problem and I solve it, that's all. It's legitimate. And I don't charge a lot, y'know? The amazing thing is that men just love to pay. That's the turn-on. They really dig the cash transaction. That's how they get their thrills." She laughed. "*Some* thrill, huh?"

Getting up from the sofa, Penelope began to move around the room, her breasts darting in and out of her blouse. She continued to eat her apple. "Do you mind if I watch TV while we talk, baby?" She turned it on. "The Beverly Hills is a very homey sort of place, don't you think? I really like it. I've been really comfortable here. It's got class." She fell back on the bed. And then, an odd thing happened. Tears suddenly welled up in her eyes. She didn't say anything. She just wiped them away, ate her apple, and began to watch Marilyn Monroe playing a ukelele.

Somewhat later we returned to the Polo Lounge. As Penelope had pointed out, she *was* a working girl. Antoine showed us to a corner table. Although it was past midnight, the Lounge was still crowded, for the most part with men.

"Well, how will you do it?" I said.

Penelope laughed. "It's easy, the easiest thing in the world, baby. I've already got my man. Don't look, but there's a blond guy in the corner booth. He's got his eye on me."

Getting up suddenly from her chair, Penelope ambled from the room. I couldn't see whether she looked at the blond man or not, but moments after, he rose and followed her. Less than five minutes later, Penelope returned. "I told him you were my ex-husband," she said.

In a matter of minutes, the blond had paid his bill and left. He didn't look at our table.

"Well, I guess I'd better split," said Penelope. "Wish me luck." She kissed me on the cheek. "And remember," she said. "No names."

I nodded and watched her leave. At the door, she waved. She was a very beautiful girl. She didn't chew gum or bite her nails and she had a way of bringing tears to her eyes that was particularly admirable. Antoine sent over another margarita. It tasted sour. I walked out into the Patio, closing the door to lock the noise in the Polo Lounge. It was one o'clock in the morning and there were still a hundred people there.

I was drunk. I sat down under the Brazilian pepper tree. The dark hotel rose up around me. From one of the bungalows came the sound of low laughter. A couple, whom I had seen in the Polo Lounge, walked arm in arm to bungalow one. It was cold. The sedge had withered from the patio wall. And no birds sang.

RIAN MALAN

The World's Biggest Newspaper

T HE LOS ANGELES TIMES is big. Really big. The biggest, richest newspaper in all the world. It has dominated Southern California since the turn of the century, when it already was America's fattest newspaper, and for the last two decades it has had no competition worthy of the name. In a good year—which means most years at the *Times*—it is bloated with advertising, twice as much advertising as the *New York Times,* ten times more than the opposition *Herald Examiner,* more than L.A.'s twelve commercial television stations put together, more than any other newspaper on the planet. On this spring day in 1982, in the abyss of a near depression, the *Times* is a little slimmer than usual, but with its seven daily sections, seven additional Sunday supplements, and eight suburban editions, it remains a monolith of a newspaper. Spread out end to end, it covers most of the deep-pile brown carpet in the office of Tom Johnson, its publisher.

"It's like a supermarket," Johnson observes proudly. "We have tremendous inventory. We provide more, I think, than any other newspaper." Johnson is an earnest and forceful young man, very charismatic in a boyish, Jaycee way. His strong, open face is topped by a vigorous thicket of dark brown hair. He wears dark business suits and metal-rimmed spectacles, and the overall effect smacks strongly of Clark Kent. Tom Johnson was born poor in Georgia, and his rise in the world has indeed been Kryptonian: a business degree from Harvard ("business degree," he says, a last lingering southern inflection in his speech); eight years in the service of President Lyndon Johnson, eight more under the tutelage of Otis Chandler, scion of the dynasty that has controlled the *Times* since 1882; and, finally, in 1980, command of the great *Los Angeles Times.* He was just thirty-eight—the definitive bright young man, and the first non-Chandler in almost a century to run the newspaper.

Intoxicating, to be so young and hold such power. For an hour or so, Johnson bullishly expounds about this gargantuan creation scattered at his feet, this behemoth that holds sway over a market richer than Sweden or Belgium and sells well in excess of a million copies on the average weekday, more than the combined circulation of its twenty suburban competitors. He produces a four-inch-thick, blue-bound tome—the *Times*'s master plan, he says, for quelling uprisings in the outlying reaches of its empire and ensuring its dominance well into the next century. He talks about the vast resources the paper throws into the journalistic fray—8,500 employees, including 746 editors, reporters, and photographers, the largest editorial staff in the country. The telephone rings, and he learns that President Reagan is coming to lunch the following Tuesday. Intoxicating indeed.

Even the view from this second-floor suite must quicken Johnson's blood—city hall right across the street; the gray massif of the federal courthouse rising beyond it; pedestrians bound for the State of California Building and the county seat, both a stone's throw away. Things have been ordered thus for a hundred years in downtown L.A., the *Times* and government wheeling around one another, twin galaxies of ultimate, elemental power. The *Times* has always been the voice of the Southern California establishment, the *Pravda* of Times-Mirror Square. "We aspire to be a newspaper of national and international excellence," Johnson states emphatically, but later he settles back into his off-white sofa and grows curiously dejected. "In my judgment," he says, gazing at the sea of newsprint at his feet, "this newspaper is quite good. But it could be better."

"Better." The word haunts the executive suites of Times Mirror Square. The *Times* has held so many records in the newspaper business—biggest, richest—for so long that they mean nothing; they are the given, and they are not enough. The *Times* wants to be better. It wants to command the respect accorded the *New York Times* and *Washington Post*—respect that somehow, year after year, eludes it. It wants to be the best newspaper in the world.

Otis Chandler craved that status from the moment he became publisher of the *Times* in 1960. He was a perfectionist, a world-class athlete, a virtual ascetic who seemed indifferent to the trappings of his immense wealth but who possessed a Midas touch all the same. Under his leadership, the Times Mirror Company grew into a $2 billion media conglomerate, master of eight newspapers in five states, seven television stations, the nation's seventh-largest cable system; the *Times* itself improved vastly, but it still was not the best. Growing weary, Chandler retreated to the chairman's suite in 1980 and passed on the sacred charge to Tom Johnson.

Chandler was quite specific about Johnson's mission. The young southerner was, of course, expected to take care of business, but his true charter was contained in a handwritten letter he received soon after his arrival in L.A. in 1977.

"So, my young friend," wrote Otis Chandler, ". . . together we are going to push the *New York Times* off its perch. Somehow, someday, in spite of the geography, traditions, eastern snobbery, and the like, there will be recognized only one superior newspaper, and it will be located, of all unlikely places—way out West, in Indian and smog country—L.A.!!! That's your challenge (and mine)."

Johnson eagerly set off in pursuit of the grail. He created daily business and entertainment sections, moved to beef up the paper's coverage in areas where it had been slack, refurbished the way it looked, hired more reporters, and led the *Times* to new pinnacles of prosperity. But the true goal—to be the best—remained achingly out of reach. At every turn the *Times* was slighted. The *Newspaper Design Notebook* ridiculed its new look—"We can't help but wonder why the *Times* bothered," it said. The trade journal *Adweek* pointedly omitted the *Times*'s William Thomas from its list of America's twelve best editors. In newspaper circles, people would make polite remarks about how much the paper had improved over the years, then weigh in with their reservations—too long-winded, too cautious, too close to the establishment, too hard to read. These are judgments with which many *Times*men do not quibble.

God knows, the *Times* is a good newspaper, but there's a torpor about it, a genetic caution that stymies even the most determined efforts to make it a truly great one. "There aren't a lot of dazzling things left to do with a newspaper like this," says Johnson, staring at the newspaper on the floor. A crushing inertia seems to have settled on his broad young shoulders. "Even after having been here five years I don't think I'm as forcefully in control as I would like. It takes a Herculean effort to move the *Times*." There is something about this newspaper—so rich, so powerful—that pulls it up short of true grandeur, and Tom Johnson, like Otis Chandler before him, seems to have run smack into it.

THE FIRST STREET lobby of the *Los Angeles Times* is a corporate shrine, a cool, dark marble sanctuary in the center of which a great white globe turns slowly on its bronze axis. The old union-busting Chandler war cry, TRUE INDUSTRIAL FREEDOM, is carved in granite alongside the doorway, and at each of the globe's four compass points stand busts of the Chandlers, the dynasty that founded and still controls the paper: General Harrison Gray Otis, the apoplectic old warhorse who drove around town at the turn of the century with an ornamental cannon on his car, striking terror into the hearts of trade unionists; Harry Chandler, the shrewd son-in-law who built the family holdings into a real estate empire the size of Connecticut by the thirties; Norman Chandler, the grandson who used the *Times* as a flack sheet for Richard Nixon and like-minded Republicans in the forties and fifties; Otis Chandler, the great-grandson who tore up his forefathers' bigoted legacy in the sixties and played fair.

Beyond Otis Chandler's likeness the visitor enters a warren of interminable corridors that lead eventually to the third floor, editorial hub of the newspaper that responds so sluggishly to Tom Johnson's "Herculean effort."

A forest of signposts point the way to Food, Real Estate, Foreign, Fashion, National, Business, Calendar, Metro—the *Times*'s plethora of departments.

Follow any of these signs and in time you will find yourself in a room so vast that it disappears into a point at the far end, a full city block away. The decor evokes a bank, an insurance company. The carpet is a soothing gray green, the fittings chrome and white. Light flows out of tall beige bins, reflects off the ceiling, and diffuses softly through the room, which is alive with the green flicker of video terminals. This is the *Times*'s newsroom, where the paper's newsgathering army labors in a hushed, orderly ebb and flow of shifts. Journalists from horizon to horizon, the best journalistic talent money can buy, so many reporters that they often lose track of one another.

Earlier this year a note appeared on the newsroom bulletin board announcing the death of one Harry Klissner, former *Times* reporter. "The world is a little poorer at this time," it said, adding that Klissner left "a vast multitude of friends" at the newspaper.

"Who the hell was Harry Klissner?" asked reporter Eric Malnic, glancing at the note. He flipped through his *Times* directory, a two-inch-thick list of his fellow employees' phone extensions. No Harry Klissner. A crowd was gathering around the bulletin board. Nobody remembered Harry Klissner. Malnic removed the note, scrolled it into his typewriter, and typed, "Who was Harry Klissner?" across it.

"There are people in this very room I don't know," said a bystander. "I've been here for twenty-four years," exclaimed Malnic, "and I didn't know who he was!"

For the record, Klissner had quit the *Times* at least a decade before his death, and in this respect, too, he occasions mystery. Few *Times* employees leave of their own accord, and fewer still are fired. The *Times*'s newsroom is a very pleasant place to work—"a Cadillac," says reporter Charles Wallace, likening his previous job with United Press International to a mere VW. He and his colleagues earn, on average, about $35,000 a year—fifty percent more than the industry norm, seventy-five percent more than the average wage at the opposition *Herald Examiner*. Top reporters pull in close to $60,000, and editors even more. *Times*men and -women are cosseted with paid sabbaticals, annual cost-of-living increases, and generous expense accounts. Best of all, they don't have to work very hard. "You take all this too seriously," a copy editor told one newcomer. "The trouble with you is you're a hyper New York Jew. Why don't you take up jogging?"

Unlike most dailies, the *Times* is not built on ulcers and broken marriages. *Times* reporters are often given unlimited time to prepare their stories, an unheard-of luxury in a profession so grueling that its practitioners suffer fearfully high rates of alcoholism and burnout. Staff writer Jerry Cohen, for instance, had been working on an opus on aging for fifteen months at the time of this writing, while some newsroom grunts over at the impoverished *Herald* were churning out a story a day. There is no star system at the *Times*, none of the intense competition that drove *The Washington Post*'s Janet Cooke to cheat for her Pulitzer prize. This is, after all, what some sacrilegious reporters call "the velvet coffin," despite new metropolitan editor Noel Greenwood's efforts to make his reporters' lives less serene.

"I think things were running at half speed for a period," growls Greenwood, who assumed power eighteen months ago. "No sense of pursuit, no curiosity about Los Angeles." A blunt and businesslike newsman, Greenwood inherited a staff whose news instincts had atrophied to the extent that they were no longer capable of recognizing a major story on an LAPD blotter. (The police shooting of Eulia Love, a cause célèbre in L.A.'s black community in 1979, took more than three months to surface on the *Times*'s front page.) Greenwood and his sidekick, Dave Rosenzweig, have tightened the screws somewhat and drummed up several solid investigative pieces since taking over, but two men can do only so much to accelerate the comfortable rhythm of this newsroom. "God forbid that anything should happen after the first edition goes to bed [at 7:30 P.M.]," says one scofflaw. "Short of a major quake or a 747 crashing into the Music Center, the *Times* isn't interested."

The odd thing about the *Times* is that it is full of would-be dissidents, men like Greenwood, Rosenzweig, city-county bureau chief Bill Boyarsky, national editor Dennis Britton, men who struggle against the prevailing mood of complacency but can't quite eradicate it. Consider media writer David Shaw, who is often allowed to critique the *Times*'s foibles on its own front page. Most recently he authored a devastating analysis of the paper's obituary policy. The *Times*, Shaw wrote, was devoting more space to entertainers (Jimmy Durante) than to statesmen (Moshe Dayan) and seemed quite nonchalant about the fact that many of its subjects had been dead and buried for so long that they were fading from public memory. The powers that be at the *Times* agreed that their obit policy rated a mere "six and a half or seven" on a scale of ten, but were perfectly content to let it stand until recession-mandated cutbacks killed off the obit page entirely eight months later. "It's mildly frustrating," admits Shaw. Mildly? Well, let's forgive Shaw his equivocation, because he is probably as reluctant as the next reporter to court expulsion from this journalistic Eden. When Kay Mills was ordered to soften an editorial calling for the resignation of the local PBS station chairman (who happened to be Tom Johnson's neighbor), she knuckled under. "I'm just a worker bee," she says. "Sometimes it's safer that way." When national editor Britton disagreed with his paper's initial indifference to civilian casualties in the recent war in Lebanon, he kept his peace. "I speak out only when I'm really inflamed," he says. In for the long haul, most *Times*men are reluctant to rock the boat. "Lower-level editors look at copy as a source of danger," says one reporter. "They don't want anyone coming up and saying, 'How the hell did that get in the paper?'"

Reporters are prey to the comfort syndrome as well. "It's real easy just to get by here," says one. "I've begun to realize that I can just hang around and do a piece every couple of weeks. That's what makes me realize it's time for me to go." But he's going nowhere soon—and know's it; he came to the *Times* at the pinnacle of his career, and now, in terms of salary and prestige, there is nowhere to go but down. "Most people just roll over," he admits. "They can cut off your balls, and you just say, 'Okay, where's my next check?'"

IT IS LATE on a Friday afternoon. *Times* associate editor Jean Sharley Taylor has kicked off her shoes and joined her visitor at the conference table in a corner of her office. "This is going to be the newspaper of the eighties!" she says. A coy and gracious woman in her fifties, Taylor oversees the *Times*'s eight "soft" sections—Calendar, View, Travel, Home, The Book Review, Real Estate, Food, and Television Times—and she is waxing enthusiastic about the newspaper that has been her professional home for eleven years.

"We're coming down the middle in terms of being moderate," she says, illustrating her point with an airy gesture of the hands. "We're also coming in on a high plane in terms of news coverage versus sensationalism. You can destroy a woman by saying her voice rose shrilly, rather than just rose. When I see those things coming through, I stop them."

Taylor continues at some length about the *Times*'s politeness, its abiding sense of caution. She mentions that she has, this very week, "toned" a column—not a straight news story but a signed column of opinion out of Washington that "talked about the administration in a way that was very negative." As originally written, the column mentioned a Capitol Hill luncheon at which alternative funding for the arts was discussed. The meal, wrote the *Times*'s Sylvie Drake, was "a basic lunch, perhaps devised as penance for this administration's attempt to elevate catsup and relish to the rank of vegetables." By the time Jean Taylor had worked over this offending passage, the repast in question had become "a basic no-frills lunch, in keeping with this administration's emphasis on cost cutting."

"It was, just to my ear, fair," Taylor says. Does she think the same sort of toning down is done elsewhere in the *Times*? "Oh, I hope so!" she says.

"All of this may make us a little dull occasionally," she adds.

A little? Occasionally?

In some respects the *Times*'s toned-down primness could be considered quite admirable, depending, of course, on how much titillation you expect for your quarter. The *Times* hired Roderick Mann to replace gossip columnist Joyce Haber, then forbade him to use unnamed sources—forbade him, in other words, to gossip. The *Times* sniffs disdainfully at lurid stories, generally abandoning them to the exploitation of "lesser" newspapers, which are all too happy to oblige. It plays few crime stories on its front page and downplays such reader pleasers as this summer's congressional sex-and-dope scandal. It even bounced Richard Pryor's 1980 self-immolation off page one in favor of a story on elections in South Korea.

It may be all very well for the *Times* to hold itself aloof from such tantalizing stuff—most newspapers that aspire to greatness have stiff Victorian spines—but it recoils as well from controversy in considerably more substantive areas. Last year a Bank of America spokesman told a *Times* reporter he wouldn't be bothered if the Soviet Union were to invade Poland. An invasion, he suggested, could stabilize the country's economy and safeguard the bank's loans. When the story reached the desk of economic-affairs editor John Lawrence, he blanched. This was a very hot quote, especially given the enthusiasm with which the cold-war drums were being thumped in Washington at the time. Lawrence sent his reporter back to the banker three or four more times to make sure he realized what he was saying. By then, of course, the banker was nervously equivocating, and the *Times* was spared having to use the quote.

John Lawrence has a long-standing reputation for journalistic skittishness, a trait that obviously has not hindered his career at the *Times*. In June the Commerce Department released figures indicating that American business was not taking advantage of massive Reaganomic tax breaks to reinvest. To many observers, including *The Washington Post*, a cornerstone of supply-side economic theory appeared to have crumbled, and the *Post* proclaimed as much on its front page the following day. The Business section of the *Times*, under Lawrence's fastidious stewardship, mulled over the figures for a month before reaching a similar conclusion.

Or consider the way Lawrence and the *Times* handled the death of Jack Tripp. Tripp was a local Shell Oil salesman who committed suicide in 1979 and left behind a note blaming his superior at the oil company for his despair. His wife claimed in a lawsuit that he had been forced to threaten service-station owners who refused to sell gasoline at prices dictated by Shell; Shell settled the case out of court for $50,000. This incident eventually found its way into the opening paragraphs of a story prepared last February for the *Times*'s Business pages by reporter Debra Whitefield—a compelling illustration of what she alleged was an oil industry-wide campaign to break independent gas retailers.

Most newspapers would have been delighted to lay Tripp's death at the door of a scheming oil company. Whitefield's story was sound—sound enough, Lawrence admits, for a bolder newspaper such as *The Washington Post* to have to run it. Nevertheless, the Tripp anecdote made Lawrence queasy—after all, you can't ask a dead man to interpret his own suicide note—and he ordered Whitefield to rewrite the story twice, diluting it further each time. In the published version, Tripp's suicide was mentioned only in passing, along with a quote from a Shell spokesman that this was "a tragedy with no readily apparent answer." The telling suicide note was not mentioned at all.

"We do have a different approach on this kind of story," says Lawrence, "but we're not afraid to be tough." As evidence, he produces an article in which the *Times* exposed the nefarious dealings of a minor banker with long hair. "When you're a strong newspaper," says Lawrence, "you're more credible if you don't try to get the last ounce of charge out of your stories."

It would be wrong to assume that Lawrence toned down the Tripp story to protect Shell. Rather, the *Times* simply becomes squeamish in the face of ugly, "negative" (a favorite word), or nakedly controversial stories. In the *Times*, a massacre in El Salvador remains "alleged," even after the London *Times* prints photographs of the dead; a *Washington Post* news service story about planned CIA capers in Nicaragua is undercut by the prominent insertion of a White House disclaimer. Journalistic jaws sagged all over town last February when the *Times* allowed industrialist Justin Dart to call President Ford a "dumb bastard" on its front page. This was wildly out of character for a paper that is usually unremittingly nice, even in its editorial pages, the very place where opinionmongers are supposed to wield their biases. A few days after Ronald Reagan's election, for instance, editorial pages editor Anthony Day ordered the last-minute excision of a Mike Royko piece. The Chicago columnist had jeered the new actor-president and those who had voted for him and Day considered the piece too vulgar and inflammatory for his dignified pages.

Day, forty-nine, speaks slowly, chain-smoking Merit cigarettes, often stopping in mid-sentence to grope for precisely the correct construction, the right word. He comes from an old newspaper family, holds a degree in classics from Harvard, and, beneath his abstracted, slightly rumpled academic façade, he has the burnished manners of a Brahman—and that, perhaps, is why his part of the newspaper is so innocent of coarse passion, or of any passion for that matter.

"The influence of the *Times*'s editorial pages," he says, peering over the brown rims of his spectacles, "is cumulative, say, over the period of a generation. We are influential not so much in the positions we take but in the

way we think about things. Which is fair. Reasonable. Moderate. Educative."
And, with the exception of the *Times*'s celebrated call for Interior Secretary
James Watt's head, congenitally cautious.

Times editorials are erudite, exquisitely balanced little essays, long on
hand-wringing, short on bold solutions, even for problems as mundane as
earthquake planning (the *Times* said the next governor should think about it)
or poor management at the local PBS station (the *Times* said it deserved
good management). H.L. Mencken believed newspaper editorials should
"stir up the animals," but the *Times* prefers to let sleeping dogs lie. Especially
big, fierce dogs such as those that snapped at NBC's John Chancellor when
he ventured to criticize "imperial Israel" at the height of this summer's war in
Lebanon. Israel's pulverization of West Beirut chilled many Americans—
"and well it should," said Day at the time, although his newspaper said
nothing of the sort. Pulling in its head at the start of the siege, the *Times*
waited seven weeks to voice its first quavering criticism of Israel's tactics.
"The positions we adopt," says one of Day's eight editorial writers, "are so
objective as to be utterly indifferent."

So objective, in fact, that cartoonist Paul Conrad was banished from the
editorial page nine years ago. Conrad is a merciless iconoclast who has won
two Pulitzer prizes, and the *Times* was distressed to think that readers might
confuse "the voice of the *Times* with the pen of Conrad," as an editorial put
it. "As Conrad is fond of saying," explained the editorial, "he works in black
and white; the editorial writers work in shades of gray." Indeed. On the same
day that Conrad was relegated to the op-ed page, another color was wiped
off the *Times*'s editorial palette with the announcement that the paper would
no longer make endorsements in major political races. In so doing, the *Times*
pontificated, "we shall strengthen [our] ability to comment on the issues and
candidates with impartial vigor." When Mike Curb mounted a strong
candidacy for the Republican gubernatorial nomination last summer, however, there was no "impartial vigor" in evidence—the *Times* simply held its
nose, even though it viewed the sleek opportunist with grave misgivings. To
do otherwise might have caused a commotion, and the *Times* loathes
commotions.

Once Curb had gone down in flames in the primary, however, Day was
quite prepared to share his views. "To be quite honest," he said, again artic-
ulating an editorial that was never written, "Curb is not a respectable
character."

Neither, for that matter, was Big Tony Peraino, boss of a small-time
Brooklyn mob that infiltrated the Hollywood movie industry in the mid-
seventies. In early 1981 the *Times*'s Sunday Calendar section sent two
freelancers on Peraino's long-cold trail. Authorities had already hounded the

Perainos out of business, but no matter—the *Times* is never obsessed with being first on a story. After eighteen months and the expenditure of at least $80,000—yes, $80,000—the story was ready for publication, but the *Times* was suddenly beset by qualms. Running unfavorable stories about Hollywood is a recent departure from *Times* tradition—this is, after all, the newspaper that first ignored the 1977 David Begelman forgery and embezzlement scandal and then printed a stomach-turning apologia in which arts editor Charles Champlin termed Begelman's liberties with other people's checks "a crimeless crime."

Widely mocked as a show-biz toady following this debacle, the *Times* resolved to keep a more vigilant eye on Hollywood. It took the paper's old guard a while to adjust to the new approach, though. Just last year, an exposé of the Teamsters' activities in the movie industry was "toned" by Jean Taylor, and a damaging story about producer Robert Evans was spiked at the insistence of his friend Champlin. The three-part Peraino story offered the *Times* another chance to prove that it was no longer a softy, but once again it grew tremulous. "This wasn't the sort of breezy, entertaining thing people are accustomed to reading over Sunday brunch," says a *Times* editor. Anxious not to cause Sabbath indigestion, Sunday Calendar editor Irv Letofsky decided to open the series with a foreword in which he first groveled for running such unusual fire, then argued that it was "not-unusual information," thus tying himself into an inextricable semantic knot.

"I wasn't quite apologizing," says Letofsky, ensconced in an office papered with old movie posters, "I was trying to tell people what it was doing there." He explains that most *Times* entertainment writers have a positive attitude and that when a nasty story comes along, there are "a lot of wrenching decisions" to be made. "I'll explain that," he says. "Or try to explain that." He seems uncomfortable. "I can't explain anything exactly, but I can always try." He tries, but finally there is no explanation. This is just the way things are done at the *Times*, newspaper of the eighties.

IN THE FINAL analysis, the way things are done at the *Times* is decided in this sprawling second-floor office, on this broad, clean desk, by this deeply tanned man—William F. Thomas, editor and executive vice president of the *Los Angeles Times*. On the bookshelf behind him are biographies of generals Douglas MacArthur and Omar Bradley. Thomas is fascinated by the military mind, an appropriate passion for the editor of a newspaper so vast that some of his minions refer to him as "The," to distinguish him from the legions of lesser editors.

Thomas, however, looks less like a general than an affable shop foreman, with his graying hair slicked into a quiff and his speech peppered with old-fashioned profanities. "Son of a gun," he says. "Son of a bitch." At North-western University on the GI bill, he earned side money as a jazz pianist, and if his life had followed a different trajectory, if he were wearing a shiny suit, he could merge unnoticed into a Vegas lounge combo. Merging unnoticed—that's Bill Thomas's public relations problem.

Things might be different if Thomas shared Joseph Pulitzer's belief that the purpose of a newspaper is to "afflict the comfortable." But moderation, not affliction, is the note Thomas wants to sound in the pages of the *Times*—a worthy attitude, perhaps, but not one that's likely to drive an impeachable president from office. Thomas is plainly suspicious of the inquisitorial journalism that came into vogue after Watergate—in fact, he says, he wasn't quite comfortable with the press's role in Watergate itself. "The main thing I try to do in this job," he says, "is to give people a fair shake."

A fair shake! Such humility is profoundly out of sync with the moxie of his counterparts Ben Bradlee and Abe Rosenthal, editors, respectively, of *The Washington Post* and the *New York Times*. It is his curse to be constantly compared to them and found wanting. Bradlee and Rosenthal goad and bully their subordinates, whereas Thomas's managerial touch is so light that one of his chief lieutenants says working for him is like "being in a seance." Bradlee and Rosenthal are cocktail party and media superstars in their cities; Thomas is "Bill who?" in L.A.

A reserved man, Thomas is scarcely visible even inside the *Times*, where reporters see so little of him that some jokingly doubt his existence. He steers clear of the newsroom, delegates by telephone, and spends his spare time golfing—in fact, he was on the course one weekday morning in 1971 when Otis Chandler decided to make him editor, and he had to scramble back to the office for the laying-on of hands. Some regard his relaxed style as proof that Thomas is a weak editor. He is not inclined to defend himself on this score. "It's like saying I'm not a crook," he says. Were he to rise to the bait, however, he could note the extent to which the *Times* mirrors his personality—cautious, nonjudgmental, thoughtful, a little bland. These are precisely the hallmarks of the "special kind of journalism" of which the *Times* has often boasted in full-page ads in the *Wall Street Journal* and the *New York Times*. It's a brand of reportage that is very much Bill Thomas's creation, and it is the cause of much that's wrong with the *Times*. Most newspapers strive to stay abreast of the breaking wave of history, to print news that's urgent and immediate—the sort of hard-edged information that's not available in magazines or on television, with its fleeting attention span and ratings-dictated agenda. Thomas, however, has turned the *Times* into a daily newsmagazine that's sometimes content to mop up after the news breaks—an easier, safer task, and ultimately, a denial of a daily newspaper's central charge.

Son of a Michigan banker, Thomas came to California in the fifties to run a foundering weekly in Sierra Madre, and even then he felt that newspapers would have to change to survive television: "I figured out that traditional newspaper journalism was an exhausted field, for an earlier time, when people were poorly educated and had to have their stuff packaged in little bite sizes." Thomas's ideas dovetailed neatly with Otis Chandler's, and he rose swiftly after joining the *Times* in 1962, becoming metropolitan editor in 1965 and editor in 1971. This was the *Times*'s golden age. It was stronger than ever financially, its suburban competitors were comatose, and the *Herald Examiner* was enfeebled by labor strife. The *Times*, like some ancient civilization at the height of its power, no longer had to worry about the barbarians on the border. In this safe and sheltered environment, Bill Thomas shaped the *Times* into a very unusual newspaper. He had two maxims: "Do it once, do it right, do it long," and "The reporter's words go into the paper." He vanquished hard-line copy editors who wanted to hold the *Times* to traditional styles of news reporting. He encouraged reporters to take their time, to add a magazine dimension of thought and anecdote to their stories. He nurtured those reporters whom he thought of as poets.

As Thomas's concepts took root, the *Times* began to lose its edges, its muscle definition. It developed instead a Southern California looseness, an expansiveness, a fondness for the why of a story instead of the traditional what. With its rambling stories and soft focus, it became less of a newspaper with each passing year.

Thomas's *Times* was sometimes strikingly different, sometimes just long-winded, a great, grave newspaper carrying out its somber duty. "We know," admits Mark Murphy, former metropolitan editor, "that if one percent of our readers get to the bottom of one of our long pieces, that's a lot." The *Times*, in other words, is readily prepared to bore more than a million readers on any given day.

It would be unfair to Thomas and the *Times*, however, to dismiss its "special journalism" as merely boring, because on occasion it can be very special indeed. Consider the work of Charles T. Powers, the Byron of the *Times*'s national staff until he was elevated to the foreign desk in 1980. He had always been a feature writer rather than a hard-news reporter, a dashing prose stylist who was not, by several accounts, much interested in politics or economics, the glum grist of daily journalism. Not quite the man most newspapers would choose as a foreign correspondent, but then, the *Times* foreign desk is not quite like any other.

The *New York Times*, for example, requires its international correspondents to grind out dispatches about everything that stirs in their sector of the globe. *Los Angeles Times* correspondents are told to overlook hard-news stories—"spot stories" in the argot—unless, of course, there is a war, coup, or famine. Instead, they are meant to wrestle with the grand sweep of events and seek out the illuminating human-interest angle—a task at which Powers is a past master. His first foreign post was Nairobi, and something about Africa went to his head like champagne.

Powers profiled a tribal patriarch who had 40 wives and 349 children and who slurped mud-colored beer through a six-foot straw. He filed stories about the rain, garage mechanics, coal merchants, forlorn sailors—wonderful, exotic stories, in spite of their utter dearth of news value. "Imagine the city as a drawing by M.C. Escher," he wrote of Tananarive, capital of the Malagasy Republic, "an illusionist's trick where fish turn into birds, water runs uphill, and steps leading down take you back where you started."

Those were the opening words of an enchanting Powers story that appeared on the *Times*'s front page last May 5. Meanwhile, back in Nairobi, representatives of more than one hundred countries had gathered under the auspices of the United Nations to discuss the world's rapidly deteriorating ecology. There they were, the first, second, and third worlds, discussing something no less urgent than the preservation of the planet while the *Los Angeles Times*'s correspondent pursued ancestral spirits through the winding streets of Tananarive. The *New York Times* carried three stories on the Nairobi conference; the *L.A. Times* dispatched it with a two-inch summary.

And this, of course, is the downside of the *Times*'s approach to journalism. So many of its soldiers are off on scouting expeditions that they miss battles along the front line. Not a day goes by without the *Times* ignoring a relatively important news story or relegating it to a paragraph in the page-two news wrap-up. Israeli officers denounce their own army's barbarism on the occupied West Bank—two inches in the *Times*. South Africa throws its forces deep into Angola—two inches in the *Times*. The University of Central America alleges election fraud in El Salvador—not a word in the *Times*. Former Health, Education, and Welfare secretary Joseph Califano rakes the Reagan administration—not a word in the *Times*. Critics of the paper see this as some sort of grand conspiracy to distort the news, but it's really just the world according to Bill Thomas. "We don't necessarily want the day-to-day stories," says George Cotliar, the *Times*'s amiable managing editor. "Are they of real importance? I don't think so."

What Cotliar and his colleagues do seem to want is a newspaper that is frequently less concerned with world events than with the sideshows that happen to intrigue the folks at Times Mirror Square. More inclined to cover the weather in Cairo than massacres of Indians in Guatemala, the *Times* remains a good paper, but not a great one.

But since that is good enough to hold a million-plus subscribers, to say nothing of $580 million in annual revenues, it is probably unreasonable to expect the *Times* to self-tinker much. "They care about the paper, but they don't have the passion to make it as good as it could be or should be," says Jim Bellows, a former *Herald Examiner* and *Washington Star* editor who held Jean Taylor's job at the *Times* from 1966 to 1975. "Their attitude seems to be, 'Don't fix the thing if it isn't broken.'"

"Son of a gun," says Bill Thomas, running his fingers through his hair with just a trace of exasperation. "We don't stick to traditional newspaper subjects. Sometimes we overshoot. Sometimes we're verbose to the point of stupefaction. Right now I'm on a kick of editing a little harder. The goddamn pendulum never stops. It's always here or there." Or wherever. Earlier this year the *Times* did seem to be somewhat more tightly edited, but by midsummer the paper was back to its old ways—a sprawling seven-part series on Orange County, a psychoprofile of Police Chief Daryl Gates that occupied much of the *Times*'s news space on two successive days. Fascinating, if you happened to be interested; if not, you were in Mark Murphy's ninety-nine percent. The stories were long. They were esoteric. They were impenetrable. They were a special kind of journalism.

DAN NOYES, MAUREEN O'NEILL & DAVID WEIR

Operation Wigwam

12:30 P.M., MAY 14, 1955

As the countdown approached, five hundred miles off the California coast, Dr. Alfred Focke hesitated. The weather was bad. Fifteen-foot seas and twenty-four knot gusts had smashed into the thirty ships arrayed along two wide arcs away from Focke's command post on the USS *Mt. McKinley,* knocking some of them out of their assigned positions.

It was not too late. Years of top-secret government planning, millions of dollars of the U.S. Navy's sophisticated scientific gadgetry and a task force of 6,500 men could be brought to a halt up until the last tenth of a second. But the time for that decision had come.

At a quarter to one in the afternoon, Focke put aside his remaining doubts and pushed the button.

The USS *Mt. McKinley* was five miles from "Surface Zero." It would take fifteen minutes for a sequence of electrical impulses to navigate a mass of complex circuitry and equipment and reach the bomb buried two thousand feet under the ocean, in the center of the array of ships. But close by, something had gone wrong, and Commander Richard Purdy was desperate. His ship, the USS *Marion County,* was supposed to maintain an elaborate arrangement of buoys in their proper positions for the blast, but the weather had tangled the ship in cables attached to the buoys.

Meanwhile, aboard the USS *Molala,* a seventeen-year-old seaman named Barry Nicoll was below deck cleaning latrines. He had no warning of what was about to happen; he only knew that his ship was out "on maneuvers."

At a tenth of a second before 1 P.M., an awesome rumble came from far beneath the turbulent Pacific. History's first deep underwater nuclear blast sent a force two and a half times as powerful as that released at Hiroshima hurtling toward the surface, and Operation Wigwam was officially under way.

This is the story of that operation, a one-bomb atomic battle off the coast of California. It is an eyewitness account, based on the memories of the men who planned and executed the explosion as well as those who were its victims. Because many of the official records and movies have recently been declassified, it is probably the most detailed inside story of atomic sea war ever made public. It is a story that changed the lives of Focke, Purdy, and Nicoll forever.

NINETEEN FIFTY-FIVE, the year Albert Einstein signed the Pugwash Manifesto renouncing war, was a time when Americans were learning the fears of the nuclear age—fear of the Russians, of spies both inside and outside our borders and of the terrible dangers of radioactive fallout. There was a rush to build bomb shelters, and school children were drilled to crouch under their desks when mock air raid sirens sounded.

As part of an intensive effort to find out what our enemies could do to us before they did it, the U.S. government detonated fifteen nuclear bombs during 1955. There were no enemies at these explosions, only thousands of American servicemen.

Wigwam, an operation so secret even its code name was a classified term, was one of the fifteen. Planning for it began at least two years before H hour. In complete secrecy, Focke, at that time a navy explosives expert, started working as scientific director of the project. He was quietly transferred from the Naval Electronics Laboratory at Point Loma up the coast to the University of California's Scripps Institution of Oceanography at La Jolla. There, working ostensibly as a marine physicist, Focke started devising the scientific components of the test.

The peaceful Scripps campus, high on a scenic cliff above a wide Pacific beach, looked like a relaxed academic outpost devoted to understanding the ocean at its doorstep, but the task force of Scripps scientists quietly working within held the highest government security clearances. They knew that what they were readying was an experiment—no one had ever shot off an atomic bomb deep below the sea before—and an experiment involving human life. But the navy officers and the scientists assigned to the project felt that they had good reasons for that experiment.

In the aftermath of World War II, antisubmarine warfare was one of the U.S. Navy's major preoccupations (it remains so to this day). According to an "operation plan" developed by the Armed Forces Special Weapons Program in 1954, "the chief objective of Operation Wigwam is to determine with satisfactory accuracy at what ranges, under various conditions, a submarine or surface vessel will be destroyed by a deep underwater atomic explosion. The second objective is to determine the hazards to the delivery vehicle and its supporting forces." In other words, the naval personnel being assembled for the blast were unwittingly participating in a nuclear "war games" experiment.

This work was complicated, as another navy report later observed, "by the inability of anyone to predict to any satisfactory degree the extent and type of surface and subsurface phenomena." No one knew, for instance, whether the ocean would be able to contain the shot or whether the radioactive blast would explode out into the air and contaminate the surface. Unknown, too, was how powerful a shock wave would be created by the explosion—and what that would do to the ships near the blast site.

The uncertainty surrounding the test was not surprising given the overall lack of scientific knowledge about the oceans at the time. "Oceanography," a Scripps public information officer recently confided, "only really came of age after World War II, when the military became interested in the oceans." The navy, for example, underwrote almost the entire Scripps budget during the fifties, and the institute's director was Roger Revelle, a former navy expert in the oceanographic aspects of atomic testing.

The Wigwam task force of Scripps scientists, including Focke and Revelle, was given the task of locating a suitable area between 200 and 600 miles off the California coast for the blast. They chose a spot at 28° 44' north latitude and 126° 16' west longitude, 450 nautical miles southwest of San Diego, and declared the area a "biological desert."

By mid-April 1955, a month before D day, the Wigwam planners were caught up in a whirlwind of secret sessions, classified memos, top-level security clearances and emergency conferences.

On the morning of April 12, six key officials plotting the test gathered at Point Loma for an urgent meeting. They had three big worries: the press, the public and the tuna. Present at the meeting were Focke; Rear Admiral John

Sylvester, commander of the navy's Wigwam task force; Focke's military assistant, Captain Jack Lofland; two marine biologists from Scripps; and Dr. W.R. Boss, an Atomic Energy Commission (AEC) official. The AEC was worried about the public. "It must be acknowledged," noted an internal AEC memorandum, "that in the event of an unanticipated accident involving radioactive contamination, public opinion might exert sufficient pressure to cause delay or cancellation of future testing."

In addition, the AEC's Division of Biology and Medicine had protested the idea of an atomic blast so close to the West Coast for fear it might disrupt the ailing tuna industry.

A year earlier, during a series of nuclear detonations code-named "Castle," at Bikini atoll, Japanese tuna boats had reported landing 480 metric tons of radioactive fish, and panic had swept American supermarkets.

The U.S. tuna industry was already in dire straits, thanks to the intense competition from Japan. Canning executive G.C. Van Camp Sr. had told the AEC that another scare would "wreck the industry," throw thousands of people out of work and focus public anger on the entire nuclear testing program.

Now, at their Point Loma meeting, Focke, Sylvester and Lofland were told by the AEC's Dr. Boss that the Food and Drug Administration (FDA), which normally monitored tuna for radioactivity, didn't want any part in checking tuna after the Wigwam blast. This news greatly upset the military planners.

Boss then explained that the FDA could still be convinced to take part if the navy would provide the expert personnel. But Sylvester said that all the navy's radiation safety experts would be needed at the test site in case the "shot vents and some of the water or mist hits ships of the task force."

The planners' major concerns were for the scientific and military results of the test; concern for the possible hazards facing the thousands of men stationed at the blast site appears to have been secondary. In fact, the navy originally wanted to stage a much larger operation, but the event had to be scaled down because of a "reduced budget." Radiation standards set for the operation allowed exposure to ten times the amount of radiation considered safe for the public in 1955. On the afternoon of April 12, after the morning meeting at Point Loma, the AEC's Boss toured one of the tuna canning plants, posing as a Scripps scientist in the company of bona fide Scripps scientists, in order to plan a monitoring program. The AEC scrupulously avoided letting anyone know that it was involved in monitoring tuna for radioactivity—the agency even discussed using UCLA as a front to reimburse fishermen for any "hot" fish that might have to be discarded.

The Wigwam architects would have preferred to keep the test secret, as some of the other nuclear blasts had been. But the large scope of this test, involving 6,500 men on thirty ships, as well as what they termed their "public relations" tuna-monitoring effort, made a news leak inevitable. Furthermore, there was the "serious international problem" that Mexico and South American nations were major consumers of Pacific fish. The AEC worried that President Eisenhower's Atoms for Peace program might be undermined as a result.

So, during the weeks leading up to the blast, AEC officials fabricated their strategy: "If the test operation is conducted as planned, without any untoward incident, it is felt that by development of a proper public information plan, adverse public reaction can be held to a minimum." A draft press release written two weeks before the blast set down the official line: "No radioactivity at all has been found in commercial fish arriving from the area."

Despite the best efforts of Scripps and the AEC, however, when a carefully worded press release was finally issued several days before the detonation, it aroused anger in the West Coast fishing industry and in some state officials as well. Seth Gordon, director of the California Department of Fish and Game, sent a letter to the AEC contesting the "biological desert" label Scripps had pinned on the blast site: "We know there are no deserts in the ocean. Fish in greater or lesser abundance are found everywhere."

The protest died quickly, however, when the AEC quietly pointed out to industry officials that "the less said about the affair to the press the better."

As part of its "public information plan," the Pentagon also lied about the size of the bomb. The *San Diego Tribune* was leaked the story that the blast's yield was "thought to have had an energy equivalent of one to five kilotons, certainly smaller than twenty kilotons... The bomb was actually thirty kilotons. As for press coverage of the blast itself, an internal AEC memo bluntly stated, "There will be no access by correspondents." As the countdown to H hour began, Focke and his small circle of atomic warriors reviewed every detail of their heavily classified operation. Each stage of the test was code-named, according to a common theme, dating from earlier military glories. The tuna-monitoring effort was labeled "Pow-Wow." Pretest sub models were "Papooses." And the simulated submarine hulls that were to be used as targets of the blast (to determine the "incipient lethality" of underwater nuclear bombs) were called "Squaws"—because, according to Focke, "that is what gets squeezed inside the Wigwam." With the press, the public and the tuna industry all under control, the only variable the navy had not prepared for was the weather. For Commander Richard Purdy and his crew, the weather made all the difference.

1:00 P.M., MAY 14, 1955 — H-HOUR

FIFTEEN MINUTES after Focke pressed the button on the *Mt. McKinley,* the bomb exploded, propelling three giant radioactive gas bubbles toward the surface 333 fathoms above. The water rifled skyward at a speed of 200 miles per hour breaking into the atmosphere with poetic symmetry. Surface Zero became a boiling white circle two miles in diameter. Domes, then plumes, of churning water rose up, each higher than the last, until a column of water higher than the World Trade Center towered above the midday sea.

Shock waves from the blast thundered through the ocean, slamming into the circle of barges, tugs, LSTs, destroyers and an aircraft carrier. Among the shock waves was one that had rebounded off the hard rock bottom 16,000 feet below.

Some of the ships were tossed up like bathtub toys. A barge at Surface Zero disintegrated; another nearby roller-coastered forty feet up and down in the roaring white foam.

Lying flat on the deck of the command ship, *Mt. McKinley,* not far from scientific director Focke, a chief petty officer looked up to see the king post superstructure "vibrating like tuning forks." A military report later said two of "the ships appeared to flex as the shock wave traveled from bow to stern."

Aboard the USS *Fort Marion,* boatswain's mate Walter Johnson felt a fine mist rain down on him.

On the *Molala,* seventeen-year-old Barry Nicoll was ordered up on deck from his job cleaning the latrines. Halfway up the ladder he felt the blast. Like many around him, he had no idea what was happening. He looked toward the white mountain exploding out of the Pacific and gasped.

A twenty-eight-square-mile area of ocean churned like a giant caldron. The displaced water crashed noisily down again, this time pushing a new wall of boiling water out from Surface Zero—toward the ships. Suddenly, a gargantuan white wave over 600 feet high threatened the ships. It surged for more than a mile and then died down, shooting out breaker after breaker in concentric circles away from Surface Zero.

Downwind from the blast, beneath the 330-billion-cubic-foot radioactive plume drifting southward, Captain Ross Pennington readied his ship, the USS *George Eastman,* to sail near Surface Zero. The ship's power had been knocked out by the initial force of the blast, and Pennington and several of his crew members had to leave their shielded control area to get it going again. A secret report later noted that the men were working under "extremely hazardous respiratory conditions." Once the *Eastman* got moving, it looked from the other ships as if it were sailing into a mountain of radioactive water.

Upwind of Surface Zero the *Marion County* was still trying to get out of the blast area. Commander Richard Purdy was trying to calm his men, who were screaming and running around uncontrollably in the face of an advancing 1,900-foot wall of water. Purdy kept his senses, stabilized the ship, and put the engines into reverse. The *Marion County* started to back away from the blast area—it could no longer go forward because its bow door had been damaged in the rough seas.

The research ship, the *Horizon*, that carried most of the Scripps scientists, also was incapacitated by the blast. The scientists panicked as the ship drifted helplessly into the circle of radioactive water downwind. "Inside the bomb area it was so hot you'd be killed," remembers Dr. Theodore Folsom, a Scripps oceanographer. "When we drifted into the hot water, the needles on the radiation range finder went way off. I yelled, 'Get the hell out of here.'" Folsom took advantage of the situation, however, by dropping measurement devices overboard. The ship finally got going and moved quickly out of the danger area.

Within ten minutes of the blast, the land masses ringing the Pacific echoed the sound of the explosion. At that time, the Coast and Geodetic Survey reported the rumble as an earthquake. Instruments at Cal Tech measured it at the equivalent of 4.1 on the Richter scale. The shock wave reached a Greek freighter more than 600 miles away from the blast site, steaming off the Golden Gate. The ship radioed the Coast Guard, "Has San Francisco just been hit by a severe earthquake? We have been badly shaken but are all right and will return to render assistance if needed."

Thirty-two minutes after H hour, the sound of the explosion reached Hawaii. Echoes from each of the islands in the Hawaiian chain reverberated back to Point Sur. Later the sound-bounce from each of the Aleutians off Alaska came in, followed by an echo from Japan.

NOT LONG AFTER the volcanos of water subsided, sharp bursts of automatic gunfire erupted from ships deployed around Surface Zero. It was cleanup time, and some of the radioactive debris was being sunk by gunfire. Barrels scattered over a three-mile radius were sunk to 16,000 feet below, where they joined one of the three sub hulls and a barge that had already sunk.

Other waste-disposal activities were more complicated. The simulated submarine hulls designed and built especially for Wigwam, surface barges, instrument platforms, buoys, pontoons and cables used in the test were now the record of history's first deep underwater nuclear explosion. The buoys and pontoons were retrieved by designated ships and placed on deck for the return voyage home. The barges and two surviving sub targets were rigged up for the 500-mile tow back to the mainland.

Then there was the 3.1-square-mile circle of foam that defined the perimeter of the most highly contaminated water from the blast. Scripps scientists followed this "hot" water for forty days before losing its track 120 miles west of Surface Zero. Any migrating fish that came in contact with what the scientists labeled the "undulating sheets" of radioactive water would have absorbed it and possibly have become dangerous to eat. (As anticipated, the one-month tuna-monitoring effort after the test did not find any radioactive fish from the Wigwam site, although it did detect a few "hot" specimens from the 1954 Castle area.)

The process of retrieving radioactive debris naturally exposed the ships (and their crews) to high levels of contamination. According to one report, "the main deck and topside spaces [of the USS *Chanticleer*] were contaminated from 2,500 to 25,000 counts per minute as a result of the ship's work in a contaminated water area." Eugene Gordon, a seaman on the *Chanticleer*, remembers that "men went around the deck with Geiger counters. The ship was hot. We had to deep-six a lot of the stuff on deck, including a vat of potatoes."

According to the report quoted above, "personal clothing contamination up to 50,000 counts per minute was experienced. [However the Geiger counters were calibrated, 50,000 counts would have been highly radioactive.] Attempts to launder contaminated clothing in shipboard facilities were not successful in a reduction to permissible levels. Holding for decay, in addition to laundering, appeared to be necessary." The report went on to state that "highly contaminated sinkable objects, not essential to the mission, were discarded oveboard."

Among the largest pieces of radioactive waste were the two surviving submarine hull targets. Each was 132 feet long. In order to raise one of the subs to facilitate towing, groups of divers had to enter the radioactive water and readjust the cables and weights holding the subs down. The navy placed a high priority on salvaging these target hulls because expensive, delicate instrumentation had been placed on board in order to measure the effects of the blast.

Once the sub hulls were ready, two ships began the arduous job of towing them toward San Diego. Halfway back, however, the main cable holding one of the sub hulls broke, and it sank to the ocean floor thousands of feet below.

The next day the cable towing the third sub hull started tearing apart. The radioactive hull was carefully maneuvered to about 100 feet of water somewhere off either Santa Catalina or San Clemente island (there are conflicting reports on exactly where). There it was sunk in waters that are used by abalone divers, fishermen and recreational boaters. As late as five years later, in 1960, a diver who had been involved in Operation Wigwam reported seeing the sub hull still in place. (Checks of navigational charts of the region have failed to locate the sub hull in 1980, however.)

The possibility that low-level radioactivity might have been released into these recreational waters off the California coast cannot be discounted, though it is not addressed by any of the declassified reports released by the navy to date.

While the radioactive sub hulls were being towed back to land, the ships carrying "hot" buoys, pontoons, cables and boxes of contaminated water docked in San Diego. Large cranes lifted this radioactive debris from the test onto the docks. Its ultimate resting place is unknown, but according to Dr. John Gofman, a nuclear critic trained in both nuclear physics and medicine, it was "very irresponsible" to bring the test waste back to land.

Finally, two ships involved in Operation Wigwam—the USS *George Eastman* and the USS *Granville S. Hall*—were purposely exposed to radiation. The *George Eastman* was equipped with a special "wash-down" system, which essentially consisted of spray-type garden hoses. This system was only fourteen percent successful, however, according to a recently declassified military report. Radiation levels on the *Eastman*, for example, reached 500 milliroentgens per hour one day after the blast. This level, though undoubtedly short-lived, indicates that the ship became "hot" enough to constitute an extremely hazardous environment for its crew—especially since it went on to its next assignment at Operation Redwing, farther out in the Pacific.

Fourteen months later, in August 1956, Captain Ross Pennington and his crew stood on deck as the *Eastman* approached the Golden Gate.

Suddenly the tug sent to meet the ship appeared. To Pennington and his crew the tug was a ghostly sight, completely draped in canvas, with crew members wearing what Pennington's wife, Mary, waiting for him at berth at Hunter's Point, recalls as "white, spacelike suits."

As the ship docked at Hunter's Point, a radiation detector was placed at the bottom of the ladder. Mary Pennington watched as her husband descended the ladder. Her heart dropped when he was turned back. He and the crew had to change their shoes, which were "hot" from walking around on the deck of the radioactive ship, before they were allowed back on land.

After this chilling start to their reunion, Pennington explained to his wife what had happened at Wigwam and Redwing—that the "*Eastman*'s purpose was to be exposed to as much radiation as possible."

AFTER THE BLAST, Richard Purdy had to back his damaged ship, the *Marion County*, 500 miles to San Diego. Then he went home to the cottage in Encinitas where he lived with his wife, Ruth. Purdy seemed all right for a couple of days. He took Ruth to a party for all the commanders involved in the operation, although as usual he did not tell her what had happened at sea. At the party several officers mentioned to Ruth that her husband deserved a medal for the way he had calmed his crew and navigated the damaged ship back to port.

Richard Purdy had participated in many of the hottest firefights in the Pacific during World War II, including Okinawa and Midway. Purdy said that after one battle he was responsible for towing two boatloads full of dead friends and companions, whose bodies were decomposed beyond recognition, out to sea and then sinking them. After completing this mission, Purdy said he was given two bottles of bourbon and told to "go to the officer's club and drink it off." He was not the type who could forget, however—time and again the standard commendation forms filed in his naval record indicated the deep and unusual compassion he felt for the men serving under his command.

Purdy had enlisted in the navy, refusing an appointment to the Naval Academy arranged by a congressional contact of his father's. He had quickly risen through the ranks and was pinstriped captain of his first ship at the age of twenty-eight, just as World War II was breaking out.

Although he felt he had seen the worst of war's horrors, Commander Purdy had not been prepared for his first glimpse of nuclear devastation. That came in 1954, when he was ordered to tow a nuclear bomb-blasted ship back to the mainland from the South Pacific. Purdy's ship, the *Marion County*, towed it all the way back to San Diego. A newspaper report called it the longest ship tow in naval history.

Ruth Purdy says her husband could not get the image of that ship out of his mind. Nothing he had seen in the war had prepared him for the advent of weapons that made commanders and seamen and human judgment itself irrelevant.

Steaming backward into San Diego after Wigwam, Purdy said later, was like reliving the towing of the disabled ship from the South Pacific the year before. At home with his wife, Ruth, in Encinitas in late May 1955, Purdy was even quieter than usual and had trouble sleeping. Within days, after viewing an executive showing of the film clips of Wigwam with the assembled naval brass, Richard Purdy suffered a complete nervous breakdown. He was transported off to the psychiatric ward of a nearby veterans' hospital, where he was kept for six months. He refused the navy's offer of a 100 percent psychiatric disability and demanded to return to sea. Because of his record, the navy complied. He was given charge of the rescue effort to pick up anyone who went down at sea in airplane crashes off San Diego. There wasn't much to do, and a few months later, at the age of forty-four, he retired, his brilliant naval career a shambles.

NOT LONG AFTER the blast, while Richard Purdy was slowly backing the *Marion County* toward San Diego, seventeen-year-old Barry Nicoll, aboard the *Molala*, started vomiting. As soon as the ship reached San Diego, Nicoll was transferred to a nearby VA hospital, where other symptoms started appearing in rapid succession.

Nicoll was told he had been hit by 390 roentgens of radiation from the blast (a dose of 300 is considered potentially lethal by some experts). The admitting physician noted in his official health record that Nicoll had suffered chills, general malaise, loss of appetite and headaches after "exposure to radiation on maneuvers consisting of atomic warfare."

Nicoll's hair stopped growing—he didn't need a haircut for the next six months—and the hair on his chest fell out completely. (These symptoms were omitted from his official health records.) He developed severe thyroid trouble. Part of his thyroid was removed, but other symptoms kept appearing. His spleen hurt; his lymph nodes were swollen. The hair loss and gastrointestinal problems were classic indicators of radiation exposure.

During his six-month stay at the hospital, Nicoll continued to have the terrible headaches and other symptoms. All this time he was afflicted by a mysterious quenchless thirst. Nicoll was told he was suffering from mononucleosis, but he felt the doctors were hiding something from him. "Every day, groups of doctors would come in to look at me—five or six of them at a time. Some were foreign—they couldn't speak English. It made me feel important to have so many interesting people coming in to see me—I was only seventeen. But it also got me worried." Nicoll says he was visited at the hospital by a navy captain who said, "Under no circumstances are you to mention what you've seen or where you've been. If you do, I'll take care of you." (Recent attempts to locate the officer have failed.) Nicoll says he obeyed the command for the next twenty-five years.

FOR ALMOST A quarter of a century silence surrounded Operation Wigwam. For the men who had devised and executed the maneuver, these were years of success and achievement. The scientists at Scripps rose to the top of their fields. Their names achieved prestige in the marine labs that ring the coasts of the world's great oceans. Many of them directly benefited from their involvement at Wigwam, publishing papers on the tendency of radioactive pools of water to resist diffusion by the ocean or the relative lack of biological productivity in the eastern tropical Pacific.

Members of Scripps's Wigwam task force publicly downplayed the threat of radioactivity to fish on several occasions. In 1957 testimony before a congressional subcommittee probing fish contamination from the Castle nuclear blasts, Scripps director Revelle suggested that just because fish were "hot" didn't mean they were inedible. He stressed that only "one-half of one percent" of the catch in question, which was landed by Japanese fishing fleets, was radioactive. This, however, did amount to 480 metric tons.

While they were publicly minimizing the threat of radioactivity in the oceans, Scripps scientists were also publishing research papers in journals such as Limnology and Oceanography that indicated that marine organisms exposed to radioactivity concentrated many dangerous isotopes (including strontium 90) to levels thousands of times that found in the seawater itself. This "biomagnification" represents a serious health threat to people (such as the entire population of Japan) who rely on fish for a large part of their diet.

Scripps also was involved in the navy's controversial ocean-dumping practices, monitoring sites like the Farallon Islands area off San Francisco, where nuclear waste was dumped for twenty years. In 1957 Scripps reported no "easily detectable amounts of radioactivity" at the Farallons. But recently, evidence has surfaced that leaking drums have released radioactivity thousands of times higher than the background levels.

Furthermore, Scripps performed atmospheric research for the CIA, which critics charge is investigating weather modification schemes; developed technology for the CIA's mysterious *Glomar Explorer* mission; constructed a prototype of a "floating island" that could serve as a mid-ocean airfield; and conducted undersea research for the navy. Press speculation on the latter has centered around the potential use of low-frequency sonar in submarine warfare or the firing of benthic nuclear missiles. The institute's current director, William Nierenberg, who is an expert in antisubmarine warfare, consulted on Project Agile, a Department of Defense-funded counterinsurgency operation. Scripps has carried out extensive nondefense research as well, including deep-sea drilling and manganese nodule mining work, useful to industry.

The technical evaluations Scripps scientists prepared of the Wigwam blast have now been released, along with other military and AEC reports, under the Freedom of Information Act.

They reveal that:

● Largely because of the adverse weather conditions, seventy percent of the experiments planned for Wigwam were failures.

● "The Wigwam detonation produced sufficient airborne activity to have given radiation doses many times tolerance to exposed personnel located approximately five miles downwind." (At least two ships—the *Eastman* and the *Granville Hall*—were about five miles downwind at H hour.)

● Air monitors stationed at San Diego measured a higher level of radioactivity over that city within four days of the blast. The radioactivity skyrocketed from ten to twenty times normal background levels over the next nine days.

● The frightening "base surge" created by the blast was characterized as an "insidious hazard" that turned into an "invisible radioactive aerosol."

IN SEPTEMBER 1979 one man finally broke the twenty-five-year public silence about Wigwam. In Honolulu, Elroy Runnels, forty-six-year-old father of four, announced to a room packed full of television lights, cameras and reporters that he was suing the government for exposing him to lethal radiation at Operation Wigwam. Two days later Runnels was dead of leukemia.

At this point, a determined activist named Tony Hodges entered the scene. Hodges, an old friend of Runnels's attorney, was outraged by the government's refusal to pay Runnels's disability claim. He managed to obtain the navy's declassified film and official written report of Operation Wigwam and scraped together enough money for an early December budget-fare flight from Honolulu to San Diego. His mission was to force the Wigwam story into the public arena.

Hodges's effort was only a partial success, but the publicity he engineered did indirectly help unravel the conspiracy of silence about the blast. A graph of high levels of radioactivity over San Diego, after Wigwam, was shown on local TV and alarmed residents concerned about fallout and cancer.

Mayor Pete Wilson directed his Quality of Life Board, headed by sociologist Joseph R. Gusfield of the University of California at San Diego, to investigate the possibility that the city's air had been contaminated by Wigwam. "We were very skeptical of the military people the Pentagon sent out to talk to us," Gusfield said in a recent interview. "We knew they were just PR people." Nevertheless, when the commission issued its report last April, it concluded that there was no evidence to dispute the official version of events at Wigwam—and that the air over San Diego had not been dangerously radioactive. The report suggested that another atomic bomb set off at the Nevada Test Site around the same time may have been responsible for the measured increase.

Officials of the Department of Energy (DOE), which has taken over some AEC functions, flatly deny that the Nevada test could have been the culprit. "All of our fallout was blown due east on those particular days," stated information officer David Jackson in Las Vegas. "The sharp increase in radio-active half-lives over San Diego was probably due to Wigwam," said DOE physicist David Wheeler.

Amid the finger-pointing back and forth, neither side was disputing the main issue: that radioactive fallout had been injected into the atmosphere. Although it may not have created an immediate health threat to San Diegans, this burst of fallout contributed to the globe-circling belt of man-made radioactivity that endures to this day. At its peak, in 1962, the weapons testing was cumulatively responsible for approximately thirteen percent of the background radiation hitting people in the Northern Hemisphere.

One of those watching the Wigwam controversy on San Diego TV last winter was Richard Purdy. By December 1979 Purdy knew he was dying of lung cancer. His nervous breakdown had led to a drinking problem during the years of quiet retirement in Encinitas.

Once he realized that Operation Wigwam was declassified, Purdy ended his long silence about the test. Ruth was shocked: Her husband had never mentioned the test except once, nine years after the explosion, when he had developed painful cataracts in both eyes. That condition had caused an experienced Navy physician to ask him whether he had ever witnessed an atomic explosion because, according to the doctor, "it's the kind of condition many atomic veterans suffer."

Now Richard Purdy started reliving his personal nightmare once again. He told Ruth about the wall of water charging his ship, the *Marion County* seeming to bounce eighteen inches off the ocean, the men screaming, the damaged bow door, his crippled ship drifting toward Surface Zero—all as part of a"peacetime maneuver" staged against his own men. For the first time in twenty-five years, Ruth Purdy began to understand why her husband had gone crazy.

On his deathbed, Purdy called in a young neighbor, Ron Josephson, and spoke haltingly into a tape recorder, detailing everything he could remember about the blast. The sick man's voice explained why he was finally setting down his record of Wigwam. "It's too late for me, son, [but] I feel they were all left holding the bag—all those crews. Not just on my ship—hell, no—but all those crews."

Three weeks later Ruth Purdy watched her husband bleed to death in the final stage of his cancer. A special bed, ordered weeks earlier from the VA so Purdy wouldn't have to leave home at the end, arrived too late to be of any use. Ruth Purdy was now a widow of the nuclear age.

WHILE SAN DIEGO was still in tumult over whether Wigwam had doused it with "hot" air, Tony Hodges, whom the mayor's PR man had dubbed "Johnny Atomseed," was telephoning Sacramento, trying to interest aides to Governor Jerry Brown in the test. A few days later, Brown held a midnight screening of the declassified Wigwam film, to which he invited dozens of antinuclear activists who were staging a five-week sit-in at his office.

After viewing the blast movie, Brown issued an immediate call for the federal government to publicly release the names of all servicemen involved in Wigwam so they could receive suitable medical treatment.

The following day, at his home in West Covina, Barry Nicoll noticed a small news account of Brown's statement. Despite the catalog of repercussions he had suffered after Wigwam, Nicoll had eventually recovered enough to finish his navy duty. He married, started raising a family and found a job. In spite of recurring illnesses—including a second operation in 1959 to remove the rest of his thyroid—Nicoll became a successful teamster, made good money and acquired a nice house with a swimming pool. But in 1979 Nicoll fell out of a truck-trailer while unloading it.

That accident seemed to unleash his post-Wigwam symptoms in exaggerated form. "The doctors told me I was like a loaded gun. What happened to me in '55 put me in a condition where the trauma of my accident triggered my diabetes, my headaches, my thirst—everything."

Now, Brown's call for the identity of Wigwam victims raised Nicoll's hopes for government compensation. "All these years I kept quiet about it," he explains. "It was under a cell in my mind that was not to be opened. I never even told my family. But once I started talking it spilled out like water over the falls."

Nicoll wrote Brown a letter, explaining how he had been exposed at Wigwam. But the governor never answered, apparently because of a staff oversight. "That hurt me more than anything else," he says. "When I saw that notice in the paper I felt a togetherness with Governor Brown. But now I wish I had never seen it. It's too painful. I'd like to come face to face with Governor Brown and ask, 'Why'd you call for our names?'"

Rocking in his chair, gulping gallon after gallon of fluids, Nicoll says he today suffers severe headaches "two-thirds of the time." He has to go to bed by 9 P.M. every night because he feels exhausted, even though he cannot work. If he wears his glasses longer than twenty minutes at a time, his vision blurs.

Two radiation-illness experts consulted for the preparation of this article stated that no definitive diagnosis could be made of Nicoll's multiple health problems. His exposure at Wigwam has been complicated by years of intervening events, particularly his accident in 1979, and the possibility that he may have suffered from unknown inherited conditions. Both doctors, however, felt his problems may have been exacerbated by exposure at Wigwam. "Nobody has done a study to see if there is a connection to radiation of any of these diseases," points out Dr. Gofman. "Virtually nothing has been done to find the effects of low-level ionizing radiation on these diseases or other health problems. Although good evidence exists that cancer and leukemia are induced by low-level radiation, other medical disorders simply have not been studied."

Today Barry Nicoll is trying to decide how to meet his growing medical bills. He says he is a loyal citizen—both of his oldest sons are in the air force with his blessing, and he still raises and lowers his American flag every day. "But what burns my butt is how they went about covering this all up—all these years." He has retained a lawyer to look into suing the government.

"It's a disgrace that the government is not at least studying these men," observes Gofman. "The reason they aren't is that they would frighten the public and the military planners. But the government has an obligation to find out what happened to them. The servicemen weren't even like guinea pigs—you study those at least. These men were like sheep."

During a six-month investigation for *New West* and ABC News's "20-20," the Center for Investigative Reporting found thirty-six men who participated in Operation Wigwam. Fourteen of them had suffered from diseases that could be traced to radiation exposure at Wigwam:

● Charles Fleming, a civilian technician for Scripps, was in a small airplane that flew directly into the radioactive plume above Surface Zero to measure radioactivity after the shot. He developed a mysterious condition that caused his bones to crumble and died last summer of a heart attack.

● Walter Johnson, the boatswain's mate who felt a fine mist filter down on him after the explosion, developed a severe skin rash within a year and a half of the test. The VA says it has lost his medical records from that period. Today, twenty-five years after Wigwam, he still has to keep a sign above his bed: DON'T SCRATCH!

● James Heiner, a third-class petty officer on the USS *Curtiss*, also developed a painful skin disorder, resulting in welts, discoloration and severe itching. The condition has come and gone since the test and does not respond to any medication.

● Archie Gary, who was on the USS *Comstock*, suffers from a similar skin condition.

● John Stillwell was on a salvage tug that towed one of the contaminated submarine hulls back from the test. He developed cancer and had to have half of his jaw surgically removed.

● Earl Branham, a pipe welder temporarily on the USS *Comstock* during the test, has leukemia. He was told by the VA that his medical records are missing.

● Robert Wilhite, from the USS *Wright*, recalls being "appalled that the navy would allow its men outside during the blast without any protective clothing." Wilhite had his right lung removed due to cancer in 1971 and now has cancer in his left lung.

● Marche Rothlisberger, administrative officer to Task Force Commander Admiral Sylvester, developed tooth and gum problems as a result of a strange bone condition that appeared in 1966. His periodontist stated, "The underlying cause for his condition could have been radioactive exposure."

• John Brewer, who was on the USS *Fort Marion*, has skin cancer and cancer of the knee. He does not feel Wigwam was responsible for his diseases.

• Richard T. Fellis, who was on the USS *Chanticleer*, died in 1977 of cancer.

• Elroy Runnels is dead of leukemia.

• Richard Purdy is dead of cancer.

• Barry Nicoll suffers from undiagnosed disorders.

• Captain Ross Pennington, who sailed the USS *Eastman* toward Surface Zero, died last December of leukemia. He received a 100 percent disability evaluation from the government for his exposure to radiation in nuclear tests—apparently the only serviceman from Wigwam to be compensated so far.

Many of these men are hindered in their attempts to get compensation by the fact that they were not wearing radiation detection badges during the blast. Others have had their records lost or misplaced by the authorities. The government has not performed a comprehensive survey of the health effects of the Wigwam blast.

The Defense Nuclear Agency's (DNA) spokesperson, Lieutenant Colonel Bill McGee, stated pointedly, "We are not in the health defense business."

The DNA's official report on the Wigwam test, released last February, amounts to a whitewash of what actually happened at the blast. This 250-page version compiled by the Jaycor consulting firm of Alexandria, Virginia, suffers from the following major failures:

• Although a few high-level officials reviewed a draft, not one of the 6,500 participants in Wigwam was interviewed for the report.

• The report downplays the chance that Wigwam caused the radioactive "spike" over San Diego four days after the blast. An independent meteorologist and two radiation experts consulted by *New West* determined that radiation from Wigwam may indeed have been responsible.

• The report neglects to mention the substantial pretest concern that tuna or other commercial fish might be contaminated by the test. It also does not report that, despite AEC advisory committee recommendations that Mexico and other South American fishing nations be forewarned of the test, no international announcements were made.

• The report claims that all personnel were familiarized with the radiological hazards before the test, but few of the thirty-six participants interviewed for this article could recall any such briefing. Many, in fact, were not even told they would be witnessing an atomic explosion.

• The report claims that every participant was given a radiation detection film badge to wear during the test, but fourteen of the thirty-six men interviewed for this article say they were given no badges.

● The report does not mention the full extent of damage sustained by ships involved in the test. No mention is made of the severe damage inflicted on the USS *Marion County*, described to *New West* by three eyewitnesses, or the *Eastman*.

● At one point the report claims that no servicemen received more than 0.425 roentgens of radiation from the blast, but elsewhere it says that the deck of the *Eastman* received 400 roentgens. According to John Gofman, "The ship would have remained radioactive, at low levels, for months afterward, representing serious health consequences for the men on board in terms of eventual cancers."

It is apparent from this report and other similar documents that the U.S. government does not want to know whether its seventeen-year nuclear war had any victims. The official position is that the tests simply had to be done. Governor Brown is still the most prominent public official who has taken issue with the government over Operation Wigwam. Brown's aide Phillip Greenberg told *New West* that a detailed letter from the DNA earlier this year, which reiterated the conclusions of the official Jaycor report, answered all of Brown's questions about the blast at that time. Now, based on the new information in this article, it appears that he should reconsider calling for studies of the health effects of Wigwam, the government's obligations to California veterans and the hazards of materials dumped off the California coast.

TODAY THE Scripps Institution of Oceanography is the largest center of its kind in the country. It no longer has to rely on the navy for most of its budget, and the days of coordinating nuclear blasts in the Pacific are a somewhat embarrassing memory.

The man who pushed the button at Wigwam, Dr. Alfred Focke, lives about ten miles from Barry Nicoll. He says that he would do it all over again today. But he also feels that "every prospective head of state should be required to stand within five miles to witness one of these small atomic bombs. The savings in eventual damage to humans could be incalculable."

Scripps officials were nervous during a recent round of interviews about their role in Wigwam. An internal memorandum, circulated by public affairs officer Chuck Colgan, advised that the staff hold a special meeting "to review the subject areas of Wigwam to be discussed with the reporters."

In addition, Nierenberg tried to deny that Focke was employed by Scripps while acting as Wigwam scientific director in 1955.

"No, we checked our records, and Focke was working for the Naval Electronics Lab at that time, not us."

Reminded that the institute's official history states that Focke was a

Scripps employee at that time, Nierenberg then consulted with deputy director Jeffery Frautschy before returning to the phone: "Ah...yes, it seems Focke was with Scripps at that time, after all." His voice was unenthusiastic.

From his office overlooking the institute's picturesque loading pier for its fleet of research vessels, Frautschy recently reviewed Scripps' involvement in Operation Wigwam. Frautschy admitted that if the navy asked the institute to coordinate a similar test today, "We would have to take into account the shift in public opinion before agreeing to do it. We probably would say no."

ANNE LAMOTT

Almost 86'ed

Love is not kind or honest and does not contribute
to happiness in any reliable way.
—ALICE MUNRO

A ND SO WE all know, neither does wealth or fame, neither does being an artist. Show me a group of at least reasonably successful writers, actors, filmmakers, fine artists, and dancers, and I'll show you a litter of weird, tortured puppies.

For one thing, they have to spend a lot of time alone. Some say Too Much Time—thinking, shaping, creating, creatively destroying, reshaping, alone except for the tools of their trades, and other inanimate objects, and various leering specters. None of these are on the side of the artist. Take the walls of one's work space, for instance. After Too Much Time alone, hour after hour, day after day, the walls warp, pulse contract, taunt, in cahoots with the ghost of Edgar Allan Poe. And critics perch on the artist's shoulders, like the angel and the devil of conscience in cartoons. Somebody once said, "A critic is someone who comes onto the battlefield after the battle is over and shoots the wounded." So the artist cries out, The *hell* with the critics, and the critics smile.

Just get the work done, we cry to ourselves and each other. Keep the faith! Trust in GM and take short views! Onward! And one has to pretend that it doesn't matter what happens when the final project comes out of the chute—whether in the public eye one emerges sovereign or goat. No, this doesn't matter; what matters is the process, the artistic growth, the integrity, the vision. Work is the gimbal of the artist's life—Matisse, when asked if he believed in God, replied, "Yes, when I work."

Even if one receives praise and attention, the artist may end up feeling like the squat and pompous Renaissance king in the old New Yorker cartoon, who is studying a just-completed royal portrait of himself in which he is depicted in all his squat pomposity, with angels soaring down to greet him, singing hallelujahs. "More angels!" he cries to the painter, who stands beside him at the easel. "And make them happier to see me!"

So when the work is done for the day and the project is still spinning around the artist's medicine-ball head—spinning like a Tibetan prayer wheel, to the exclusion of being able to care much about anything else—the artist heads for the places where his or her cronies hang out, fellow artistic sociopaths and sympathizers. Who listen, commiserate, gossip, exhort, share the excitement or despair.

North Beach San Francisco's Tosca Cafe has always been one of the prime places where artists of one persuasion or another met in the evenings, from the Beats in the fifties to the local movie luminaries in the eighties. It has also always been a place for hip San Franciscans, for North Beach regulars, and socialites, upwardly mobile aging youth, business gentility, local politicians, and illustrious visitors. Mailer used to drop by in the sixties, Louis Malle was there the other day. People all over the world know about it and come by for a drink when in town. It is a grand old place, beautifully lit, with opera on the jukebox and a long, fine bar with ancient towering espresso machines at either end. Behind the bar are fresh flowers, and Mario, arguably the world's most perfect bartender, who has been here since 1946.

Jeannette Etheredge has been the owner since 1980. Her mother, Armen Bali, the legendary benefactor of the great Russian ballet stars, brings them by when they are in town, and Francis Coppola, whose Zoetrope Studio is in the Sentinel Building one block away, brings his people by. In 1982, when production of The Right Stuff began in San Francisco, director Phil Kaufman and his actors—Sam Shepard, Ed Harris, Fred Ward—began hanging out there nighily. Hunter Thompson, Robin Williams, Harry Dean Stanton... Tosca is a confluence of artistic greats—actors, directors, dancers, writers— and sophisticated San Franciscans. People feel special there. They belong.

What a lovely hat belonging is! You walk into the right room, and you pick up this hat and put it on, this hat of belonging, and you wonder, What was all that fuss about? The anguish, the loneliness, the lack of connectedness.

It is an exciting and secure feeling to belong at Tosca.

I used to, pretty much, more or less. Until February 5.

JEANNETTE is a powerful, attractive woman in her forties, a rabid fan of movies and ballet. She has an exemplary relationship with her employees, and entertains her friends, famous or not, with concern and generosity, six nights a week (Tosca is closed on Mondays). It is rare that a customer acts up: on those rare occasions, Jeannette can deliver a look of pure, withering, horrified disdain. She is like the woman in the P.G. Wodehouse story, "known in native bearer and half-caste trader circles as 'Mgobo-'Mgumbi, which may be loosely translated as She On Whom It Is Unsafe To Try Any Oompus-Boompus."

She does not like drunks, or drunk people. We have discussed this on a number of occasions (previous to the incident on February 5, an event to which I shall return). Granted, there probably aren't a lot of bar owners who rejoice when a group of loud, mindless drunks arrive at their bars, but Jeannette *really* doesn't like drunks. As much as anything (she has told me), she can't stand to see what they do to themselves. She has created an atmosphere where civilized people can drink in a grand old bar with an illustrious history, where they can safely assume that the other customers will not start acting up. (On occasions when customers at the bar started becoming obnoxious, Mario has been known to sidle over and casually mention his large son, a large son to whom Mario must still show a thing or two.)

So you go in to talk to Mario and Jeannette and your cronies, and maybe you go in because there are apt to be some celebrities there, and you go in to have a drink, or two. Tosca is, after all, a bar, and bars are about alcohol.

Alcohol is a drug dealing with one's sense of personal power. It seems to me that two kinds of people drink a lot: those who feel powerless, and those granted an irrational amount of power. For the former, alcohol diminishes the feeling of powerlessness; it makes you feel more capable, while, ironically, it is making you less so. It gives you the feeling that you can do it, which is what power is all about. And for the latter, those with an irrational amount of power—doctors, lawyers, the rich and/or famous—it takes away the guilt, the internal squirminess. It makes you feel a benevolent amusement about your power. It makes you feel that it is okay.

In this scheme of things, it is still a great advantage to be a male.

I have been at any number of parties and bars, full of erudite and successful people, where popular, powerful men arrived, or ended up, drunk—I mean, really drunk, three sheets to the wind drunk—and proceeded to tear up the pea patch. I have repeatedly heard them spout words so crude, rude and socially unacceptable that they made what I said to Jeannette on February 5 sound like something by Kahlil Gibran. These men ruin evenings, and they keep getting invited back. They are men, bread-winners, they are just blowing off steam. They can also let themselves go, can bloat, sag, wrinkle, gray, whatever, and still be thought attractive, more powerful with every passing year. But women with however much power and fame damn well better stay attractive—so what kind of real power is this? As Roy Blount Jr. wrote, "Power that worries about whether its hiney is beautiful is not power."

(And furthermore: have you ever noticed that if you're a man with badly pockmarked skin, you can still be an actor—whom women will desire? Bill Murray and the head of the vice squad on "Miami Vice" come to mind. Can you think of any pockmarked actresses? I rest my case.)

JEANNETTE AND TOSCA offer you shelter from the storm: Reagan will almost surely send us to war in Nicaragua, and your shy neighbor may be constructing a huge sex box, and if he doesn't kill you, your cheese might, and the book and movie industries are, for the most part, run by men with the vision and honor of cattle ticks, and too many people out there are hungry and homeless and decompensating. Outside all hell seems to be breaking loose, so what are you going to do?

Go inside.

The lighting in Tosca is golden, elegant, and there are, as always, fresh flowers behind the bar, and Mario is zizzing up one of Tosca's famous brandy-laced cappuccinos, and there is Francisco gentility in the clothes and carriage of the people who sit at the bar or at the red Formica tables and naugahyde booths in the big room, talking. There is opera on the jukebox, and Caruso does not yet have to compete with the blaring disco which will start up downstairs when the Palladium nightclub opens. (When it does, its beat will have a congealing effect on the opera in here, not unlike the liturgical sound track in movies like *The Omen* or *Damien: Omen Two* when the adorable young anti-Christ begins to act up.) But for now, the opera adds to the atmosphere of animated civility.

My cronies are here, the people I "run into" rather than "have to dinner." Tony Dingman tells me about the movie his boss Coppola is making; Sara Strom—Francis's secretary—and I discuss a wonderful slutty nail polish I have discovered; Al Wiggins discusses Stanley Cavell for a while and then tells me that people who come to Tosca before 8:30 are like the people in Elmore Leonard who get to airports an hour or more before departure time, they are People who do not have enough to do. I greet Jeannette, who is at her stool by the espresso maker at the far end of the bar. She asks me about my work. I tell her, and ask if I can cash a check. Yes, of course, she says. I talk to Curt Gentry about J. Edgar Hoover, wonderful squalid stuff, and then to Peggy Knickerbocker about a mutual friend of ours, and about meat loaf. I ask Jeannette if I can practice pool by myself in the back. She says, Yes, of course.

I belong, pretty much, more or less.

I play pool by myself for a while, and then, lonely, go back to the bar. Everyone in the place is talking or listening, or, as Fran Lebowitz suggests, talking and waiting.

Half of the people who are listening (or waiting) appear to be meeting the eyes of whoever is talking to them, but they are wearing psychic bifocal contact lenses: they can look into their friend's eyes while at the same time peer through the bottom part of the contacts to check out their friend's teeth, or neckline, or lack of it thereof. Then they can look through the top part of the contacts to see if there is someone more interesting around, or if anyone famous has arrived.

I am aware of what they are up to because I am doing the same thing.

I can't help it. It is an automatic response. I do not like to admit this, but I am, in a figurative sense, a star-shtupper. Many of us here tonight are. It is another major reason we hang out at Tosca. Maybe coming in here caters to everything cheap in us—the desire to see celebrities, the desire to be seen as a local celebrity. Maybe if you are mentally sound—if you have a reasonably healthy balance of confidence and humility, you do not have these needs. I have a friend who knows one of you. But most of the people I know are driven by a blend of arrogance and secret, crippling self-doubt, and many of the people I know are star-shtuppers. I'm not sure that this is a bad thing—I mean, it's not as bad as putting people into huge sex boxes, and it's not even as bad as going to the movies wearing digital watches that go off every half hour. It's just sort of silly or sort of sad or something. (One of my best friends—a brilliant and discerning man in his late forties, a man who has read *Ulysses* half a dozen times—recently covered a day's shooting of "Dynasty," and wrote in a letter to me, "Linda Evans wasn't there, drat, because I was sure she would fall in love with me; poor Mickey.")

Watching for stars at Tosca is like watching for whales from the Point Reyes lighthouse: it is a splendid place to be even when you don't see any spouts or tails, but when you do, when all of a sudden *fush!*, you see the geyser of a whale, it makes the world bigger for a moment. Or when all of a sudden Sam Shepard comes in, and you've been in awe of his pure, beautiful writing, and his charisma as an actor, and he's standing a few feet away, talking to Jeannette: it rolfs the Sam Shepard file in your head, and all those memories of awe and admiration rush out like bubbles.

Memories of the great good people who happen to be famous are like Fabergé eggs: in Marin this spring. Huey Lewis draping the gold medal around the neck of a retarded ten-year-old sprinter at the Special Olympics—"Chariots of Fire" blasting from speakers behind them, ecstasy on the girl's face when he kisses her cheek. Ecstasy on my face at ten years old, when Vivian Vance dropped by for a visit. (She was married to John Dodds, who was my father's editor at the time, and she was dressed to the nines and wearing this marvelous fandango eye makeup. Ethel Mertz! The three little Lamotties, raised to be Politeness Children, greeted them ladies first, of course—I had been trained to curtsy, and the Politeness Boys to bow at the waist. And then when we turned to greet Mr. Dodds, Vivian waved away the very *idea*, as if it were smoke, and, with her head held high, announced, "Oh, but you don't even have to bother with him: *I'm* the famous one.")

I cannot remember to whom I lent my only suitcase three months ago, but I can perfectly remember the exact shade of Vivian's eye shadow.

Tosca is a place where San Franciscans can feel special, aristocratic in an egalitarian kind of way, and it is a place where celebrities can go and for the most part avoid being pestered by star-shtupping people like me. Jeannette protects her friends, both by offering them sanctuary in the private room in the back where the pool table is, and by making it quite clear that they are not to be bothered when they are hanging out at the bar or in a booth. They are here, but not really approachable.

I, on the other hand, being a medium-small fish, am approachable by people who recognize me from dust-jacket photos. All right, maybe it doesn't happen all that often, but they do come up from time to time at Tosca, and they say nice things about my books, and I hang my head and shuffle, and then begin bowing and scraping with embarrassed pleasure. I think I must look like a trained horse answering the question, How much is three plus three? (But then there was the time a rich and slightly scary-looking woman came up and asked, "Are you Anne Lamott?" and I nodded, and she said, "You wrote *Rosie*," and I nodded and blushed and began the bowing and scraping. "God," she said. "I just *hated* it.")

But if you're famous, Jeannette can and will protect you. During the Democratic National Convention, any number of stars hung out, either with her at the far end of the bar, or in the poolroom. The place was packed. Hunter Thompson was there, Robin Williams was there, and Ronald Reagan Jr. was there. I watched him mingle nicely with Jeannette and the other stars, and it was perfectly clear that I must not approach him. Must keep my distance. ("Hey! You're Ron Reagan, right? God, I just *hate* your father.")

Tosca can be a magical and relaxed place, whether or not any stars come in. The only thing you have to do to be a part of this exclusive club is to not act up. That is the only rule, and I broke it.

IMAGINE IF YOU will a meter such as the one on the old "Queen for a Day" show that registered the misery applause, only in this case it will measure Human Excellence. If the needle moves all the way to the right, you've got a person whose life personifies grace and excellence: David Niven, say, or

Chris Evert, or Yehudi Menuhin, or E.B. White. If the needle moves all the way to the left, you've got Muamar al-Qaddafi, or people who blow up cats.

My performance at Tosca on the evening of February 5 sent the needle racing over to the left: it stopped in the area occupied by the scores of Martha in *Who's Afraid of Virginia Woolf?* and Linda Blair toward the end of *The Exorcist,* and Frances Farmer out on the town a few years before the lobotomy.

I went into Tosca that night with my friend Curt Gentry, with whom I had had several drinks at Gino and Carlo. It was a quiet night. Jeannette was playing dominoes with an elegant male friend. We said hello, and she invited us to a party the following night, a party at Tosca to welcome Tony Dingman home from Rio. Some of our cronies were there. We mingled nicely. Then Curt left, and another friend arrived, and I had a couple more with him, and regaled him with stories of the twenty-two-hour Greyhound bus trip I had taken from Seattle the day before. I had begun to crack in Portland; Portland is only an hour away from Seattle. He bought me another drink, and left for the bathroom, at which point I took the opporunity to traipse over to Jeannette, and—under the illusion that I was continuing to mingle nicely— began making jocular comments.

For some reason it seemed amusing to call Jeannette unprintable names, in front of her friend. The terms of endearment my best friends use with me, along the lines of "you ignorant slut" and "you incurable troglodyte" and "you godforsaken moron" and worse. I was gregariously insensitive to the fact that Jeannette was having to sit there being verbally attacked by a loud, mindless drunk, in front of a friend.

Then I dusted off my hands and left for home.

The next morning I did not remember those last fifteen minutes at Tosca.

I was looking forward to the party for Tony all day.

When I walked into Tosca that night, around seven, Jeannette was sitting with Curt Gentry and Peggy Knickerbocker at the far end of the bar. I said hello to each of them in turn. Peggy and Curt said hello back. "Aren't you going to say hello?" I asked Jeannette, only somewhat nervous. "No," she said.

Curt and Peggy, stiffly, anxiously, turned to each other and began discussing the weather.

"Well, why not?" I asked.

And she began to tell me just how profoundly uncute and unfunny I had been the night before, and how I had humiliated her in front of her friend, and just what a general ass I had made of myself, and then she nailed me on two or three of my gravest personality defects. It was almost uncanny.

I stood listening, in a rapt, wired state of Cobra Hypnosis.

Then I apologized six ways from Sunday; I was nauseated with remorse. I bowed and scraped, and sort of begged for forgiveness. Jeannette cleared her throat, and said, "Well," and then Tony and some more of our cronies arrived.

We all hugged him and said welcome back. I began to cry. Curt got out his handkerchief and mopped me up. I made small jokes and told Tony about my twenty-two-hour Greyhound bus ride, and tears kept pouring down my face, and Curt kept mopping me up, and I kept making little jokes and really mingling rather nicely, under the circumstances. And then I thought, well maybe I'll go home now and have a nice glass of Drano.

I went up to Jeannette, apologized some more, and said I could not remember feeling so ashamed, and she ended up accepting my apology: she was really pretty nice about the whole thing.

But things just haven't been the same between us since.

I've gone in about once a month since then, and I sit miserably behind the espresso machine at Mario's end of the bar, and I talk to him or to Tony Dingman or to Curt or whomever, and it is clear that Jeannette does not want anything to do with me. I have not yet been eighty-sixed, but I am on the bad persons list, and I worry every time that Mario will come over to tell me about his big son.

The Ontology of the Pitch

YOUNG AGENT on the phone—two blinking lines. He is dressed like a chic Italian shoe importer, permanent smirk, well-appointed feet on desk. He is sipping Evian water.

> AGENT: . . . My fingers are burning. they're so hot. These guys just sold a script to Disney for 250,000. Katzenberg[1] is dying to take them off the market. They won't be available after this for three years. But they happen to have a corridor for one pitch. Tomorrow they have a second breakfast open because Dawn Steel[2] cancelled,[2] and I'm going to give it to you . . . because I'm crazy about you!

AGENT hangs up phone, turns to secretary.

AGENT: Who was that?

CUT TO: INT. FEMALE EXEC. OFFICE—DAY

The office is lined with sports paraphernalia, reflecting the general gender confusion in Hollywood EXEC in Armani suit, fishnet stockings and cowboy boots, is glancing at the trades and talking on the phone to shrink, lover or boss.

> EXEC (to secretary GIDGET): Who's next?

> GIDGET: You can't cancel these guys. They're downstairs.

> EXEC: Bring in the troops.

ENTER TROOPS

Fleshing out creative assemblage are two EXECS: one JR., on JR. JR. The JR. EXEC has read half of the script sent by the agent as a writing sample for this pitch. The JR. JR. has read all of it He says nothing.

---

1. Jeffrey Katzenberg, chairman of motion pictures and television for the newly reconstituted Disney, one of the two or three best barometers of "heat" in development. This is the process in which studios select and commission movie ideas to be scripts and then collaborate in their creation through the dread exercise known as a story meeting.

2. Don't believe this. Since Dawn Steel became president of production for Paramount, she doesn't have time to take pitch meetings.

EXEC: Who read these guys' script? Can they write?

JR. EXEC: They did *Hollywood High* for Lorimar, *Cheap Thrills* for Kings Road, and *Trust Me* for Guber/Peters.

EXEC: I've never heard of any of these movies.

JR. EXEC: That's because none of them has been made. But they just did a rewrite for Grazer and they're fast.

EXEC: Good. That means they'll pitch fast. Bring'em up.

CUT TO:

Your classic comedy team: two writers and a PRODUCER.[3] The writers, PHIL and BILL, dress in 501s, college or Lakers T-shirts, well-worn sneakers. BILL sports a baseball cap. (This is good at some studios for small talk.) The PRODUCER is easy to pick out: he's dressed like a cross between Miami Beach and "Miami Vice" and the resemblance doesn't end there.

GIDGET: Can I get you something to drink?

PHIL: Perrier?

BILL: Ramlosa?

PROD: Pellegrino?

GIDGET distributes Evian water all around. Everyone looks pleased. PRODUCER whips out Emergen-C Pack, tears it open and fizzles it into his glass.

PROD: Ever since I've been going to AA I've been hooked on this stuff.

The writers shift awkwardly in their seats hoping the PRODUCER will get them through this crucial small-talk section of the pitch.

PROD (to EXEC): So...How's your divorce?

---

3. A writer should bring a producer to a pitch meeting at his election if it is necessary for social savvy and political leverage. Some producers are irresistible to some studio executives. The writer should know this and not bring the wrong producer to the wrong studio. Some producers are wonderful at relaxing executives, creating a casual, party-like atmosphere. Some producers are taken seriously intellectually (whether or not they deserve to be), and this is important to know in case you are pitching a drama (also known as a movie with a downbeat ending). Classically, producers "wind up" that is, prep the group for the right mood, and intrigue them with the "area." The writers do the "pitch"— the actual telling of the story. Producers should try to navigate the meeting for the writers—save it from dangerous twists and deviations from their mutual intentions. They cannot wrest control completely, though, as the real control is always with the buyer—on the other side of the table.

> EXEC: It's fabulous. I got the Nautilus equipment, so I'm in good
> shape....And yours?

Now that they've touched on the intimate aspects of both their lives, the
PRODUCER must execute the critical segue into the pitch.

> PROD: I still have my wheels—and that's all I need in this town. In
> fact, that's how I got this idea....[4] I am driving down PCH in my
> new Ferrari at 2:00 A.M....And I'm riding high...All of a
> sudden, I realize the car is my date...I'm bummed because I
> can't bring her upstairs. It's then I realize my fantasy. A Ferrari
> that turns into a woman. Car by day, woman by night. I call it
> *Hard Drivin' Woman.* (He looks at EXEC.) That's why I brought it
> to you—it's right up your alley. It's a cross between *10* and *Splash,*
> with a touch of *My Mother the Car.* I see two videos already.[5]

Everyone is stunned. EXEC reachs for Evian and lights up a Camel.

> EXEC: Have you got the story worked out?

Writers respond to this moment of pressure by speaking simultaneously.

> BILL: Phil, why don't you start?

> PHIL: Bill, why don't you start?

---

4. The windup: generally there are two kinds. One is the first-person-fake, a media-related
quasi-intimate anecdote, a version of which is here. The second is the so-called true story,
the true-to-life incident which inspired the story. This is vital in television, and actually
useless in movies, but few buyers know this. Often they are impressed with the mere fact
that some aspect of the notion has been verified by reportage—giving it the illusion of life
or importance. Either way, it is a very handy' transition technique.

Tips on the subtle aspects of the windup: the windup anecdote is a common and
opportune place casually to name-drop: parties, people, restaurants, vacation spots (Aspen
being the most frequently heard last year) or critical screenings. Famous People Present
when the idea you are about to pitch suddenly occurred to you is a standard.

5. Peak of the windup, and the mark of a truly gifted pitcher, is the presentation of the
high-concept "miniaturization" of the idea. It must be said succinctly—as in its seminal
influence, the *TV Guide* log line. The tag line of the windup occurs when the producer
(usually) combines the names of past solid hits to form genetically engineered new movie
ideas. This is a neat trick, and is preferable when only two movies are hybridized—the
three here are too much.

BILL: I don't really have this down yet, I mean it's not engraved in stone....[6]

PHIL: (interjects) This is the first video.

BILL: In it we see NORMAN,[7] a nerdy, twenty-five-year-old, unfulfilled dreamer fantasizing a parade in which every woman he has ever desired becomes an exquisite car. We see that NORMAN ha a long way to go to make his fantasies real. He's not popular with girls and he's a terrible driver, too.

He's planning to buy a Ferrari tomorrow to change his life.

JR. EXEC: How can he afford the Ferrari?

BILL: Inheritance.

PHIL: Life savings.

PROD: Tax refunds?[8]

EXEC: You can work out the backstory later.

PHIL: Then one day...

PROD: Here's where we suspend disbelief...

PHIL: So, then one day NORMAN figures out that no matter how wonderful his car is, it's no substitute for the love of a woman.

---

6. Listed are all the clichés habitually given as excuses for half-baked, shoddy thinking. The glibbest can "wing it" through unprepared story pitches, but this isn't necessarily a good sign for the eventual script. Being quick on your feet isn't the same as being good on the page, or consider the almost axiomatic observation: Good writers pitch badly and bad writers pitch well. Some good writers pitch well, but this is merely a function of gifted personality: they're charming They make good money, too. Writers for whom solutions come too easily are suspect—it means they're thinking like producers. The best writers write from character and story, but seem to be driven by character. The most adept pitchers tend to be "story over character"-type writers. They can make up a simulation of a story structure on any workable premise—but their characters can be interchangeable.

7. Introduce your character to humanize (read: cast) the pitch. The right age for your protagonist is critical. It should be a part right for Anthony Michael Hall (or is it Michael Anthony Hall?), or any member of the Brat pack. Here "nerdy" is selected because it is an easy route to "character change." Whatever condition you choose for your central character, it should contain within it the seeds of his evolution. This is your crucial "character arc"—all characters improve their lot, that is, unless they are the antagonists, in which case they get theirs in a big scene called the "payoff."

8. Wrong. Terrible error not to have anticipated this question and worked out a mutual answer at least on the ride over. The Jrs. are clever and are listening carefully to score points on mechanical details.

That night NORMAN pulls into his garage, goes up to his bedroom and there, parked on his bed, is a fully equipped, sleek, dynamic woman dressed in a custom-colored, candy-apple, metalflake, Ferrari red negligee.[9]

JR. EXEC: How did it turn into a girl?

BILL: Fairy Godmother.

PHIL: Remote control garage door opener.

PROD: Special effects?[10]

EXEC: You can work out the device later.

PHIL: Now, NORMAN runs to the garage and the car is gone! He runs upstairs and realizes it's true. His fantasy car has become his fantasy woman.

PROD: This is our second-act crisis.[11]

EXEC: What is the issue?

PROD: Does he go for the car, or does he go for the girl?

JR. EXEC: Sounds like "Let's Make a Deal."

EXEC: So, what does he do?

PHIL: He picks the car.

BILL: He picks the car.

JR. EXEC: What's his motivation?[12]

---

9. Hyperbole is an excellent indicator of potential ad copy. Used sparingly, it can be effective to executives so they can imagine the poster.

10. Try to avoid at all costs internal disagreement on central points.

11. This notion of the second-act crisis is relatively new in pitch meetings, now that a certain popular story-structure class has become the rave in Hollywood. Everyone knows about the three-act structure, borrowed from theater, which implies that our hero is in desperate shape—the furthest possible distance from his goals—at the second-act break.

12. The all-important "motivation." You can count on arguing about motivation, because unbeknownst to you, all members of the pitch meeting are closet psychoanalysts. Each of these experts will dazzle you with his ability to debate the fine points of any motivation, venal or otherwise. Once again, this is a good point to agree upon before the pitch, though not inflexibly. You must allow the geniuses to flex their intellectual muscle here because it's through this process that they begin to possess the idea as their own, and thus want to buy it. Motivation is therefore something you must have considered opinions about but be willing to give up. Pitch meetings try on motivations like yentas try on bargains in the dressing room at Ohrbach's.

BILL: He has to get to work.

PHIL: Lack of emotional maturity.

PROD: It's a coming-of-age story.

EXEC: Coming-of-age stories are over.

PROD (sweating): It's not a coming-of-age story exactly, what I mean is it's a Bigger-than-Life, Fish-out-of-Water, Action-Adventure...You know, like *Beverly Hills Cop.*[13]

EXEC: Perfect.

PHIL: So, NORMAN picks the car, but he isn't happy. It's not working well. He tries diligently to fix it and fails. He takes it to the best Italian mechanic in L.A, who keeps it for months. NORMAN goes to the mechanic to retrieve her, but no go. The mechanic bawls him out: "What's a matta with you? A high-performance machine like this, you ever tune her? You gotta take a baby like this to the limit, you know, torque her three, maybe four times a week minimum, to keep her happy. She's happy now."[14]

JR. EXEC: Is this a triangle?

BILL: Yes.

PHIL: No.

---

13. Genre/tone section of the pitch: Here, a potentially devastating error is made in evaluating the studio's current position vis-à-vis genres. Read your studio carefully before going in, and be aware of potential gluts with respect to ideas already in development. (This is one of the things some good agents know about—though they often get it wrong.) This producer brilliantly ripostes from his low moment with his creation of a compound genre.

14. Don't go into excruciating detail in telling the plot. Remember this is a condensation. Think of it as the *Reader's Digest* condensed-novel version of a screenplay. These people have short attention spans and they hear stories all day. Also, the people they turn around and sell your story to have even shorter attention spans than they do. Tell them the salient points, the series of beats (more on beats later). Do tell about subplots if they involve hot or cute casting like Madonna, David Lee Roth or Tina Turner. It's common for some pitchers to break into dialect when describing plot. This seems to replace character description. Fortunately, this is most frequent in comedy, and comedy writers do funny dialect. (This raises the age-old question: If the meeting is funny, does that mean that the script will be funny? Hint: The answer is no.)

PROD: It's a beat, a subplot.[15]

BILL: Then we cut to the chase scene.

PROD (interjecting): This is a very realistic sequence, cut to a driving sound track...ZZ Top is wild for this.

EXEC: I get the general picture here, what kind of casting do you see?

PROD: Daryl Hannah and I have been looking for something to do together.[16]

JR. EXEC: I bet you have.

EXEC: Daryl is unavailable.

PROD: Anyway, this is a director's picture. Ivan Reitman and I have been trading phone calls all week.[17]

BILL: And now we come to the emotional payoff.

PHONE RINGS. GIDGET bops into office with enthusiasm.

---

15. Beats: Epistemologically, this is a curious notion. It has something to do with the rhythm of the plot—those consecutive moments in the plot that create the structural underbelly of the story. Beats are related to one another by both narrative and emotional causality. A subplot: a bunch of beats carried by actors other than your star.

16. Notes on casting: Imagine all of the roles in your story cast by big box-office stars. People over fifteen do not count unless it is a "drama" (recall the definition in note four) and then only about four stars count. Know which stars are basically unattainable and/or unavailable to save yourself from looking dopey. But under no circumstances ever allow a pitch to hinge on the casting of one particular person This is the easiest route to a pass. Also, know what actors your studio has standing deals with and what ideas that star is looking to develop. They need to justify the astronomical fees paid to keep these stars off the market and gobble material for their commitments like candy.

17. Most meetings (you're in trouble if they don't) have a wish-fulfillment segment assigned to discussions about directors. Most of these conversations are moot, because the directors the studio wants to hire don't have to or want to make studio-developed films. They want to make their own films with no interference, and most of the best select their own writers and collaborators. Once in a blue moon a good script is in development and attaches itself to an A-list director (most recent examples include Peter Weir on *Witness*, Barry Levinson on *Young Sherlock Holmes* and Ron Howard on *Cocoon*), but these are exceptions and triumphs of development. After one schlock comedy the filmmaker is ready for Medea. In comedy the situation is a deteriorating disaster for studios who cannot get directors for commercial comedies—the movies they most want to make. The unattainables, Harold Ramis, Ivan Reitman, Ron Howard, Rob Reiner, Bob Zemeckis, John Hughes, et cetera, can now basically write their own ticket and are extremely unlikely to take on an assignment again.) In your next life, plan to be a comedy director.

GIDGET: I hate to interrupt, but Spielberg is on line two.

EXEC bolts. The meeting comes to an abrupt stand still...Awkward silence as GIDGET distributes a second round of Evian to everyone. EXEC returns.

EXEC: Well, I guess we've wrapped it up. That was terrific, thank you. I know how busy you are, I'll call you first thing in the morning....I think this is very fresh. Let me speak to my people and get back to you.[18]

PHIL, BILL, PROD all leave. They do not know what to think. They share a shocked silence only broken in the parking lot where they discuss the EXEC's ridiculous outfit.

Back at the pitch table, the three EXECs push back their seats and exchange glances, all look at GIDGET lurking in the door.

GIDGET (shrugs): It's a PASS.

EXEC: Who's next?

---

18. How to read the meaning of "Let me speak to my people": It's not a good sign, but not necessarily a bad one. Maybe she's being political, or maybe she's passing the buck. On the other hand, maybe she's not paying attention. What's clear is that she can't say yes by herself, and you may have to go through all of this again with her boss. This is dull news.

The after-politics of the pitch, or what to do the next day, when they pass, to change their minds: (1) you could get Anthony Michael Hall or John Hughes attached (this will be hard); (2) you could go out to dinner with the conglomerate head in New York and mention the idea casually to him at Regine's; (3) you could get the idea on the cover of this magazine; (4) you could sell it to Disney.

MERRILL SHINDLER

How Success Almost Spoiled Chez Panisse

I T WAS A clear case of being too good which isn't actually a fault, but it's always hard to watch your favorite quiet little restaurant fall prey to mass media praise, rendering it popular and crowded. Stripping it of the stuff of which rendezvous are made.

That was the case when Chez Panisse made a hit in the *Chronicle* and in the October, 1975, edition of *Gourmet*. Double-knitted hordes massed at the doors and the phones went mad with calls for reservations (too often unkept). Darrel Corti of Sacramento's Corti Brothers specialty food markets sent a funeral wreath to Alice Waters, Panisse's manager and guiding spirit.

"We thought for a while that perhaps we should close," says Alice. "I just don't know how to express how—how torn we felt about the review, particularly the one in *Gourmet*. In a way, the review told us that this is the time to reevaluate the way we see Chez Panisse. In another way, the challenge was taken away—we almost lost that energy struggle that kept us going, that kept pushing us where we wanted to go."

Actually, it was something of a double tribute to the quality of the food that the restaurant was so well reviewed, since the kitchen has a reputation for perversity and irreverence. During a recent visit by Robert Finigan of *Jack Shelton's Private Guide to Restaurants*, chief chef Jeremiah Tower became so annoyed by Alice's insistence that flawless food be sent to the reviewer (whom she recognized) that he sent Finigan's three companions picture perfect plates of gigot rôti aux herbes while sending Finigan "inordinately gristly pieces hacked inexpertly from the leg. I quietly instructed the waiter," said Finigan in his review, "to ask the chef for more appetizing slices. He was back in moments, the same plate in hand. 'The chef says, tough,' he announced to our general astonishment. Had I not been visiting Chez Panisse in a professional capacity, I might well have decorated the waiter with gigot rôti and then set out for the kitchen, but instead I cooled my outrage with sips of the remarkable 1972 Pinot Noir, Mt. Eden...."

"I almost died," says Alice in retrospect. "Jeremiah just got fed up."

Unfortunately, Waters and Tower (along with their other working partners, pastrymaker Lindsey Shere, headwaiter Tom Guernsey and wine steward Jerry Budrick) were forced to deal with a new breed of customer before they could adjust to their sudden leap to restaurant stardom. "People who came after reading the reviews didn't seem to care about the quality of the food. They'd come because it was the thing to do. I'd get letters that were so depressing, as if I didn't care about what we serve. How could they say we're disinterested? I'm utterly obsessed! I almost cry if everything isn't perfect..., yes, sometimes I do cry."

One result of last year's panic at Panisse was that the restaurant was put up for sale. "It really got to a point where it was frustrating to everybody," says Alice, "and we all wanted to go our own ways. It was serious, but it wasn't serious." During the months that the restaurant was for sale, there was only one serious offer (the going price was $500,000, not including the services of Waters, Tower, et al.), which, Alice says, "scared me half to death."

At the end of 1976, unsold, Panisse went off the market.

On a recent Saturday morning, Alice was in the kitchen trying, simultaneously, to finish off the restaurant's luncheon orders, run interference around the cooking class in progress under the auspices of Jeremiah, and prepare for that night's specially designed Valentine's Day dinner—a $15 prix fixe affair consisting of lamb hearts cooked en brochette with a beamaise sauce, oysters on the half-shell, sautéed duck breasts served with sour cherries, hearts of artichokes and a dessert of coeurs a la creme la cream cheese heart of sorts served with fresh strawberries and red currant glaze).

Chez Panisse has existed at this extraordinary level of hysteria since Alice and a pair of partners (long since departed) opened to the public in late August 1971. The restaurant—named for an old man who appears in Marcel Pagnol's cinematic trilogy, *Fanny, Marius* and *César,* began with the same basic five-course meal that is served today. The difference was that the meal cost $4.95. Today, it costs $11 and up.

As the Mutt and Jeff of Chez Panisse's kitchen, Alice and Jeremiah make for an odd, if not often crazed couple. Alice, thirty-two, a one-time Montessori teacher, discovered France and French food at age nineteen. Jeremiah, thirty-five, has a somewhat more exotic past. English-born, Tower began polishing his palate at an early age while traveling about Europe with his family. When he left England for Harvard, he had in his steamer trunk a case of 1894 Malmsey Madeira, a recipe for a chicken liver omelette bequeathed to him by an aunt, and an insatiable love for the culinary philosophy of Curnonsky, whose *belle é*poque gastronomy pervades Chez Panisse.

But for a favorite local French restaurant to be truly loyal to its local patrons, it must do more than just emulate the Continent. Panisse blends the old world with the new, using many of the excellent ingredients indigenous to Northern California.

During a dinner last fall, Panisse paid homage to the foodstuffs of Northern California. For $20 per person, the meal began with Tomales Bay bluepoint oysters, then moved on through cream of fresh corn soup, Mendocino-style, with crayfish butter; Big Sur Garrapata Creek smoked trout steamed over California bay leaves; Monterey Bay prawns sautéed with garlic, parsley and butter; preserved California-grown geese from Sebastopol; Monterey Jack cheese from Sonoma; and walnuts, almonds and mountain pears. The meal was accompanied by champagne from Schramsberg, a choice of four Napa Valley wines, and a local port from the East Side Winery.

One problem confronting Waters and Tower is their search for fresh food among the arches of McDonald's. "It's so hard to run a restaurant in a city," says Alice. "We're constantly at the mercy of the suppliers. We're lucky about some things—we have a fellow who gathers mussels for us, for instance. But the biggest problem is meat—it's very hard to get meat that doesn't go through big wholesale packing houses."

To get around part of this problem with suppliers, Chez Panisse is establishing a garden on a single acre in Amador County to grow all the produce they'll need for the year. "It'll be totally organic, and we hope to be getting ninety percent of our produce from there by the end of the summer.

I've also thought of creeping the cuisine down over the border, getting it hotter and spicier. And one thing I'd love to have is a barbecue or grill, a big fireplace where I could do ninety percent of our cooking." A touch of her Montessori background rises in Alice's voice. "I want people who are interested in food to be able to come here and use this restaurant as a learning experience. I want people to eat real stuff, that's my mission."

EHUD YONAY

The California Defense Establishment

I N 1961, WHEN retiring President Dwight D. Eisenhower warned his countrymen to watch out for the "conjunction of an immense military establishment and a large arms industry," the Department of Defense was spending (at today's rate of exchange) $85 billion on the research and procurement of new weapons. While that seemed like a lot back then—still does—the annual expenditure of the defense establishment remained remarkably constant for the next twenty years. In 1980, the figure was actually $68 billion. But in 1981, Ronald Reagan became president. By 1983, defense expenditures stood at $118 billion. By 1984, $124 billion. By 1985, $134 billion—an escalating spending frenzy that would surely alarm Eisenhower were he alive today.

But this is the space age, a time when technology can design any sort of weapon desired as long as the money can be found to make it. Where prudence ends and profligacy begins is an open question. Suffice to say, the Reagan years have seen defense contractors win some of the most lucrative weapons orders in history—$20 billion for 100 B-1 bombers, for example— and with congressional approval of $1.4 billion in preliminary research into the Strategic Defense Initiative Technologies, the sky has now literally become the limit. The ultimate budget for technology's assurance we may all continue to sleep safely at night is expected to reach a trillion dollars, a sum as difficult for the taxpayer to perceive as the weapons his money would buy.

To put the simplest face on it, defense spending is largely a matter of keeping up with the Joneses. At the moment, according to U.S. Department of Defense estimates, the Soviets devote from fifteen to seventeen percent of their gross national product to the military, as against our seven percent, and they spend fifty percent more on weapons than we do. Our competitive fervor spreads throughout the rest of the world, where nearly everybody now has somebody to watch out for—Pakistan worries about India, Saudi Arabia about Iran, Greece about Turkey, Israel about the Arabs, and so on, and vice versa. As best we can, we try to sell our side what weapons they think they need—as the Soviets do theirs.

Consequently, at the midway point of the twentieth century's penultimate decade, the weapons business is booming. It has indeed become one of the great economic enterprises of our time, providing gainful employment for ever-increasing numbers of the world's work force. Nowhere is this immense concentration of money, technology, and enterprise more apparent than here in California.

In up-to-date terms, the most reliable defense of the free world is based roughly on something called the Triad system, an interlocking network of three kinds of armament: missiles launched from the ground, missiles launched from the sea and strategic bombers. If California should suddenly put an end to its defense production, two of the three legs of the Triad would cease to exist. Lockheed Missile and Space Company, which is located in Silicon Valley, has built all U.S. submarine-launched ballistic missiles since the 1950s, from the Polaris and Poseidon through the latest, the Trident II D-5. In Southern California, Rockwell and Northrop are building the next two strategic bombers, the B-1 and Stealth.

But the state's involvement does not end here. Of thirty-two companies with prime MX (ground) missile contracts, sixteen are Californian, including Rockwell, Aerojet, Northrop, and TRW. Moreover, General Dynamics'

Convair Division in San Diego builds both sea- and ground-launched cruise missiles. The Big Four of the defense industry—McDonnell Douglas, Rockwell, Lockheed, and General Dynamics, all here—take in a full third of *all* defense prime contracts.

If it is true that power follows money, California (whose number one son is President) is at the heart of the defense establishment.* Defense spending here comes to $40 billion a year (including $11.5 billion in military payrolls). No other state runs even a close second.

With agriculture at $13.8 billion and tourism at $31 billion, defense has become California's largest industry. At last count, more than one quarter of the Reagan administration's record budget for research, development, and acquisition of new weapons was spent in California. And the future looks even brighter. Because California enjoys a comfortable lead in high-technology research, a good part of that Star Wars trillion will have to be spent here.

"Conjunction" was not the sort of polysyllabic word anybody expected to hear from Dwight Eisenhower—and certainly not in a warning against the growth of a system in which he had so prominently figured. How insidious has become the intersection of such powerful interests in our society today? If coffee brewers are charged off at $7,622 and ashtrays at $659, what can be going on with the really heavy stuff? "Waste, fraud, and abuse" has become standard rhetoric for Congress in reviewing defense planning. In 1982, Department of Defense officials spent 1,453 hours trying to explain themselves before ninety-one congressional committees and subcommittees. In turn, the Defense Department has undertaken criminal investigation of forty-five of its top contractors, all of whom plead they are innocent victims of government bureaucracy, forced to spend almost as much time filing forms as making guns.

None of this Sturm und Drang is very likely to affect the way weapons will continue to be sold to the military. Those inside the system argue that fraud and abuse are nothing against the monstrously inefficient ways in which the system has evolved. Within the military purchasing system (unlike virtually any other business), deals are not cut over lunch. To secure an order, a would-be military contractor must start at the bottom of the ladder and

---

*There is little reflection of this power among the California delegation in Congress, however. No truly influential positions are held in either the Senate or the House on the important armed services, procurement, or budget committees. For years the late Senator Henry Jackson was known in Washington as the Senator from Boeing. Today, the two most powerful members of the House Armed Services Committee are from New York (the *second* largest defense state). In the Senate, Sam Nunn of Georgia and Barry Goldwater of Arizona watch carefully over the interests of the defense industries in their states. In most important matters of defense, California's delegation is out of it.

work his way up, seeking approval from scores of military people who can kill his project without explanation. Having made it to the top, he must then win the unanimous consent of half a dozen general-grade officers and top DOD officials who, from his vantage, have the power of emperors. Then of course there is still Ronald Reagan....

So ensnarled has become this maze that the major contractor will keep on call large staffs inside and outside his organization so as to secure the unimpeded movement of his project. A friendly call from his lobbyist to an old service buddy at the right time can help a lot. (For small fry, without Washington offices, there are always the "Beltway Bandits," retired officers, usually field grade and above, who can for a fee make a call, too. Also available is the sometime potent subcontractor network, which often consists of *thousands* of companies working on the project all over the country. If every employee of every company petitions his congressman for a weapon's safe passage, the resultant deluge can be persuasive. Whether any agency or institution, including the President and the Congress, may ever untangle this mess remains to be seen.

IV.
Archetypes

The Founding Mother

U NTIL ABOUT 1980, the rest of the world had practically no idea at all about architecture in California, what it was like, how good it was, if it even existed. Through the fifties the situation had been mending slowly because *Arts and Architecture,* a Los Angeles-based monthly, had been publishing the work of outstanding modern California architects like Richard Neutra and a whole brilliant younger generation of Angelenos: Charles and Ray Eames, Pierre Koenig, Craig Ellwood and so forth--and publishing it so stylishly under the editorship of John Entenza that the world was beginning to take notice. Then this extraordinary book came out in 1960, and—suddenly—California architecture had heroes, history and character.

It was called *Five California Architects*; it described the careers of earlier architects whose works are now objects of international pilgrimage but were then hardly names to most of us: Charles and Henry Greene, Irving Gill, Bernard Maybeck, R.M. Schindler. The author, Esther McCoy, wasn't even a name outside California, barely known in Los Angeles, where she lived. But it was clear that she knew her stuff, was a real scholar, though she seemed to belong to no known academic faction or school of thought, and could write—the book was so damned readable it was in a different league than most architectural literature.

So, as a newcomer to the Los Angeles scene in 1965, I had been looking forward to meeting her with some awe. There was a clarity, a plain-spoken directness about her writing that, to me, was engaging as well as informative, but, later, I discovered that her plain speaking had caused some concern among our mutual friends. I myself have a bit of a reputation for saying it like it is—"acerbic" they call both of us—and the expectation seemed to be that we would try to shred one another conversationally when we met.

We didn't, and from that afternoon I date my acquaintance with two of Southern California's greatest architectural treasures; one was the Gamble House, that 1908 Craftsman-style masterpiece by Charles and Henry Greene ...and the other was Esther McCoy, who had kindly driven me up to Pasadena to visit it and was by then established as the presiding genius of architectural writing in this part of the world.

Esther was eighty in November. EIGHTY!...but as sharp as ever when I went to visit her last summer, still living in that strange house in Ocean Park whose upper floor is an unpublished nonmasterpiece by R.M. Schindler himself. I say "himself" advisedly, because Schindler is how she got involved in architecture in the first place; looking for a job after her wartime work as an engineering draftsman at Douglas Aircraft, she finished up in his office. Schindler was difficult, vain, Viennese, brilliant, the site architect for some of Frank Lloyd Wright's California masterpieces, and himself a world-class talent—but so thoroughly unknown outside Los Angeles that there are still histories of modern architecture that don't mention his wonderful, radically modern houses of the early twenties. He may have been a weird employer, but what a subject for a writer to discover!

For a writer is what Esther has always been, by avocation and since her college days. Effectively self-trained as an architectural historian, she has always been a careful craftsman with words, and neither wastes them nor minces them. She is acerbic, but never for effect, a cheap laugh or to score off an opponent. She does not suffer fools gladly (and the pains of age have added a dash of vinegar to her judgments), but she is unfailingly gentle-womanly about it, in that unmistakable voice of hers, at once fluting, grating and elegantly fatigued. And her writing remains direct, businesslike, purposeful, animated by a determination that certain things about art, literature, architecture, cities, California should be recorded, narrated, published—a determination in which there has lately been a hint of awareness of the running out of time, of the certainty of mortality. As she said to one of her fellow laborers in the vineyard of architectural history a couple of years ago, "Get that damn book finished, I want to read it before I die!"

No ONE CAN write about architecture in California without acknowledging her as the mother of us all. Robert Winter and David Gebhard saluted her at the beginning of the first version of their inimitable *A Guide to Architecture in Southern California*, and in all subsequent versions. Myself, I could not but do the same in my book on Los Angeles. Even the cautious scholars of Berkeley call *Five California Architects* a "classic." That classic, founding work was not only the beginning of California architectural history as we now know it, whatever other studies may have come before, but it was also a beginning for her. She put California architecture on the map and became almost overnight the state's leading architectural sage. There followed books like *Modern California Houses*, on the experimental and influential Case-Study Houses sponsored by *Arts and Architecture*; on the work of Craig Ellwood, most stylish of the steel-and-glass architects of that connection; on the correspondence of R.M. Schindler and his fellow Viennese Angeleno, Richard Neutra; and most recently, a companion to *Five California Architects*, reviewing the lives and works of *The Second Generation* (as she calls them) of California modernists: Gregory Ain, Raphael Soriano, J.R. Davidson and Harwell Hamilton Harris.

All this, and magazine articles all over the place, has done a power of good for California architects and for the art of architecture itself in the state. But someday her benign influence on the other arts will also have to be saluted, for quite a few California artists and writers seem to be in some sense her intellectual godchildren. And so are generations of architecture students, for she has taught or lectured at campuses all up and down the state, and nationwide, spreading the word, observing the scene.

She was in Santa Cruz on one of her trips not long after we moved into our present abode, a much-modified little stucco number that had subsequently acquired bigger windows and an external clothing of diagonal redwood planking that gave it some pretensions as a pioneer of vernacular Post-modernism. She offered no comment on our domestic setting until she was leaving, when she looked back from the front gate and with a chuckle said, "And there's Professor Banham sitting in his modern California corner window!". . .which effectively put both house and householder in their places.

She is a great putter-down of pretensions. If you wanted to hear real sharpness of judgment and inability to tolerate pomposity, you should have heard her and John Entenza raking over the foibles and personalities of the ongoing architectural scene—indeed, one of the few real comforts of Entenza's difficult last years was to have her call and bring him up-to-date on all the gossip, even old gossip which he missed the first time round. And she made those calls because she knew the pleasure they would bring him. She has the gift of friendship, as they say, and is profoundly concerned about people. . .and that is one of the special strengths she brings to her architectural writing. There may still be days when her friends are tempted to echo the Hungarian proverb, "With friends like that, who needs enemies," but she really doesn't have a malicious bone in her body. She speaks as she finds, with sympathy and honesty, and relevantly to the matter in hand.

Our last public encounter was entirely characteristic. I had been lecturing about those Case-Study Houses she had helped to make famous, and had been going on about the much-copied diagonal bracers that stiffened the steel frame of the Eames's epoch-making house of 1949. With customary and probably laborious art-historical methodology I had set out to show that the choice of a diagonal bracing must have had deeply felt aesthetic motivations, as well as a presumed structural necessity.

Before the questions could begin, Esther, from the floor of the house, set the record straight by the usual recall of apposite but unpublished gossip. "You know. . .the engineer told Charles Eames that he didn't need to have that diagonal bracing [pause], but Charlie said, 'I *wannit!*'"

It was enough; the facts, not the theoretical speculation. Long may she continue to speak thus plainly, and continue writing all those books we want to read before we die.

GLADWIN HILL

Your Browns and Reagans May Come and Go, but Jesse Endures...

I F CALIFORNIA WERE to have an official elder statesman, as it does a poet laureate, few would question that the designation should go hands down to State Treasurer Jesse Marvin Unruh. Browns and Reagans may come and go, but Jesse endures. Currently he is marking without fanfare thirty years in politics (with one brief hiatus), during most of which he has been, as now, a force to reckon with. Actually, the appellation of Elder Statesman, while Unruh rather likes it, is not quite apt, with its intimations of senility and Olympian detachment. At sixty-one, Unruh doesn't look too different from the burly, moon-faced Democratic persona that brought him the sobriquet of legislative Big Daddy in the 1960s. But regular gym workouts have slimmed him down from 280 pounds to around 210.

And while he dispenses sagacious counsel to the less experienced, he functions not from a position of detachment but from very much in the thick of things. He directs the ebb and flow of billions of dollars in state and related monies, instigates legislation, and has an important part in shaping state fiscal policies. He was, for instance, one of the chief designers of the emergency bank financing that saved California from a humiliating cash shortage in the wake of Proposition 13.

But Unruh's biggest distinction is as a Survivor. California politics are so fluid that each election is a new ball game, and one defeat often means oblivion. Unruh has weathered more notable setbacks than anyone else.

The son of dirt-poor Texas sharecroppers, Unruh served in the navy in World War II and then went to the University of Southern California. In 1954 he was elected to the state assembly from the blue-collar Los Angeles airport suburb of Inglewood. Gregarious, canny and toughly pragmatic, he quickly sized up the power structure at Sacramento and fitted himself into it. It took him only seven years to maneuver his way into the speakership, a position of power in doling out committee assignments and steering legislation—and in the elicitation of campaign contributions.

Unruh shepherded dozens of progressive measures, like the 1964 fair-housing act, into law. But such accomplishments were recurrently over-shadowed by his style. His autocratic direction of the assembly's proceedings evoked occasional mutterings about Simon Legree and Captain Bligh. (He once kept the chamber doors locked for hours until he got a desired vote.) And he attained a degree of immortality with his celebrated aphorism: "Money is the mother's milk of politics"—uttered in defiant rejoinder to comment about his keen interest in campaign donations for himself and his allies.

Unruh held the speakership for a record seven years, until the Democrats lost their chamber majority in 1968. But along the way he suffered some poignant reverses. He had sedulously ingratiated himself with the national Kennedy apparatus, with all that implied in political potential. Two assassinations shattered these prospects.

In 1970 he quit the legislature to make a try at dislodging Ronald Reagan from the governorship. But it was almost foredoomed: in his preoccupation with the political technics of Sacramento, Unruh had never expanded his grass-roots electoral base much beyond his original Inglewood constituency. He sat out the next three years running a medical service corporation. Then he struck out again in 1973, running for mayor of Los Angeles against Tom Bradley.

But counting Unruh finished in politics, as many did, proved a classic case of underestimation. In extremis Unruh fell back on his own maxim about the nutritious aspects of money. On the California scene a preeminent concentration of money was the state treasury.

The state treasurership had always been an obscure office—a bookkeeping job only a few pegs above capitol janitor in luster. But forces were at work setting the stage for a dramatic transmogrification. Soaring interest rates were putting a premium on deft management of the state's flow of funds. Market conditions were also engendering a spate of low-interest, tax-exempt revenue bonds for everything from housing projects to industrial pollution abatement; the proliferating flotations needed watchdogging. Concurrently, inflation had ballooned supervision of retirement funds of state employees and school teachers into a big responsibility. In 1974, the year after he had lost out in the mayoral race, Unruh drew a bead on the state treasurer post. With his name recognition, he easily beat an obscure opponent, as he has twice since.

ODD GROUND RULES of California politics preclude the building of conventional political machines. But, just as he had made the assembly speakership an extraordinary power center, Unruh set about weaving a network of political ties with the treasurer's office as the hub. In 1981 he persuaded the legislature to establish a commission to review every proposed public-agency bond issue—with himself as chairman. When the $2 billion Los Angeles-San Diego "bullet train" project came up in the legislature, Unruh got himself named chairman of a new commission to monitor it. He now sits on about thirty boards and commissions, more than he can keep numerical track of.

California state and local governments currently have about $15 billion in bonds outstanding. The constant turnover of obligations on this scale represents big business for about ten large Wall Street firms that compete on virtually even terms, to market the bonds for lucrative commissions. Unruh says he plays no favorites in placing bond issues and investing state cash. But a degree of rapport with him is plainly no handicap. His roster of campaign contributors is speckled with names of securities houses like Merrill Lynch, Bear Stearns, Bache Halsey and Kidder Peabody. "What I say to these people," Unruh explains bluntly, "is: 'We've got a certain amount of business to give. I've got a campaign to run. If I have to pick and choose, I'm going to pick my friends....'"

Through such diplomacy, Unruh has accumulated a war chest of more than $600,000 toward his 1986 campaign, which he figures may require $1 million. He sets his personal net worth at "about $600,000." Along with other investments he owns condominiums in Sacramento, Los Angeles and Long Beach. He has residences in Sacramento and Los Angeles, and constantly shuttles among offices in Sacramento, San Francisco and Los Angeles. Divorced years ago, he has five grown children; one of his four sons runs a political-data computer service in Los Angeles.

Legend has him, from speakership days, acting as a major clearinghouse for campaign contributions, corralling them and parceling them out to cohorts. He acknowledges occasional personal beneficences—such as $25,000 to Assembly Speaker Willie Brown in 1982—but says, "Generally I don't like the idea of raising money centrally. With me it's mostly a matter of directing campaign contributions to people I think should have them."

Whenever ethical questions about cultivating contributions are raised, Unruh says: "Any time people don't like it, they can adopt public campaign financing. I've been advocating that for twenty-five years. But I don't think it's going to happen next year...."

A more pressing need of state government, he thinks, is longrange planning. "By its nature state government is preoccupied with coping with today's brushfires," he says. "Almost nobody is looking forward beyond this year. Every time the economy changes, we fall back into a financial mess. We have to have something out there saying that in three, five, ten years, thus and so is going to happen. Potential problem areas are obvious—finances, taxes, education, employment, water. The trick is allocating resources to apply them in the right places.

"My big idea for the future is interfacing the public and private sectors. They're like siamese twins, with a single circulatory system. You can't do anything in this state without massive business support. I'd like to work out some kind of arrangement where we'd swap people back and forth between government positions and research."

Unruh's lifelong ambition has been to be governor, but he sees little chance now of realizing it, if only for the fact that hustling up the requisite $15 million or more of campaign financing seems unduly onerous. "It's not becoming for an older statesman like me," he says.

For Unruh, the governorship would be largely a matter of prestige, and he's always been less interested in prestige than in power. And as things are, one of the financiers he deals with observed, "he's the most powerful man in the state—he's got his hand on the money."

JAMES HAMILTON

Look, Then, at Harry Bridges

J ULY 9, 1934, SAN FRANCISCO. The procession began at the Ferry Building and stretched for miles up Market Street. Leading the way, with as much dignity and solemnity as a horse-drawn caisson, was an old flatbed truck with two coffins, perfectly spaced, side by side. Then came the longshoremen, thousands of them marching slowly eight abreast, hatless, their faces hard and grim in the brilliant sunshine. A union band played a Beethoven funeral march. The men moved to its slow measure. Behind the longshoremen and matching their formation came 40,000 citizens of San Francisco, an endless river of humanity; make it 80,000 feet tramping slowly to the cadence of the dirgeful music, and no other sound. And not a cop in sight. The police had agreed to stay away if the stevedores promised to control the crowd. This they did, adorning hundreds with blue armbands to direct traffic and control the crowds, and to stare down any dispassionate onlooker who did not remove his hat.

Labor was burying its dead. Howard Sperry, a longshoreman, and Nick Bordoise, a member of the Cooks Union, found their separate ways into those flower-bedecked coffins by receiving, one each, one apiece, a bullet in the back from the random firing of San Francisco riot police during the climactic battle that became known as Bloody Thursday, a battle that was the culmination of eight weeks of tension and strife during the maritime strike of 1934.

The operative word in the San Francisco newspapers was blood: "BLOOD FLOODS GUTTERS AS POLICE BATTLE STRIKERS!" "Blood ran red in the streets of San Francisco yesterday." "Drip, drip, drip, went the blood on the white tiled floor."

In a desperate attempt to break the strike, the shipowners had hurled riot police, 800 strong, against the picketing longshoremen. Thousands of spectators lined the steep Rincon Hill above the waterfront at 8 A.M. sharp to watch the action, serviced by hustling vendors selling chocolate bars, chewing gum and cigarettes. The air was thick with tear gas and vomiting gas, the crack of pistol fire, the whine of bullets, the screaming of sirens, and that deadliest of sounds—the sickening dull thump of hardwood riot sticks against human skulls. Bullets smashed through the windows of streetcars, and bystanders fled with burning eyes from the tear gas.

When the battle was over and the dead and wounded carted away, and the jails filled to overflowing, the governor of the state, Frank F. Merriam, decided to call in the National Guard. A man named Harry Bridges, head of the Strike Committee, said, "We cannot stand up against police, machine guns and the National Guard bayonets."

What no one had counted on—not the shipowners, or the businessmen, or the Hearst newspaper chain—was the extraordinary and dramatic impact of the funeral march—those 40,000 people, the incredible outpouring of sympathy which led directly to the great General Strike of 1934. There had been other general strikes—Seattle just after the first world war—but they were brushfires compared to what happened in San Francisco following that magnificent demonstration. An entire labor population laid down its tools; not a wheel turned. The city was entombed in silence.

This remarkable event reached its fiftieth anniversary in recent weeks. It not only strengthened the nascent International Longshoremen and Warehousemen's Union, but it brought upon the national scene one of the most unique and controversial labor figures of his time, a man now battle tested and ready to go, one Harry Renton Bridges.

He was born in a fairly prosperous suburb of Melbourne, Australia, the son of a real estate broker. He received a parochial education at the hands of the Jesuits, perhaps learning some of the inexhaustible argumentative skills that would serve him well across many a negotiating table. A romantic, he resisted being pressed into service for the landed gentry and went to sea. He sailed in barkentines, twice surviving shipwrecks. Angered by working conditions aboard ships, he eventually came ashore in San Francisco and became a longshoreman. Though his father was a conservative, Bridges had been exposed to Australian trade unionism by two of his uncles. Conditions in the maritime industry on the West Coast were barbaric during the first decades of this century. Sailors and stevedores were looked upon as dregs and misfits in a burgeoning industrial society, men who deserved enslavement. Corruption, nepotism, kickbacks and favoritism were standard.

Perhaps the worst, certainly the most degrading, practice was the shape-up. Longshoremen, hundreds more than were needed, would gather at one of the piers just before dawn and await one of the company men to choose which of them would work that particular day. It was a labor marketing device conceived by men whose warped sense of humanity blinded them to the possibilities of uprisings based upon indignity alone; never mind the other, less abstract abuses.

After nearly twelve years as a working longshoreman, Bridges began to see the struggle in strictly class terms, and was quoted a few years later as saying, "We take the stand that as workers we have nothing in common with the employers." A radical dream began to take shape: a democratic, rank-and-file union, unheard of at the time in the labor movement, controlled by the membership with a central hiring hall serving as the unbreakable backbone. They would have control over their working lives (and control over the employers' products on their way to market, of course) and in this way live with a measure of pride and dignity.

Working carefully and in secret to avoid being blackballed by the companies, he built a power base. The demand for a hiring hall was to be the crux of the matter, the uncompromising anvil upon which so many men were to risk getting their skulls split open.

When the employers made their move, Bridges and his union came together with all the force and resonance of railcars coupling; he may have lost the battle of Bloody Thursday but he won the war, and the longshoremen got their cherished hiring hall.

It was not the end of the struggle, by any means. There would be other strikes, other stands to make, as both sides refined their positions for mutual gain. The wiry, hawk-faced Bridges dominated the negotiating tables with his arrogant personality and an unyielding determination to fight tooth and nail for better conditions for his men. George P. West wrote of him in the *New York Times* during those years: "Facing the shrewdest of corporation lawyers, he makes them seem a little helpless by contrast."

BILL BAILEY, a bit of a legend himself on the San Francisco waterfront and a key figure in the recent documentaries *Seeing Red,* about the American Communist Party, and *The Good Fight,* about the Abraham Lincoln Brigade in Spain, said that "Harry had the amazing ability of stayin' one jump ahead of the bosses. He seemed to know what they were gonna do next." Maybe because of the cut of Bridges's working-class sails and his Australian twang, the "bosses" didn't know that a part of him was one of them. It's been said that he had contempt for intellectuals who confined their radicalism to talk and theory, and that a hard-nosed employer represented a man of action, somebody he understood—and could outsmart.

He became a hero to his men, they could identify with him as working class, and above all they trusted him. Richard L. Neuberger, writing in the Forum in 1939, mused over the conundrum. "Many labor chieftains are aloof and distant from the men they lead. They use a sort of superiority technique and enjoy filet mignon and ride in sedans, though their followers eat goulash and travel on streetcars." He spoke of men like John L. Lewis, Phil Murray, Dave Beck and William Green, of colonial residences, expensive cigars, trips to Europe, tailored clothes...hors d'oeuvres at an ambassador's reception. "Look, then, at Harry Bridges as he stops at a sailor's hotel, eats seaman's food and drives a Ford. See him as he goes on relief during a strike and turns back his salary to the union treasury...[And] his objective is that no union official shall receive more money than the average member of his union...." Bridges made good on this objective. And today he still lives on the fringes of the workingclass Mission District of San Francisco, in modest, no-nonsense comfort.

So word went out: Harry couldn't be bought.

But he left his flank open, he was vulnerable. When he came ashore in 1920, having earlier paid the $8 head tax, he neglected to push through the necessary paperwork to gain citizenship. A conservative cry arose: "Can an alien rightfully come here, without accepting the obligations of citizenship, stir up men to militant action and violent hatreds?" He was accused by the government of being a communist, and the witch-hunt was on. Deportation proceedings began and went on for years. The FBI lived in his pocket. In 1939 he was acquitted by a fair-minded judge, the dean of Harvard Law School, James M. Landis, when it became apparent that the opposition had brought in stool pigeons from all over the country to testify against him—felons, small-time hoods and communists who wanted off the hook. The vendetta continued with the trials of 1945 (after which he received his naturalization papers), 1950, and 1953, when the Supreme Court at last set aside an earlier conviction of perjury. After nearly twenty years, his dues to democracy were paid in full.

In the cold, modern, impersonal world of containerization it may not be so easy to search out and define Harry Bridges's legacy, but it's there. His high-spirited defiance still courses through the blood of the union. It is written in these words: "The basic rule of this union is that the rank-and-file comes first, second and third. Even when we're wrong we're right."

I once asked a longshoreman I knew to tell me why his union was so unique. After a rather disgusted pause he answered: "Orneriness and humor. It's a brotherhood. When we start up the gangway of a ship we're sayin' to the employer, 'Move aside, we'll load or discharge the ship as you see fit, but you better stand clear. And if you have to talk to us, do it through channels. We ain't here for your pleasure, just our own. And remember: the waterfront is our world, not yours.'"

Even though he was an alien for most of his fighting years, Harry Bridges is a throwback to radicals like Eugene Debs and Big Bill Haywood, men who paved the way for the deal makers to come, until the American labor movement was driven inevitably toward a centrist position in American life. Alien or not, he is very much in the American grain. He somehow passed on to longshoremen a belief in personal sovereignty and independence, and above all a rugged dignity that freed them from a sense of drudgery and oppression.

Maybe the legacy should be scaled down to a smaller image, but one that is no less reverberating. They tell the story about an old pensioner who, some years back, long after Bridges had retired, still attended the monthly meetings. At one heated, rancorous affair, marked by bitter arguments over whether to ratify an upcoming contract, the old-timer leaned his head back, closed his eyes and, in a loud, dreamy voice, intoned a litany: "I wants to hear it from Harry, I wants to hear it from Harry, I wants to hear it from Harry...."

DAVID EHRENFELD

Garrett Hardin Is the Original Thinker's Original Thinker

T HERE AREN'T MANY people in California—or anywhere else—whose mere thoughts are more interesting than their way of making money, their private sex lives, the story of their miraculous recovery, their method for training police dogs or losing weight, or their six gourmet recipes for leftover broccoli. Garrett Hardin is one of the precious few: the original thinker's original thinker.

So forget the usual stuff of magazine biography: the peripatetic life as a younger son of a father employed by the Illinois Central Railroad, the lonely exciting days on his grandfather's farm in Missouri, the polio that left him, at the age of four, partially crippled for life, the swimming, the wife and four children, even the details of his pro-abortion battles of the 1960s. What matters are Hardin's ideas, the shimmering, crystalline creations of his mind that never fail to astonish his admirers and that leave his many enemies feeling as if they were trying to ward off a giant with a willow twig.

In the story of the emperor's new clothes, the emperor's nakedness was finally exposed by a little child who lacked the sophistication to rationalize away what he could plainly see. Hardin's role in life has been that of a child pointing at naked emperors (the title of his most recent book of essays is *Naked Emperors*). He is a hunter of taboos, of the concepts and practices we declare sacred, out of bounds to criticism and rational discussion. And like anyone who questions the sacred, he has aroused more than his share of opposition from all quarters.

Both liberals and conservatives can find plenty to make them nervous in Hardin's writings. In fact, if you can read Hardin for more than ten minutes without getting mad, you are probably (1) a saint, or (2) brain-damaged, or (3) a very slow reader. Liberals he dismisses, using Michael Novak's explanation, as people with no human "middle term" between individualism and universalism. Conservatives he embarrasses by rejecting such contemporary right-wing causes as "right-to-life," efficiency, and perpetual growth. Truly, the professor emeritus of human ecology at the University of California at Santa Barbara has never worried about his public relations image.

The article on earthquake prediction in his book of essays called *Stalking the Wild Taboo* is a case in point. This essay, he writes proudly by way of introduction, was rejected by more magazines than anything else he has written. And no wonder. In it, Hardin makes the case for not spending any federal money on new research in earthquake prediction. (Note that he lives in Santa Barbara; at least he can't be accused of cowardice.) "At best," Hardin says in the essay, "if the research were unsuccessful, $137 million would be wasted." This is the best that could come of such a scientific endeavor. The worst? You guessed it: the research might succeed and we might learn how to predict earthquakes. "And then what?" he asks.

There is a fundamental difference, Hardin observes, between earthquakes and hurricanes. Hurricanes already exist when we start to predict their behavior. Storm forecasts give us at most a day or two in which to take fright and do whatever we are going to do—batten down or flee. But earthquakes are another matter. "On the basis of all we know about earthquakes, it is almost certain that in an earthquake warning system, lead-time and reliability would be *directly* related." In other words, if scientists learn how to predict earthquakes reliably, the chances are that such predictions would be made six months rather than six days before the actual quake. (It appears that the Chinese, years after Hardin wrote about earthquake prediction, were able to evacuate one city shortly before a major quake, with a resulting saving of life. But this kind of last-minute warning is not the sort of forecasting system that is at issue here.) So assume that scientists do learn to predict earthquakes several months before they happen. "And then what?" he asks.

All hell would break loose. What could anyone do, knowing that a quake was probably coming during the next six months? Pack the china away? "...what do you eat off of in the meantime?" Hardin wonders. Think of the psychological effects on a population already enduring the multiple stresses of life in the fast lane. Think of what would happen to real estate values and home sales, to the insurance industry, to banking, to stock values of local industries, to construction....It would be inevitable, Hardin continues, that as soon as a hint of a forthcoming prediction of a quake became known, powerful interests would combine to suppress it. Such an act would be followed by the equally inevitable rumors, leaks, and profiteering, all adding to the social turmoil. Some people would be leaving the earthquake zone, some would be staying, others—experts at exploiting chaos and human misery—would be arriving in unsavory droves. Could the quake, itself, when it finally comes, possibly cause as much damage to society as its prediction?

This is already enough to make us stop and think, but Hardin is not yet finished. The dangers of earthquake prediction are much greater for a so-called free, capitalistic economy than for a controlled economy like Russia's. Thus earthquake prediction becomes a political weapon that will harm us but not our enemies, and the fact that the wounds will be unintentional and self-inflicted will not make them any less serious.

What bothers Hardin most is that—regardless of whether they would agree or disagree with him—the federal agencies that have considered whether to fund earthquake research have never even thought about the side effects of prediction. "Nowhere," he writes, "do they indicate that they have the slightest inkling of the psychological and sociological dangers of the scientific advance they hope for. Their analysis is a beautiful example of the pathology of specialism....In their bland indifference to the total meaning of earthquakes these geophysicists remind us of the apocryphal surgeon who 'solved' the problem of the weeping patient by extirpating her tear glands."

The method of Garrett Hardin's inquiry is organized around one critical question: "And then what?" This is the ecologist's question, par excellence. Ecology, the study of living organisms in their environments, is above all concerned with interactions and their consequences. What Hardin has done is turn an ecologist's eye on processes and happenings that most of us take for granted, and to look beyond at the consequences. He likes nothing better than to take our society's most beloved ideals, the ones we have painted a gleaming white, and apply a few coats of intellectual paint remover. Even the titles of his essays reveal his method. "In Praise of Waste," "The Moral Threat of Personal Medicine," "Vulnerability—The Strength of Science," "The Threat of Clarity," "Nobody Ever Dies of Over-Population." Do such themes seem paradoxical to you? You didn't look far enough, says Hardin. Ask the question "And then what?" and the other fellow's paradox will become your common sense.

Hardin is a taboo-hunter, and such game is plentiful, but he doesn't scatter his shots at random. His principal target—pursued with a near-obsessional zeal for more than a quarter of a century—is the democratic and liberal notion that what is good and true for the individual must by extension be good and true for everyone. His great assault on this doctrine—and certainly his best-known work—was an article originally published in the journal *Science,* in 1968, and since then reprinted in many places. He called it "The Tragedy of the Commons." At the heart of this profound and indeed tragic essay is, as we might expect from Hardin, a paradox—a deceptively simple one. Consider a "commons" such as the original commons or public grazing land. Any herdsman has the right to graze cows there, as many as desired. Assume that the commons is already crowded, and you, a herdsman, want to add another cow to your herd. What is the benefit to you? Clearly one cowsworth of benefit, because all the profits will come to you. And what are the costs? Because grazing is free, the ongoing costs are primarily those related to overgrazing. But the one cowsworth of overgrazing costs contributed by your extra cow is shared by everyone who uses the commons, and you will only perceive a tiny fraction of it. The profits are yours but the costs are everyone's. With this kind of accounting, why not buy another cow? And then another. That's the tragedy of the commons: what's good for you alone may be awful for you plus your neighbors.

Although Hardin has identified deteriorating commons in many areas of modern life, from medicine to pollution, his *bête noire,* the commons that frightens him most, is the right to multiply, with its result not of overgrazing but of human overpopulation. In "Nobody Ever Dies of Overpopulation," a short essay wrtten in 1971, he made clear his belief that the world is already overpopulated. Describing a storm that had just killed a half-million people in East Bengal (now Bangladesh), he asked; "What killed those unfortunate people? The cyclone, newspapers said. But one can just as logically say that overpopulation killed them....In the web of life every event has many antecedents. Only by an arbitrary decision can we designate a single antecedent as 'cause'....Were we to identify overpopulation as the cause of a half-million deaths, we would threaten ourselves with a question to which we do not know the answer: How can we control population without recourse to repugnant measures?...Instead we say that a cyclone caused the deaths....Fate is so comforting."

How can we control population, given the tragedy of the commons? Enclose the commons, says Hardin, restrict the right to multiply. Keep our distance from other places which have refused to enclose their commons. "Mutual coercion mutually agreed upon" is his phrase. Limit some personal freedoms in order to preserve others more precious.

And how do we—even a simple majority "we"—mutually agree upon and bring about such mutual coercion? On that subject he is less clear. But if we turn aside from the writings of Garrett Hardin with the feeling that he is better at exposing naked emperors than he is at sewing new clothes, we must not hold it against him. An overpopulated world needs clear-sighted children. And he never claimed to be a tailor.

NEELA CAMPBELL

Gene Scott: A View from the Pew

Neela Campbell of San Francisco, a born-again Christian writer and community organizer, has been watching Pastor Gene Scott on KVOF with great interest. Campbell was appalled—and, at the same time, fascinated—by Scott's "innovative" fund-raising methods, and took careful notes while watching in preparation for an FCC complaint that she intends to file shortly. The following is a brief account of some of her more interesting moments with Channel 38.

G ENE SCOTT SEEMS as deeply convinced about the integrity of his complaints—mostly against government bureaucrats and other ministries—as he is about his religious faith. The result is that getting hooked on Channel 38 is much like getting hooked on a soap opera: You want to quit, but you're afraid the episodes you'll miss will be blockbusters. The *Festival of Faith*, which runs from three to eight hours, depending on Scott's mood, is the most astonishing show on television. Scott often says, "There ain't no other show like the *Festival*, folks." He's right.

Where else would you see a network president fire an entire TV station's staff right on camera? I saw Scott do it on a local replay of a show aired on Channel 18 in Hartford, Connecticut, when employees tried to form a labor union. Scott believes the TV station is part of his church and that churches shouldn't be unionized. So he ordered one camera locked in position, and a second camera manned by a trusted personal staff member—then he fired everyone except the station manager, whom he had brought from California. Employees were told—on the air—that they could have their jobs back if, by morning, they agreed to Scott's terms: no union, no complaining, much smiling, working any hours Scott wanted. The case is currently pending before the National Labor Relations Board.

Where else would you see a network president vent his anger on a watermelon? Scott was furious with the *Hartford Courant,* because it once refused to call Faith Center a "church" in a story about Channel 18. His anger resulted in his introducing as a guest "a watermelon that alleges to be a newspaper." The watermelon bore the banner "The *Hartford Courant.*" Scott put a microphone in front of it. "Can you say *church?*" he screamed. "See, it can't say nothin'," he said. "It's too full of seeds."

On September 27, Scott read a story from the *Courant* about his lawsuit against the city of Avon, Connecticut, for its locking up of the Channel 18 transmitter during the spring tax battle. This story used the word "church" four times. Now pleased, Scott produced another well-labeled watermelon and held a funeral service for it, complete with pallbearers and funeral music on the organ. "There'll be a viewing in the hall after the program," he said. Then he added, "This watermelon may return from the grave. There'll be a resurrection if this newspaper ever again forgets to say 'church.'" Barely pausing for breath, Scott then announced a funeral service for the Reverend Raymond Shoch, founder of Faith Center and its pastor for twenty-six years, who had died less than forty-eight hours before.

Scott often says that barely a dozen pastors support him in the three areas Faith Center serves. Many Christians are disturbed by Scott's attacks on other ministries, his theological position in not submitting to government authority (many believe that the Bible teaches this submission) and his antics. During his program, Scott instructs his counselors to hang up the phones on critics. Scott boasts that he has all critical letters thrown out so he does not see them; his secretary maintains a list of persons who write critical letters.

Scott says he is "a loner in the church world." In contrast, Paul and Jan Crouch, who run Trinity Broadcasting Network (TBN)—which airs the more conventional *Praise the Lord* program on Channel 26—receive a lot of involvement from local pastors. This involvement philosophy is being followed by Pastor Ron Haus of the First Assembly of God Church in Vallejo, who is attempting to bring a second Christian TV station to the Bay Area. The Crouches have signed a contract for their *Praise the Lord* program to be aired on the new station. The FCC ruling on this license will come in December. Scott is clearly furious over this. "The last thing the Bay Area needs is another Christian imitation of the 'Johnny Carson Show'," he fumes. He refers to the Trinity Broadcasting Network as "my competition."

Channel 38's license is up for renewal December 1. Scott says, "If you are not for us, you are our enemy. If you are against Channel 38, you are not only against me, you are against God."

MICHAEL PARRISH

Portrait of the Surfer as a Middle-Aged Man

A T SIX A.M. on an overcast day, Greg Johnson, forty-one, picks a surfboard from the fifteen or so in his backyard and waits for a couple of friends before walking down the hill to the beach. He's a little behind schedule this morning. If he gets up at quarter to six, he can often be in the water five minutes later, which gives him a bit more than an hour of surfing before he has to come back, shower, and get ready for work.

Surfing is mostly a young man's sport. It takes time, the sort of time older people, with the responsibilities of job and family, don't have. And it is not exactly a socially acceptable form of recreation. While it may be appropriate for a kid to pop open a few beers with friends at the beach, a middle-aged man is better off inviting his boss to his tennis club. Some great surfing competitors go on to launch surfboard shops or the like, but most drift away in their mid-twenties, when adult demands intrude.

Greg Johnson has never seriously considered drifting away. He caught his first wave in 1953, at age twelve. He and his friends had to hitch out from Inglewood to get in the water. Now he lives in a house that overlooks the ocean in Manhattan Beach. And when the assorted professionals in his neighborhood are browsing through their *Wall Street Journals*, Johnson is out there in the cool, gray ocean, catching the morning surf.

Johnson is no aging beach bum. He's a family man, and he pays his taxes. But when the subject of freedom is raised, he has clearly given the matter considerable thought. Freedom is, for him, surfing and the sea. Since he first decided this as a teenager, his master plan has been to get to the beach, and to stay. Over the years, what was once summer fun has become an obsession.

His passion for surfing began to develop while he was in Catholic school. Johnson started out at St. John the Evangelist—a grammar school where the nuns addressed him as Gregory—and then moved on to the now-defunct Mt.

Carmel High School in central Los Angeles. His father, an accountant at Northrop for thirty-five years, steered him toward a career in the postal service. At school the football coach wanted blood. Johnson learned his athletic principles in the days when it was not enough to play a sport—you had to win.

"Johnson," yelled the coach one halftime, "why are we here?"

"To have fun, coach," Johnson said with a grin. Whereupon the coach slammed Johnson up against a locker and screamed, "No, no, no!" until Johnson changed his mind.

Meanwhile, on weekends and through the summer, Johnson surfed. Floating around between thrilling rides, wearing only his baggy swim trunks, free of constricting shoes and shirts and creased pants, just watching the pattern of incoming swells and feeling himself rising on their great backs as they rolled underneath—all this was a soothing, rhythmic experience. He was fascinated by the everchanging waves—he had much to learn about how they are formed, how they break, where he had to position himself to catch the big shove. But as much as anything, Johnson, a city boy, enjoyed the soul-warming experience of space. As far as he could peer out across the ocean, he could see no telephone poles, backyard fences, or automobiles.

So at first light most mornings through the summers—and to the distress of his mother, who thought it rude that people didn't come to the front door—his friends stood under his window and called, "Gre-eg," and he would go surfing. At first they had to negotiate rides to get out to 22nd Street in Hermosa Beach. Then, in 1956, in his sophomore year in high school, Johnson solved the problem by spending $300 on a '46 Ford woody.

He took the usual summer jobs—box boy, gas station attendant, laborer. But he hated them. His feet were always tired; he watched the clock. He was a lousy employee, even for a kid. What he really wanted to do was surf. He liked the sport and the scene at the beach. And he liked to raise a little hell. Every now and then he and a couple of his buddies would "gas and run"— gas up for a surf trip and drive off without paying—"donut and run," or "Twinkies and run." And they did take off their clothes a lot. One had to change clothes by one's car, after all, and if it blew the tourists' minds to see all those bare asses flashing along Pacific Coast Highway, it was their problem. Johnson and his friends once had the rewarding experience of hearing a judge solemnly announce: "The report here has it that your penises and testicles were hanging below your fannies as you drove by the lady who reported you...."

By the time Johnson went off to college, he was torn between the conventional sports programs he excelled at—he spent most of his college days supported by football scholarships—and surfing. School was comfortable and the responsible thing to do, especially since he realized that he would someday have to get a job. But he was hardly a spectacular student.

Meanwhile, friend after friend consigned his fate to surfing and dropped out to make a life of it. Johnson joined them whenever he could, but he didn't want to jump in head-first. Although he wanted to end up at the beach, he knew that he wanted to find a way to make a living there. He loved to surf, but he had a practical streak in him that kept his obsession in check. Johnson spent five years at three local colleges pondering the matter. Then at Cal Poly Pomona he met Deanna.

She was a "heavy-duty" student, a biology major, not to mention a former princess of the Los Angeles County Fair, and she came from a wealthy family. He was one of the "animals," the athletes, and too much a screw-up to be real husband material. Still, he was charming. On their first date, they got a six-pack of beer and parked in a walnut grove. Deanna bought the beer.

Matters now became serious for Johnson, and he worked hard at becoming a teacher. Teachers have decent hours and summers off. If the master plan was going to work, it was time to push. He quit football and hit the books. A few months before his graduation, he and Deanna said their vows—and they moved to a neat if monotonous housing tract in Alhambra.

"OUR FIRST YEAR of marriage had to be the worst year of my entire life," says Deanna Johnson, stretched out on a couch in their Manahattan Beach home, facing her husband. "Greg was student teaching, and then he started teaching. I was still in school, carrying sixteen to eighteen units—the science major trying to graduate. And so—Miss Studious—I spent hours studying in the bedroom while Greg was building models out in the living room. Watching TV and building models. He'd want to do something, and I'd be studying. It was just—it was horrible."

"I'd never built a model boat in my life," says Greg. "I hated that. I didn't have any identity. I wasn't living here. This gives me a lot of support and strength, you know, the beach."

In 1965, what then seemed like the final brick in the master edifice fell into place. They moved to Manhattan Beach. Greg had a job with a nearby school district, and to his surprise he found that for the first time in his life he loved going to work, he loved teaching kids. Now it was time to get back into the water. It sounded is if it were going to be simple. It wasn't.

"I think that when we moved here," says Greg, "Deanna thought I liked the beach and my friends and all that better than I liked her. I would go so often—and I would have liked to include her, but it wasn't the same for her; it wasn't the same feeling. And so it became my friend Roger and his first wife and myself against her." Greg and some friends took up volleyball.

Soon they were playing five nights a week. And every spare moment they went surfing.

"You know," says Deanna, "you go along with it for a certain number of years, and then it finally accumulates and comes out in the open. We did what Greg wanted to do, and I resented it a lot. And I wasn't very nice to Greg, and I wasn't very nice to his friends, either. They thought I was a real bitch. There were people who chose sides, who went to Greg's side and said, 'Well, get rid of her!' It was really a bad scene."

So bad that one night at a party in their backyard, one of Greg's surfer buddies threw a pitcher of beer on Deanna when she told everybody it was late, that they ought to break it up. And Greg—although he later came in the house to try to put an arm around her shoulder—at first laughed along with the rest.

Soon after that, they hit bottom. "We were going to split," says Deanna. "I was going to take the kids, and I was going to do what I wanted to do. And at that point it was so bad there was no anger involved; it was pure apathy. It was past the point of dickering and fighting. I'd say it had gone a year or two beyond that."

Instead, they ended up in marriage counseling for most of four years. And that didn't start off with great optimism, either. For one thing, the therapist wasn't your average surfing type. Greg had some trouble taking him seriously. "He's little and has a beard, and he's soft-spoken," says Greg. "Immediately after I walked out the first time I thought, 'I'm gonna kick his ass. I'm gonna kick his butt.' And I meant it. You know, everything about him was 'little' and 'pimp.' Well, Deanna kept going [for the first year], and then she asked me to come back. So we went back, and then they put us in a group—so there were four couples. It took a few times, but for whatever reason, and I can't remember the incident, I somehow gave up my power to him. I followed one of his suggestions. And it worked. I learned from that."

Both of them learned that if Deanna knew Greg loved her more than the beach and his friends, she would no longer resent them; and all that Greg had to do was say that he did, which he did. "But we really are different," says Greg. "And she lied to me. She said she was a real beach bunny. Then when we got to the beach, she said, 'I'm not going into the water.'"

"Another thing we're going to rectify is that he's off in the summer and I'm working," says Deanna, who is a medical technologist. "For the three weeks after school's out, I want a divorce because there's a lot of adjustment having him around."

"But I *work* in the summer," says Greg through his teeth. "I have other jobs. I work my little butt off."

"Oh, I know, I know," says Deanna in mock sympathy. "That's why you're at the beach every day when I get home. But whether or not he's working at his other jobs is irrelevant. There's a certain resentment in me when I go to work and he's home, going to the beach, or playing volleyball."

"I'M SORT OF A focal point because I'm between places," Johnson says, pulling on his wet suit, getting ready to head down to the beach one morning. He has friends living in towns on either side of Manhattan Beach, and a varied assortment arrive every good surfing day to go down to the beach with him. In recent years the underwater sand formations have been such that Manhattan's waves are particularly good. Johnson also has a convenient outdoor hot water shower for his friends to use.

Johnson's substantial though unpretentious home sits astride the main Manhattan Beach sand dune, a half dozen short blocks to the sea. He has already noted the wind direction from the flapping of the large American flag attached to the right corner of his third-floor balcony. He has checked out the surf from his living room windows, which offer a wide-angle view of the bay from Point Dume to the Palos Verdes Peninsula. He could also have checked it from his bathroom, or, had he felt the need for a better look at the waves breaking closer to shore, he could have gone higher yet, to his "super check spot," through the trapdoor he's cut in the roof.

"The older I get the more definite I am about what I like to do," he says, now standing in front of his house. "So, I'm always available, I'm always there for surfing. You have to have a passion for something. Like, if I asked you right now, 'Where would you like to be?' and you knew right away you'd want to be, I don't know, at Alta skiing or down at San Onofre surfing—those are the kind of people I like to be around." Some of Johnson's friends begin to arrive. First there is "Travelin' Bill" Saunders, forty-three, who began surfing in the mid-fifties and met Johnson when they were on the El Camino Junior College football team together. Then comes Roger Mercier, formerly "Crazy Roger," another old teammate. Mercier, who was a brilliant student, despite the prodigious amounts of wine he consumed (and despite the fact that he lived for some time in a station wagon near campus), is now a vice president and general counsel for Denny's, the restaurant corporation. Mercier arrives with his sixteen-year-old son, John, who is a regular in the morning lineup. Finally, Brian Sweeney, another friend from the late fifties, who now owns a real estate firm, pulls into a parking space across the street. They walk down to the water. In a few moments, all are astride their boards, arms resting on their hips, waiting through an unremarkable series of swells.

"I have a good story," says Johnson with a grin. "Last year at school a kid said something about surfing. And I said, 'Oh, yeah, I was in the water this morning.' Well, they don't believe you. I mean, they just got out of bed. They just got to school. And this kid was giving me some crap and saying, 'No way. That's bullshit.' "You know how water collects in your sinuses? Well, I put my head down, and all the water from my sinuses went into my nose, and then I lifted up and all this water poured out onto the floor. And I just looked at him. It was the perfect proof."

The conversation ends as a couple of guys take one of the few waves of any consequence that morning. Meanwhile, Greg George and Jeff Eick (better known as "Peff"), two more old-timers, have come up from 8th Street and pushed their boards out through the shore break.

Thirty years ago these guys used balsa long boards, on which subtle and graceful movement—rather than skateboard-style acrobatics—were prized. As boards changed many old-time surfers were unwilling to endure the embarrassment of relearning their sport. Johnson's friends are the exception. Today, their hairy chests taking on a bit of gray, they carry short, modern surfboards down to the water.

Another thing has changed over the years. Each has made a little money. In fact, most of the men in the water this morning are millionaires.

Fifteen minutes later Johnson steers his late-model VW van toward the Criterion restaurant, his breakfast spot in downtown Manhattan Beach. He is explaining how inflation and the real estate boom were godsends to a lot of older surfers. He is not yet a millionaire himself, though he could well be on his way. "There was a feeding frenzy about ten years ago," says Johnson with admirable understatement. "And I was lucky to get in on it. I loved houses and I loved property. I bought a house, and when it went up a couple of years later, it was worth, like, $4,000 more than what I'd paid for it. Well, $4,000, that was half my salary. I couldn't believe it. So I told a friend, 'We have to do it again.' And finally I got my first little group together."

This investment group—made up, in large part, of old surfing buddies—is now known as the Yukon Weinnies, after a faculty athletic team Johnson helped found at Yukon Intermediate School. (The spelling seems to have been the decision of the not entirely fastidious young surfer who printed up the group's T-shirts.) The Yukon Weinnies own some fifteen smaller properties around South Bay beach towns. Johnson manages the places, collecting rents and so forth, and Travelin' Bill Saunders—a former Shell Oil Company chemist who dropped out to work for himself—does most of the construction and maintenance, when he's not in the mountains or in Mexico.

"I take great pleasure in being an entrepreneur," says Johnson. "It's like being free of the system. I'm free of the school district. I like to teach school, but now I don't need them.

"A lot of those guys in the water this morning quit," Johnson goes on. "They graduated from college as engineers or accountants or business majors, went into business, and quit. That shows how aggressive they are— they quit after, like, three years and went into real estate."

And they became millionaires.

Now, every afternoon after teaching school, Johnson falls by Naramore Associates, a Redondo Beach real estate outfit with whom the Weinnies are loosely connected. And from seven-thirty to eight o'clock each weekday morning, Johnson makes himself available at the Criterion for contract signing or other brief real estate-related business. At the same time, he has breakfast with whichever surfing friends happen to come along.

This morning Johnson and his son, Christopher, twelve, Travelin' Bill Saunders, Roger Mercier, and Mercier's son, John, crowd around a booth. Since no one drops by to talk real estate, the conversation turns to the psychology of being an older surfer.

"My teaching job gives me respectability," says Johnson. "I mean, I have a job—I'm okay, you know. So I can go surfing. Otherwise, I don't think I could."

"Yeah," agrees Mercier, chin resting on his fist.

"If you're a surfer and you're twenty-five, you're not a bum," says Johnson. "But if you're a surfer and you're forty and you—"

"And you don't have any bread, you're poor," muses Mercier. "Think about it—it's not fun being forty and poor."

"We're fortunate," says Johnson. "The way I look at it, it was just luck. We wanted to stay at the beach; we knew that. And we ended up here.

"We have an old friend who has been surfing as long as we have," says Johnson softly. "But he didn't act, you know. He was a school teacher. And now his life is kind of sad. He lives in a little apartment, and he's down on the beach. And we kind of like to envy him, but we don't want to be him. He's got all the young chicks with him and everything—he's divorced—and he surfs all the time now. But he's lost; his life isn't in order. He doesn't have real freedom because he's always going to have to work. We're going to be able to retire, you know, and quit."

"Then you surf," says Saunders.

"Yeah," says Johnson. "And we're almost there."

IT IS SOMETHING of a personal tradition that every day Johnson parks his van and steps in front of his lined-up students mere seconds before the pledge of allegiance begins. "It's my way of fighting the establishment," he says, glancing at his watch. This is but one of the eccentricities his fellow teachers have noticed. He also likes Reyn Spooner shirts, at $35 a crack—the first reverse prints made in Hawaii—which are revered by surfers. He wears *huarache*-style loafers and sandals and a waterproof watch, so that when he's surfing he can tell when he has to get out of the water to go to school. Yet his coworkers do not dislike him. He is considered a rather lovable, if not altogether effective, fellow.

Johnson is a special-education teacher, and he takes on students with normal intelligence who are too restless for regular classes, or who are, as he puts it with affection, "my young gangsters." Stories abound in the hallways of every public school about the maddening challenge of teaching special-ed kids. But according to a few fellow teachers, Johnson is remarkably efffective. "Yet the teachers can't get away from this surfer-Mr. Nice Guy image, his infectious personality," says one. "And so they never think he does anything. And then we have all these kids who just dramatically improve."

"I'm not a real good teacher," insists Johnson. "In fact, I'm pretty lazy. But what I am is, I'm easygoing. I never really get too upset with most of them, and so they come to school—their attendance is nearly one hundred percent—every day."

Peewee Roller, A-Dog, Babyman, Nasty, Doctor Dookie, even a girl who terrorized the school and was later found to have human bite marks on her arm—all the juvenile characters of a television sitcom can be found in Johnson's class. "They're just little kids who have trouble making it," says Johnson, leaning back on one of the brown, flower print couches in his living room. "Really, just the kids who need to go surfing, right?"

Then, lest this seem embarrassingly profound, he leans back farther, laces his fingers together behind his head, and starts talking about his flag and his cannon. "I've always liked flags, you know. But Deanna hates them," he reports gaily. "She says it looks like a headquarters, this house." The flag also helps him spot his home when he's floating around between waves— something else that gives him a small ping of pleasure.

The cannon is a seventy-five-pound brass Civil War replica. As soon as the cannon is mentioned, Paige, Johnson's fifteen-year-old daughter, looks up with a grimace and says, "Oh,God." The details are unclear, but apparently Paige is often elected to apologize to the police when they arrive to complain about an especially heroic blast.

"The cannon just came about," says Johnson innocently. "On special occasions I fire it. I start the race in Manhattan [the annual 10-K Manhattan Beach Old Home Town Fair run], and I fire it at tournaments, or I fire it when I get drunk."

In Johnson's life, while much has changed, much has remained the same. And it seems a reasonable bet that for the rest of his life there will be those calls to go surfing.

"Gre-eg," calls Travelin' Bill now when he shows up in the misty mornings.

"Goddamn it," growls Deanna, who likes to sleep in. "I thought I married a man! I thought you were going to grow up!"

But Greg Johnson loves every minute of his life. "My friends who still surf all have that look, like, 'God, I'm still doing it! I still go in the water! I can do it and not be a bum!'"

ANTHONY COOK

Good Wine, Bad Blood

T HE FIRST AWKWARD moment came after the Lord's Prayer. Monsignor William Serado, pastor of the St. Helena Catholic Church, stood before the tightly packed congregation of 250 mourners and offered a blessing for the "dearly departed," Rosa Mondavi: "Let us offer each other the sign of peace." Almost in unison, the mourners shifted their eyes to catch a glimpse of Rosa's two sons and two daughters standing in the first three pews with their families. What would they do? Time stopped, as the morning sunlight filtered through the stained-glass figure of St. Helena, the mother of Constantine. Then, reluctantly, Rosa's children exchanged tentative, embarrassed hand clasps. The moment passed, and they turned away from one another to stare straight ahead at the altar.

Even a prayer for their mother had failed to unite the family, especially the two men, now in their early sixties, who were fighting each other over the family winery in Napa Valley, valued at more than $40 million and grossing $17 million a year. The battle had grown ruthless—it was beyond business, beyond reason. No matter which brother won—Peter or Robert—each was out for blood rather than just money.

Father Sixtus Cavagnaro, a close friend of Rosa's during her last years, stood up to speak. His words were Italian, and they rolled forth with an intensity that riveted even the few in the crowd who couldn't understand a word. Father Sixtus pointed to Rosa's coffin. Signora Mondavi is gone, he said. So what good does this fighting do? What good does this greed do? Let your mother rest in peace. Stop this family war before you are all six feet under!

As the service drew toward its end, the brothers, Robert and Peter, sat like stone. A group of mourners approached the bier. Joe Alioto bent to grasp a handle. His friend, Fred Ferroggiaro, reached for the other. Then Rosa's brother, Nazzareno Grassi, joined them, along with Andrew Johnson, manager of the St. Helena branch of the Bank of America. These were the pallbearers, all picked by Peter. The four carried Rosa's coffin down the blue carpet, past her friends and family and out into the July heat. Rosa's children followed at a distance, girding themselves for the last rites at the family mausoleum.

FIVE DAYS LATER Robert and Peter and their teams of lawyers walked into the Napa County Courthouse to resume the battle that some say hastened their mother's death. The court case had dragged on for ten weeks; then Rosa Mondavi, who was eighty-six and ailing, died of a stroke on the morning of the nation's Bicentennial.

Alternating between high drama and low comedy, the trial provided vignettes of the unraveling of a talented and emotional family that had devoted itself to quality winemaking, a lucrative business with a special mystique.

Out of the ordeal emerged a picture of two brothers locked in a sibling rivalry that evolved into a major business impasse—two brothers whose differences were so great they could not even agree on how to pronounce the family name. Peter called himself a MonDAYvi; Bob said MonDAHvi. In the end, the judge handed down an unusual judgment that threatens to change the character and quality of the C. Mondavi Winery, one of California's legendary winemaking companies.

Cesare Mondavi anglicized his name after he got off the boat from the province of Ancona during the wave of Italian immigration at the turn of the century. Cesare's friends in the new world thought MonDAYvi sounded more American. Such seemingly small considerations were important in a town like Ely, Minnesota, where Cesare began work as a pick and shovel man in the iron mines. He prospered. Soon he had saved enough to return to his birthplace of Sassafarento and marry Rosa Grassi, a young peasant girl who worked in the kitchen of a middle-class family.

In 1908 Cesare took his Italian bride back to Minnesota, and they opened a boarding house in the town of Virginia for local miners who wanted the cuisine and fellowship of the old country. Rosa enjoyed the work, partly because it allowed her to display her talent for cooking. Even late in life, when money was no object and she held the title of president of the Charles Krug winery, Rosa was happiest in her kitchen. As one of the family explains it, "Her thing was chicken broth."

Rosa's work load at the boarding house was overwhelming: the care and feeding of ten men, plus, soon after, her own four children—Mary, Helen, Peter and Robert. She thrived on the routine, however, and began making more money on the boarders than Cesare did pouring drinks in a saloon he had bought. After awhile, he sold the saloon and bought a grocery store. By the twenties, the Mondavis were worth roughly $30,000.

Then the tight band of Minnesota Italian-Americans honored Cesare by picking him to go to California and ship back grapes for the production of their home-fermented wine. Prohibition was going strong, but each family was permitted by law to make up to three barrels of their own wine per year.

Cesare traveled to California's San Joaquin Valley and shipped back cattle cars full of grapes. In two years, he sent enough grapes east to bring his family west. In 1922, they settled in Lodi.

As the children grew, the shipping business became a family enterprise, manned by the industrious, frugal and closely knit Mondavis. Mary helped with the records, the boys did handiwork and Poppa made all the decisions.

Robert, who was eighteen months older than Peter, enjoyed the prerogatives of being the eldest son; he was eager to set an example for his brother. From an early age, the deliberate and restrained Peter was compared to energetic and outgoing Bob.

Bob turned even the simplest chores, like nailing boxes for their father, into contests. Bob perfected a way to economize his hammering to the point where he could nail three boxes a minute (with twenty-two nails per box) for a total output of 1,500 boxes a day. He was easily the fastest box maker in Lodi—but he pushed his brother to work at his pace. "Come on Pete. Don't lose your rhythm. Keep it up!"

Later, in high school, Bob played football; he was the fullback that the team called on for clutch yardage. He would lower his head and bull his way forward. His senior year, he led the Lodi Flames to a state championship.

Peter, on the other hand, disliked contact sports; he preferred tennis. But he had his brother's reputation to live up to. Grudgingly, he went out for football, and played fullback, too. With him running for the tough yards, his team had only a so-so season.

To make matters worse for Peter, he was constantly reminded that he was the baby in the family; his family called him "Baby." When he followed his brother to Stanford University in 1933, he suggested it was about time they dropped his childish nickname. The family agreed; they changed Baby to "Babe." Even now, at sixty-one, his nephews and nieces call him "Uncle Babe."

By the time the bouncy athlete and his kid brother went to college, the seeds of the current battle were rooted in their characters. Friends didn't see the built-in conflict; all they saw were two sons of an immigrant miner and his shrewd but barely literate wife walking around California's blue-blood college with change in their pockets—in the middle of the Great Depression. The family's frugality had given the brothers the chance to be Stanford men.

They studied hard, joined Phi Sigma Kappa (together) and drank Blue Boar Ale and Cuba Libres. (Their taste for wine came later.)

By the time they started college, the nation's "noble experiment" with Prohibition had ended. For Cesare, it was a short step from shipping grapes to crushing them, and he began toying with the idea of a family wine business. When the sons showed interest, he showed his foresight by acquiring part of the Sunny St. Helena Winery in the Napa Valley, an area which he believed would produce great table wines some day.

Napa Valley was also the home of the Charles Krug Winery, one of the oldest wineries in the state. It had been reopened after the repeal of Prohibition by Lou Stralla of St. Helena, who was sending wine in tank cars to distributors like Schenley.

The Krug winery had been founded in the nineteenth century by a Prussian emigré, Charles Krug, who had failed as a revolutionary but succeeded as an American newspaperman. He came to California in 1852 to write for a German paper on the Pacific Coast, the *Staats Zeitung*. Then, after a short-lived investment in a gold and silver refinery, he sank his savings into a Sonoma Valley vineyard and found paydirt. With a small cider press, Krug made 1,200 gallons of the first wine produced in Napa since the days of early Spanish winemaking. He then took his first profits and bought richer land in St. Helena.

WHEN KRUG DIED, the ranch buildings and surrounding vineyard passed to his daughter. Then, when the family defaulted on a loan, the property fell into the hands of James K. Moffitt, a San Francisco banker who hoped to find another family who would restore the Krug wines' early reputation for quality. Moffitt's heirs held on through Prohibition by making grape juice. Then in 1943, at the urging of his son Bob, Cesare Mondavi bought the winery.

At the time the Mondavis purchased Krug, half of the Napa Valley was producing a less-than-glamorous crop: prunes. And the Krug winery, despite its rich history, had seen better days. The Teutonic granite buildings were still grand, but ill-equipped. The surrounding 147 acres of grapes were fit only for bulk wines. Recalls Bob: "We were bottling the wines on dirt floors and shoving the cases through the windows." Still, the operation turned a profit for the Mondavis from the beginning. Cesare paid $75,000 for Krug; in the first year the family made $77,000.

During the war, as the family worked to establish their new winery, Peter was away fighting. Bob was the winemaker. When Peter returned from England in 1945, Cesare put him in charge of production, while Bob ran the sales program designed to turn the family's old grape customers into wine buyers. That combination of talents looked ideal, except for one sorry detail: From the start, Bob and Peter couldn't agree. "He resented my coming back to join him in the first place," says Peter. "I was going faster than him," Bob replies.

The conflict flashed into the open in 1946. With his father's approval, Bob amassed a huge inventory of crushed grapes after signing some big contracts with a group of Eastern wine distributors. It looked like a master stroke at first. Wine was in short supply and the price of bulk wine spurted from around fifty cents per gallon to $1, then $1.50. But other winemakers jumped in, too. Within six months, increased production overran even the boom-time demand. The price of bulk wine plummeted, and the price of grapes dove, too, from $125 to $36 per ton. Bob's Eastern distributors broke their contracts, and the Mondavis were stuck with their inventory—and $371,000 in losses. They went into debt to save the company.

The problem, as Peter saw it, was that Bob was moving too fast for comfort. As Bob saw it, Peter couldn't keep up. But Cesare stepped in, and the dispute died—on the surface. A traditional Italian father, who smoked short stogies and kept a brass spittoon near his desk, Cesare ended the boys' disagreements simply and effectively—he pounded his fist on the dinner table. But though the brothers stopped talking about the 1946 debacle, the memory of it haunts them to this day. "If it weren't for Dad we would have lost this place," says Peter. "He [Dad] went along with my policies," says Bob.

Their disagreements multiplied as the years went by. Bob, the super-salesman, wanted to keep boosting production; Peter, the hose and barrel production man, wanted stricter quality control. Bob wanted more higher-priced "premium" wine to sell; Peter complained they were shipping wine when it was too young. Bob wanted open tastings among the winery staff to improve the vintages; Peter didn't want to share his winemaking secrets with employees. Bob wanted to keep plowing money into the business; Peter wanted to take a little cut. Bob wanted to spend a buck to make a buck; Peter wanted to make it before he spent it.

Peter thought Bob was treating him like a feckless kid brother. "I was working like a dog, and he'd come back from a trip and tell me I was doing everything wrong. Meanwhile, he was out promoting, overspending, over-projecting, never catching up with any of his projects. He was uncontrollable!"

But Bob has a different view: "I was working for an idea." That "idea" was to make Krug a brand identified with quality wine, and to deliver that wine in volume nationwide. And despite their differences, the Mondavis were succeeding. Sales of their premium vintage varietals and C.K. Mondavi table wine increased from 12,000 cases in 1950 to 500,000 cases in 1960. Although the profits were still marginal, the value of the business was increasing with every bottle sold.

Then in 1959 Cesare died. His will left his interest in the family partnership to Rosa during her lifetime and appointed Robert and Peter as co-trustees. The family partnership, known as C. Mondavi & Sons (as is the corporation), controlled the company. The remainder of the shares, some forty percent, were owned by the children—Robert had twelve percent; Peter, twelve percent; Helen, eight percent; and Mary, also eight percent. This complicated structure of ownership became a crucial factor when the family dispute erupted in court this year.

With Cesare gone, there was no one to arbitrate Bob's and Peter's disputes. Rosa had assumed the title of president, but her true expertise revolved around antipasto and tortellini. She treated the company she served as president with a touch of humor. In restaurants, she invariably ordered Charlie Krug wine.

She approached her sons' disputes like a mother rather than an executive. Her instinct was always to side with her baby, Peter. Her advice to Bob was: Try to get along with your brother.

Bob spent even more time on the road promoting the company's wine and dazzling friends in the industry. That galled Peter; Bob seemed to get all the credit—the pats on the back and the chairmanship of the Wine Institute.

Peter complained—louder and louder—that Bob's promotions were costing the company too much money. Bob argued they were necessary for sales. Then one fall morning in Lodi in 1965, Peter told Bob he was ripping off the company with twenty-four-karat expense accounts—he called his brother a thief. Bob said, "Say that again, and you're in trouble." Pete said it again, and Bob warned him again. Pete repeated it one more time, and Bob started swinging, and wrestled his brother to the ground. When Peter returned to St. Helena, he had purple bruises marking his throat.

That was too much for Rosa. She met with Peter, Mary and Helen. Then they filed out of the room and a friend gave Bob the news: The family wanted him to take a six-month "leave of absence." Bob was miffed. "There we were gathering momentum, and all of a sudden, I was cut off at the pockets."

To make the point even more dramatic, Rosa took Bob's eldest son, her grandchild Michael, aside in her kitchen and told him she was sorry to spoil his plans, but there would be no job for him at the winery when he graduated from college in the spring. It was another way of forcing Bob to make way for his brother.

BOB LEFT, but didn't go far. He went down the road six miles and started a new winery. By recruiting two partners and floating a loan, he raised $100,000 and formed Robert Mondavi and Sons at age fifty-four.

Meantime, nothing much changed at Krug, except that Peter was installed in Bob's old corner office and Rosa was elevated to board chairman. They, in turn, recruited another board member, a man who loved good wine, good food—and a good fight: San Francisco mayor-to-be, Joe Alioto. At board meetings, Rosa and Joe would work at what each did best. She would call the meetings to order and then disappear to the kitchen while he ran down the agenda. When the pasta was done, the meeting would adjourn and the feast would begin.

At first, Alioto tried to make peace with Bob, but that failed. As the Robert Mondavi Winery started to turn out wine, the Mondavis at Krug tried to discourage him from using the family name on his bottles. It didn't help that he was *pronouncing* it differently. He was a Mondavi, and a competitor. But when Bob insisted, the family reacted in a typically ambiguous way. They helped Bob crush and bottle his first vintages with Krug equipment. Then they had Alioto send him letters telling him not to compete.

The strain was even more pronounced on holidays, when the family gathered at the beautiful oak-shaded grounds of the Krug estate. Rosa would cook a sumptuous meal—baccala, salami, chicken soup with cappelletti, pasta asciutta, ravioli—and serve the Peter Mondavis at her house on the property. Then she would walk over to Bob's house a few yards away and hand some healthy portions through the door. Same meal, separate tables. No matter how much the social insults hurt him, the business rift bothered Bob even more. He remained a director of C. Mondavi & Sons, as company sales topped $7 million in 1970 and the value of his stock kept climbing. But the shares were restricted. He could only sell them to a family member—and at a family price, rather than at its true market value.

Bob still held his interest in the 1943 partnership set up by his father. By accident, the family had discovered that the partnership could be used to avoid double taxation of dividends from Krug. Profits on sales of wine could go directly to the members of the partnership, without being subject to corporate taxes. Bob, who needed all the money he could get to support his own winery, liked that arrangement. But then his brother Peter decided the family would form a new partnership reducing Bob's status to a limited partner with a smaller percentage of shares.

"They made him an offer he could only refuse," said Bob's attorney. Bob took a radical step. In 1972, he sued his mother, brother and sister to force the sale of the family corporation; he claimed the new partnership devised by

Peter violated his rights as a minority shareholder. Rosa, Peter and Mary countersued (Helen joined Bob), and the case finally went to court in 1976.

In the words of one of the participants, the trial was "like a button-down alley fight." Crowded into the trailer converted into a temporary courtroom in Napa were the feuding families, and their scrappy lawyers—John Martel, a long-haired forty-five-year-old with an encyclopedia of facts, representing Bob, and the bombastic master of trial law, Joe Alioto, representing Peter and his mother. The opening round histrionics, said one lawyer, "made the Scopes trial look like a cotillion intermission."

Because it was a big case in a small town, both Superior Court judges disqualified themselves. The job of dignifying the affair fell to a visiting judge, Robert Carter, who comes on like country, but is exceptionally sharp. He became a circuit rider after a coronary bypass operation allowed him to return to the bench. He pulled into Napa in his silver Airstream trailer prepared for a tough job. And he got one: The trial lasted 103 days.

As the trial dragged on, the warring family sat together in the jury box. And Bob continued to live on the Krug ranch in the home next to Rosa's "little brown house." In the evening he would walk over to her place, enter through the side entrance and step into Rosa's kitchen. There was always something on the stove, and Bob, who loved his mother's cooking, would take a small dish, compliment his mother on the food and then make idle conversation. That was his way of paying respects. But the next morning he would go back into court to press his suit against her for excluding him from Krug.

IN THE END, Judge Carter issued a tough-minded decision—that Krug was "no longer the family corporation originally envisioned, but instead has in reality become a corporation for Peter and his family." He concluded that Krug should be sold so it would no longer divide the Mondavi family.

As Carter saw it, the real trouble began after Peter and Rosa began worrying about his children. She wanted to transfer shares in Krug to Peter's children, but her accountant wanted to avoid heavy gift taxes. The amount of the tax depended on the winery's earnings, which had been increasing steadily. Peter decided that if he could make Krug's profits decline, Rosa could transfer the shares and Peter's family would gain a tighter hold on Krug.

The way they accomplished the stock gift was ingeniously simple. Peter and his family partners, acting as middlemen, sold wine to Krug at inflated prices, and Krug paid more for crushed grapes than the other growers were paying. Down went the company's profits, while the partnership earnings kept going up. Result: Krug was "worth" less, so gift taxes were lower when

Rosa passed on her shares to her grandchildren. The only problem was that Bob decided the ploy was depriving him of his rightful share of earnings. He was, said Carter, the victim of a fraud.

Peter claimed that his brother was an unfair competitor. He pictured Bob as a man who was trying to sell the family heritage—for the right price. He accused him of trying to arrange a takeover of Krug by his partner, the Rainier Brewing Company, a Seattle brewer that held a seventy-five percent interest in Robert's winery.

Peter's argument didn't sway the judge. Instead, he concluded that Peter, Rosa and Mary had concealed a 1972 offer from Schlitz to buy out the family for $32 million as part of their scheme to put control in Peter's hands. The judge decided that Bob had been excluded from Krug, and was entitled to damages totaling $535,885.21.

PETER MONDAVI SITS subdued in his cluttered office on the Krug ranch these days. Portraits of Cesare and Rosa stare down from the walls, and stacks of company records and correspondence in boxes, stamped with the black and red Krug label, surround him, gathering dust. "It doesn't seem fair," said Peter. "One man can force you to sell what you've worked your whole life for."

In a disarming, almost melancholy way, he recited the history of his differences with Bob—"I respected him as my senior brother until he went overboard." Then he earnestly retold his version of events, which was rejected by the court but accepted by his friends, because Peter doesn't seem like a man who would chisel a brother.

"I was always the runner-up," he said. "I'm not that fast; I'm a detail man. Bob was an ultra-perfectionist; I was kicked around." Even his brother's departure didn't make Peter content. "I'm not enthusiastic about being on top."

Peter will appeal Carter's ruling to divest the winery—a process that could take up to two years. Meanwhile, offers are pouring in from public companies anxious to cash in on the wine boom with one of the last of Napa Valley's family-owned premium wineries. Krug earned $3 million in its last fiscal year, so the asking price could exceed $50 million—sixteen times the annual earnings.

Peter could take his share of the proceeds, of course, and go down the road to build what he has always wanted: a winery for Peter Mondavi and Sons. But instead, he said he is planning a $5-million expansion of Krug's storage capacity, overseeing the 1976 crush and shoring up morale. As he walked across the shaded lawns of the historic ranch wearing a white shirt, checked jacket and a tight smile, an approaching workman in overalls doffed his cap. Peter is still the Mondavi in charge at Krug.

Down the road at the Robert Mondavi Winery. the mood is more ebullient. On the day I visited, Bob was sitting at a round revolving table with a line of glasses circling the edge, half-filled with the juice of freshly crushed white grapes. It was the regular morning tasting; he compared notes with his attractive blond winemaker, Zelma Long, his son Tim, his financial man George Schofield and even his lawyer. He and John Martel have a lot to celebrate: the court decision couldn't have been better if they'd made it themselves.

Bob sprints around the new white Spanish mission winery like a man half his age. The pace shows in the growth of the Robert Mondavi label. From 2,000 cases to 229,000 in ten years is a remarkable accomplishment, especially considering the winery's reputation for unexcelled quality. "It's a way of life," enthuses Bob. "It takes dedication."

Bob hasn't yet managed to cash in on his quality reputation, however. In fact, the winery has lost money in all but three years, as rainier has pumped in some $12 million for up-to-date equipment (including an IBM computer for controlling fermentation), as well as plantings and inventory. Two years ago Rainier itself was plunged into the red, when bulk wine prices turned sour, and the Mondavi winery lost half-a-million dollars. Peter Mondavi would call that too fast for comfort.

Bob says his quality will eventually pay for itself. Peter, who has raised just one price in three years, pledges value for money. Bob's obsession is making fine wine; Peter's is running a prosperous business.

With glasses and half-empty bottles spread out on a table before him, Bob conducted a private tasting for me. He poured a 1970 Château Lafite, a 1970 Château Margaux and a 1970 Robert Mondavi Cabernet Sauvignon—the best of France up against the best of Napa. All three were superb, the quality indistinguishable to me. "There," beamed Bob, "that will show you the future of winemaking in this country."

Bob still runs up $150 lunch tabs sampling the competition's best bottles. Peter still worries whether he is paying too much for his grapes. Had they combined their talents, they might have been the Ernest and Julio of fine wines: a promoter who needed a backstop; a detail man in search of a visionary. Each brother tried to make the other more like himself. They needed each other. But they had no use for each other.

Sissy Het

IT'S A LITTLE before dark on Saturday night when the Full Moon Empowerment ("Faerie") Circle gets under way. Scores of men, and a couple of women, join hands in a high-stepping snake dance, leaving the center of camp for the twilit forest. The snake hisses loudly, like a furiously deflating beach toy, as it goes. There's a lot of hissing at this seventh annual California Men's Gathering—hissing as applause, hissing as celebration. Like almost everything here, this takes some getting used to. A large contingent of Radical Faeries is attending this year's CMG, and the hissing is thanks to them. Last night, after the welcoming ceremonies, one of the Faeries explained to the gathering that the Radical Faeries have elected to "reclaim the sound of the snake as a positive sound." Now other people have taken it up, and all weekend long, when someone says something that goes over big, there's an almost deafening hiss of approval, and a wave of fists bobbing in the air in imitation of snakes' heads.

The line dances past a man in a long, black, druid-style robe who holds a finger up for silence, and the hissing subsides. Then the line enters a clearing that has been ringed with odd decorations: every few yards a foot-thick slice of a tree rests on the ground, and weighted to each slice by a white candle is a sign bearing the name of a California community: SANTA BARBARA...SANTA CRUZ...OAKLAND...SAN FERNANDO VALLEY.

In the clearing the circle coils tighter and tighter, then stops, and everyone sits down to hear remarks by Alan Acacia of Berkeley, who is wearing a dress. Alan is a "Sissy Het"—a heterosexual who wears a dress to declare his solidarity with women. In a flier headlined: WHY ARE MEN WEARING DRESSES AT CMG?, which he distributed earlier in the weekend, Alan wrote, "The fact of the matter is that the majority—perhaps two-thirds of the men here—are heterosexual. And many of the men holding hands or wearing dresses are het, too....Society tells us that only HE-MEN are 'real' men....The truth is that real men are tender, are colorful, are sweet to each other. Everything we do—from calling a man 'dear' to wearing pretty clothes, to hugging another man—is male....For us, the skirt is a symbol of our freedom to choose, freedom to live, freedom to love."

The late-summer heat is mild here in the San Bernardino foothills, but the mosquitoes are maddening, and as Alan Acacia and some Radical Faeries tell the gatherers about magic, and about the two-inch-tall spell-casting faeries who lived under the earth in pre-Celtic times, and about the relevance of all this to the present-day anti-sexist men's movement, there is a counterpoint of slapping so loud that it occasionally threatens to drown out the hissing.

Out here in the clearing and back in camp, there are about two hundred men—an occupational mix heavy on therapists, teachers, and artists, but not without its executives and laborers—who will tell you that they are the new model in masculinity, a sensitized marque built for the demands of the eighties. Along with the National Conference on Men and Masculinity, the California Men's Gathering is a major annual event in what is loosely called "the men's movement"—California, typically, occupies an early-warning edge of the cause. The men here have come to a rented church youth camp one hundred miles east of Los Angeles to attend workshops, do movement business and politicking, sing, dance, socialize, and talk, with as much bemusement as passion, about the state of contemporary men. If male roles today are in flux or in question, the California Men's Gatherers have dwelt on the matter with as much concentration as all the Donahue-guesting shrinks and pop sociologists in captivity, and with somewhat more colorful results.

The men's movement is a lumping of causes and organizations of various political bents, but the wing of it that gathers at the CMG is organized around opposition to sexism as practiced by men toward women and by straight men toward gays. The organizations represented here include CAMP (California Anti-Sexist Men's Political) caucus, MEN (Men Evolving Non-Violently), NOCM (National Organization of Changing Men), Men Against Rape, and the Los Angeles Men's Collective.

The notion of a "men's movement" seems initially odd and, over most of a casual tour of the territory, stays odd. If any group seemed not to need a movement, it was men, who are seen as enjoying an embarrassment of material advantages and a history of dictating social discourse. In fact, the men's movement has its roots in consciousness-raising groups that formed almost immediately after the late-sixties rise of such groups for women, and an unkind observer might perceive some male jealousy there: women were not going to have even rap groups to themselves. The men's movement has, in fact, been characterized by some feminists as an ultimate exercise of male privilege: at last, for the sex that has everything, a place to go fret about it. But by the mid-seventies, the big cities and college towns were home to weekly gatherings at which men could talk (and cry) to their sympathetic fellows about their relationships with their fathers, about attacks of impotence and other sexual anxieties, about their confusion over what the hell liberated women wanted out of men—about the difficult business of tooling up a personality that was acceptable by contemporary lights and also honest. They were reading books such as *A Choice of Heroes,* by Mark Gerzon; *Men in Difficult Times,* edited by Robert A. Lewis; and *Men Without Masks,* by

Michael Rubin. They were talking about "homophobia"—the socially induced fear of being gay or being thought gay, which is believed by the
movement to promote a fear of touching and trusting other men—and taking
up protracted man-to-man hugging as a countermeasure.

To an extraordinary degree for what is supposed to be a concerted social
drive, the men's movement is given to self-conscious puzzling over the
contradictions and ironies that its very existence seems to produce. As an
example close at hand, the California Men's Gathering attracts a few sympathetic women, but each year there is an earnest debate about barring them
altogether. The result would be an anti-sexist gathering as purely male as the
most staunchly chauvinist businessmen's club—a Bohemian Grove using real
bohemians. Such contradictions abound because there are at least two
impulses at the root of the movement: a desire to make common cause with
feminists against sexism, and a desire to redeem and celebrate what is good
about being male. The second impulse may follow from an overdose of the
first, but in any case we're in ticklish territory: where is that just-right, fine-
tuned male role, that self-invention that is neither a macho cartoon nor a
blanded-out wimp? The tone of conversation at many CMG workshops is
tentative, wistful, conditional, as if the movement's agenda has yet to extend
beyond the agreeable homilies.

It's tempting to write off the men's movement as a fringe, but there is the
nagging feeling that this is just what people did whose first contact with the
women's liberation movement was through newspaper photographs of
people burning brassieres. However, it's presently impossible to say whether
the men's movement will also develop into a movement in the march-on-
Washington sense, with programs, issues, and political moxie. Tom Mosmiller,
an Oakland activist who devotes himself full time to antibattery and men's
health programs, argues that the movement is becoming a full-fledged
political cause. "There will develop a greater agenda of things men want," he
says, "things like paternity leave, flex-time, better occupational safety and
health, divorce reform, custody reform, nonconscription. Take the battery
stuff: five years ago there were maybe five [counseling] programs [for wife-
beaters] in this country, and now there are over a hundred."

The ultimate political effectiveness of the men's movement aside, its
growth over the past ten years indicates that there is, for some men, a
troublesome sense of estrangement from other men, and that the movement,
with its confessional sessions and tribal gatherings, remedies that feeling for
them. Ed Silberman, a thirty-two-year-old child-care worker, joined a men's
group because "there was something I was craving in my life that had to do
with masculinity." The movement, he says, has "made me a lot more
confident about myself, helped me own up to who I am. I walked into a

men's group, and read books, and the message I got was, 'As long as you've got a penis between your legs, you're a man, and don't let anybody judge you because of something they think masculinity is.'

"I think my relationships with men, and not just men's movement men, are improving. There are times I can say I like men, I dig who they are, they're a nice animal. Four years ago, I couldn't say that."

Illijana Asara is one of the female partisans of the men's movement. A thirty-six-year-old counselor from Santa Cruz, she has collaborated with a poet named David Steinberg on a presentation of erotic poetry and slides that they've given around California and at the CMG. "I've been much more involved with the men's movement than I ever was with the women's movement," Asara says. "One thing that's drawn me to this branch of the movement, and to CAMP in particular, is that the politics don't include blame. I gobbled up a bunch of the early feminist stuff very fast, but I've never found the women's movement very forgiving. They're saying that half the population is to blame for the situation and they want to trash that half of the population. I haven't been able to sit down in a women's group without hearing all these trashy tales about men, and I got sick of it. I live with a man. How am I supposed to go home and establish an intimate relationship with a man after sitting there and condoning that kind of stuff, which cuts off communication between people?

"We're just at the beginning of the expansion of the men's movement now, but I think the men's movement is going to challenge the women's movement on the next step that has to happen in order for men and women to really get it together with each other."

To BE SURE, the issue of male identity is not so pressing for most men—many men already feel reasonably secure being who they are, getting up every day and living their lives and feeling no need to drive out into the California desert and hug each other. But if these questions—however awkwardly asked and uncertainly answered—are in the air for a dedicated minority such as the men at the CMG, experience teaches that they may be coming soon to an air near you. That's what the "empowerment" part of the Full Moon Empowerment Circle is about: the power to spread the movement's message in the coming year. So, the organizers explain, we are now going to gather around the signs that name our home cities. To get there, though, we have to get past the robed Gatekeepers, who ask each of us, "Are you prepared to be emotionally honest with yourself?", a question we doubt ever got asked by real Druids at the turnstile to Stonehenge. If we answer yes, the Gatekeepers say, "Then go in peace, brother."

In each city circle, a "facilitator" from the city in question explains the plan for this ad hoc men's group: each of us in turn must tell what has hurt him as a man and kept him separate from other men. Some of the answers are on the analytical side—the sexual psychology of it all, the sexual politics—but some of them are real horror stories, from bad dads forward, little fifth-year psychiatric breakthroughs alfresco, and soon the darkening forest is dotted with the sporadic sounds of men screaming or weeping, and the silhouettes of men breaking down on the ground and other men's hands reaching to comfort them.

Then the facilitators hand out acorns to symbolize the empowerment we're taking away with us, and each of us is asked to say what he plans to do for the movement this year. The circles break up, and we stumble past the Gatekeepers—this time, they sprinkle us with water, saying, "Be blessed by the tears of your Mother Earth, be blessed by your own tears"—and down the hill to join an arms-over-shoulders circle around a searing campfire. The circle does some loud, dissonant humming and moaning, which gives way to a long round of a neo-Gregorian drone that is heard frequently during the weekend:

> *We are an old people, we are a new people,*
> *We are the same people, different from before.*

Then some of the men in the circle call out the "big steps" they hope to take this year: "Nurturing children," "wearing my dress more often," "being silly," "stopping AIDS," "stopping violence," "honesty," "trust," "reclaiming belching and farting," "forgiving my father," "forgiving myself." Then these steps are all blessed, and there is more dissonant moaning and tumultuous howling, and another song:

> *Listen, brother, listen to my heart's song,*
> *I will never forget you, I will never forsake you.*

And Alan Acacia closes the Faerie Circle by saying, "Go tell the twelve million men of California that we do have a choice in how we live our lives."

The Faerie Circle is the most elaborate ceremony in a weekend that is long on ceremonies. There are also dances, evening entertainments, and dozens of workshops. Some of these are in the mainstream of men's feminism—"Homophobia," "My Father, Myself," "Working with Other Men to Stop the Violence," "How to Cope with Sexist Remarks in Social Situations," "Rape," "What It's Like to Be a Man." Others are less evidently germane: "Mime and Mask Movement," "Group Oil Acupressure," "Slide Show: Our Trip to Nicaragua," and the one listed in the program booklet as "Coming Together: The Jack-Off Network." ("In the past few years, hundreds of men have been finding support and recreation, friendship and erotic adventure with jack-off buddies in groups....Many find affectionate attention and exuberant sport provide them a basis for firm, gentle bonding with other men through regular j-o meetings....Straight, bi, gay, and others interested are all welcome.") As is typical of a certain kind of California gathering these days, the CMG draws together a number of strains that aspire to counterculture, from serious social programs (particularly counseling for men who practice battery) to Esalen-style humanistic psychology, to elastic hippie superstition, to timeless mimeo leftism. There is a babel of jargons, and a sometimes harrowing concern for political correctness. To spend three days here is to feel as if a tiny, importunate Pacifica radio station has been implanted in your thymus. One morning, outside the camp dining hall, a man urges another to make known at the next day's plenary meeting his feeling that "In the Evening by the Moonlight" should not have been sung the night before because of its reference to "darkies." The man who was upset by the song says, "I hear you saying that I should put that feeling out at the meeting, and I thank you for saying that," but then a third man points out that "I've Been Workin' on the Railroad" is also objectionable because of all the people the railroad exploited and that he was made uncomfortable by "Clementine" as well because "the forty-niners, when they came to California, really murdered and mutilated. These things have to be *examined*." In general, the gatherers are most comfortable with the lyrics of Holly Near ("We are gentle, angry people/Singing, singing for our lives"), a latter-day radical songsperson who is like Pete Seeger without the glitter.

At the plenary meeting, a marathon Sunday planning session for next year's gathering that draws most of this year's turnout, voting is done by an exhaustive consensus. Alan Acacia begins the meeting by requesting that we "raise our voices"—another hand-holding circle, more humming and moaning—to "create a spirit of love and energy for the many issues to be discussed," but in the debates that follow much of the energy is nervous tension. As Tom Mosmiller, who cofounded the CMG and cochairs this plenary meeting, says later, "This will go down in history as the year the CMG met the Radical Faeries." It happens that this year's gathering immediately follows a week-long Radical Faerie encampment outside San Diego, and the impulse to party-hop has led to a larger than usual complement of Radical Faeries at this CMG, with all the snake-hissing, hippie-style belief in Magick, winged-phallus earrings, and sexual flamboyance that this entails. The men's movement generally, and the CMG in particular, sees itself as a unique place for gay and hetero men to hang out together, but the Faerie presence seems to be stretching that coalition in places. At Sunday morning's breakfast, an announcement that the family of a church-camp staff member was upset by a display of "overt sexuality" in the parking lot last night has set the stage for a sharp debate on a Radical Faerie proposal that next year's planners choose a site that will accommodate "men's considering privacy, nudity, and male sexuality important." ("Wait till you hear this one," a gatherer who does press-liaison work for the event tells me before the resolution is introduced. "It's about whether they can run around naked and f—— in the bushes.")

The more conventional CMG elements, particularly some members of this year's planning committee, bristle at the hiss-applause that greets Radical Faerie floor motions, and even a debate over a resolution favoring Newer Age food at next year's CMG becomes testy. A planning committee member takes exception to the pro-vegetarian position of a Faerie who argues that the gathering should have "food that's enlivening, as opposed to food that is endeadening." Another speaker asks that the proposal specify whole-wheat bread at the next gathering, because the white bread served this year has caused "feelings of hurt and isolation."

But it is the nudity/privacy/sexuality number that brings things to a head, with the proposal introduced by a speaker who says that he "cannot explore my maleness unless I can wear women's clothes, or wear a top and no bottom, or be sexually aroused when I want."

"I'm very concerned," says one of this year's planners. "I see the gathering becoming much more radical by virtue of its membership, I want middle-class men to be able to come here. What's our direction?"

"Clothing is a barrier," a supporter of the proposal says. "Clothing is a way we say, 'I have more money than you do, I have things that you don't.'"

"There are costs to freedom," argues another of this year's planners. "As I see it, the cost of this kind of freedom we're being asked for is that we'll lose the participation and comfort of men from the other end of the spectrum. The Radical Faerie gatherings have been described to me as providing a lot of freedom, and I don't understand why we're being asked to provide another Faerie gathering."

One of the few black men at the gathering says that there aren't enough third-world people here and that "these proposals might keep third-world people out. A lot of them are going to be put off by having vegetarian food, or by having open sex and nudity." He also notes that when he offered a workshop on minorities and racism in the men's movement only one person showed up.

Alan Acacia says he has "a personal need to acknowledge that the Radical Faeries are the most radical men in California" but that he is concerned about "losing those twelve million California men" from future gatherings.

Gordon Clay, the meeting's co-chair, says the proposal shouldn't be voted down on that basis because, with a "heavy gay presence" and men in dresses,

"we've already excluded those twelve million men. You've lost them already
....Now where do you draw the line?"

Both sides remain patient and conciliatory as the matter is talked to death,
though there are flare-ups: after one long round of snake-reclaiming applause,
a planning committee member says testily, "I move that we stop having this
hissing. I know it's supposed to be applause, but it sounds like hissing to me."
Somewhere in the third hour of the discussion, your correspondent slips out
to catch a plane. (A few weeks later, asked what finally became of the
nudity/sex proposal, Tom Mosmiller, despite having co-chaired the meeting,
cannot for the life of him remember.) Turning onto the highway, I notice that
the handmade road signs directing gatherers to the camp are still up on the
phone poles. CMG STRAIGHT AHEAD, reads the first yellow diamond. PREPARE TO
NURTURE, says the second.

THERE ARE, OF course, other kinds of men's movements, and A. Justin
Sterling's is about as other as they come. Sterling, a fast talker with some
good Werner Erhard moves, leads weekend-long "seminars" in California
and New York for men ("Men, Sex, and Power") and women ("Women, Sex,
and Power"). His qualifications are hard to pin down: a spokeswoman for the
Sterling Institute says, "Justin's credentials are the results he gets. We don't
like to give people a lot of information to intellectualize about." But Sterling
will tell you, with fetchingly arrogant certainty, that he knows precisely who
the new-model man should be.

Politically, Justin Sterling couldn't be farther from the CAMP and NOCM
men. But the success of his weekends (at $400 a head) suggests that he has
tapped into the same longing that the antisexist men's movement addresses—
the longing on the part of some men to be more comfortable with other men,
and to have simple answers about what men are supposed to be now.

Like other pricey weekends that promise the Truth, the Sterling seminars
encourage their graduates to bring fresh recruits to get-acquainted evenings.
At a public building in Berkeley on a Saturday night, hundreds of well-
dressed, bright-looking people gather and greet one another in a happy
atmosphere of reunions and introductions: it could be a singles mixer or a
sales convention, except for that special eye shellac you see on recent
converts to human-potential nostrums.

The evening is called to order by Dianne Hertzberg, a stylish woman with
a fixed smile who works for the institute. She calls a group of women who
recently took the "Women, Sex, and Power" seminar to the front of the room,
so "we can see what a group of women celebrating being women looks like."

The women at the front, giggly and a little dazed looking, pass around a
wireless mike, enthusing about their seminar experience in vague terms that

are familiar on this circuit—about how they didn't "get it" at first but then they *really got it,* and now everybody smiles at them all the time. "I didn't used to like *manly* men," one graduate says, pauses coyly, and adds, "Now I do!" When Hertzberg offers one of the graduates the chance to introduce Sterling, the chosen woman bursts into tears as she takes the microphone. "This is such an *honor,*" she sobs. "He brought me back to *life!* And I want you to know him...because to *know* him is to *love* him!"

Also Sprach Zarathustra blasts from the P.A. speakers at top volume as a portly little man in a brown suit enters the hall to a standing ovation. The women graduates surround him, hugging him. He gives his mike to a lesbian couple who beam at him, basking in his attention, as they tell the audience how the seminar gave them the power to make their relationship work.

"Now, all these women have been open with you," Sterling tells the crowd. "At this point, I'd like to do a little research by asking: How many people will say, 'Yes, I want to take the seminar'?" As soon as hands are raised, volunteers rush to drop registration cards into the respondents' laps. Then Sterling explains what's going on with men and women: "Twenty years ago, women said, 'Okay, the next step is to emasculate men. Take away everything masculine.' Men went along. They were taught to act and speak in a new way. But women like to change their minds. It's a woman's prerogative. And lo and behold, women changed their minds, and you know what they say now? 'We want our *men* back! It's no fun not having any *men* around!'

"The men's seminar gives men the thing that every man in this room is looking for: the man they've always wanted to be." A group of men's seminar graduates replace the women at the front of the room and stand arms over shoulders, beaming. Sterling asks one of the men how his work has been going since the seminar. "It's been *wonderful* for my work," the man says. "I counsel people for a living, and now, instead of a lot of theoretical bullshit, I simply know that men need to be men and women need to be women. A lot of people are trying to do it backwards and it just doesn't work."

Sterling opens the floor to questions. A young man who identifies himself as Mike asks, "What could I learn in your seminar that I wouldn't learn in Actualizations?"

"You will get the twentieth-century *initiation into manhood,*" says Sterling. The men at the front of the room approve with an apelike cheer: "HOO HOO HOO HOO HOO HOO HOO!"

"It used to be that men were initiated into manhood by other men," Sterling says, "but now you are the man some *woman* wanted you to be." He points to the apemen. "The reason they made that noise is that we went back thousands of years, to the time when men could be men with other men.

Men are nearer to the animal level. Women have more social consciousness, whereas men are more comfortable in caves." The men from the seminar, he says, "don't have to be men for women anymore. They'll be men for themselves, which is what women *really* want."

Mike asks if women and men shouldn't be in the seminars together, since the idea is to make man-woman relationships work. The seminar men hoot and jeer. "You see," Sterling tells Mike, "you, like so many other men, are scared shitless of being in a room with two hundred other men and no women. We say 'seminar,' but really that's not what it is—it's an initiation. But if we called it that, the press would go crazy and say I was a cult and whatever else the press likes to do with good things. It's not a seminar, it's a *crazy two days*. You want to enroll?"

"I don't think so," says Mike.

"What's the most important thing in your life?" Sterling asks him.

"Personal growth."

"No," says Sterling. "The most important thing in your life is *your balls*."

There's some embarrassed hemming and hawing from Mike—if this is a prepared routine, it's a beauty—and finally he says, "Well, if I lost my balls, I could still experience personal growth."

Sterling turns triumphantly away from Mike, pointing at him. "And *that* is where men have been for the last fifteen years!" he shouts. "Trying to experience personal growth without their balls! They'd go on doing it, except women changed their minds! Now men are saying, 'Whoops, where are my balls?' And—" he turns back to Mike—"there is *nothing* like getting your balls back! You won't *need* any personal growth! Be the man you always wanted to be!"

"I want to be the *person* I always wanted to be," says Mike.

"Bullshit!" yells the seminar graduate who counsels people for a living. "I can see through you, Mike," says Sterling. "You have no secrets from me. Just don't be *cunty!*" Huge ape applause. "What you're saying is, you're not ready."

"I'm ——"

"That's good. We don't want you enrolling if you're not ready. This is the kind of seminar," he says to hundreds of people into whose laps registration cards have lately dropped, "that nobody can sell to you. When you do the seminar, you discover that you can do anything you want. You can do the dishes! But you do them the way a *man* does the dishes. There's something *different* that happens to those dishes because a *man* does them."

Tom Mosmiller says that the existence of the Sterling seminars demonstrates the need for the antisexist men's movement. That may be. But watching the men at the front of the room, listening to their ape cheer and remembering the Radical Faeries' snake applause, I'm as struck by the similarities as by the differences: the ersatz tribal mumbo jumbo, the big deal made of men touching each other, the rush by all these people to make up in a hurry for connections they're sure they've missed. A few years ago, the Sterling Institute might have offered the "Give Yourself Permission to Be Rich" weekend or some such. But sexual identity is the hot, bollixing property of the moment, and the audience listening to Sterling is spellbound.

"For the past twenty years," he continues, "men have been apologizing for being men. Twenty years ago, women came out with *rules* for men: Don't be macho, don't be aggressive, don't be a bully—and this is how the *women* of the eighties are acting! The way they told men not to act! When you apologize for being a man, everything you do, everything you touch, *reeks* with that apology! Once you stop apologizing, you can be anything you want to be! You'll find out who your friends are! And as for your relationships with women, every woman is secretly looking for a man who first and foremost won't sell himself out! And every man *has* sold himself out...." Sterling adopts a sarcastic, namby-pamby tone: "The *gentle* man, the con*side*rate man, caring about *your* sexual needs, trying to find *your* G-Spot...."

He whirls to address a group of women in the audience, resuming his normal voice: "And those are the men you don't trust! Those are the men you have domesticated! The men you have turned into house pets! You know what a house pet is? *A PUSSY!!*" This zinger gets the loudest applause of the evening from all these well-dressed, bright-looking people. It's possible, of course, that in this crowd, they clap when they mean to hiss.

DAVID EHRENFELD

The Science of Edward Teller

E DWARD TELLER, ONE of California's best-known and perhaps most influential current residents, was born in Budapest in 1908, the son of successful, nonobservant Jewish parents. Showing an early talent for mathematics, he was trained in that subject and in chemical engineering, but eventually gravitated toward theoretical physics. In 1931 he became a part of the celebrated Gottingen group of physicists and mathematicians, which included such names as Heisenberg, Hilbert, Franck, Fermi, Bohr, Gamow and a youthful pair who roomed at the same villa, Paul Dirac and J. Robert Oppenheimer. Driven from Germany by the rise of Hitler and the Nazis, Teller made his way, with Rockefeller Foundation support, to Niels Bohr's institute in Copenhagen, where he shared lodgings and the love of poetry with a German aristocrat and talented atomic physicist, Carl Friedrich von Weizsacker. In 1935 Teller traveled to the United States and the first of a series of university appointments.

By the summer of 1939 there were only a dozen people in the world who appreciated the full significance of nuclear chain reactions. Among these, it had become plain that there would be no cooperation to suppress the development of nuclear weapons. Moreover, Heisenberg and von Weizsacker, two of the dozen, intended to remain in Germany, where they eventually headed (and perhaps deliberately led astray) Hitler's unsuccessful effort to develop the bomb. On August 2 Teller, with Leo Szilard—another of the twelve—drove out to the Long Island cottage that was occupied by Albert Einstein. According to Einstein's and Teller's recollections, Szilard handed Einstein the draft of a letter to President Roosevelt urging the need for a secret program of atomic research.

Much later Teller commented that "Einstein only signed his name. I believe that at that time he had no very clear idea of what we were doing in nuclear physics." Einstein agreed with this interpretation. After the war he said to his biographer, Antonina Vallentin: "I really only acted as a mailbox. They brought me a finished letter and I simply signed it." He also is said (by atomic historian Robert Jungk) to have remarked, "If I had known that the Germans would not succeed in constructing the atom bomb, I would never have lifted a finger."

For Teller, the August meeting with Einstein was his "first atomic assignment." That letter launched both the American atomic bomb project and the near half-century nuclear career of Edward Teller, "Father of the H-bomb." Neither history nor mythology offers us an example of a single human being who has been as successful in creating weapons of mass destruction.

As an active member of the Manhattan Project, from 1941, Teller found his way to the laboratory of Enrico Fermi at the University of Chicago, and then to the fission and fusion bomb study group led by Oppenheimer at Berkeley.

In 1943 he moved to Los Alamos, still as part of Oppenheimer's group, but he became increasingly dissatisfied with the direction the research was taking. Impressed with the enormously greater power of atomic fusion compared with fission, Teller pushed for the early development of the H-bomb. Oppenheimer and the majority disagreed. In 1951 Teller left Los Alamos, first for Chicago and then for the newly created Lawrence Laboratory at Livermore, which he had successfully lobbied for in Washington. In the next year the U.S. exploded Teller's H-bomb, causing a Pacific island a mile in diameter to disappear in a fraction of a second. About that explosion, Teller later wrote: "We would be unfaithful to the tradition of Western Civilization if we shied away from exploring what man can accomplish, if we fail to increase man's control over nature." The explosion of the H-bomb brought Teller to a pinnacle of influence and power in the Western World.

In 1954, at the height of the McCarthy era, Teller testified before the Atomic Energy Commission's security board that Oppenheimer, although loyal, was not to be trusted with the "vital interests of this country," because of his failure during the war and immediately afterward to pursue the development of fusion weapons. Unavailable at the time, for security reasons, was a sharply differing account of the controversy. As claimed by Hans Bethe, atomic pioneer, Nobel laureate and once Teller's supervisor at the Manhattan Project, Oppenheimer's decision to downplay fusion research after the war was based in large measure on some faulty calculations made by Teller himself. Not until the severity of these mistakes was appreciated did Teller and the mathematician Stanislaw Ulam discover, in 1951, a correct way to design an H-bomb.

After his denunciation of Oppenheimer, Teller was shunned by many of his former colleagues in physics and applied mathematics. Yet he maintained both his academic and weapons connections in California—at the University of California, Berkeley, and indirectly, at Davis, later at Stanford's Hoover Institution—and always, in one capacity or another, played a leading role at Lawrence Livermore National Laboratory. In the quarter century after the fall of Oppenheimer, Teller, although in partial eclipse, nevertheless guided Livermore into a preeminent position as the nation's designer of advanced nuclear weapons systems. And he became a public champion of many nuclear and militantly anticommunist causes—from nuclear arms buildup to atmospheric testing to civil defense to nuclear power and other "peaceful" uses of atomic energy to the Vietnam War. In 1962 Teller wrote: "We cannot be strong unless we are fully prepared to exploit the biggest modern power, nuclear explosives. Nuclear weapons can be used with moderation on all scales of serious conflict. . . . We should be prepared to survive an all-out nuclear attack."

LET ME NOW speak for myself. As a biologist reviewing this brief outline of the scientific career of an atomic physicist, I am struck not so much by what I find as by what is missing. It is as if Teller and I inhabit different universes with different fundamental laws. Or perhaps we see the same universe but with different organs of perception. Although we nominally live on the same planet, the attributes of our environment that matter to each of us are worlds apart. I can illustrate this better with an example—one tiny part of my scientific world that matters and speaks to me:

There are more than three hundred species of often brilliantly colored Euglossine bees in the American tropics; many of them are the sole pollinators of their own associated orchid species. Among certain orchids of the genus *Coryanthes,* male bees gathering scent from one part of the flower become intoxicated by the odor and fall into a bucket-shaped, water-filled lip of the flower positioned immediately beneath the scent glands. The only way out for the bee is up a ladderlike structure in a narrow passageway leading into the heart of the orchid flower. When it reaches the male column, a part of the flower shaped to fit the anatomy of this species of bee slips in between the thorax and abdomen and holds it fast. The bee struggles for fifteen to thirty minutes, pushing back a cap covering the sticky pollen sac, which becomes attached to a specific part of the bee's abdomen by a stalk. The bee frees itself. As it flies off, the rush of air dries the stalk, which contracts, reorienting the pollen sac so that it is positioned to be deposited directly on the female part of the next orchid flower that the bee visits.

In the vast panoply of life this is but the merest fraction of a speck; after all, there are between five and twenty-five million species on earth, each with its unique life history. But that fact in itself is the place to start the comparison of Teller's perception of the world with mine. His scientific world is one of general laws and elementary relationships, which when understood can be manipulated, as technology, for desired ends such as the manufacture of nuclear weapons. The scientific thrill comes with the discovery of the basic laws, and this thrill is reinforced by the power that rewards the successful technologist. I cannot be sure, but I imagine that, to a mind like Teller's, *specific* things and *specific* events are just so much clutter until they can be seen as part of a general pattern.

Of course, biologists also look for generality, especially if they want to be employed. General laws are important, yet to a real biologist much of the wonder is in the richness, the diversity of life. Thousands and thousands of kinds of plants are pollinated by insects—only *Coryanthes* uses that particular bucket-and-ladder mechanism. Diversity is a primary manifestation of biology, as precious and wonderful to those who study life as the laws of mass and energy are to those who study physics. To destroy such diversity, for any reason, is unthinkable.

Another example will take the comparison a little further.

At coral reefs in all tropical oceans, many divers have observed an extraordinary process taking place. Little fishes, usually wrasses, gobies or juveniles of other species, set up territories, either singly, in pairs or in small groups. These "cleaner fish" often have the same color pattern: blue and black longitudinal stripes. Before long, much larger fish assemble at the cleaning station, frequently ordering themselves in patient, mixed-species queues of as many as fifteen to twenty individuals. Assuming special postures and sometimes colors, the large fish at the head of the line are cleaned of parasites by the cleaner fish, which scrape them off and eat them. In the course of their work, the cleaners swim in and out of the mouths of the larger fish without harm. After being cleaned, a fish moves peacefully off and its place is taken by the next in line. Many of the clients of these stations are predators accustomed to eating wrasses and gobies when they find them in other situations.

It is natural for observers of other forms of life to find in nature things that seem applicable to human society. This is the so-called anthropocentric approach, and although it has its dangers it can be useful and even inspiring. True, each generation finds the things it wants to find in nature, but eventually a complete picture begins to emerge. Nineteenth-century biologists living in a society in which the working classes were brutalized by a newly emerging, raw industrialism found plenty of examples of subjugation, exploitation and brutalization in nature.

Although this ruthless view of nature still exists, many biologists are now sensitive to the other side of the story. As the reef fish tell us, enemies can cooperate to their mutual benefit even while they remain enemies. Nature abounds with such examples—the more diverse the natural community, the more positive relationships occur within and between species.

Unfortunately, complex living systems with their myriad positive and negative interactions are especially vulnerable to outside interference. The more complex, the more vulnerable, as seemingly small changes resonate destructively throughout the system. When people introduce technology to the natural world, unexpected and unwelcome things can happen.

Pueblo Bonito was a large communal dwelling built by native Americans in Chaco Canyon, New Mexico, in the year 919. A success from the start, it was greatly expanded and remodeled in the middle of the eleventh century, becoming a masterpiece of passive solar design. With an orientation such that the first ray of sunlight on the morning of the summer solstice struck exactly parallel to the front of the semicircular pueblo, it attained near-maximum theoretical efficiency of heat retention in winter and heat loss in summer. Less than one hundred years afterward, Pueblo Bonito was abandoned, for no obvious reason. It is speculated that the deforestation occurring when timber was taken from the canyon for the expansion of the pueblo caused soil erosion, increased runoff of rainwater, a slow draw down of the water table and ultimate failure of the Pueblo's agriculture and water supply.

Old Pueblo Bonito was an outstanding success: it offered its residents the chance for a stable and probably comfortable existence. But its success spoiled it. New Pueblo Bonito was technologically more sophisticated; however, it was out of scale with its natural environment. The late Rene Dubos, microbiologist, philosopher and environmentalist, observed that many natural systems are totally unsuited for receiving sudden inputs of large amounts of energy. This is especially true when the energy is in a form that the community has not previously experienced. All successful technologies consciously or unconsciously recognize this principle. Technological cleverness has to be accompanied by restraint or it destroys life, including the life that created it.

WHAT HAS BROUGHT Edward Teller back into the forefront of national weapons policy, even as a sick man in the twilight of his career, is Star Wars. Indisputably this is a Teller creation, nurtured for decades in the fastness of the Lawrence Laboratory and finally brought to fruition by the bright young men of the Department of Applied Science. Fellowship support for these bright young men has come from the little-known Hertz Foundation, whose official address is a post office box in Livermore, and one of whose directors is—Edward Teller.

They are the bright young men (scarcely any women) of O-Group, led by the bearlike, combative Lowell Wood, Teller's protégé and intellectual son, spewing futuristic weapons ideas like sparks from a welder's torch. And there is Peter Hagelstein, inventor of the nuclear X-ray laser—medical dream turned into weapons dream. Or Rod Hyde, MIT graduate at age ninteen, who came to Livermore to design a starship engine that might help him leave this limited planet. And others with other devices to invent: microwave weapons, particle beams, electromagnetic pulse weapons and the ones, perhaps most important of all, that we don't know about yet, all sharing the commonality of unimaginable power.

To Teller and his disciples, Star Wars offers the hope of a world free from the nuclear shadow. Opponents counter that if so, it will be the first time in human history that any technologically advanced defensive weapon has proved impregnable or has conferred a lasting advantage, and the first time that such a technological advance has not led quickly to a permanent increase in the destructiveness of war. Nor, they assert, is there any scientific reason to expect that Star Wars will prove an exception.

It was the X-ray laser, Teller's apparent favorite and O-Group's major announced success, that convinced President Reagan in March 1983 to accede to Teller's promptings and opt for Star Wars. But paradoxically, it is the same nuclear bomb-pumped X-ray laser that has alerted both the public and Washington to the fact that Teller's antinuclear defense is itself nuclear powered. Whether the delivery system is "pop-up" or orbital, X-ray lasers are likely to mean nuclear bombs going off above our atmosphere. Furthermore, X-ray lasers have offensive capabilities. And finally, nobody but the President seems to believe that devices such as X-ray lasers could stop all incoming missiles, let alone nuclear bombs, perhaps already of convenient carry-on size and capable of being smuggled into the country in suitcases. This awareness constitutes the biggest cloud (apart from its titanic cost) in the Star Wars firmament and the greatest challenge to Teller's vision.

There is no way of telling exactly what a nuclear war would do to life on earth; all the supercomputers in existence could not begin to keep track of the variables that might matter. However, the impact of so much concentrated energy on so many parts of the biosphere could not be other than catastrophic. Vietnam is still devastated by the ecological consequences of its limited, nonnuclear war, and ecologists estimate that extremely serious effects will persist on a time scale measured in hundreds of years, perhaps in millenia.

Here is one scenario of the effects of nuclear war on the living planet, prepared by physicists and biologists working together:

> Extreme cold, independent of season and widespread over the earth, would severely damage plants, particularly in mid-latitudes in the Northern Hemisphere and in the tropics. Particulates obscuring sunlight would severely curtail photosynthesis, essentially eliminating plant productivity. Extreme cold, unavailability of fresh water and near-darkness would severely stress most animals, with widespread mortality. Storm events of unprecedented intensity would devastate ecosystems, especially at margins of continents....Light reductions would essentially terminate phytoplankton productivity, eliminating the support base for many marine and freshwater animal species....Extreme temperatures and low light levels could preclude virtually any net productivity in crops anywhere on earth. Supplies of food in targeted areas would be destroyed, contaminated, remote or quickly depleted....Survivors of immediate effects...would include perhaps fifty to seventy percent of the earth's population....Societal support systems for food, energy transportation, medical care, communications and so on would cease to function.
>
> —Paul Ehrlich, et al
> "Long-Term Biological Consequences of
> Nuclear War," Science, December 1983

And what are we to make of the exceptional career of Edward Teller? Life scientists confront the immense and glorious complexity of life each day. Physicists, by contrast, deal with systems of stark simplicity. Moreover, in living systems irreversibility and uniqueness are ever-present conditions of existence. Entire classes of objects and even processes disappear, never to return again. This matters.

In physics such things are rare. The physicist observing a bubble chamber sees evidence of two elementary particles that collide. The particles disappear and are replaced by another kind of particle with a different mass and maybe energetic waves of certain lengths and frequencies. The old particles are gone, but it doesn't matter. If we wait a few minutes, weeks or months, we will see the identical process happening again. There is no cause for concern about the loss of the original two particles. Perhaps working with these sorts of physical systems is what keeps the Tellers of this world from coming to grips with the peculiar fragilities of life and the human meaning of destruction.

As a Jew, Teller is heir to a legacy of unnumbered persecutions; indeed in his own lifetime he has personally experienced the nightmare of the Holocaust and the iron claw of the Russian beast. For millenia his ancestors have suffered persecution and enjoyed fantasies of escape—even of revenge. But it is not recorded that any of them in their wildest dreams before now considered that it might be worth risking the world in the struggle against oppression.

The issue is not whether we are to abandon our miraculous cleverness, but how we are to allow ourselves to use it. As the farmer and poet Wendell Berry wrote, "The use of the world is finally a personal matter, and the world can be preserved in health only by the forbearance and care of a multitude of persons."

Ultimately, the biological and the theological perspective fuse into one, and we come to understand that certain acts of destructive creativity cannot be justified or excused for any human reasons. This is the message of the Catholic bishops to those who work on weapons of mass destruction, whether "offensive" or "defensive." The message is central to the other great faiths as well. And the reasons why it is true, as in the case of all-important truths, is very simple.

"Man remains a partner of God in the ongoing creative process," suggests Norman Lamm, a Talmudic scholar. "However, here we must distinguish between two Hebrew synonyms for creation: *beriah* and *yetzirah*. The former refers to *creatio ex nihilo* and hence can only be used of God. The latter describes creation out of some preexistent substance, and hence may be used both of God (after the initial act of genesis) and man. God has no 'partners' in the one-time act of *beriah* with which He called the universe into being, and the world is, in an ultimate sense, exclusively His. He does invite man to join Him as a co-creator, in the ongoing process of *yetzirah*. Hence, man receives from God the commission to 'subdue' nature by means of his *yetzirah*-functions; but because he is incapable of *beriah*, man remains responsible to the Creator for how he has disposed of the world."

v.
Necrology

KEITH ABBOTT

When Fame Puts Its Feathery Crowbar Under Your Rock

W HEN I REVIEW the eighteen years that I knew Richard Brautigan, one incident comes back to haunt me. It happened on a hot July 5 in Montana. I had spent my first day in Montana at the Fourth of July Livingston Rodeo with Peter and Becky Fonda. After breakfast the next morning, Richard said he had something to show me and he went into his cabin/bedroom off the main ranch house. When he came back to the kitchen, Richard put a .22 rifle, a beautiful old Remington pump action, on the table. "Isn't this a beauty?" he said. I picked up the rifle and admired it, and Richard said that he'd never had it sighted in.

"I'll do it," I said. "There's time before we drive into Livingston this afternoon. Where's a good place to shoot?"

Richard pointed out the window, indicating the old creek bank behind his barn. He said that the ranch garbage dump was out there and that I could shoot at old tin cans against the bank.

"This really sends me back to childhood," I told him. "I spent years shooting tin cans at a quarry."

Richard smiled; he had a way of acknowleding such emotions so gracefully—it was one of the pleasures of being around him. "Oh yeah, so did I. A .22 rifle, a box of shells and an old sandbank—that used to be heaven to me."

I asked him if he wanted to come along. Suddenly the smile was gone. Richard turned away from me. "No," he said. "I don't like to go shooting with anyone else. I had an accident when I was young. Maybe you can take my daughter out. No one has shown her how to handle a rifle. She should learn."

"Oh sure," I said. I was a little nonplussed by the quick change of mood. I added that if Ianthe came back, I'd be happy to instruct her.

Richard got a box of .22 ammunition from the cabin and put it on the table. I picked it up and walked out the back door and across the high grass of the back lawn and continued up the path past the barn. Back in the low ranch house I could see Richard watching me from the kitchen windows. There was a strange look on his face. I realized I had forgotten to ask where he would be. I should have told him to call me rather than come and get me. I didn't want any accidents.

After a while I stopped shooting. I thought about my own worries about someone coming around the barn and straying into the line of fire. Then I realized that it wasn't me, it was Richard; I had gotten some contact paranoia off him. Then I reran the look on his face as he stood on the porch. It was the pleased, guilty look of a boy who was about to risk something vicariously by sending a pal out to do something he wouldn't do himself. Then I explored that look a little further, and I knew that it was as if he were expecting me to have an accident.

That realization really spooked me. I took the rifle back to the house, cleaned it, and put it in the corner of the kitchen where Richard could see it when he came back in. I never shot the rifle again, and Richard never mentioned it again. But when he took it back out to his cabin that evening, he picked it up and glanced back at me with that same look—guilty complicity —and it made me extremely irritated. It was as if I were seeing something unhealthy in my friend, something so creepy and adolescent that I never should have seen it.

SAN FRANCISCO, 1966-1975

IN 1965 I HAD come from Seattle to live in Monterey. There I had made friends with Price Dunn, the model for Lee Mellon in Richard's first published novel, *A Confederate General from Big Sur*. From Price's stories about Richard I learned that we had much in common. Like Richard, I was born in Tacoma, Washington, and I felt an affinity for Richard's short stories about his Northwest working-class childhood and especially for his marvelous imagination.

Early in 1966 I moved to San Francisco, and when Price came up from Monterey he introduced me to Richard in his slum apartment on Geary Street. Without Price acting as a catalyst, it probably would have been difficult to make friends with Richard, as he was very shy and reserved. But once Price got Richard going with his stories, it was easy to join in. Despite being a loner, Richard had a great capacity to let other people into his life. His fiercest allegiance was to the imagination, and once he felt you shared that with him, his loyalty and friendship were total.

Richard was the most willful person I have ever met. As a young, almost completely unpublished writer, I was impressed that he was living on whatever money he made from his writing. He was determined to make it as a writer on his own terms. Coming from his background of poverty, neglect and practically no formal education, it was a miracle that he should have written anything at all. In 1966 he had three unpublished novels, no agent, no publisher—and yet he seemed supremely confident of his talent and work.

In those days, going around with Richard was like traveling inside one of his novels. With friends he talked just as he wrote. Outrageous metaphors and loony-tune takes were commonplace; one-liners, bizarre fantasies and lightning asides darted out of him one after another. He loved to improvise verbal games, but he would do them deadpan; he seldom cracked up. One of the few people who could get Richard laughing was Price, who had a runaway imagination and a life to match. We spent hours trading skewed dialogue from a Bogart movie or talking in weird rewrites of Beatles lyrics.

Richard's willfulness played a part in these routines, too. Although he was open to inspired changes, he liked to control the games. He often dictated what the shared reality was to be for the day. For example, one afternoon as we passed the hamburger joint ouside his apartment, he sniffed, "Ah—the smell of grease on the winter wind." Then, very solemnly, "Li Po, I believe." While we went about our errands for the rest of the day, we improvised fake Chinese poems randomly, always careful to end them with fictitious attributions and the pompous phrase, "I believe." Richard liked to say these routines "disappeared in their becoming." He believed in the magic and spirit of play and worked very hard to get that quality into his writing.

For Richard, writing was serious business, and his apartment showed this. His long, dark hallway was lined with posters for his readings, pasteups of the covers for his poetry pamphlets, mimeo poetry broadsides and fan letters. Each new publication was propped up in a place of honor in front of his aged mason jars and rusty mementos of his bleak Northwest childhood— almost as if they were offerings to the demons he had fled there.

When the Haight-Ashbury became nationally notorious in early 1967, Richard's work was appearing in free mimeo editions of five hundred copies. In the space of two years he was selling books in the hundreds of thousands and had his picture in *Life* magazine. His novel *Trout Fishing in America* brought him a huge audience. At a time when New York publishers were looking for the "*Catch-22* of the hippies," this small-press novel became one of the media symbols for the Haight, quickly running through several printings, then going on to sell thousands in trade paperbacks.

The strength of Brautigan's best writing came from the same source as his weakness in life: an awesome ability to ignore common sense and concentrate on the uncommon sense which his mind was constantly stewing up. If it is true that the brain contains layers of filters for experience, then Brautigan's lacked some, for he could see things in startlingly primal ways—his major connection to the psychedelic generation. When he wrote in *Trout Fishing in America* that a mother's nagging voice was "filled with sand and string," it made sense to kids who were listening to the Beatles' Eleanor Rigby keeping her face in a jar by the door or to Bob Dylan's song about a conductor who "smoked my eyelids and punched my cigarette." And, for people who were being busted down to point zero by LSD, Richard's use of simple and direct speech was a natural. The irony is that he himself never took psychedelic drugs, preferring wine or whiskey.

From the first, Brautigan's popularity had circumvented the established literary routines, and so his work was held up to a withering critical crossfire from, in Tom McGuane's words, "the pork and beans reviewers." The bottom line was that, in the beginning, Brautigan didn't need critics and that was enough to doom his good writing to mediocre reviews, with the exceptions of his fellow writers—such as Guy Davenport, John Barth, Tom McGuane and Don Carpenter—who were able to articulate the immense discipline, seriousness and skill with which Richard wrote. He never bowed to anyone else's opinions, although he himself could be quite candid about the qualities of his writing. Around 1970, when his poetry was being bought in editions of thousands and getting trashed in the few critical articles written on it, he was puzzled and a bit incredulous. After showing me one such review, he remarked, "I'm a minor poet. I don't pretend to be anything else." He always returned to his fiction, but by then his work had become an emblem of something far larger than his skill as a writer.

If pride sustained Richard through his lean years, once he was famous it only allowed him angry amusement and skyrocketing sales as defenses against parody and ridicule. When sales dropped, his amusement turned to just anger, and thence to bitterness and fear, and lastly to a kind of loathing which poisoned his spirit and partially eliminated his ability to respond to life and its small happinesses. When "fame puts its feathery crowbar under your rock," was how Richard ruefully phrased it.

In 1975 Richard finally moved out of his Geary Street digs and into a new apartment on Union Street. The move was fraught with the usual nuttiness— Richard ducking out for this and that reason—but it was enjoyable enough for me, and on the last day, I brought along my daughter Persephone, age seven. Children generally liked Richard, recognizing an ally in anarchy, but that day Persephone was grumpy. Richard, who was hung over, was quite solicitous. He immediately promised her ice cream goodies at Enrico's when we finished loading his stuff on my truck. Persephone would have nothing to do with him. She sat in the kitchen with a Coke Richard had bought her at the corner store.

The last things to go were stacked in the living room, and I carried them out, leaving it bare. Now, Richard had a habit of emptying his pockets of change on the floor. So, around the front room floor there were all kinds of coins. He once told me the story of how he had acquired the habit.

One spring he had been totally broke in San Francisco when a friend had called and promised him a job in Reno as a laborer on a construction project. Richard had borrowed enough money to get to Reno, but when he got there, he was told the job wouldn't start for three days. He had no money for a room. On his first night he had a series of comic encounters with a Reno cop who had a genius for finding him curled up somewhere. Threatened with jail, Richard hiked to the outskirts of town and found an old easy chair abandoned in the corner of someone's yard. For three nights he would wait until their lights went out and then he would sleep in the chair with his three sets of clothing on to ward off the cold. "The last thing I put on was a quilted jacket, and with all those other clothes on, I looked just like a Chinese communist," he said. "You can imagine what those Nevada folks would have done if they woke up early and found one of them in their backyard." His first day on the job, Richard drew an advance. After he got a motel room, he was so happy to have any money at all, he yanked out his pockets and sprayed change over the room. He had continued the practice ever since.

Anyway, on this moving day, Richard was facing reality from inside one of his mental whirlwinds, hung over and sour with worry. More to distract him than my daughter, I suggested that he give Persephone the job of sweeping the floor. At first Richard didn't understand what I was saying—he thought I was suggesting child labor or something—and then he recognized what was on his floor. He got a broom and dustpan and brought them to Persephone, who was staring at the gas range in terminal boredom.

"Persephone," he said, "would you like to sweep my floor?"

Persephone looked up at me with the universal *Do I have to, Dad?* question in her eyes and I nodded. She sighed and took the broom and dustpan from Richard.

"No, not the kitchen floor," Richard said, playing dungeon master and pointing. "The floor in there."

As she passed by me, Persephone gave me one of her sideways looks— *your weird friends*—and dragged the broom into the next room.

Richard was in an ecstasy of expectation as Persephone tiredly dropped the dustpan on the bookshelf and then looked down at the end of the broom for that first sweep. There was a wonderful moment as her eyes saw the money and then glazed over with childish greed. Richard could barely contain himself. In his glee he hopped to his back porch and came out with an empty mayonnaise jar and held it out to Persephone. She glanced up, jerked it out of his hand, put it on the bookshelf, and then the broom really began to fly, sweeping piles of quarters, dimes, nickels and pennies.

Whenever I remember Richard, I like to think back to that day, the look on his face as he stood in the doorway, his hangover banished, watching delightedly as Persephone swept his floor clean in a daze of joy. He knew that this would become a legend of her childhood. It was a good way to leave his Geary Street apartment and the 1960s.

MONTANA, 1976

Too many things were out of proportion in his life in
relationship to their real meaning. (Sombrero Fallout, *1976*)

WHEN BRAUTIGAN INVITED me up to his ranch in 1976, I had not seen him very much in the past year. He had been staying alternately in Japan and Montana. The acceptance of his work by the Japanese intelligentsia had culminated in his forthcoming novel, *Sombrero Fallout*, being published simultaneously in the United States and Japan. Richard was quite proud of the welcome he received in Japan. He showed me a Japanese edition of his short stories and told me that this was now being used as a textbook for teaching English. "Not bad, huh, pal, for a guy who took a couple of years to get through first grade?" he said. He found it delightful that his work should be taught in Japan when he had learned to read from the 1941 headline: JAPS BOMB PEARL HARBOR.

Richard had been in Tokyo all spring and had not been able to return to Montana in time to arrange for the ranch work to be done. He called me and asked if I could come up and help him get the place in shape. I told him I had not done any ranch work since I was nineteen. He was so desperate that he offered to pay my way plus wages to compensate me for canceling a job I had lined up in Berkeley. I considered it a paid vacation and took a flight up, planning to stay a month at the most.

The ranch turned out to be a large one-story house, a barn and an outbuilding which Richard had converted into his bedroom. He had built a writing room in the loft of his barn, facing east. It was clear that Richard was not exaggerating about the ranch. It was in bad shape. Although he had no livestock, the fences required mending, the fields needed cutting and the irrigation ditches had to be dug out.

Besides his helplessness at ranching, Richard had another handicap: he didn't drive. To get around he relied on neighbors or the Livingston taxi service. When I arrived, he had Peter Fonda rent a car for us on his charge card—Richard had no cards. He claimed that credit card companies routinely denied writers cards because of their bad credit histories and bad characters. The way Richard told it, the denial was like a badge he had been given for being judged dangerous to banking. So, instead of a peaceful house away from it all, Richard had put himself in a situation where he was at the mercy of others.

After the July 4 rodeo and partying were over, I set to work on the ranch. But almost immediately I realized that my real problem was not my rusty ranching skills; it was Richard: he was going through a serious crisis. I tried to set up a work routine. In the morning I got up early, around 5 A.M., made breakfast and then went out to the fields to mend fences before it got too hot. The late July afternoon temperatures were brutal in Montana, so I used that time for siestas. The first few days, Richard would come rocketing into the kitchen, compulsively talking up a storm even though he looked haggard and distracted—he'd clearly not slept. In the afternoons, when I wanted to nap, he wanted to drink wine and talk. The talks quickly became very one-sided, consisting mainly of Richard's byzantine grievances about running the ranch. For the remodeling, he had hired some people from Seattle, friends from the Haight-Ashbury days, and they had done a bad job. He was afraid to hire local people, wanting to preserve his privacy.

I was used to Richard's ineptness at scheduling his daily life, but I wasn't prepared for how he literally had lost all sense of proportion, both about his writing career and his social life. It was frightening to me. I had seen him loopy before, but not all the time. There were very few instances when he regained his old detachment that created his sense of humor. Except for some grim, rather macho kidding—of which the term "pal" was a new affectation for him—he seemed harried, manic and humorless. Instead of the little vignettes of daily life that he habitually told (and later would turn into writing), there were stories of hobnobbing with Hollywood stars. His store of anecdotes began to resemble *People* magazine filler—how Warren Oates put down X or the time Richard beat Jack Nicholson one-on-one in basketball for $50 (neglecting to mention that Nicholson was perhaps half a foot shorter than him). These little fillers all had power-tripping as their subject.

Since Richard was incapable of planning anything as complex as the food for two days running, let alone anticipating his other needs, he kept calling me in from the fields to make trips into Livingston, sometimes three times a day, until I told him that I couldn't do both jobs—ranch hand and driver. So he hired a housekeeper, a friend of the Fondas who was staying in Livingston. At night his behavior became so erratic that the housekeeper and I arranged to take turns staying up with him and trying to talk him down from his often paranoid rants, while also trying to restrain his alcohol consumption.

One night he told me that he couldn't go to sleep because he was afraid of his dreams. I don't think I've ever heard a fellow writer confess a more disheartening thing to me. To me, dreams are essential to any imaginative process. Richard added that he had a prescription for Stelazine, which he said knocked him out for two or three dreamless hours.

I was very disturbed by this admission. I had never known Richard to take any drugs other than caffeine and alcohol. At the time I judged his alcohol intake to be up to three liters of wine at dinner, often ending with whiskey past midnight, so I told him to stop taking the drug because he'd kill himself. I also said that I didn't think Stelazine was supposed to be used as a sleeping pill; it was a long-term anxiety medication with a huge list of side effects. He didn't seem to take my warnings very seriously, but by then I noticed that Richard didn't seem to be taking advice from anyone, including Tom McGuane and William Hjortsberg, two of his closest friends in Montana.

I decided to limit the amount of alcohol bought on our shopping trips, cutting the wine in half by buying fifths rather than the half gallons of Almaden that he liked, and "forgetting" to pick up brandy or whiskey. I noticed that most of the time Richard wouldn't drink alone, so I also took car trips during the afternoon and thereby aborted any early starts on the evening's drinking. Less booze combined with a fly-fishing trip seemed to calm him down for a few days.

About this time the jacket copy and bound page proofs for his novel *Sombrero Fallout* arrived. Apparently Brautigan had final say over the jacket copy, and he enlisted my help in rewriting it. I spent a couple of evenings listening to Richard as he obsessively wrote and rewrote the description of the novel. What he was trying to find was a way of talking about his work that avoided the 1960s hippie buzzwords. Richard called the project the "dewhimsicalizing" of his literary reputation.

This notion serves both as a measure of his determination and of his naiveté. Dust jackets don't convince reviewers, and they are certainly ignored by critics. In Richard's mind he was the only one who could effect this change in the critical climate; he was scornful of the copy Simon and Schuster had sent him. It was a heroically misguided notion. The novel seemed an unlikely candidate to rescue Brautigan's critical reputation; it was thin, unreal in an unpleasant way, without engaging characters. With its strained attempts at humor, I judged it unlikely to be a popular book with his fans either. I found one detail fascinating, though: in *Sombrero Fallout* the hero, "a humorist," tears up a false start on a story and the pieces of paper go on to have a life of their own, enter reality and start a war. I took this as an artistic recognition by Richard that his work was out of his control.

As we worked on the jacket copy, Brautigan talked about what he was tryng to do with his latest novels by combining genres in their subtitles. He called *The Hawkline Monster* a "Gothic Western," *Willard and His Bowling Trophies* a "Perverse Mystery," and *Sombrero Fallout* a "Japanese Novel." It became clear that Richard, with his belief in names—that giving something a label made it that thing—was trying to influence his critics. Another of his gambits was shortening the time span of his stories. *Willard* had occurred in twenty-four hours, *Fallout* in an hour, and he predicted his next novel would take place in the space of a minute. He was also consciously writing about serious concerns: violence, irrational hate, grief, and loss of innocence via the modern sexual diseases. He was trying to do all this with his usual writing skills: irony, startling metaphors and juxtaposition of images. Unfortunately, these genres and themes demanded either psychological characterization or bold dramatic action, neither of which he could use effectively, given his style.

Brautigan could not face the fact that he was losing his popular audience. From his comments I began to suspect that his stay in Japan had done the worst possible thing—restored his inflated image of his importance as a writer without giving him new material or insights. A friend who accompanied him to Tokyo said that Brautigan had an audience of top Japanese authors, intellectuals and avant-garde artists; in America he had nothing comparable.

Taking advantage of Richard's preoccupation with his book, I conjured up an excuse to leave early and arranged for a flight out. Needing someone to oversee the irrigation-ditch digging I had set up, Richard called our old friend Price in California and asked him to fly up and take my place. Afterwards I felt bad that I didn't warn Price about Richard's unstable state of mind. Since they were the oldest of friends, and since Richard always had an immense respect for Price, I thought that perhaps his benevolent presence would help Richard find some peace. As it turned out, a week later the friendship of over twenty years ended in a scene straight out of a B-grade gothic horror show.

At the Bozeman Airport I left the car keys at the rental desk for Price, who was flying in that night from San Francisco, along with one of Richard's girlfriends. I felt very happy to get out. A couple of weeks later, I received a series of grim late-night calls from Richard. Price had betrayed him. They could never be friends again. He told me an incoherent story about Price "abandoning" Richard at the ranch and destroying the rental car. Richard claimed that this act had "almost wrecked" his friendship with Peter Fonda. It wasn't clear what was going on, only that Richard was obviously in one of his manic drinking phases again, making late-night calls to all his friends and detailing his grievances in the monotone voice he used for such tales.

With some cross-referencing to other friends whom Brautigan had called, and finally a call to Price himself in Monterey, I found out what had happened. Richard's girlfriend had caught a ride into Livingston on Friday to do some shopping. Richard had asked Price to go in and pick her up around six that night. Price found her at a local bar being entertained by several local cowboys. Price tried to convince her to leave, but she was drunk and her admirers did not want her to leave. Price was not foolish enough to try to argue with a bunch of cowboys on their Friday night out, so he bided his time. Another woman in town who fancied Price shanghaied him away for a while. When he returned, Richard's girlfriend had drunk herself out of enough admirers that Price could separate her from the remaining hopefuls and sober her up with coffee for the drive back.

At the ranch Richard was waiting in a jealous rage. He had taken all of Price's clothes out of his room and thrown them on the front lawn. Price and the girl retreated to a neighbor's house and slept there that night. In the morning Price changed his clothes, put the old ones in the trunk of the rental and absentmindedly left the car keys in his pants pocket. After Richard refused to talk to him, he decided that he had had enough craziness. But the keys were in the trunk now, the car locked, so Price took a cold chisel and knocked a hole in the trunk. Then he drove to the airport, turned in the rental car and flew back to California. The rental car people billed Fonda for a new trunk. Fonda called Richard in his own rage over the large bill, which Richard paid.

The most revealing thing about the episode was that Richard never admitted to his jealousy. In his arrogance he simply could not tolerate the *idea* that Price could have stolen his girlfriend, nor that she might have found life in town more interesting than Chez Brautigan.

When I got back, I noticed that Richard had written—under his signature on the proof copy of *Sombrero Fallout* he had given me in thanks for my work on the dust-jacket copy—"Montana Faust." It was an act of such Olympian delusion and hubris that it astounded me. When I told Price of it, he said simply, "Richard's gone insane."

CALIFORNIA, 1977-1982

FROM 1977 UNTIL 1982 I saw Richard infrequently, but I knew him to have two periods of calm during that time, when he seemed like the person I used to know. The first was some months after my stay in Montana. Richard had gone to Tokyo and had returned with a broken nose. When he described how this happened, he quite frankly said that he was bad-mouthing someone (he used the phrase "running them down viciously"). A man sitting next to him, whom he didn't know, had turned around and flattened him, breaking his nose. This rude and deserved punishment seemed to bring Richard back into the real world for a time. He actually inquired about my life, seemed interested in my replies, and acted as if he cared.

His marriage in 1977 to a Japanese woman, Akiko, also seemed to help him at first. Most of the personal, though often solipsistic stories in *The Tokyo-Montana Express* were written while she was with him. Once the marriage soured, Richard became more and more alcoholic and depressed. His isolation increased, as did his late-night phone calls, all recounting over and over as if his memory were gone, the details of his impending divorce. Fueled by calvados, they were unbearable conversations.

During this time Richard told me that "I guess the only thing I can do is write. If that's so, then that's all I'll do." He seemed to be saying that he was going to forego any other contacts with people, and I think that he did just that and it killed his spirit. Writing alone cannot sustain a man, but in his willfulness, Richard thought it could.

My last face-to-face contact with Richard occurred after *The Tokyo-Montana Express* was published. He was determined to hustle the book and make back the money he felt he was going to lose on his divorce settlement. When he got back to reading at various colleges, he was dismayed by how badly his audience had shrunk. He found that he was no longer even known by young readers. "They don't read," was what he said, but what he meant was that they no longer read him.

When I read his last published book, *So the Wind Won't Blow It All Away*, I found a possible explanation for the incident with the .22 in Montana. In a strangely disjointed narrative, the book's teenage protagonist relates how he accidentally shot and killed a friend with whom he was out plinking. Had this adolescent trauma—whether real or imagined no one seems to know— haunted him all his life? I took it as another sign that he was in the worst shape of his life when, for the first time I could recall, there were clumsy, badly written sentences in his fiction.

Whenever Richard called, it was as if he were drunkenly playing a tape of the last conversation we had, constantly referring to his status in Japan and lack of it here. His anger, his bitter self-imposed isolation, were magnified by his now-unrelenting arrogance. Compulsively in need of friends, he was just as compulsive now about abusing them. From his German translator, Günter Ohnemus, I received a report that during his European trip in 1983 he had become uncontrollably alcoholic, had skipped or trashed readings, had lost his agent, and was now claiming that a computer in a Tokyo hotel was going to handle all his writing business. Günter also said that through botched business deals Ricard had also lost a considerable amount of money. Even though his death by drink or misadventure seemed inevitable to me, I didn't think he would kill himself. At the wake, when asked if he had expected it, his first publisher, Don Allen, said, "I wasn't surprised."

For my part, all I can say is that no man had more need for friends, or less use for them.

PAGE STEGNER

A Poisoned Pen

E ARLY IN HIS CAREER, John Steinbeck wrote to a friend that in spite of his state of abject poverty and the difficulty he was having inspiring publisher interest in his work, "the pen feels good to my hand. Comfortable and comforting. What an extension of self is this pen." The measure of that extension is the foundation of Jackson Benson's formidable biography retracing the steps of one of America's most admired, most read, least critically respected authors from his birth in Salinas, California, in 1902 to his death in New York City in 1968—entitled "true adventures," one presumes, because much that is known about Steinbeck's private life is the product of myth, rumor, the sour grapes of critical wrath, and the author's own habit of inventing and embellishing the facts of his personal history. Reclusive and shy as a young man, he spent a great deal of his time in the privacy of dreams and fantasies, and, like many endowed with an active imagination, was not always able to maintain a distinction between the story he lived and those he made up. "No writer is ever willing—even if able—to portray himself as seen by others or as he really is," Edward Abbey once remarked. "Writers are shameless liars."

At its simplest level (if thirteen years of research can be so categorized) Benson's biography straightens out the truth from the fiction and gives us a detailed chronology. There are the adolescent years in Salinas and Pacific Grove, the influence of various Stanford professors on an otherwise recalcitrant Steinbeck, who refused to accommodate himself to institutional proscriptions and failed to graduate, the struggle to become a published writer, and the accompanying fear that success might alter the pleasures of simple living (not to mention the joys found in the act of writing itself). And there is the overwhelming realization of that fear with the popular reception of *Tortilla Flat, Of Mice and Men, In Dubious Battle,* and *The Grapes of Wrath.* Steinbeck was transformed by the popularity of his major works from unpolished rustic, his favorite pose, to international celebrity. He suddenly acquired both a circle of ideological enemies, who accused him of everything from Communist-Zionist plots to sexual perversion, and a circle of classy new friends, including Charlie Chaplin, Spencer Tracy, Burgess Meredith, and Darryl Zanuck, whose lives were somewhat more stylish and fast paced than those of his previous associates. The very circumstances he most wanted to avoid began to materialize. He became, as Benson puts it, "a prisoner of his notoriety." And while he "hated the disadvantages of fame," he was nevertheless seduced in large measure by its benefits.

In consequence (at least in part), his first marriage, to Carol Henning, collapsed. His second marriage, to Gwyndolyn Conger, a singer and aspiring actress he had met in Hollywood, endured a rocky tenure of five years before she left him, claiming, among other absurdities, that one of their two sons was not his. Gwyn's defection was a bitter pill to swallow. According to Benson, Steinbeck had idolized her—had played Lancelot to her Guinevere— and her rancorous departure meant not only the end of a relationship but also the death of a romanticism he had embraced, in one way or another, all his life. "The sadness of Steinbeck's plight was that he had brought a literary-inspired passion to his writing, and it drove him to success, but when he brought it to his life, it nearly destroyed him. There was further irony in the circumstance that one of the major themes of his writing had been the destructiveness of myth when it is used as a pattern for living."

More than half of Benson's 1,038-page work is devoted to the post-*Grapes of Wrath* period—an extended tour for the New York *Herald Tribune* as a war correspondent, first in North Africa and later with the Fifth Army's invasion of Italy, his collaboration with Ed Ricketts on *The Sea of Cortez,* his love affair with Zachery Scott's wife, Elaine, whom he ultimately married and with whom he lived out the rest of his life, his travels with and without Charley, and throughout it all his endless search for new material. Benson devotes considerable discussion to the gradual severance of Steinbeck's ties with California and the psychological rejection of his "roots" engendered by the furious reaction to the publication of *The Grapes of Wrath* in 1939—a reaction, he wrote to his agent, Elizabeth Otis, that truly frightened him. "It is completely out of hand—I mean a kind of hysteria about the book is growing that is not healthy." And to his friend Carlton Sheffield he remarked that at least the Associated Farmers (meaning California agribusiness) couldn't shoot him "because it would be too obvious and because I have placed certain informations in the hands of J. Edgar Hoover in case I take a nose dive." Small wonder he began to find California repugnant. While he returned to his family's cottage in Pacific Grove several times after fleeing to New York in 1941, he grew increasingly disenchanted with the place—and the place as subject in his fiction. Today, of course, he is regarded in Salinas, his hometown, as a saint. Today, of course, he is also dead.

In 1962, Steinbeck was awarded the Nobel Prize for literature. In a curious parallel to the reaction following the publication of *The Grapes of Wrath*, success again spawned vilification, and he was pilloried by the arbiters of literary taste, most of whom seemed to live east of the Hudson River. The sneering scorn of Arthur Mizener of *The New York Times* set the tone, but

Mizener was probably taking his cues from earlier monuments of intellectual snobbery written by Edmund Wilson and Alfred Kazin. "Crude and limited people do certainly feel some emotion in connection with work that is limited and crude," Wilson had written, and had gone on to use Steinbeck's novels as examples of the kind of work that does not speak to the emotions of "the more highly organized man"—meaning, he explained, "people who can distinguish Grade A and who prefer it to the other grades."

Mizener, in his turn, questioned the judgment of the Swedish academy in awarding the world's most distinguished literary prize to someone whose "limited talent is, in his best books, watered down by tenth-rate philosophizing." As these remarks appeared in America's leading newspaper, their effect, Benson points out, was "to take away the Nobel Prize before it was even given." It hurt, as California's rejection had hurt, and it most certainly contributed to the frequent mood of ill-tempered cynicism and self-pity that characterized most of Steinbeck's remaining years. In the last note he ever wrote, to Elizabeth Otis, he remarked, "I have owed you this letter for a very long time—but my fingers have avoided the pencil as though it was an old and poisoned tool"—a long, circuitous route from that comfortable and comforting pen.

A great many literary critics and teachers of college literature courses have never been very fond of books, it seems to me, and the more a writer is loved by his audience the less he is liked by his reviewers. Jackson Benson's biography is perhaps too long, and at times anecdotes seem to be included primarily because they have been collected, but the great strength of his labor is that he obviously cares deeply for both the written works and the man who wrote them. Steinbeck's personal flaws are acknowledged and commented on, but Benson doesn't feel the need to demonstrate himself morally and intellectually superior to his subject. In setting down his facts, and in the presentation of his opinions concerning Steinbeck's works and life, he draws a portrait that is both penetrating and compassionate—one that succeeds, as any good biography must, in bringing a complicated existence into focus and restoring it with life.

NEIL MORGAN

The Long Goodbye

R AYMOND CHANDLER IS number 1577 in San Diego's Mount Hope
Cemetery, a graveyard on the wrong side of town, where the city
buries its indigents. If you give the graves' keeper Chandler's name and the
date of his death, he will direct you to a slope where there are few flowers
and only the most modest of markers. The mystery writer seems as lonely
and out of place in death as he was in life. It is the kind of hard joke that
would make Philip Marlowe, Chandler's not quite brittle detective, reach for
his bottle.

When I reread Chandler's novels, the cityscapes of Southern California
through which I move each day seem thick with ghosts. The lifetime that
Chandler gave Marlowe extended from the stark 1930s into the era of Elvis
Presley, and Marlowe risked his lonely life in these streets as he railed against
corruption. Along this restless edge of Southern California that seems an
aeon ago, but the settings of Chandler's five big Marlowe novels are still
here—shoved back away from the route of the parade, sunbaked and
fading, but here. They are not along the eight-lane freeways or in the flossy,
gimmicky shopping centers, but on the gritty back streets of Hollywood and
Santa Monica and Manhattan Beach, in Pasadena and down the coast where
I live, and Chandler lived, in La Jolla. If you do not care to seek out this
California for yourself, you may find it all there, forever and unyielding, in
the pages of *The Big Sleep* (1939), *Farewell, My Lovely* (1940), *The High
Window* (1942), *The Lady in the Lake* (1943), and *The Long Goodbye*
(1953).

Although Chandler died in 1959, Philip Marlowe remains very alive
indeed. He has been discovered by oncoming generations and is more
widely celebrated in Anerica now than he was during most of Chandler's
lifetime. Marlowe is a man of excruciating bluntness, in open revolt against
injustice and hypocrisy. He has a kind of heathen idealism that now seems
surprising for the times in which he moved. Yet the reason he lives on is not
that he is a rebel but that Chandler wrote him brilliantly, in corking stories.

Marlowe seems to have evolved from a character named Mallory in the
stories Chandler wrote for the revered pulp magazine *Black Mask* in the
1930s. Both author and character were scarred in the Depression. "Marlowe
and I do not despise the upper classes because they take baths and have
money," Chandler wrote, "we despise them because they are phony."

Marlowe appears to remain about thirty-eight, slightly over six feet tall, with brown hair and eyes. He does not look tough, but he does not back off. He is unmarried but carnal. Chandler called Marlowe "a simple alcoholic vulgarian who never sleeps with his clients while on duty." Later he amended that in an essay called "The Simple Art of Murder": "I think he might seduce a duchess and I am quite sure he would not spoil a virgin; if he is a man of honor in one thing, he is that in all things." Marlowe was once an insurance investigator and later lost a job as a district attorney's investigator because, as Chandler speculated one evening, "I think he was a little too efficient at a time and in a place where efficiency was the last thing desired by the person in charge." He has a barren sixth-floor office with a reception cubicle and a two-drawer file that holds a bottle of whiskey. He sometimes carries a Smith & Wesson .38 with a four-inch barrel, longer than that carried by most lawmen and harder to hide, but surer.

"Marlowe is a failure and knows it," Chandler once said. "But a lot of very good men have been failures because their particular talents did not suit their time and place." It was difficult, when Chandler talked like that, to know whether he was thinking of Marlowe or himself. He even seemed, in later years, about to try to become Philip Marlowe. Maybe he finally killed himself trying. He was too intricate for the role—a complex, moody man who wanted to write lyric poetry but settled for icy-hard prose. Chandler envied Marlowe for his self-containment, for his casual appeal to women. Marlowe was not simply Chandler's alter ego, as critics insist, but his Walter Mitty. Of course, Chandler would have sneered at all of us for such speculations. He said Marlowe was being written about too much by quasi-intellectuals, by critics he called "primping second-guessers"—so much that they were making it hard for Marlowe to spit or talk out of the corner of his mouth.

What seems to drive Marlowe is his pride. "You will treat him as a proud man or be very sorry you ever saw him," Chandler said. Marlowe reflects Chandler's sense of chivalry and sentiment but has a hard-boiled mien that Chandler only practiced, and never convincingly. "There are times," Chandler said, "when Marlowe wishes he were not a private detective, just as there are times when I would rather be almost anything than a writer."

Chandler had at first awed me, a cub reporter when I met him, but for thirteen years until his death we were kind to each other. He was a man about five foot ten who managed to look slight. He had a shock of unruly hair to run his hand through when his typewriter stalled. His mouth was a thin tight line. All the humor was in the eyes behind the thick glasses. The eyes were his giveaway. They telegraphed mischief or anger or tenderness or hurt, and they kept busy.

Before his death, Chandler wrote to me that he did not know how much longer he could last. At the tag end of his creative years, a time of self-doubt and self-abuse, his only good writing went into private letters crowded with loneliness and bravado. Chandler left Marlowe to the world. To me he left his pipes, their bits chewed through where he clenched them as he typed, and his big red Universal English Dictionary, which he pored over lovingly until near the end. He left me, too, those intimate letters, which marked him beyond any talk that ever passed between us as a tormented human being.

CHANDLER HAD BEEN reared by his Irish-born mother in the Midwest. When Chandler's alcoholic father deserted them, she took her son to England. At Dulwich College he was an unspectacular student, but he worked at his Latin and Greek and began to write poetry. He stunned his mother later by resigning a civil service job in the Admiralty and taking work as a journalist. At twenty-three he returned with her to America and worked odd jobs in California. In World War I he enlisted in Canada and served with the Gordon Highlanders in France. Back with his mother in Los Angeles, he held a series of junior positions in oil companies. The Depression ended this and nudged him into writing, first for the pulps. His stories in *Black Mask* led him into detective novels and a short, troubled career as a screenwriter. Chafing at the restraints of film writing ("I imagine everyone ought to meet Samuel Goldwyn this side of paradise," he said, typically. "I've heard he feels so good when he stops."), he retreated from Hollywood in 1946 to a house on Camino de la Costa in La Jolla. It was the kind of house in the kind of village to which a man might go when he had tried to be a public person and knew he had failed. I found him there in 1946 when I was a twenty-two-year-old newspaper reporter.

Chandler's house seemed out of place along this street of private beaches and pretentious rich. It was on a rise overlooking one of the cliffs where swimmers and divers find public access: a white stucco bungalow with brick steps up from the sidewalk, a shaded courtyard with potted geraniums, fuchsias in hanging baskets, and purplish bougainvillea creeping along the eaves. It was a caricature of Chandler's Southern California. Inside, his study was lined with books more often found in the studies of professors of English literature. His desk and typewriter were littered. Pipes were abandoned with their ashes beside his reading chair, and ashtrays teetered on stacks of open books. The long living room, dominated by a Steinway concert grand, led to a picture window looking over the sparkling surf line that hooks and twists around Point Loma.

Chandler was gracious that first afternoon. He was, after all, at the crest. His first four big novels had been written. He was full of future work, but only one major book would lie ahead—*The Long Goodbye*, which most critics found softer than the first four.

That day Chandler hastened to describe La Jolla as a boring, gilded suburb "entirely too proper...a town of arthritic billionaires and barren old women." His overriding impulse, he went on, was to stand naked at high noon on the main business street and shout four letter words. When I had gotten all that down, he poured us a couple of drinks and sat back looking pleased with himself. It was his warning shot to the community that he might better be left alone, and he was.

His wife, Cissy, lived with him there for eight years before her death, but I saw her only once. She was fragile and wan, dying slowly and hard from fibrosis of the lungs, and on the night I met her she sat at the Steinway and played Chopin waltzes. The scene is heavy with lavender and magnolia in my memory. Chandler hovered over her and later took her away and helped her to bed. To her death Chandler idealized Cissy as young and beautiful, as the "light of my life, my whole ambition." He wrote that "anything else I did was just the fire for her to warm her hands at." In the final months he cooked Cissy's meals and served them to her inside her oxygen tent, convinced that no one else could take proper care of her.

She died eight weeks before their thirty-first anniversary. Chandler was brusque. He stored her ashes at a San Diego mausoleum, and then he went home to La Jolla to look at the ocean and drink. He drank through their anniversary and for two weeks more. He had done this before, but not this big. He had married Cissy just fifteen days after the death of his mother, whom he had protected until her death. Now, for the first time, no one was dependent on him. "All that is really the matter with me is that I have no home," he would later write, "and no one to care for in a home, if I had one."

The police were nearby one afternoon when two shots broke the quiet of the sea cliff. The police, who admired Chandler and had already helped him through three suicide threats, decided to lock him away in the county psycho ward. Their report read that he was sitting on the floor of his shower, trying to get his revolver into his mouth. When one officer asked Chandler for the gun, he laughed his hard cackle that came when he cared about someone or something and wanted it known that he did not care at all, and he handed it over. There were two holes in the shower ceiling. Neither bullet had been through Chandler.

It was simple to explain later that his act was theatrical, a classic cry for help. In *The Long Goodbye*, published just a year earlier, is this passage: "Then he opened his eyes and that weary smile played on his lips. 'Nobody hurt,' he muttered. 'Just a wild shot into the ceiling.'"

But Chandler's pain was real. I first learned of his pantomime through a small item in the next morning's *San Diego Union*. On a hunch that there had been no one else to do it, I stopped by the county hospital on my way to work. The superintendent waved me into his office, and I explained that I knew Chandler. He flipped through the night's admission sheets and whistled. He knew who Chandler was; he read. He got up and unlocked the white iron door and nodded to me to follow. It was an old hospital then, without any forced cheerfulness. It smelled of puke, and the eyes behind the heavy wire mesh were like those of caged animals.

Chandler stood among them like a wet puppy that had been bad. He had written of such places, but his pale face showed his shock at waking up in one.

"You want to get out of here?" I asked. "I'd like that very much indeed," he said. The English public school accent stayed with Chandler throughout his American years, but it was not there that morning. He looked like a man about to cry again.

The superintendent nodded, this time with hope. "How do you feel now?" he asked.

"I feel like a bath," Chandler said, "and some decent coffee."

"I can't release you now unless you go to a private sanitorium under a doctor's care," he said.

"Why?" Chandler asked.

"The law. You were brought here as a suicide attempt."

Chandler managed a smile. "If you'll let me go I won't do that again."

I signed him out and drove him to a private sanitorium. It was just a trace more pleasant than the county hospital and cost a lot more. Chandler would have had considerable money except for his wife's long illness. As it was, he had enough. But this was not where he intended to spend it. He also knew the law. Six days later he released himself and called me to take him home. He was buoyant. Two pretty nurses slipped their arms through his and walked him to the car.

"If I am sufficiently sane to charm these ladies," he said, "I am weller than I have been in years."

So I drove him home, much like the reporter Lonnie Morgan, who drove Marlowe home one night in *The Long Goodbye*. Chandler said he remembered nothing and would never know whether he had meant to kill himself. He said he was sorry to trouble a friend. We didn't talk much. It was the kind of moment between people that is too revealing to risk small talk and too unsettling to permit much more. When we reached Camino de la Costa he asked me in for a drink. I felt not at all like drinking, but Chandler did, and the house was empty. We went in. He fixed drinks first and called a real estate agent second, to say he would sell the house to the first buyer.

AFTER CISSY DIED and Chandler had no excuse for remaining at home, I invited him to a small dinner. He discussed the invitation for days before agreeing to come. "I am doing this as a favor to a friend," he said finally, "and I have no idea how I shall behave." When he arrived he was tidy in tweeds and sober. Throughout the evening he wore a bemused smile. He talked of English manners and social sense, the banalities of Hollywood, and the joys of proper language. He derided Marquand for his blandness. For Hemingway he reserved soft sarcasm. He lingered until the other guests had left and then presented himself like one of his beloved cats preening against its owner's leg. "Was I properly charming?" he asked. "I can do that quite well, you know, if there is any incentive."

Yet he was sometimes an irascible companion, even sober. One rainy afternoon after he had given up the house on Camino de la Costa, I sat with him in his apartment over Windansea Beach while he read aloud poems that Atlantic had just rejected. He bristled with self-fury. I was a newspaperman with no ear for poetry, and here was Chandler, the most stylish writer of his genre, writing verse that seemed to me maudlin and mawkish. We were a pitiful pair. I was trying to do a television script for a mystery series and was in need of counsel. He listened patiently to my story line and concluded that there was no future for me in the field. Nor for him. "I love words," he said. "I live for syntax. I was a lousy film writer because language doesn't count. I would never be a good television writer for the same reason."

We discussed a common bond. Friends inevitably get around to asking newspapermen when they are going to write something "really good"—the usual way of putting it—as opposed to fragile journalism. Now Chandler pulled out a letter to him from a reader, one that gnawed at him. "You write so well," he read aloud. "When are you going to write something without murders in it?" He had recently been in London, where he had talked about a play he wanted to write. But he had not settled down to it. His excuse was that his tax man had pointed out that he would be taxed on both sides of the Atlantic for its profits.

That afternoon Chandler suggested that I take with me his copy of a gruesome little volume, Gustav Schenk's *The Book of Poisons*. It had something to do with helping me find a way past a roadblock in my television script. I did not manage to return it before his death. Later I realized that Chandler had penciled only one passage in the book, about a form of alcoholic insanity that the author called "delusional jealousy." Perhaps he had marked this passage because he had seen himself in it. The affairs that Chandler had with younger women in those final years were macabre and recriminatory. It is a measure of Chandler's writing talent that

Marlowe moves so blithely among attractive women, for his own relationships with women never matured.

Alone much of the time, Chandler began drifting between England and
America in search of attachments. He was back into long sieges of drinking.
He talked much of remarriage and proposed to several women. He either
changed his mind or was rejected. Women found him alternately charming
and boorish; his need to possess them seemed to them overwhelming and
disturbing. If they sought more conventional male company, he fell into
sullen depression and took cover in alcohol.

Once from his bed at New York Hospital, where he had been dried out,
Chandler wrote: "What was the matter with me—and has been for a long
time—was a total mental, physical, and emotional exhaustion masked by my
drinking enough whiskey to keep me on my feet, and then a severe malnutri-
tion. The causes for all this are complicated; some of them you know, some
you don't. It has never been difficult for me to stop drinking, but what have
you got left?...Don't give me up. I need friends."

CHANDLER LOVED THE English countryside and the flowering of Spring; novel
by novel, the serenity of the Southern California landscape weighs more
heavily on author and reader. Yet he retained the regional California setting
he had long used so masterfully for his seventh novel, *Playback*, and for his
last, fragmentary novel, *The Poodle Springs Story*. This was Palm Springs in
disguise—because Chandler fancied that every local walked one or more
poodles by leash—and a pale caricature of Chandler at his prime. Marlowe
had become, for the first time, an overtly sexual creature, and had even,
incredibly, gotten himself married. Chandler complained to me in a letter
from England of the rootlessness of life in Southern California. Banished
from the hallowed confines of the Connaught Hotel for senile womanizing,
he sought to play Marlowe among the admiring London literary set and
boasted in letters of his conquests, real or imagined. He longed to recapture
domestic stability and gave it instead to Marlowe.

For two years or so before his death, Chandler was close to the Australian-
born widow known then as Jean Fracasse. They spent a great deal of time
together; Chandler referred to her as his secretary. In May 1958 he made her
his sole heir, though by now he was overspending his income on travel, gifts,
and alcohol. On one of my last evenings in his home I watched in awe as a
delivery man brought in a case of fifths of Rose's lime; Chandler used a few
drops of it with vodka in each of his gimlets.

Chandler's English literary agent, Guinness heiress Helga Mary Greene,
sought to order his affairs. She had been among the objects of his anguished
adoration. In February 1959, through a handwritten codicil, she became

Chandler's sole heir. (Jean Fracasse would contest the codicil, and later withdraw her suit. It was found that Chandler had suggested to other women that he would make each of them his sole heir. His estate was valued at $60,000—Helga Greene still serves as his executrix.) She agreed to marry him, but at a dinner in New York City, when Chandler chivalrously sought her father's sanction, the gesture turned to disaster. Her father, H.S.H. Guinness, of the beer and banking family, was chilled by the idea—the two men were close in age.

During that same New York visit, on March 4, 1959, Chandler, leaning on a cane, attended a coctail party given by the Mystery Writers of America after his election as its president. Helga Greene was at his side, and they had tickets to London, where she had leased a honeymoon flat. He spoke graciously to the assembled writers, returned to his hotel, and got a pleading phone call from Jean Fracasse to return to her and California. Deciding that he was too ill to go on to England, he canceled the reservations. Helga Greene flew on to London. Chandler flew back to La Jolla. He was drinking heavily again despite an attack of hepatitis, something that doctors had told him could be fatal.

His physician moved him from his apartment to Scripps Memorial Hospital in La Jolla, and Chandler died, alone, at 3:50 P.M. on March 26, 1959. The cause of death listed was bronchial pneumonia. He was seventy years old. I read about it in the papers. This time there was nothing I could do.

The specter of Chandler's loneliness followed him to his grave. Seventeen people attended the service at Mount Hope Cemetery. At the newspaper I helped with the obituary but could think of no reason to go to graveside. Helga Greene was represented only by her accountant; because it was a bank holiday in London, she later explained, she was unable to send flowers. No one heeded Chandler's request for cremation and for his ashes to be placed next to those of his wife in a San Diego mausoleum.

Marlowe would have gone back to his bleak office, taken the bottle out of the file drawer, and poured a couple of stiff ones.

VI.
Hometowns

TRACY JOHNSTON

Confronting the Sea Gods
of the Northern Coast

I'VE LIVED IN California almost all my life, never more than an hour away from the beach, and I think this fact has something to do with my religion. I was two years old when my parents moved to Los Angeles from New York. It was just after the war, and there were no houses for rent, even in the suburbs, so they found a duplex on the tiny island of Balboa near Newport Beach. I dimly remember the sunlight and the noises and the sand castles of those early days, but one of my clearest memories is of the afternoon my mother, a good swimmer, encouraged me to dog-paddle behind her out beyond the boat dock of our beach and into the channel. The water was dark and shimmered in places with oil slicks from passing boats. Far below me was another realm, teeming with strange and scary creatures—stingrays, jellyfish, eels, and forests of seaweed.

"Isn't it nice," my mother said by way of comfort, "that we can stay right on top?" I gasped for breath and flailed my scrawny arms and legs even harder, but I loved her for taking me out there to commune with the mysterious and thrilling forces of the sea.

In time, I was humbled some by the sea gods—a few rough waves let me know who was master. But my love for the sea and the sun, for the simple forces of nature on the Southern California coast, remained firm. One summer during adolescence I drove to the beach every day with a boyfriend who had bet a friend that he could tan his palms.

It was only when I discovered the Northern California coast that the mysteries began reappearing. The waves are large, the water freezing, and the cliffs steep and rugged. At low tide rocks covered with sea urchins and kelp rise out of the water like ancient gods—shoulders hunched, hair streaming. One confronts the Northern California coast mostly alone and without bias or motive. One merely witnesses; one merely wonders.

Several years ago my husband and I lived in the only town on the Point Reyes peninsula, just north of San Francisco, a beautiful place of rolling grassland, cow pastures, damp forests, and almost continuous wind and fog. Its north side, which faces the wind and waves swooping down from Alaska, is, I think, the wildest beach on the entire coast.

We were both writing at the time, so at about four o'clock we could break for walks, the most memorable of which brought us to the ocean. At Northbeach the surf crashed in rows of three and five deep, the wind creating plumes at the crest of the waves, and incoming tides were so dramatic that we constantly ran like children from the swift tongues of particularly big waves. It was like having a monster in our backyard, my husband said. I remembered the story of the Norse king who taught his subjects once and for all that he was not God. He took them to the ocean and stood at the edge of the surf. "I command the waves to stop coming in," he said, holding his hand in front of him, palm out. We liked to confront that God, my husband and I, after a day of arid mental gyrations. In a strange way the monster was comforting.

The monster is also fascinating. The lighthouse at Point Reyes is, from December to April, one of the best places to watch whales migrating along the coast, and the tide pools on Tomales Point are full of bizarre and curious surprises: sun stars, tube worms, and nudibranchs living peacefully and undisturbed in the pools are revealed at minus tides. Further south you can go night diving off the Channel Islands and watch scallops dance on the bottom of the ocean floor, opening and closing their fluted shells in odd, bouncy rhythms.

In California, as my mother showed me so long ago, a commune with the sea gods is never far away. Some day soon I mean to go with my husband to the Marin headlands at sunset and walk down to one of the little coves west of the Golden Gate Bridge. We will stand there on the beach, looking at the lights of the city, bracing ourselves against the wind, hugging each other and feeling our warm bodies beneath our jackets in the sweet, seaweed-scented air. It will be a little like standing inside the cathedral in Notre Dame.

STEVE ONEY

Adventures in Paradise

THERE ARE MANY WAYS to understand Newport Beach, California's gilded realm of the new rich. But central to any fathoming of this sea-kissed retreat from the rabble and the rebels is a basic truth that Eloise Popeil, wife of Ronco corporation magnate Samuel Popeil, failed to comprehend, and that is why she went to jail.

Samuel Popeil, as any viewer of late-night television can attest, is the man who gave the world the Popeil Pocket Fisherman and the Veg-O-Matic. For these contributions, he earned a fortune believed to be in the vicinity of $200 million, and he chose to move from his native Chicago to Newport, where he took his place among other self-made tycoons. Newport Beach has long been a favorite stomping ground for product mavens such as Elmer Hehr, the mobile-home aluminum window sash king, Dr. Robert Beauchamp, founder of Dr. Beauchamp Credit Dentists, and Alan Rypinski, the man who made Armor All protectant the force it is today in the landau vinyl-roof preservation field. Thus, Popeil must have felt at home when he moved onto Linda Isle, one of the city's eleven "gated communities"—and one of its swankest. But neither his new neighorhood's guard kiosk nor its elaborate amenities could keep misfortune at bay. Popeil's marriage deteriorated, and in 1973 he returned to Chicago and filed for divorce, leaving Mrs. Popeil at sea in a world whose tribal rites demand grand gestures and extravagant expenditures.

Mrs. Popeil soon was reduced to seeking employment at a dog-grooming shop in order to pay for the upkeep of her cars—a Rolls, a Mercedes, and a Jaguar—and the Harbor Road pied-a-terre she had taken with a lover while the Popeils' Linda Isle home was being remodeled. In the end, wildly mounting bills drove Mrs. Popeil to formulate a desperate plan: she would hire a killer. To gain control of her inheritance, she was willing to pay $400 in cash and some $50,000 in diamonds for her husband's execution.

Whether the chosen assassin intended to slice, dice, or chop Samuel Popeil will never be known. He telephoned Popeil and informed him of the plot, dreaming that the Veg-O-Matic baron would up the ante in order to call the whole thing off. Instead, Popeil called the police.

Nine months after her arrest, on the day Eloise Popeil was convicted and sent to prison, Los Angeles Superior Court Judge Mark Brandler pronounced the would-be murderess "vicious, cunning, and depraved." But such a judgment, moral in nature, did not address what in the last analysis was a failure of perception on Mrs. Popeil's part. She should never have trusted her freelance killer; she should have known that in Newport, paradise for grand acquisitors, everyone eventually catches the entrepreneurial spirit.

NEWPORT BEACH, fifty miles south of Los Angeles, is an oasis for the self-made. It is unlike other cities in that it is not, to any significant degree, economically stratified. Although there is a thin layer of old salts and random factotums here, there are primarily the prosperous, the rich, and the ridiculously rich. (The filthy rich, save for a Roosevelt and a Guggenheim, are still back east in Newport, Rhode Island.) It is Newport Beach, not Beverly Hills, that supports America's biggest Rolls-Royce dealership, along with the richest pleasure-craft harbor in the west, one of the most successful yacht brokerages in the country, and a haute couture boutique whose clients jet into the John Wayne Airport (one of the busiest small-craft airports in the nation, of course) from other kingdoms of Croesus. On graduation night at Newport's Harbor High, where thirty members of the class of 1983 drove BMWs to school, there was a screening of *The Great Gatsby.*

Of Newport's 62,556 residents, fewer than fifty receive welfare payments. (The average annual income in the city is more than $42,000.) There are 144 blacks living in Newport—one of them is Reggie Jackson. When the city's largest landholder, the Irvine Company, offered to help the municipality deal with a fair-housing suit by developing "affordable housing units" (that meant homes priced between $85,000 and $126,000 and targeted for people earning between $28,000 and $34,000 a year), a Newport resident rose up at a public hearing to proclaim, "Do we really want this kind of element here? People already get upset when they can't join our yacht clubs. At that level of income, we are talking about nonskilled labor, and they can't afford to pick up a credit card at Neiman-Marcus."

This remark should not be construed to suggest that Newporters are uncharitable. Charity balls and cocktail parties highlight the social season. The South Coast Repertory Theater, the Newport Harbor Art Museum, and the Hoag Memorial Hospital—all symbols of the city's apotheosis—are frequent beneficiaries. Newporters do look after their own. And that's the point.

At a recent dinner party hosted by an ex-city council member for a number of the town's movers and shakers, the conversation came around to the joys of living in Newport. The table talk was animated, but it was the president of one of the city's biggest real estate agencies who spoke with the voice of the people. This was just, for in Newport, realtors play nearly religious roles. They deliver their clients to terrestrial glory. "What is wrong with hedonism?" the broker asked. "What is wrong with clear-skinned people raising their children and living athletically? What responsibility do these people have to those who live elsewhere?"

In essence, Newport is America's radiant shore for the conspicuously acquisitive. It has long been so, yet now more than ever before, Newport is approaching its zenith. This summer ground was broken for a major regional cultural center. The Four Seasons Hotel chain, North America's most exclusive, will soon establish an outpost in Newport. In 1982, the Ritz, an elegant new restaurant whose chef cut his teeth at L.A.'s Scandia, opened to happy throngs. Other tony troughs are imminent.

What we have here, then, is California's newest and haughtiest gathering place for the rich, a town that now joins—some might say, eclipses—the state's other monied dominions. Newport is where it's happening, and if you can maintain an appreciation for the days when America was a great country —where you could drive around in a big, black fuel guzzler, throwing beer bottles out the back and listening to Sinatra—it is a fun place to spend some time. Of course, you have to walk with the dinosaurs. This is where Bob Haldeman and John Erlichman waited out the Watergate summer with folks who still don't think Richard Nixon had a thing to apologize for. But if you accept this world, you can have a helluva party.

ONE BRILLIANT JULY afternoon, Duffy Duffield is puttering across Newport Harbor at the helm of a nautical conveyance officially named the Newport Electric Packet but popularly known as either "the cocktail boat" or "the booze cruiser." Duffy invented it. In 1970, his father, Marshall (a retired car dealer and liquor distributor who vaulted to prominence in 1930 as the all-American quarterback of USC's Rose Bowl team), gave Duffy $300 and challenged him to take a golf cart's electric motor, stick it in a boat, and make it work. Some four hundred cocktail boats later, Duffy is the Henry Ford of Newport's waterways, and at $16,000 apiece, his craft—with their perky canopies and teakwood cockpits—are yet another highly visible index of wealth, Newport-style. "You can't do anything in this boat except get out the wine and cheese," Duffy says proudly. "You sit in this boat, turn on the stereo, and you see that it's a totally new thing to do....CEOs and company presidents, they need a thing like this."

This afternoon Duffy's mission isn't as relaxing as those for which the boat was designed. He is touring the harbor to leaflet his customers with maintenance advice. Duffy put out from his dad's slip at the Balboa Bay Club, Newport's principal playground for parvenus. The club includes Holiday Inn-inspired apartment units surrounded by a barbwire-topped wall, a tidy beach, and an embarrassment of yachts. Here, Richard Nixon often sailed with friends during the dark ages that followed his 1962 gubernatorial defeat, ex-*Playboy* centerfold models disco with stout entrepreneurs, and younger men never have any trouble meeting older women at the bar.

It is midafternoon, and the harbor waters dazzle. Floating in the main channel, Duffy's boat commands a 360-degree view of Newport Beach. To the east, on the hills that ring the city like a corona, looms Newport's most ostentatious new neighborhood, Harbor Ridge. On the development's half-acre lots stand brand-spanking-new imitations of every grandiose style of manse known to humankind. A French château is jammed next to the estate of a Spanish grandee, which is squeezed against a Tudor country house next to a Venetian villa that overlooks Tara II. From Harbor Ridge's 500-foot summit, as one architect is fond of telling prospective buyers, "You can see Beverly Hills on a clear night." To the north, south, and east of the harbor is the land of mirrored cubes: South Coast Plaza, Newport Center, Koll Center, and the Fluor Corporation complex. There, in noiseless office parks, developers work their magic.

All around Duffy, bathed by the gently pulsing waters of the harbor, are the islands on which Newport began: Balboa, where the streets are named for jewels; Lido, where the byways are "Via" this and "Via" that and the sidewalks are "strada"; Bay, where there are no streets, no cars, and it takes a majority vote of the property owners before a newcomer can buy land and begin navigating around by golf cart; Harbor, a secluded keep bespeaking the Hamptons; and Linda, where Donald Bren, the man who owns eighty-six percent of the $1 billion Irvine Company, is remodeling a house next door to the place where the Popeils once lived.

And everywhere there are yachts: the *Nordic Star,* owned by electric-motor magnate George Flager; *Mercedes,* the noble barge of Southern California's largest Mercedes-Benz dealer, Jim Slemons; *Well Stacked,* which belongs to Disney World subcontractor Chadwell O'Connor. Many of these craft, which cost as much as $100,000 a year just to maintain, leave their berths only once or twice a season, and then only to promenade around the harbor while liveried waiters serve Long Island ice tea to poobahs on holiday.

Duffy is the perfect guide to Newport Beach. A blond thirty-one year old who sports rumpled shirts and corduroys and salt-eaten topsiders, he grew up on the harbor, where he sailed his tiny skiff during the years when Newport was little more than a summer-vacation and fishing village. He is unsettled by what the town has become and has an eagle eye when it comes to spotting gold chains, "LOLs" (ladies of leisure), and other signs of pretention on the beaches and porches that front the harbor. Yet, as he will confess somewhat abashedly, Duffy is now feathering his own nest by selling cocktail boats to those who have earned Newport the sobriquet "Nouveau Beach."

Floating past Bayshores, the site of the old John Wayne estate, Duffy offers wistfully, "It used to be that nobody paid any attention to status down here. It was no big deal. I remember the first time I met John Wayne. He was just a guy out in the middle of the road over there, doing Sigma Chi bear hugs and handshakes with my dad. Now his house is owned by the Bettingens"—Burtie and William. Mrs. Bettingen recently inherited a large share of the $3.7 billion Shell Oil paid for her family's petroleum empire. The newfound fortune in hand, Burtie and William moved to Newport—Beach, that is, swimming pools, movie stars. They paid $5 million for the Wayne place, but that was just the beginning. One day not long ago, Bettingen sat Duffy down and wheeled out his plans for remodeling the manor. "He told me he's gonna sell his $1 million house in Malibu, take that money and put it into the place. These people amaze me."

Across the harbor from Wayne's house is a low-slung Mayan manse known as the Ahmanson House. Built in 1938 by Lloyd Wright (son of Frank Lloyd Wright) for violinist Jascha Heifetz, the residence is best known for a later occupant, Howard Ahmanson, founder of Home Savings of America, the nation's second largest S&L. Now the property is on the market again at more than $10 million. Last year it was rented by a Saudi Arabian prince. Duffy didn't approve. "I was over there one day doing what I'm doing today, servicing my boats, and the next thing I knew, Arabs in black scarves had me pushed up against a wall." Duffy's tone is more amazed than disgusted, suggesting that he feels a bit like a young Rip van Winkle. In an instant, the town where he used to have Huck Finn adventures and build castles on his own little sandbar (Duffy's Spit) had been transformed into a torrid zone for arrivés.

"This all happened overnight," he says as he steers to the south. "I mean, one day you've got houses here on the water selling for $60,000, and the next day the same little boxes are going for $1 million. Everything good is $2.5....It's Monopoly money, and everything is negotiable....These old rich guys trade in their wives for young gals. It's a game."

Duffy ties up at a slip holding a cocktail boat similar to his own. He stuffs a flier beneath its canvas covering and, backing away, says, "See, here's a dude that just got him a new wife. Check out what she named the boat." Across the boat's stern, bold lettering spells out *Current Occupant*.

Presently Duffy docks again at the Newport Harbor Yacht Club, the city's oldest and most exclusive boating society, to get a hamburger at the snack bar. Unlike Newport's other clubs, where one simply buys in, this institution demands that new members either be born in or sail in. Under the club's orange, white, and blue burgee, Bill Ficker won the Americas Cup at the helm of the *Intrepid* in 1970. Duffy sails for the club in the annual Trans-Pac from Los Angeles to Honolulu. He sees the place as a refuge for those who belong to the original Waspy clan that colonized Newport back in the 1930s. On this day, white-haired ladies in straw hats sit on the spacious porch taking lunch while recent USC graduates in khaki pants and rep ties congregate at the bar beneath nautical paintings. On the little prayer rug of a beach that extends into the harbor, thirtyish, Catalina-suit-clad brunettes watch over their young flocks. "Megabucks, those women," Duffy says. "All those kids and no sags."

Soon Duffy is back in his boat, passing out fliers, taking the lay of the land. Though he has sold his company, Duffy is still the number one salesman for his brainchild. "I keep up with the divorces," he says. "A lot of divorces here, and if he ends up with the boat, she goes out and gets another one. God, I'm a leech."

After a while, Duffy passes beneath the Pacific Coast Highway bridge and into the back bay, a quiet expanse of water whose shores are undeveloped and whose tranquility is disturbed only by airplanes taking off from nearby John Wayne. Two speedboats purr by. Golden sun gods and bikinied sun goddesses command each vessel. "Hey, Duff," a voice yells out.

Duffy raises his hand in a wave. It's the Marino brothers and their dates. "Jim Marino, those kids' old man, owns a big car dealership," Duffy says. "They had to rent a warehouse from my dad just to store their gadgets, and they filled it up. Snowmobiles, Vespas, drum sets, classic cars, amplifiers—you name it, they've got it. There are a half dozen or so guys just like them here in Newport, and they run together. They all bought matching mopeds the other week. One of them is John Wayne's son, Ethan. He's twenty-one, and he just bought a helicopter."

The Marino brothers disappear from sight, and Duffy is alone again. Looking up at a far-off chalky cliff, he sees something move. It is big, black and white, feathered. He sails closer to it, then closer, then finally close enough to distinguish the mass of feathers as a huge owl nesting in a small crevice. Duffy shakes his head. When he was a kid, such sights were not uncommon. Now he sees the Marinos.

"I'm not against growth," Duffy insists as he sails back into the main harbor and past the Reuben E. Lee, an eatery fashioned to look like a Mississippi riverboat. "It's just that I'd like to see some control. But the Irvine Company always gets what it wants."

For a place whose residents religiously embrace the topsy-turviness of the free enterprise system, Newport is a paradox. Over the years, its growth and its look have been controlled by the nearly feudal policies of the Irvine Company, which owns one-third of the city. From where Duffy sits on the water, he can look to the east and see nothing but Irvine-owned land, which includes most of the lots now occupied by "homeowners"—who, in actuality, only hold ninety-nine-year-long leases from the company.

In 1960 the Irvine Company commissioned Los Angeles architect William Pereira to create a plan for the city's future. Pereira, best known for designing San Francisco's Transamerica Pyramid, is largely responsible for the way Newport Beach looks today. Though there have been alterations in his plan, the company has followed the basic outline.

Pereira envisioned a mall and office park that would serve as a nucleus for a city. Newport Center, including Fashion Island (which in fact is not an island but an inland shopping atoll), represents that dream. The architect also saw distinct new neighborhoods clustered around this commercial rotary.

What Pereira may not have foreseen, however, is that these neighborhoods would be marketed not as communities but as concepts, and those concepts had as much to do with what the city became as anything else. They demographically determined the kind of people who would move to Newport.

As if it were a flashy new product, the city's rapid growth was propelled by buzzwords. Harbor Ridge was for "movers up." Big Canyon was to be "the home of the presidents." Other neighborhoods were sold to "empty nesters," while still others were designed for "never nesters," who, in the words of one Irvine official, "want to sit around a conversation pit, eating French bread and spaghetti and drinking wine." Newport's new communities would offer theme-park living to the wealthy. Although there has been some cross-nesting, the company's dream has largely been realized.

As Duffy sails back to the Balboa Bay Club to tie up his boat, he plies the waters of a place that in twenty years has grown from a sleepy town of only 27,000 into a city nearly three times that size. "You know," he says as he approaches his slip, "the Pacific flyway for ducks used to come right over here, but as far as I can tell, the ducks have now moved ten miles inland. That tells me a lot."

THE DUCKS MAY have left, but for the humans who have rolled the dice, migrated to Newport, collected their property, and built houses, life is a giddy merry-go-round. Every August, during the Annual Character Boat Parade, half of Newport floats around the harbor in boats fashioned to look like anything from Cutty Sark bottles to pirate ships. In December, at the Christmas Parade of Lights, Newporters again take to the water, this time in yachts ablaze with sparkling ornaments. But these festivities pale alongside the grand affair hosted every June by Paul Salata, a wealthy sewerage contractor, who invites the last of the last-round NFL draft choices and a date to town for a five-day celebration called Irrelevant Week. The 1983 honoree was John Tuggle, a UC Berkeley fullback drafted almost as an afterthought by the New York Giants. Tuggle was met at the John Wayne Airport by a marching band, which escorted him into town. The next day there was a golf tournament in his honor, featuring the four worst golfers from Newport's four major clubs. The man who played most poorly won. There was a banquet featuring Gary Tyrrell, a Stanford University Marching Band trombonist who was knocked down during the controversial touchdown play in the closing seconds of the 1982 Stanford-Berkeley game. Throughout the week, Tuggle—a thick-necked, toothy sort—smiled and said hi to Newport mayor Evelyn Hart, the Los Angeles Rams cheerleaders, Republican congressman Bob Badham, and just about everyone else in town.

For the grand finale, there was a yacht race around Newport Harbor with no beginning or end—because it was irrelevant.

At times the merriment seems endless. Who could forget the First (and only) Annual Chickenshit Party? In the beginning, it seemed like a joke to the scores of Newport residents who received this message in the mail: "You're being considered as an invited to the First Annual Chickenshit Party in Newport Beach." Soon more letters, postmarked from all over the country, began arriving, bearing the news: "Congratulations, you have been invited to the First Annual Chickenshit Party." A couple of weeks passed, and there was another mailing—plain envelopes containing chicken feathers. Finally, engraved invitations appeared, bearing an address and a date. On the now long-awaited night, guests arrived at the home of a wealthy Newport plumbing supplies distributor to find a big chicken coop out front with numbers spread on its floor. A dozen or so chickens paraded around the coop, and those revelers who were lucky enough to bet on numbers baptized by pullet poop took home door prizes. Said one woman who attended the party, "See what we do with our discretionary income. It's a sense of play."

Keeping abreast of such playful doings can be an all-consuming affair. The pages of the modestly named local magazine, *Gentry,* bubble with party news. In this swirl of social effervescence, two names pop up everywhere: Pat and Alan Rypinski. At a recent Olympic athletes' benefit auction, they won the privilege of being picked up in a squad car, booked, fingerprinted, taken to jail, and served a candlelight dinner by the police chief. They attend concours d'elegance, the custom-car collector's equivalent of gallery openings. They are indefatigable—they never stop having fun. As Pat will offer within minutes of a first meeting, "We've had a real American dream story. ...It sounds too good to be true, but it just is."

Though Alan and Pat Rypinski are new rich, they are old Newport. Pat grew up in Corona del Mar, Newport's southernmost section, and Alan, who was raised in Pasadena, began visiting Newport when he was a boy because his parents kept their boat there. Pat and Alan married twenty-two years ago, but until the early 1970s they were just another upper-middle-class couple. Alan, who was in sales, seemed destined merely to do well in life. He nevertheless kept his eyes open, for in Newport there is no telling what might happen.

One day in 1971, Alan walked into the Briggs Cunningham Automotive Museum, a nearby classic-car boutique. He was concerned about the condition of his Jaguar. The rubber molding was cracking apart. One of Cunningham's aides brought Rypinski a bottle of some white, milky stuff called Tri-Don. It turned the damaged molding back into the prettiest rubber you'd ever want to see. Experimenting with the goop, Rypinski found that it also worked miracles on leather interiors, vinyl roofs, and whitewall tires. He'd stumbled on a Lydia Pinkham elixir for automobiles.

Rypinksi didn't hesitate. He immediately bought worldwide marketing rights to the potion, set up an office in a room over his garage, capitalized his corporation with $1,000, and went to work. The next thing he did was to name his miracle liquid ArmorAll. The rest is history.

In 1978, Alan sold the company to Foremost-McKesson for several million dollars. Understandably, Rypinski is loath to mention an exact figure, but, as he says, "We're not worried about where our next fur coat is coming from."

The fates have indeed been kind to the Rypinskis. *ArmorAll II*, their red, white, and blue fifty-foot yacht, is docked behind their Linda Isle home, and they maintain a mooring for the boat on Catalina Island. They own vacation retreats in Hawaii, Lake Arrowhead, and Rancho Santa Fe. Alan owns a fleet of some sixty cars, including an Aston Martin, a new Ferrari, a Mercedes-Benz limousine that once belonged to the president of Romania, and a green 1950 Chevrolet pickup. Just this summer he bought a Rolls-Royce from Otis Chandler, chairman of the board of the *Los Angeles Times*. Everything is looking up for the Rypinskis. Earlier this year, the stocky, mustachioed Alan had Welter "Budd" Holden, a Los Angeles interior decorator, over to the Linda Isle house. "Budd, I don't love my house," Rypinski said. "I want you to make me love it." Holden went right to work on the $4.5 million residence, and by early winter it will, in Pat's words, "better express our casual lifestyle."

This is the year when it seems everyone in Newport is redoing his house. Don Bren, of course, is working on his new place. Don Koll, developer of the executive haven Koll Center, has bought two lots on Lido Isle, torn down the expensive homes that stood on them, and begun work on a 10,000-square-foot mansion. Bob Warmington, another major developer, has just completed his dream house on Lido, a waterfront villa with a $40,000 Italian blue slate roof. The Rypinskis are in perfect step.

Pat often stops by the house to issue directives to the workmen. An energetic forty-three-year-old blond who bears a striking resemblance to Peggy Cass, she is a stylish straw boss. Today she sports a Louis Vuitton bag, two antique ivory necklaces and a matching bracelet, a huge rock, a gold Rolex encrusted with a dozen diamonds, and lavender nails. After passing through the Linda Isle guard gate, she navigates over strategically placed speed bumps until she reaches a two-story house marked by a little black lawn jockey out front. Inside, there is a flurry of buzz saws. The spiral staircase is coming down. An indoor/outdoor bar is going in. Upstairs, a sunken jacuzzi is being fitted into a show-all glass enclosure that overlooks the harbor and the Duke's old digs. As Alan has said, "We spend our time now collecting fine things. We're very creative people. We're hunters. Our life is finding treasures."

ONE OF THE Rypinski's treasures is Amen Wardy. His haute couture boutique in Fashion Island occupies a building that was formerly a J.C. Penney auto garage. Wardy, a forty-three-year-old Texan, has been in the women's fashion business since he was a young teenager who "loved to go to Neiman's in Dallas and see all those beautiful women's shoes and bags." In 1977 he opened a store in Newport, and within a few years the establishment had become the center of the city's fashion world, a place that Wardy, a gumdrop-shaped man of Lebanese extraction, characterizes as "so unique because my customers are so unique."

Amen Wardy's is where Pat Rypinski and her friends shop for everything, including Amen's special, a six-hour "Day of Beauty" makeover that starts in the morning with a pedicure, manicure, massage, and facial, continues with a light lunch, and ends in the afternoon with a haircut and new makeup. "We put them all together," Wardy says. "The bodies, the shoes, the socks, the jewelry, the furs, the hats—we've got it all here." Indeed, Wardy's larder for ladies (which he will soon be able to update instantly, using a computerized dress-search linkup) includes caches of Judith Leiber Fabergé egg bags, racks of snakeskin coats, prides of sable and mink furs by Perry Ellis and Yves St. Laurent, suits by André Laug and Brioni, Bill Blass cocktail dresses, René Caviolla gem shoes, and cases of jewelry by Cartier. To top it off, Amen features enough Galanos gowns to permanently distract Nancy Reagan from her pressing work with the Foster Grand Parent Program.

One Saturday morning, as Pat sits in the back of the store having her nails done by an attendant while another puts her eyeliner on, a small, plump woman and her college-age daughter arrive at the porte cochere. Amen, who wears a brown and white striped, collarless shirt, khakis, and leather tennies, meets his new customers at the door. They have come, the mother says solemnly, to buy the girl some back-to-school clothes. While the daughter examines a $485 sweater studded with rhinestone visions of retro-rockers doing the twist, Amen takes the mother in tow. Presently she emerges from a dressing room wearing a $685 black angora and wool sweater with leather shoulder patches, a $485 pair of shoes by Andrea Pfister, a pair of $795 Italian leather pants, and carrying a $525 brown snakeskin Judith Leiber bag. "Oh," Amen coos, "the men are going to tear that sweater off your back, honey." The woman is his. Such moments are de rigueur for Amen, and his clients expect no less. After all, their husbands earned it.

For Newport women, Amen is the director of not only daytime shopping dramas but also glitzy nighttime theatrics. On one of these enchanted evenings, he is hosting an event that promises to be special, one of the premier social occasions of the season. It is a black-tie dinner staged both to introduce his new line of fall furs and to show off a gallery exhibition of paintings by Holmby Hills doyenne Beverly Lohman Morsey. The artist is a limner of bright, "happy" floral watercolors after the grand style of the Ecole de Bored and Brazenly Untalented in Beverly Hills. Morsey frames her works—which bear titles such as *Pink Lilies Against Lavender Background* and *Pink Lilies Against Vermilion Background*—with three-inch-wide mirrors.

Amen has set up a big tent in his parking lot, imported Milton Williams of Hollywood to cater, and invited what he calls the "crème de la crème" of Newport. There is the Duke's widow, Pilar, in a tête-à-tête with Lee Minnelli, Vincente's wife. Pilar, who wears her abundant black hair glossed into an ebony conehead, is dressed in a black gown that falls off the left shoulder. Lee's black taffeta Bill Blass number falls off the right shoulder. My goodness, they say, what a coincidence. There is the oil-rich Burtie Bettingen. There are Alan and Pat Rypinski. And over there is George Argyros, a Newport resident who owns AirCal and the Seattle Mariners baseball team. Betsy Bloomingdale, confidante to the First Lady, is on the guest list but nowhere in sight.

"Where's Betsy?" someone asks.

"Oh, I don't know," someone else replies casually. "But I saw her in Paris at the couture show, and it was 'Hello, hello, hello. Darling, darling, darling.'"

The sumptuous dinner is served at round tables lining the models' runway. As angular women parade up and down, a South American rumba rhythm animates the room. This is an evening to remember. At one table, a woman of indeterminate age wearing a decollete gown makes preening gestures designed to accentuate the swell of her bosom. Near her, a jowly, white-haired man wearing a white jacket adorned with a rhinestone American-flag lapel pin bangs the table with his fists and calls the black waiter from Milton's "boy." The young woman who accompanies him stares off into space. Meanwhile, a man who has made a fortune in oil repeatedly dunks mounds of fresh currants into his water glass and jams the wet fruit into his mouth, a predilection that results in red gruel running down his chin and onto the top of his tuxedo shirt. Growing bored with this, he begins dipping plums into his wineglass and taking ragged bites out of them.

All the while, as the models parade, Sheena Easton's "For Your Eyes Only" booms through the room. Amen has fifty-three pieces in the show— linx skins, sables, minks, foxes. There is a Geoffrey Bean. There is a Perry Ellis. Gleeful yips greet a silver fox; wild applause erupts for a full-length sable; a collective sigh welcomes a mink-trimmed Persian lamb coat, which accordions in back to show a hand-painted oriental scene. Finally, the show ends with a crescendo of German music. But before the celebrants file out into the night, six of them will whisper in either Amen's or his furrier's ear. Tomorrow, only forty-seven furs will remain in Amen's fall collection. One of the pieces sold this evening, the full-length sable, brings $75,000.

IN NEWPORT, THE free enterprise system is more than just an appropriate means to an end. It is a religion, and it is celebrated every day, in every way. The high priest of this faith is Paul Salata, the sewerage contractor. If only he'd had a few moments of devotional time with Eloise Popeil, perhaps she could have been saved.

Salata—aside from making a fortune in the sewerage business, siring an airline stewardess daughter who dated presidential progeny Steven Ford, and dreaming up Irrelevant Week—is Newport's preeminent roast- and toast-master. He is noted for his scathing, scatological humor and is regularly called upon to skewer his fellow townsmen. But, more than a barb master, he is, in the words of Alan Rypinski, "Mr. Newport—the man we can count on to fix things if a bad crowd gets in at city hall, the man who is the spirit of this city."

Late on a summer evening, Newport's bluest bloods decide to turn the tables on Salata by roasting and toasting him in the main ballroom of the Newport Center Marriott Hotel. A Catholic priest starts the festivities with a prayer in which he beseeches the Lord to forgive everyone for what is to follow. Then the fun begins.

One man praises Salata for instituting a glass-bottom-boat tour of the local sewerage treatment plant.

Another man salutes "the Sultan of Squat, who's made a filthy fortune from exporting our morning sitdowns."

Someone else remarks that Salata has just bought a birthstone ring. The stone? White enamel.

Another celebrant congratulates Salata on his degree from USC—the university of sewerage contractors.

Finally, Police Chief Pete Gross goes to the podium to salute Salata as "the only man I know who could turn effluence into affluence." Then Tom Fuentes, first vice chairman of the Republican Central Committee of Orange County, rises to formally introduce Salata to the cheering throng of five hundred. "I want you to meet a man who is a vigorous believer in the free enterprise system," Fuentes says, "a man who is philosophically sound. Please stand up and toast Paul Salata."

Hundreds of chairs push back, hundreds of wineglasses sparkle in the air, and Salata, a tall, athletic, former USC football star, takes the microphone at the head table. He gets off a couple of zingers, but on this night his humor proves to be short-winded. More important topics weigh on his mind. "Free enterprise, profits," he intones. "Hey, we're here because we take care of our own."

Then, in benediction, Salata smiles down on the multitude. "I want to tell you people something," he says deeply. "Others may make fun of this, but I say it sincerely. 'Have a nice day.'"

That's what he said, and in Newport Beach—after they take the money raised at the Salata roast and put it to the good uses of the local hospital— that's exactly what they'll do.

EHUD YONAY

The Politics of Big Sur

B Y THE TIME the city slicker got to the top of the hill, he had loosened his tie and was holding his jacket in his hand. He had stopped for a brief rest in the clump of redwoods just below the house, but as soon as he stepped out into the sun he started to sweat again. Cursing the damned wilderness and the people in it, he stepped up to the door and flashed a big city slicker smile for the old man who opened it. Well into his seventies, Wilbur Harlan could still spot a hustler. The city slicker introduced himself as a land agent for William Randolph Hearst. Mr. Harlan may have heard of him. Perhaps Mr. Harlan had also heard that Mr. Hearst was building himself a little spread down by San Simeon and was looking to expand it a bit. Would Mr. Harlan consider selling his land to Mr. Hearst? Mr. Hearst sure would appreciate it. Old man Harlan said he wouldn't. The agent said Mr Hearst sure wouldn't appreciate the news. Harlan said that was too bad. The land agent skedaddled down the hill. A day later he was back. Mr. Hearst could appreciate Mr. Harlan's position and would be willing to double his offer. Harlan again said nothing doing, and the agent again disappeared down the hill, muttering something Harlan couldn't hear but could well guess the nature of. This was in the midst of the Depression, and money was scarce.

A few days later another man lumbered up to Harlan's redwood house. He was no ordinary hustler—Harlan could see that right away. Now here was someone to watch out for. The man introduced himself as Mr. Hearst and said he came to work out a deal for the land. "You don't seem to understand, Mr. Hearst, that I live here because this is where I want to live and where my family will live after I'm gone. This land is not for sale at any price," Harlan said, and there must have been something in the way he said it, because shortly thereafter Hearst left, and that was the last Harlan heard of his offers.

Nearly fifty years later, however, Democratic congressman Phil Burton of San Francisco was far more amenable when a group representing Hearst's interests showed up at his Washington office to talk about their San Simeon lands. As Burton later recalled, "their butts hadn't even hit the cushions" when he told them he had left their huge San Simeon estate out of a bill he was rushing through the House to make the whole area a federal preserve. Hearst could keep his lands, but old man Harlan's kids and grandkids could not. The way Burton saw it, the government may have given their granddaddy a piece of land nearly a century ago, but now the government wanted it back, and Burton was going to see that it got it.

GABRIEL AND ELIZABETH DANI were there first. In 1876 they took their kids and their pack mules west of King City, over the Santa Lucia Mountains, where the government had land available for homesteading. After several days of hard walking, they stopped on a magnificent ridge overlooking the Pacific Ocean in a wild territory that the Spanish missionaries in Carmel had called *el país grande del sur,* "the big country to the south," which the locals later dubbed Big Sur. They cut and split local redwoods to build a cabin and went on to have five more children. At the suggestion of a Mexican midwife, they named one of the girls Lucia, after the mountain range. Years later, the U.S. Post Office named the local post office after her, and the name stuck to that spot long after both Lucia and the post office were gone.

In 1887 another Dani daughter, Ada Amanda, married Wilbur Judson Harlan, a rakish young man with a drooping mustache who had emigrated from Texas two years earlier and staked a 162-acre homestead across a canyon north of the Dani spread. They had ten children, of whom three, Lulu Mae, George and Marion—still live in Lucia. Today no fewer than four generations of Harlans live within earshot of the place where old man Harlan told the most powerful man in the country at the time that his money was no good at Lucia—not for buying land, anyway.

Just as the Danis and the Harlans homesteaded at Lucia, other pioneer families trekked across the Santa Lucias or down from Monterey into the Big Sur Valley. The beauty of their new land was breathtaking. Tall mountains cascaded thousands of feet down to the ocean. Rising fog from the sea nurtured magnificent stands of redwoods in the deep ravines and dense forests of live oaks and madronas on the slopes above. But the beauty of the land was misleading. Big Sur was a harsh, inhospitable country. To plant anything, the land had to be cleared by hand, but once stripped of its dense brush cover it crumbled underfoot and was apt to avalanche down the steep slopes. Horses and cattle had trouble keeping their footing on the unstable soil. Coyotes, mountain lions, condors and grizzly bears preyed on the stock. Lightning-triggered forest fires raged for days, to be followed by floods and mud slides when the rains came. The high ridges and deep ravines not only isolated the settlers from the outside but even made visits to their neighbors difficult.

Only those tough enough to survive the hardship and isolation stayed. They married into each other's families, Danis and Harlans and Pfeiffers and Borondas and Trotters, so that today all of Big Sur's old-time residents are related, constituting a tribe of rugged mountain people with hands like slabs of redwood and an almost poetic reverence for their moody land. "I'll be eighty-seven tomorrow, and in all my life I've never cut down a living tree," George Harlan announced the other day as he maneuvered his pickup truck along a twisting mountain road, leaning out of the window to read animal tracks in the dust. Young Keith Harlan was asked recently if he wanted to do anything with the family land, like sell or subdivide some of it. "That's like selling your mother," he lashed back.

The pioneers branded their names on Big Sur's map, leaving us such place names as Post Summit, Pfeiffer Ridge, Partington Cove and Harlan Creek, but kept the land remarkably unchanged. When they could no longer hold on to their ranches, many signed them over to the state for parks and preserves. Today no fewer than 10,000 acres of Big Sur's most beautiful corners are in state parks. The early settlers also passed on their protective love of the land to the scores of lumberjacks, adventurers and recluse artists who moved in after them. In the 1970s the population almost doubled to nearly 1,700, but the newcomers who trekked to Big Sur with their Jacuzzis, hot tubs and four-wheel-drive Toyotas are even more zealously committed to protecting their terrain. To this day, most Big Sur homes have no sewers or TVs and are so well camouflaged in the woods that, from the highway, Big Sur looks almost uninhabited. There are no billboards, McDonald's, souvenir shops, banks or liquor stores. Most hotels have no TVs or room phones. Restaurants close early. In 1962 Monterey County adopted the first anti-development master plan in the country. In 1972 Proposition 20, the coastal protection initiative, received overwhelming support in Big Sur. In 1976 the state mandated that Highway 1 would remain a two-lane highway. The new laws stopped the population boom. Driving through the pristine mountains-meet-sea landscape, you would never believe that more people go through Big Sur each year than visit Yosemite. When talk began that someone was trying to turn Big Sur into a national park, it sounded like a bad joke. But the talk persisted, and eventually there was more than talk.

SOMETIME IN THE fall of 1977, a Big Sur gallery owner named Gary Koeppel got hold of a secret memorandum showing that a handful of affluent residents of Monterey Peninsula to the north were working to turn Big Sur into a national park. According to the memo, they had been holding meetings with county, state and federal officials but not with the people who would be most affected, the residents of Big Sur. The conspiratorial and patronizing tone of the memo went against the grain of Big Sur's cherished independence: "There appears to be virtually unanimous agreement among concerned Peninsulans that there exists an urgent necessity to...preserve... Big Sur," the memo began. While Big Sur is in Monterey County, stretching from just south of the Carmel Highlands all the way down to the San Luis Obispo County line, it is decidedly not a part of the Monterey Peninsula, which consists of the lucrative communities of Pacific Grove, Pebble Beach, Carmel and their equally lucrative suburbs. The authors of the memo thus amounted to a cabal of outsiders.

The "concerned Peninsulans" were led by Ansel Adams, America's most celebrated nature photographer and a former member of the Sierra Club board of directors. "You have to protect these things or you won't have them," he told reporters when Koeppel made the memo public, adding that "I intend to fight very hard." Adams was apparently putting all his personal and political resources into the fight. His business manager, William A. Turnage, had written the memo, while his Los Angeles lawyers had pledged $50,000 in free legal services to the Big Sur park campaign. Adams was joined by such important members of the affluent liberal establishment of the Carmel area as former California coastal commissioner and state senator Fred Farr; his son Sam Farr, a Monterey County supervisor and former member of the Central Coast Regional Commission; and Will Shaw, a local planner-architect who owns a weekend home in Big Sur. The Monterey Peninsula Foundation, a local community powerhouse (Fred Farr, Shaw and Adams have all served on the foundation's board of directors), agreed to channel tax-exempt contributions to the Big Sur campaign if the connection between the two was kept quiet.

While Turnage reported that "the residents of Big Sur itself are...deeply concerned about...overdevelopment and excessive uncontrolled tourism," it was obvious that he didn't discuss the issue with more than a handful of them, because when Koeppel polled the community on the national park prospects, 315 were against it and only 7 were for. Adams dismissed the poll on grounds that turning Big Sur into a park was "a matter of public good versus vested interests." Koeppel exploded in anger and announced that he would stop the federalization of Big Sur even if he had to turn the whole place into a town.

Gary Koeppel, forty-two, is a tall man with short, light hair, a narrow beard, blue eyes and a penchant for color-matched outfits that often include a beret. He started out as a college English teacher, took up candle-making in Topanga Canyon, then ten years ago came to Big Sur and built the Coast Gallery in two giant old redwood water tanks south of Big Sur Valley, at the mouth of Lafler Canyon. The gallery soon became the biggest art outlet south of Carmel, and Koeppel emerged as Big Sur's leading and most vocal advocate of home rule and freedom from meddling outsiders, which in his case meant the Sierra Club and anybody resembling them. The Turnage memo confirmed his worst fears that the Sierra Club was conspiring to destroy Big Sur by evicting its residents and placing it in the hands of incompetent government bureaucrats. He interpreted the results of his impromptu poll as a call for self-rule and immediately launched a drive to actually incorporate Big Sur as a town. He announced that the government may be able to condemn a piece of private land for a park, but it cannot condemn a whole town. His "Stop Adams" campaign was ironic because he and Adams share the same goal—keeping Big Sur just as it is today. The difference between the two is over the means of accomplishing that aim. Koeppel believes that the government should protect the environment only as a last resort—when the residents can't or won't do it. He likes to use the term "private stewardship of the resources," which to him means stopping development through reliance on the coastal plan, the residents' devotion to Big Sur and the "natural constraints" of the land (most parcels in Big Sur cannot be built on because the land is either unstable or not permeable enough for a septic tank, or because of a lack of water).

Painting Adams as the environmental villain was probably the worst casting job Koeppel could have attempted. If it is true that, given sufficient time, men come to resemble their wives, pets or what they do for a living, then Ansel Adams clearly belongs to the third kind. At seventy-eight, he has acquired the hue and texture of the Sierra Nevada granite he has been photographing for much of his life. He has lost none of his stature and influence since his resignation from the Sierra Club board; if anything, his fame and influence have been rising steadily. So have his finances. The price of Adams's black and white prints have increased dramatically. He has an exclusive franchise to sell photos in Yosemite. His books are selling like hotcakes in spite of stiff prices. He is at once an environmental lobbyist and fat cat. As an artist, he can donate valuable photographs without being hindered by campaign finance restrictions.

Eighteen years ago, Adams moved into a spacious house facing the ocean on the Carmel Highlands. Looking south from his picture window, he could see the suburban sprawl skip over Malpaso Creek, Big Sur's semiofficial northern boundary, resulting in a small beachfront subdivision. In his mind he could already see the rest of Big Sur covered with trailer parks and condos, and he decided that the only way to keep that from happening was to put the feds in charge. By the time Adams began his park drive, Big Sur was already on the verge of being as protected as any place could be. In 1976 the state adopted the California Coastal Act, and Monterey County, already the most environmentally conscious county in the state, was in high gear planning protective measures for Big Sur. When it comes to conservation, Adams has little faith in the democratic process, in local governments, in zoning or in antidevelopment plans. The way he sees it, good laws can be followed by bad laws, so the way to preserve places like Big Sur is to remove them from the hands of citizens or lawmakers altogether. The fact that the residents of Big Sur wanted no part of his plan was immaterial. "It always happens in such cases—people with financial interest getting panicky, worried about being thrown off their property. We heard it in Yosemite, Kings Canyon, Golden Gate Highlands, Point Reyes—everywhere," he told *New West*.

In April 1978, at the urging of Adams and his allies, Democratic congressman Leon Panetta of Carmel quietly introduced a rider to an omnibus parks bill, providing $350,000 for an Interior Department study on ways to preserve Big Sur. The bill passed the House Interior Committee on May 15. Two weeks later, the residents of Big Sur got their first inkling of what was happening when Panetta came down to Big Sur to discuss his proposals. On June 20, Panetta received a petition from 558 Big Sur citizens urging him to drop the bill. A day later, Panetta told *New West* that "in response to vigorous local debate on the issue, I am now considering several alternatives to the study commission." Several weeks later he dropped the bill altogether. That was just the begining.

Even before Panetta bowed out, Adams supporters formed the Big Sur Foundation to spearhead their campaign to preserve Big Sur under federal tutelage. Shaw was named president, Adams vice president and Virginia Mudd secretary. William Turnage's absence from the foundation roster didn't mean that he was no longer in Adams's corner. Quite the contrary. In November 1978 he became executive director of the Wilderness Society in Washington, D.C. Now the Adams drive had a made-to-order national constituency.

THE STAGE FOR the upcoming battle for Big Sur was set when, in August 1978, Gary Koeppel launched the *Big Sur Gazette*, a monthly community newspaper with an initial circulation of about 2,000.

In the second issue, the *Gazette* broke its first major news story, revealing that the state attorney general's office, in conjunction with the Central Coast

Regional Commission, had been polling scuba divers, hikers and assorted beachcombers about their use of certain private beaches in the area. The *Gazette* discovered that the questionnaire came out of an eighty-eight page state document titled *Manual of Procedures and Criteria Relating to Implied Dedication and Public Prescriptive Rights* and that its purpose was to discover whether the owners of those beach properties had in effect given up ownership by allowing the public to move across the property. If so, the state could claim those properties without compensating the owners for their land. As one irate reader responded in the *Gazette*'s following issue, "The questionnaire is trying to determine whether certain people have trespassed on other people's private property enough for the state to take that property." The *Gazette* interviewed attorneys on the implications of the prescriptive rights questionnaire and advised its readers to lock their gates and post NO TRESPASSING signs on their fences or face the loss of their land. By the time the fourth issue rolled off the presses, Attorney General Evelle Younger had called the *Gazette*'s coverage "inaccurate and highly inflammatory," and an assistant attorney general called Koeppel a yellow journalist. Community response, however, was all favorable, establishing the *Gazette* as Big Sur's main line of defense against the preservation sweepstakes and the growing number of agencies jumping into it. Koeppel's incorporation drive was less successful. By mid-1979 it became clear that the Big Sur community didn't want to become a town any more than it wanted to become a national park, and the incorporation effort was abandoned. In early 1979 the California Coastal Commission contracted with the Monterey County board of supervisors for the development of a Big Sur local coastal plan (LCP). The race for Big Sur was now down to two contesters. Big Sur would either become a protectorate of the federal government or it would be preserved by its own residents through their elected representatives and local agencies.

The residents of Big Sur clearly preferred the second course and took an active part in the discussions and debates over every aspect of the plan— criteria for building permits, treatment of the "viewshed" areas, minimum-size building lots, establishment of tax easements to keep farmland in production. For the Adams forces, this was clearly too much democracy. Rather than make their national park-hood case in public, they were quietly making democracy work 3,000 miles away. On November 6, 1979, Ansel Adams wheeled a mammoth Polaroid camera into the White House to snap President Carter's portrait. According to press reports, he also presented Carter with a memo concerning the preservation of Alaska and Big Sur, but when reporters attempted to learn the contents of the memo, both Adams and a White House press officer claimed that the memo was "personal correspondence" and "strictly confidential." In January the National Inholders

Association uncovered evidence that the Big Sur Foundation had been quietly lobbying the Senate Energy Committee about placing Big Sur under federal ownership. On January 26, 1980, the Ankrum Gallery of Los Angeles hosted a $250-per-couple fundraiser for Alan Cranston in which some $45,000 was raised. Close to half that sum was raised by raffling two black-and-white photographs donated by Ansel Adams, who joined with Cranston for the event and autographed numerous copies of his book *Yosemite and the Range of Light.*

On January 28, Cranston circulated a "Dear Colleague" letter in the Senate, describing an amendment he planned to tack on to an omnibus parks bill: "Currently there is a 3,000-acre limitation on the total amount of land the forest service can add to the Los Padres National Forest....My amendment would remove the 3,000-acre limit...so that the forest service can accept donations of Big Sur lands." It was an explosive proposal. Not only would it allow the forest service to buy up private lands in Big Sur, but, more important, it would mean that if the forest service could get title to a few strategically located properties, many more privately held lands would automatically become "inholdings," which are subject to a number of administrative land confiscation procedures. Cranston tried to minimize the importance of such issues. "The amendment...merely waives an arbitrary rule, and I see no great need for a hearing on whether to permit donations of Big Sur lands to the government," he wrote. When he asked Senator Hayakawa to support the amendment, however, Hayakawa called Big Sur. The reaction was devastating. Within twenty-four hours Cranston's office was bombarded with no fewer than 2,000 telegrams and telephone calls urging him to drop the amendment. Cranston did just that but later quietly introduced a new bill, S 2233, with literally the same wording.

On February 21, 1980, William Turnage, now executive director of the Wilderness Society, unveiled a plan to make Big Sur "the first national scenic area in the nation's history." The Wilderness Society's proposed Big Sur National Scenic Area was remarkably similar to Adams's Big Sur National Seashore concept, with one difference. In the new plan, Big Sur would be placed under the protective management of the U.S. Forest Service (which is part of the U.S. Department of Agriculture) instead of the National Park Service (part of the Interior Department). In other respects, however, the Wilderness Society plan had all the earmarks of Adams's thinking: The U.S. Forest Service would be the chief management agency for the area, all significant development and construction would be stopped, and private lands would be transferred to government ownership or control (the plan did not say so outright, but in the March 1980 edition of the society's journal, *The Living Wilderness,* the society made it clear that "up to 75,000 acres could be acquired along the coast in Monterey County...beginning south of Carmel and extending down to the county line," which just happens to be about the sum of the privately owned acreage in Big Sur). The proposed freeze on development implied adoption of Adams's "staging areas" concept—giant hotel-restaurant-parking complexes north and south of the Big Sur protected zone, from which visitors would be bused up and down the Big Sur coast. The Hearst Corporation had already notified San Luis Obispo County of its intent to build a huge tourist-facilities complex at San Simeon.

ADAMS SPARED NO EFFORT to drive home the fact that Big Sur was his last hurrah. In a February 3 public letter, he declared: "I am nearly seventy-eight years old and...the greatest joy I will ever find in my lifetime is the opportunity to protect the unsurpassed natural beauty of our coastline....If we join together to accomplish [it], I will feel I have had a life fully lived....I [will] have fulfilled my responsibility to my children and my friends." Cranston, for one, answered the call, and in April introduced S 2551, that not only called for the creation of a Big Sur Coast National Scenic Area according to the Wilderness Society plan but asked Congress to appropriate no less than $100 million to start buying up Big Sur. He scheduled one day of hearings on the bill—in Washington. If anyone in Big Sur wanted to say anything about the bill, he had to journey 3,000 miles for the privilege. Several Big Sur residents did just that. Barbara Chamberlain, a fourth-generation Big Sur resident heavily involved in community projects, was one of them. "We felt like fish out of water. I mean, here we were, common citizens, nobody from nowhere, talking to the people whose names you see in headlines. We had no idea what we were doing except that we had a cause and we wanted people to know about it. We broke into teams, made as many appointments as we could, tried to be as pleasant and polite as we could under the circumstances," she recalled recently, sitting in a rough wooden cabin near Big Sur Valley that her father had built nearly half a century ago. They began their lobbying assault on Monday. On Wednesday they were ushered into the high-ceilinged splendor of the Democratic whip's office at the Capitol to meet Cranston. "The meeting lasted an hour," Chamberlain said, "and we started by telling him our position on the various features of the bill. Within ten minutes it became clear that he had not only not written the bill, he hadn't even read it! Each time we raised a point, he'd look over our heads to one of his assistants who was leafing through the bill, and then either he or another assistant would express surprise at what we said and assure us that this certainly was not their intent, and so on. Toward the end of the meeting we presented the senator with a petition from our members explaining our views. He didn't even open the folder to look at it but put it on the floor. When the meeting ended he got up and left the office, and the petition remained on the floor."

That was only the beginning of their lesson in Washington-style democracy. When they rushed to their next meeting with another senator, they were informed that the meeting had been canceled after someone from Cranston's office called to say that since he had met with the delegation and they "were in complete accord" there was no need for such a meeting. But Cranston didn't know whom they were going to meet. He had his staff call every senator connected with the bill and say that after meeting with Cranston the group's objections had been taken care of. "We spent the next three hours calling back every senator we already met and scheduling every appointment we had originally scheduled for the rest of the week," said Chamberlain. "That's the kind of professionalism we had to deal with in Washington."

But the hearings were as far as the Cranston bill got. It turned out that the three organizations most involved in the Big Sur park drive, the Wilderness Society, the Sierra Club and the Big Sur Foundation, were practically the only ones interested in seeing it pass. Most of the testimony was negative, and the bill was shelved. Now the ball was in the House, where the park makers had the enthusiastic support of Phil Burton of San Francisco, who as chairman of the House Parks and Insular Affairs Subcommittee could get any park legislation through the House. As congressman from the affected area, however, Panetta had first crack at the bill. "Burton told Panetta, 'Either you do it or I'll do it.' That's what Burton told us," says Jim Josoff, head of Friends of Big Sur, a local antifederalization alliance. In June, Panetta introduced HR 7380 the Big Sur Coast Area Act. While opposition in Big Sur was instantaneous, it was also obvious that the Adams forces were not getting their way, either. Not completely, anyway.

LEON PANETTA, forty-two, is a small-framed man with a boyish grin and a disarming informality. One reason he is still referred to in the county as a local boy made good is the fact that he needs no reminder of how he got where he is. Few representatives keep in closer touch with their constituents or think as much about the effect of legislative issues on the folks back home. Panetta started out as a legislative assistant to then Republican senator Thomas Kuchel, was appointed head of HEW's Office of Civil Rights under the Nixon administration, but was fired in 1970 over what he saw as the sacrificing of southern education for the "southern strategy." He became a Democrat, entered politics in 1976 and was immediately elected to Congress. He is a pragmatic politician, which means that he is as likely to be described as a conservative liberal as a liberal conservative. The Big Sur issue put him in a bind. "It would have been very easy for me to do nothing and let Burton pass a Big Sur National Park bill seemingly over my objections. But that's not my style. This is my district, the issue is important, and I wasn't going to sit by without offering the best solution I could come up with," he said recently, sitting in shirt sleeves in a small walk-up office in downtown Monterey.

Indeed, if federal involvement had to take place in Big Sur, the Panetta bill was a model of responsive attention to local needs and feelings. HR 7380 did not create a national park. It placed the secretary of agriculture at the head of that preservation effort, and made him share his authority with a council of Big Sur residents with the power to develop a regional master plan that would be binding on all landholders in the area, including the forest service. Panetta's bill even mandated that the locally developed LCP would be incorporated into the new master plan.

Why, then, did such a reasonable bill draw such sharp opposition in Big Sur? The *Gazette* called it a fraud and offered a free six-by-twelve-inch "counterfeit Panetta bill" with each new subscription—an oversize drawing of a $100 million bill with Panetta's face in the middle and the signatures of Phil Burton and William Turnage below. Later, "Anybody but Panetta" bumper stickers showed up. Letters to the *Gazette* blasted the bill from every direction. First, it was suspected of being bogus. Why would the advocates of outright nationalization of Big Sur back Panetta's bill unless they thought they could use it as a first step toward an ultimate Big Sur National Park legislation? "You have to be naive to believe that what the bill says is all there is to it," said Jim Josoff. "Panetta said his bill was not a federal designation for Big Sur. Hogwash. When you create a Big Sur area you federalize it—it is under federal, not county or state, control." Ironically, Josoff's charge that the Panetta bill was no different from the Cranston bill is shared by Michael Fischer, executive director of the California Coastal Commission. The difference between the bills was largely one of marketing, Fischer said. "Cranston has a statewide constituency, and if everybody in Big Sur hated his guts it wouldn't matter to his future. Poor Leon has to depend on the Monterey Bay area constituency, and he can't allow his legislation to appear as if the big bad federal government is coming in to take over the town."

The second objection was more direct and was succinctly summed up by John Harlan: "Who needs it? Why get the feds involved in the first place?" Panetta said that his bill would assure that the U.S. Forest Service live up to the LCP and would provide federal funds to compensate landowners who would be denied building permits under the plan. Without these two provisions, he said, the LCP could not be made to work. His bill, in a sense, was an offer nobody in his right mind could refuse—federal money with almost no strings attached

On June 21, Panetta held the first full day of hearings on his bill. Unlike Cranston, he held the hearings in Monterey, giving everyone a chance to sound off. This time proponents and opponents balanced out. While the Friends of Big Sur contended that the problems noted by Panetta could be solved without giving the feds any power over Big Sur (the White House could order the Los Padres National Forest staff to abide by the LCP; levying even a small local tax on tourist facilities would raise more than enough money to compensate those who might be deprived of the right to build a house in Big Sur), they were neutralized by local officials drooling over the prospects of federal money—$30 million, to be exact—pouring in.

What nobody seemed to notice was that, by design or not, the Panetta bill was less a Big Sur bill than an attempt to short-circuit the Califomia legislative process, that its ultimate impact on the future of the California coastline could equal or surpass that of Proposition 20. What the Panetta bill really boiled down to was a proposal to turn the California coastal protection program over to the feds—a crucial decision that should have been debated in Sacramento before God and everybody, not in a small meeting hall in Monterey. The entire bill was based on the assumption that California cannot carry out its coastal protection program and should therefore shift the burden of financing—and of overseeing it—to the federal government. Had the bill passed as drafted, a precedent would have been set. If the Monterey County LCP could not be enforced without government intervention, what about other LCPs in other beachfront counties? Were the coastal protection initiative, the 1976 coastal act and the coastal commission a mere exercise in futility or, worse yet, a roundabout way of placing the feds in charge of our beaches?

The irony is that the entire Adams drive to place Big Sur under federal protection had been noted from the outset for the unusual predominance of present and past coastal commission figures. Fred and Sam Farr were both coastal commissioners. Zad Leavy, Big Sur's representative on the Central Coast Regional Commission, and Joe Bodovitz, ex-executive director of the commission, were hired as consultants to the foundation. Saunders Hillyer, a former commission staffer, is the $35,000-a-year executive director of the Big Sur Foundation. Since to justify a federal takeover at Big Sur the foundation in essence needed to discredit the state coastal protection plan, such ex-coastal commission staffers could provide expert advice about the shortcomings of the plan. But the foundation managed to get the help of more than just past employees of the commission. One of the leading advocates of both the Cranston and Panetta bills turned out to be Michael Fischer, executive director of the coastal commission. In fact, both Cranston and Panetta relied on Fischer's testimony to justify the need for their bills. Fischer has said that his support of both bills was fully discussed with Huey Johnson, California secretary of the resources, who discussed it with Gray Davis, Govenor Brown's chief of staff. "Both Huey and Gray had said on a number of occasions that I speak for the state of California [on the Big Sur bills]," he said.

Once Panetta concluded the Monterey hearing and flew back to Washington with enough public support to keep the bill alive, the fate of Big Sur was in the hands of the professional park makers. The bill was sent to the Parks and Insular Affairs Subcommittee, headed by Phil Burton. Burton held another day of hearings, where much of the testimony was in opposition to the bill. Even before the hearing began, Burton had already decided to grant the Hearst Corporation's wishes to be left out of the proposed Big Sur Coastal Area. After the hearing, he held a meeting with the Hearst lobbyists. It took him only thirty seconds to tell them they got what they wanted, he told reporters later. The following day Burton took five minutes to move the bill through a subcommittee markup (amendment and rewrite session), at the end of which 43,000 acres owned by Hearst were left out of the "protected" zone. What made it particularly ironic was Burton's public accolades to Hearst for keeping the San Simeon area pristine and undeveloped. By the time he made the statement, the San Luis Obispo County Board of Supervisors had already incorporated into its general plan Hearst's proposal to construct a huge tourist center at San Simeon, to include one motel and three lodges with a total of 900 rooms, an employee housing complex, eight restaurants, an RV park, two eighteen-hole golf courses, two commercial shopping areas and a boat docking and launching facility. Furthermore, the reason the San Simeon area had been undeveloped heretofore was not Hearst's "enlightened environmental outlook." Back in the 1960s, Hearst planned to build a town of 65,000 around the small coastal village, complete with colleges and airports.

Reporters covering the committee suspected that the reason Burton let Hearst off the hook was concern that massive litigation could torpedo the entire Big Sur project. Burton is a practical man. When asked later why he agreed to ask only $30 million for the Big Sur Program instead of the $100 million Cranston asked for earlier, he said he didn't think he'd get it.

"My concern is that a $100 million bill for California, behind a $150 million to $300 million Lake Tahoe bill, behind a $360 million Redwoods bill, behind a $150 million Santa Monica bill, behind a $30 million Channel Islands bill, $30 million in add-ons in Point Reyes and Golden Gate National Recreation Area, resulting in almost 85 percent of all the national land and water money for acquisition, well, it might just be a little bit unrealistic," he told a reporter for the *Sacramento Bee.* The implication was clear: As in all other areas mentioned, there would always be more money next year or the year after to buy more Big Sur land for the forest service. Big Sur's future was now in the hands of the experts. According to Alan Perlmutter, a Big Sur resident who flew to Washington to lobby against the bill, he was sitting in Burton's outer office when Turnage turned to him and asked, "Just who in hell do you one thousand people think you are that you should control that land instead of the people of the United States?" If there is anything Phil Burton knows well, it is how to get parks made. On Monday he held the subcommittee hearings. On Tuesday he chaired a five-minute markup session in which the Hearst lands were exempted. On Wednesday, July 23, he maneuvered it through the House Interior Committee, where it passed without a single dissenting vote after a mere fifteen-minute discussion. Had Congress not recessed for the Democratic National Convention he would have taken it right on to the House Rules Committee and the floor. As it was, he waited for the House to reconvene and on August 25 whipped the bill through the House by marshaling more than two-thirds of the votes.

Senator Cranston pledged to guide the Panetta bill through the Senate this fall, and on August 27 it was sent to the Senate Energy Committee. Although Cranston is not a member of that committee, he virtually hovered over it to make sure the bill was treated right. "Of all the bills before the Energy Committee, Big Sur is Cranston's top priority," Roy Greenaway, Cranston's chief administrative assistant, told the *Gazette*.

But Cranston was not having his way, and the bill was not moving in committee. Finally, with only two days to spare before the election recess, the Adams forces decided to gamble all on a daring legislative commando strike.

It was a two-prong operation. On the Senate side, the Energy Committee scheduled the bill for a markup session on September 30, three days before the Ninety-sixth Congress went home to get reelected. On September 29, Cranston got Senator Dale Bumpers of Arkansas, the parks subcommittee chairman, to propose six surprise amendments to the Panetta bill, and suddenly Big Sur's worst fears came true. The amendments gave the secretary of agriculture, not the local council, final authority "for the comprehensive management plan developed by Big Sur Coast Area Council"; they gave the secretary authority to develop, build and manage visitors' facilities in the area, which translated into authority to construct any new hotels, inns or campgrounds he deemed necessary; they completely reversed the Panetta bill by providing that the citizens' council had no authority over the U.S. Forest Service plans for the Los Padres National Forest; and most significantly, they gave the attorney general of the United States the power to prohibit property owners from doing anything with their land until the government lines up the funds to buy it through condemnation. The Bumpers-Cranston amendments would have done what Koeppel, Josoff and hundreds of Big Sur residents feared all along—change Panetta's bill into a flat-out national park bill.

By the end of the day on September 30 it was clear that the committee was not going to take up the Big Sur issue. It was then that the second stage of Operation Big Sur went into effect. Early that evening Phil Burton rose on the floor of the House and nonchalantly asked the Speaker to suspend discussions and get down to voting on an obscure bill sent to the House from the Senate five days earlier. The bill, S 1910, was not the sort that people were likely to argue over. In 1923 the federal government moved the entire town of American Falls, Idaho, several miles to the southwest to make room for the new American Falls reservoir. But the government forgot to transfer title for the city's parkland. S 1910 would do that, and now the House had to approve it. As soon as the House clerk finished reading the bill, however, Burton rose again and offered twelve amendments whose combined text was twenty times the size of S 1910 itself. With the exception of a few minor items, the bulk of the amendments were controversial bits of park legislation. The biggest of these was the Big Sur Coast Area Act—in other words, Panetta's bill. Since the bill had already passed the House by a two-to-one margin a month earlier, why was Burton sending it through again? Simple. The Senate had already passed S 1910. If the House now passed it, it would go back to the Senate as a House message for a perfunctory concurrence that required no committee hearings. With only days left before the Senate ended its work before the election, nobody in his right mind would quarrel over an obscure little bill to give the good people of American Falls their parks, and the Big Sur bill would slip through unnoticed. As the House clerk droned through page after page of Burton's amendments, Burton offered a thumbnail sketch of the new provisions. It took him "all of forty seconds" to get the bill approved by the full House. There was no debate or challenge. It was now 6 P.M.

The bill was then carried to the Senate chambers, but that is as far as it got. Wary of just such a maneuver, a young staffer on Senator Hayakawa's team, Bruce Keough, had earlier placed a "hold" on anything concerning Big Sur, requiring the minority leader to inform Hayakawa of any pending Big Sur amendment, bill, or House message; it also meant that the subject was controversial and should be held for appropriate discussions. Once again, Hayakawa turned out to be Big Sur's guardian angel, and the bill never came up for a vote. Three days later Capitol Hill was deserted by its legislators, and the Panetta bill was left up in the air. By the time Congress reconvened, Reagan had been elected president, and the Republicans took over the Senate. Both Democrats and Republicans agreed to pass only crucial or noncontroversial legislation. On November 19, the Senate Energy Committee held its last meeting of the year, and Big Sur didn't come up. Barring a last-minute surprise maneuver by Cranston, the Big Sur bill was dead.

AARON HARLAN, old Wilbur and Ada's elder son, had left Lucia in 1916, but ten years ago his son John returned to the family homestead with his wife, Ruth, and two sons. This year he finished building his home on a hill high above the ten-room Lucia Lodge, which his sons operate. The new house has solar collectors on the roof and patented native-stone fireplaces, which make it nearly energy independent. A few hundred feet from the house, surrounded by a fruit orchard, is Aunt Lulu Mae's house, and further up, just before the gently sloping hill suddenly tilts up and shoots skyward, is Uncle Marion's cabin. The place has changed little since Gabriel and Elizabeth Dani homesteaded on the ridge across the canyon to the south, except that a monastery now stands where the Dani home used to, and the ancient redwoods in the canyons have grown. "When I was a kid you could look straight across the canyon. Now you can't. It's incredible how those old trees just keep on growing," says Harlan. Firewood is stacked in long rows near Uncle Marion's cabin. Marion is butchering goats in the shed for his brother George's birthday the following day. Weathered wood picket fences. End of summer yellowing hillsides. Jars of freshly made apple preserves on Ruth Harlan's kitchen counter. I tell John Harlan that the environmentalists behind the Panetta bill are worried that sooner or later there will be subdivisions at Lucia. "I resent not being grouped in the category of environmentalists. The people who've lived here—we are environmentalists by birth and training. We were environmentalists before anybody found it in vogue to be one," he says, looking, not even bothering to point, at the virgin landscape, the fog crawling up from the sea. "We've done pretty good keeping the place for more than one hundred years, wouldn't you say? I don't see why it should go to hell in a hand basket just because the federal government doesn't own it."

ISHMAEL REED

My Neighborhood

MY STEPFATHER IS an evolutionist. He worked for many years at the Chevrolet division of General Motors in Buffalo, a working-class auto and steel town in upstate New York, and was able to rise from relative poverty to the middle class. He believes that each succeeding generation of Afro-Americans will have it better than its predecessor. In 1979 I moved into the kind of neighborhood that he and my mother spent about a third of their lives trying to escape. According to the evolutionist integrationist ethic this was surely a step backward, since "success" was seen as being able to live in a neighborhood in which you were the only black and joined your neighbors in trying to keep out "them."

My neighborhood, bordered by Genoa, Market Street, and 48th and 55th streets in North Oakland, is what the media refer to as a "predominantly black neighborhood." It's the kind of neighborhood I grew up in before leaving for New York City in 1962. My last New York residence was an apartment in a brownstone, next door to the building in which poet W.H. Auden lived. There were trees in the backyard, and I thought it was a swell neighborhood until I read in Robert Craft's biography of Stravinsky that when Stravinsky sent his chauffeur to pick up his friend Auden, the chauffeur would ask, "Are you sure Mr. Auden lives in this neighborhood?" By 1968 my wife and I were able to live six months of the year in New York and the other six in California. This came to an end when one of the people I sublet the apartment to abandoned it. He had fled to England to pursue a romance. He didn't pay the rent, and so we were evicted long distance.

My first residence in California was an apartment on Santa Ynez Street, near Echo Park Lake in Los Angeles, where I lived for about six months in 1967. I was working on my second novel, and Carla Blank, my wife, a dancer, was teaching physical education at one of Eddie Rickenbacker's camps, located on an old movie set in the San Bernardino Mountains. Carla's employers were always offering me a cabin where they promised I could write without interruption. I never took them up on the offer, but for years I've wondered about what kind of reception I would have received had they discovered that I am black.

During my breaks from writing I would walk through the shopping areas near Santa Ynez, strolling by vending machines holding newspapers whose headlines screamed about riots in Detroit. On some weekends we'd visit novelist Robert Gover (*The One Hundred Dollar Misunderstanding*) and his friends in Malibu. I remember one of Gover's friends, a scriptwriter for "The Donna Reed Show," looking me in the eye and telling me that if he were black he'd be "on a Detroit rooftop, sniping at cops," as he reclined, glass of scotch in hand, in a comfortable chair whose position gave him a good view of the rolling Pacific.

My Santa Ynez neighbors were whites from Alabama and Mississippi, and we got along fine. Most of them were elderly, left behind by white flight to the suburbs, and on weekends the street would be lined with cars belonging to relatives who were visiting. While living here I observed a uniquely Californian phenomenon. Retired men would leave their houses in the morning, enter their cars, and remain there for a good part of the day, snoozing, reading newspapers, or listening to the radio. I didn't experience a single racial incident during my stay in this Los Angeles neighborhood of ex-southerners. Once, however, I had a strange encounter with the police. I was walking through a black working-class neighborhood on my way to the downtown Los Angeles library. Some cops drove up and rushed me. A crowd gathered. The cops snatched my briefcase and removed its contents: books and notebooks having to do with my research of voodoo. The crowd laughed when the cops said they thought I was carrying a purse.

In 1968 my wife and I moved to Berkeley, where we lived in one Bauhaus box after another until about 1971, when I received a three-book contract from Doubleday. Then we moved into the Berkeley Hills, where we lived in the downstairs apartment of a very grand looking house on Bret Harte Way. There was a Zen garden with streams, waterfalls, and bridges outside, along with many varieties of flowers and plants. I didn't drive, and Carla was away at Mills College each day, earning a masters degree in dance. I stayed holed up in that apartment for two years, during which time I completed my third novel, *Mumbo Jumbo.*

During this period I became exposed to some of the racism I hadn't detected on Santa Ynez or in the Berkeley flats. As a black male working at home, I was regarded with suspicion. Neighbors would come over and warn me about a heroin salesman they said was burglarizing the neighborhood, all the while looking over my shoulder in an attempt to pry into what I was up to. Once, while I was eating breakfast, a policeman entered through the garden door, gun drawn. "What on earth is the problem, officer?" I asked. He said they'd got word that a homicide had been committed in my apartment, which I reconized as an old police tactic used to gain entry into somebody's house. Walking through the Berkeley Hills on Sundays, I was greeted by unfriendly stares and growling, snarling dogs. I remember one pest who always poked her head out of her window whenever I'd walk down Bret Harte Way. She was always hassling me about parking my car in front of her house. She resembled Miss Piggy. I came to think of this section of Berkeley as "Whitetown."

Around 1974 the landlord raised the rent on the house in the hills, and we found ourselves again in the Berkeley flats. We spent a couple of peaceful years on Edith Street, and then moved to Jayne Street, where we encountered another next-door family of nosy, middle-class progressives. I understand that much time at North Berkeley white neighborhood association meetings is taken up with discussion of and fascination with blacks who move through the neighborhoods, with special concern given those who tarry, or who wear dreadlocks. Since before the Civil War, vagrancy laws have been used as political weapons against blacks. Appropriately, there has been talk of making Havana—where I understand a woman can get turned in by her neighbors for having too many boyfriends over—Berkeley's sister city.

In 1976 our landlady announced that she was going to reoccupy the Jayne Street house. I facetiously told a friend that I wanted to move to the most right-wing neighborhood he could think of. He mentioned El Cerrito. There, he said, your next-door neighbor might even be a cop. We moved to El Cerrito. Instead of the patronizing nosiness blacks complain about in Berkeley, I found the opposite on Terrace Drive in El Cerrito. The people were cold, impersonal, remote. But the neighborhood was quiet, serene even—the view was Olympian, and our rented house was secluded by eucalyptus trees. The annoyances were minor. Occasionally a car would careen down Terrace Drive full of white teenagers, and one or two would shout, "Hey, nigger!" Sometimes as I walked down The Arlington toward Kensington Market, the curious would stare at me from their cars, and women I encountered would give me nervous, frightened looks. Once, as I was walking to the market to buy magazines, a white child was sitting directly in my path. We were the only two people on the street. Two or three cars actually stopped, and their drivers observed the scene through their rearview mirrors until they were assured I wasn't going to abduct the child.

At night the Kensington Market area was lit with a yellow light, especially eerie during a fog. I always thought that this section of Kensington would be a swell place to make a horror movie—the residents would make great extras—but whatever discomfort I felt about traveling through this area at 2 A.M. was mixed with the relief that I had just navigated safely through Albany, where the police seemed always to be lurking in the shadows, prepared to ensnare blacks, hippies, and others they didn't deem suitable for such a neighborhood.

In 1979 our landlord, a decent enough fellow in comparison to some of the others we had had (who made you understand why the communists shoot the landlords first when they take over a country), announced he was going to sell the house on Terrace Drive. This was the third rented house to be sold out from under us. The asking price was way beyond our means, and so we started to search for another home, only to find that the ones within our price range were located in North Oakland, in a "predominantly black neighborhood." We finally found a huge Queen Anne Victorian, which seemed to be about a month away from the wrecker's ball if the termites and the precarious foundation didn't do it in first, but I decided that I had to have it. The oldest house on the block, it was built in 1906, the year the big earthquake hit Northern California but left Oakland unscathed because, according to Bret Harte, "there are some things even the earth can't swallow." If I was apprehensive about moving into this neighborhood—on television all black neighborhoods resemble the commotion of the station house on "Hill Street Blues"—I was later to learn that our neighbors were just as apprehensive about us. Were we hippies? Did I have a job? Were we going to pay as much attention to maintaining our property as they did to theirs? Neglected, the dilapidated monstrosity I'd got myself into would blight the entire block.

While I was going to college I worked as an orderly in a psychiatric hospital, and I remember a case in which a man was signed into the institution after complaints from his neighbors that he mowed the lawn at four in the morning. My neighbors aren't that finicky, but they keep very busy pruning, gardening, and mowing their lawns. Novelist Toni Cade Bambara wrote of the spirit women in Atlanta who plant by moonlight and use conjure to reap gorgeous vegetables and flowers. A woman on this block grows roses the size of cantaloupes.

On New Year's Eve, famed landscape architect John Roberts accompanied me on my nightly walk, which takes me from 53rd Street to Aileen, Shattuck, and back to 53rd Street. He was able to identify plants and trees that had been imported from Asia, Africa, the Middle East, and Australia. On Aileen Street he discovered a banana tree! And Arthur Monroe, a painter and art historian, traces the "Tabby" garden design—in which seashells and plates are mixed with lime, sand, and water to form decorative borders, found in this Oakland neighborhood and others—to the influence of Islamic slaves brought to the Gulf Coast.

I won over my neighbors, I think, after I triumphed over a dozen generations of pigeons that had been roosting in the crevices of this house for many years. It was a long and angry war, and my five year old constantly complained to her mother about Daddy's bad words about the birds. I used everything I could get my hands on, including chicken wire and mothballs, and I would have tried the clay owls if the only manufacturer hadn't gone out of business. I also learned never to underestimate the intelligence of pigeons. Just when you think you've got them whipped, you'll notice that they've regrouped on some strategic rooftop to prepare for another invasion. When the house was free of pigeons and their droppings, which had spread to the adjoining properties, the lady next door said, "Thank you."

Every New Year's Day since then our neighbors have invited us to join them and their fellow Louisianans for the traditional Afro-American good luck meal called Hoppin' John. This year the menu included black-eyed peas, ham, corn bread, potato salad, chitterlings, greens, fried chicken, yams, head cheese, macaroni, rolls, sweet potato pie, and fruitcake. I got up that morning weighing 214 pounds and came home from the party weighing 220.

We've lived on 53rd Street for three years now. Carla's dance and theater school, which she operates with her partner, Jody Roberts—Roberts and Blank Dance/Drama—is already five years old. I am working on my seventh novel and a television production of my play *Mother Hubbard*. The house has yet to be restored to its 1906 glory, but we're working on it.

I've grown accustomed to the common sights here—teenagers moving through the neighborhood carrying radios blasting music by Grandmaster Flash and Prince, men hovering over cars with tools and rags in hand, decked-out female church delegations visiting the sick. Unemployment up, one sees more men drinking from sacks as they walk through Market Street or gather in Helen McGregor Plaza, on Shattuck and 52nd Street, near a bench where mothers sit with their children, waiting for buses. It may be because the bus stop is across the street from Children's Hospital (exhibiting a brand-new antihuman, postmodern wing), but there seem to be a lot of sick black children these days. The criminal courts and emergency rooms of Oakland hospitals, both medical and psychiatric, are also filled with blacks.

White men go from door to door trying to unload spoiled meat. Incredibly sleazy white contractors and hustlers try to entangle people into shady deals that sometimes lead to the loss of a home. Everybody knows of someone, usually a widow, who has been gypped into paying thousands of dollars more than the standard cost for, say, adding a room to a house. It sure ain't El Cerrito. In El Cerrito the representatives from the utilities were very courteous. If they realize they're speaking to someone in a black neighborhood, however, they become curt and sarcastic. I was trying to arrange for the gas company to come out to fix a stove when the woman from Pacific Gas and Electric gave me some snide lip. I told her, "Lady, if you think what you're going through is an inconvenience, you can imagine my inconvenience paying the bills every month." Even she had to laugh.

The clerks in the stores are also curt, regarding blacks the way the media regard them, as criminal suspects. Over in El Cerrito the cops were professional, respectful—in Oakland they swagger about like candidates for a rodeo. In El Cerrito and the Berkeley Hills you could take your time paying some bills, but in this black neighborhood if you miss paying a bill by one day, "reminders" printed in glaring and violent typefaces are sent to you, or you're threatened with discontinuance of this or that service. Los Angeles police victim Eulia Love, who was shot in the aftermath of an argument over an overdue gas bill, would still be alive if she had lived in El Cerrito or the Berkeley Hills.

I went to a bank a few weeks ago that advertised easy loans on television, only to be told that I would have to wait six months after opening an account to be eligible for a loan. I went home and called the same bank, this time putting on my Clark Kent voice, and was informed that I could come in and get the loan the same day. Other credit unions and banks, too, have different lending practices for black and white neighborhoods, but when I try to tell white intellectuals that blacks are prevented from developing industries because the banks find it easier to lend money in communist countries than to American citizens, they call me paranoid.

Sometimes when I know I'm going to be inconvenienced by merchants or creditors because of my 53rd Street address, I give the address of my Berkeley studio instead. Others are not so fortunate.

Despite the inconveniences and antagonism from the outside world one has to endure for having a 53rd Street address, life in this neighborhood is more pleasant than grim. Casually dressed, well-groomed elderly men gather at the intersections to look after the small children as they walk to and from school, or just to keep an eye on the neighborhood. My next-door neighbor keeps me in stitches with his informed commentary on any number of political comedies emanating from Washington and Sacramento. Once we were discussing pesticides, and the man who was repairing his porch told us that he had a great garden and didn't have to pay all that much attention to it. As for pesticides, he said, the bugs have to eat, too.

There are people on this block who still know the subsistence skills many Americans have forgotten. They can hunt and fish (and if you don't fish, there is a man who covers the neighborhood selling fresh fish and yelling, "Fishman," recalling a period of ancient American commerce when you didn't have to pay the middleman). They are also loyal Americans—they vote, they pay taxes—but you don't find the extreme patriots here that you find in white neighborhoods. Although Christmas, Thanksgiving, New Year's, and Easter are celebrated with all-get-out, I've never seen a flag flying on Memorial Day, or on any holiday that calls for the showing of the flag. Blacks express their loyalty in concrete ways. For example, you rarely see a foreign car in this neighborhood. And this 53rd Street neighborhood, as well as black neighborhoods like it from coast to coast, will supply the male children who will bear the brunt of future jungle wars, just as they did in Vietnam.

We do our shopping on a strip called Temescal, which stretches from 46th to 51st streets. Temescal, according to Oakland librarian William Sturm, is an Aztec word for "hothouse," or "bathhouse." The word was borrowed from the Mexicans by the Spanish to describe similar hothouses, early saunas, built by the California Indians in what is now North Oakland. Some say the hothouses were used to sweat out demons; others claim the Indians used them for medicinal purposes. Most agree that after a period of time in the stearn, the Indians would rush en masse into the streams that flowed through the area. One still runs underneath my backyard—I have to mow the grass there almost every other day.

Within these five blocks are the famous Italian restaurant Bertola's, "Since 1932"; Siam restaurant; La Belle Creole, a French-Caribbean restaurant; Asmara, an Ethiopian restaurant; and Ben's Hof Brau, where white and black senior citizens, dressed in the elegance of a former time, congregate to talk or have an inexpensive though quality breakfast provided by Ben's hardworking and courteous staff.

The Hof Brau shares it space with Vern's market, where you can shop to the music of DeBarge. To the front of Vern's is the Temescal Delicatessen, where a young Korean man makes the best po' boy sandwiches north of Louisiana, and near the side entrance is Ed Fraga's Automotive. The owner is always advising his customers to avoid stress, and he says goodbye with a "God bless you." The rest of the strip is taken up by the Temescal Pharmacy, which has a resident health adviser and a small library of health literature; the Aikido Institute; an African bookstore; and the internationally known Genova Deli, to which people from the surrounding cities travel to shop. The strip also includes the Clausen House thrift shop, which sells used clothes and furniture. Here you can buy novels by J.D. Salinger and John O'Hara for ten cents each.

Space that was recently occupied by the Buon Gusto Bakery is now for rent. Before the bakery left, an Italian lady who worked there introduced me to a crunchy, cookie-like treat called "bones," which she said went well with Italian wine. The Buon Gusto had been a landmark since the 1940s, when, according to a guest at the New Year's Day Hoppin' John supper, North Oakland was populated by Italians and Portuguese. In those days a five-room house could be rented for $45 a month, she said.

The neighborhood is still in transition. The East Bay Negro Historical Society, which was located around the corner on Grove Street, included in its collection letters written by nineteenth-century macho man Jack London to his black nurse. They were signed, "Your little white pickaninny." It's been replaced by the New Israelite Delight restaurant, part of the Israelite Church, which also operates a day care center. The restaurant offers homemade Louisiana gumbo and a breakfast that includes grits.

Unlike the other California neighborhoods I've lived in, I know most of the people on this block by name. They are friendly and cooperative, always offering to watch your house while you're away. The day after one of the few whites who lives on the block—a brilliant muckraking journalist and former student of mine—was robbed, neighbors gathered in front of his house to offer assistance.

In El Cerrito my neighbor was indeed a cop. He used pomade on his curly hair, sported a mustache, and there was a grayish tint in his brown eyes. He was a handsome man, with a smile like a movie star's. His was the only house on the block I entered during my three-year stay in that neighborhood, and that was one afternoon when we shared some brandy. I wanted to get to know him better. I didn't know he was dead until I saw people in black gathered on his doorstep.

I can't imagine that happening on 53rd Street. In a time when dour thinkers view alienation and insensitivity toward the plight of others as characteristics of the modern condition, I think I'm lucky to live in a neighborhood where people look out for one another.

A human neighborhood.

TOM HUTH

The Uncity of the Future

CALIFORNIA SNOWBIRD *(Nomadicum patriarchus)*
Markings: *White hair, tanned beak, lightweight polyester plumage.*
Voice: *Contented warbling. Turns to grating squawk when amplified through CB radio.*
Range: *Northern forests and streams in summer; southern deserts and shores during less temperate seasons.*
Nests: *Aluminum motor homes and trailers that can be pulled down the road at the slightest whim or inconvenience to body or soul.*

THE MAYOR, WHO ISN'T actually anybody's mayor, drives his sound truck through the streets of Slab City, which isn't really a city. He calls out through the loudspeaker: "PROPANE! WHO NEEDS THAT PROPANE? THE PROPANE TRUCK IS IN THE AREA! NOW IS THE TIME TO GET THAT PROPANE!" The citizens of Slab City are puttering around their gleaming high-tech gypsy wagons. Some sit in folding chairs upon their scraps of Astroturf front yard. The men, invariably, are tinkering with their rigs—peering underneath at their life-support systems. A few stand patiently in the dirt streets to flag down the propane truck. As far as the eye can see, they are living like this—the old folks at home, circa 1984—camped out by the thousands like runaway, children in a desert wasteland that is free for the taking.

"Hell," says the Mayor, who is sixty-six, "we couldn't pay the taxes in the city. The doctor bills, the medication were so stinkin' high. In the cities they've got sidewalks and curbs and all that stuff." He gestures out the window at The Slabs. "But we don't need that. Streetlights....We don't need *any* of that stuff."

Indeed, the real-estate amenities here are so few that they can best be described in the negative. Slab City has no electricity, no sewage system, no running water, not a single telephone. It is no more—and no less—than a stretch of bleached hardpan in the Imperial Valley outback whose sole creature comforts are the bare concrete-slab foundations of the abandoned military post where Patton is said to have trained his troops to fight in North Africa. The residents simply park their self-contained rigs in the dust and shove little piles of rocks together to indicate their respective turfs; or the more established campers settle on the slabs themselves, which are marvelously level.

The Slabs. It makes for a strange and stirring sight: this senior citizen army amassed in dreamy wintertime retreat, their porta-palaces bivouacked among the clumps of sage brush, ironwood, and creosote bushes, their TV and CB antennas casting up for stray signals from the civilization they've left behind.

The Mayor, a transplanted New Englander, a short, sun-ripened man with a determined jaw, reasons: "This beats the rest home all to pieces. Instead of paying $3,000 a month, we're taking that burden off the taxpayers. If we're happy in a place like this...if people leave us alone...I think this is a better deal."

The deal, unspoken, works like this: In return for accepting such rude accommodations, the people of this perennially blooming city enjoy a scandalous amount of freedom compared with the rest of us. They pay no rents, mortgages, or time-sharing fees. They answer to no one, live under the sway of no known government. The State of California, which owns the land, exerts no presence whatsoever. The officials of Imperial County pay scant attention to snowbirds, who tend to mind their own business and keep tidy encampments. The feds merely send them their social security checks care of the post office at Niland, three miles away. What's more, the Slab People resist all attempts at self-government or self-organization. They have formed no community associations, erected no street signs, posted no regulations of any kind. Slab City is just here. Except in the summer, when it's not.

Al Hilton is called the Mayor because he's such a civic minded fellow and, besides, that's his CB handle. He calls through the loudspeaker: "IF YOU NEED PROPANE, YOU DO NOT HAVE TO MOVE YOUR RIG! IT'LL BE PIPED RIGHT IN!"

An elderly gent whips past us in a three-wheeled all terrain vehicle. The Mayor explains matter of factly: "He's a member of the Apple Dumpling Gang. They roam all over the desert and the Chocolate Mountains....They go way over the Colorado River into Arizona." Other seniors can be seen scooting about on motorcycles and mopeds, riding bikes, walking.

This looks suspiciously like a movement: the gerontocracy in training for that promised day when everyone except Dick Clark will be over sixty-five. Actually, it represents several movements of the seventies and eighties—the dispersal of Americans to less-populated places, where they cluster for safety and familiarity; the segregation of Americans by age in their own residential complexes; the decline of the single-family home in favor of more economical housing that takes up less space. If it's true that we have to grow old, then we can look at the Slab lifestyle as an increasingly popular way to go.

According to Hilton, who has wintered on The Slabs for more than fifteen years, about 25,000 rigs come here for a part of each year, with a steady seasonal population of 2,000 residents. In addition to this place, tens of thousands of snowbirds migrate to other offcial and unofficial trailer parks throughout the Southwest. The Yuma, Arizona, area alone is reputed to be the nesting ground for 30,000 of them. Nationally, the number of people who live full time on wheels is estimated (no one can count them—they won't stand stlll for it) in the hundreds of thousands.

Mayor Hilton observes: "You cannot count per month or per week or per hour because they're comin' and goin' night and day."

As we ride through the uncity, we see two Air Force jets engaging in a mock dogfight high in the cloudless eastern sky. Other Slab dwellers are watching, too, from beside their rigs. In fact, out here on this flat-earth moonscape between the Salton Sea and the Coachella Irrigation Canal—a place with no theaters, no restaurants, no recreation centers, no golf courses, no swimming pools, no stores, no daily papers save The Brawley News, no badminton courts, no stop signs—the flyboys of the Army, Navy, Air Force, and Marines provide the live entertainment. Almost every evening they make spectacular bombing runs into the Chocolate Mountains ten miles distant. KA-BOOM! KA-BOOOMMM! The little metal shelters of the Slab People shudder on their trusty Goodyears.

Bulletins from the six o'clock news, CB Channel 23, Slab City:

> For people who are concerned and wanting information on Ben and Marie King, better known as Sabre Jet and Candy Apple, he's been having a medical problem, so we sent him into San Diego today for further tests. Now the word is going around that he's got cancer. We don't know this. All we know is that down in Brawley they found something up in the pancreas area that they couldn't identify....

> Breaker 23. This is the Sun Devil. We're up in Area Seven. Somebody picked up a wooden step with green imitation grass on top of it and took off with it....we'd like to have it back, if possible.

THESE ARE NOT wealthy people, mind you. If they could afford Newport Beach, that's probably where they'd be. Instead, for the most part they are solidly, steadfastly, sincerely middle class. These are the kind of people who once cherished the notion of having a hometown to call their own—a deed to some small, fenced piece of God's green earth, a yard, a garden, a tree for the kids to climb, an address, a place they could always come back to. And many of them had just that. But then, as the years went by, the kids grew up and flew the coop, and longtime friends departed for Sun City or Sarasota, and the old neighborhood changed, and it didn't feel much like home anymore.

At the same time, by the 1970s motor-coach companies were turning out units with flush toilets, full baths, microwave ovens, king-size beds, air conditioning, color TVs, central vacuum—rolling suburbanesque dollhouses with all the comforts of home plus CB systems just like the truckers had. How easy it was for Mom and Pop to trade in that four-bedroom ghost house in Cedar Rapids for a shiny new Winnebago—for a Four Winds, a Wilderness, a Commander, an Explorer, a Swinger, or a Free Spirit. They had always wanted to get out and see the country, hadn't they? They'd worked all their lives, as it turned out, for this opportunity to spend their remaining winters in a place where it was sinfully warm and their arthritis wouldn't kick up and no one, but no one, would bother them.

That was the dream, anyway.

Merrill Chapman, a retired service rep for Xerox, spends his winters on The Slabs and his summers as a campground host in Oregon. In Slab City he and his wife live on Main Street (such as it is) because he sells Honda generators in the gravel outside their thirty-five-foot Komfort Fifth-Wheel. He remembers their leave-taking this way: "After the kids grew up, we found that material things didn't mean that much to us anymore. So we gave those things to the children to help them get started, and we went to the simpler life, which is much more comfortable. You're not a prisoner of all the possessions you've accumulated." Chapman, a thoughtful, silver-haired man, feels sorry for those snowbirds who have houses to return to. "Come spring they say, 'I've got to get home, I've got to get back to do this, this, this, this. Pay the taxes, pay the insurance, repair this.' For me, I didn't want that have-to-go-back, have-to-go-back.

"I don't have a lawn to mow," he says, pointing to his yard outlined with stones. "I make this up when I come back in the fall, and in the spring I take these rocks and put them back in the bushes, and I rake this all out, and you won't see a wheel track. And that's what ninety-nine percent of the snow-birds do when they come to an area like this—they leave it cleaner and better looking than when they arrived. That's the snowbird way of life."

Virginia Martin, who belongs to a social-minded singles group called Loners on Wheels, which has nearly 3,000 members, remarks: "Oh, it's a wonderful, wonderful thing for these people who otherwise would be sitting home in a rocking chair. Our oldest member will be ninety-four years old in March and pulls an Airstream. And we had one woman who passed away a couple of years ago who had only one leg, and she pulled her own trailer."

As she speaks, about two dozen Loners on Wheels are enjoying their regular afternoon happy hour. They sit drinking out of plastic glasses and camper mugs and listening to an accordionist play songs from their youth. "The thing is," Martin says, "it keeps them alive longer, and it keeps them well. They keep going...there's something down the road; what's on the other side of that hill...? Well, I don't feel like going today, but, by gosh, I'm going to get up and go tomorrow!"

This same sense of spunky self-satisfaction runs through most conversations with the Slab People. But, you know, they're right: This is an ingenious solution. They have beaten the system, or at least finessed it. It seems preposterous that a Slab City could even be allowed to happen—that, in an age when most of us are being crowded into condos, these Americans could be permitted to plunk down their houses willy-nilly on public property, set up homesteads there, form entire cities and then abandon them to the wind, all without official sanction or recompense. Neat.

Jim Childress, who was until recently a land agent for the State Land Board Commission, which holds title to The Slabs, points out that snowbirds "don't have any inherent rights to stay there for free," and yet he quickly adds that the state doesn't have "the resources or staff to check up on all those parcels." So, Childress declares, "we let nature take its course." The federal government is equally cooperative: The Bureau of Land Management designates "long-term visitor areas" where people can live on wheels for eight months at a time, free.

Wealthier motorhome migrants live at posh RV resorts—plug-in country clubs that offer golf, tennis, swimming, and stage shows along with full utility hookups. But the Slab People and their brethren make do for themselves. They get their power from generators or from solar panels and wind chargers. They buy their propane and water from trucks that make regular rounds. They bury their sewage tubes under the sand—gopher holes, they call them—and exclaim: "Why, the ground's so dry here, it just turns this stuff to dust!"

The rigs in which they live range from piggyback camper shells that can be bought secondhand for a few hundred dollars to motor coaches and professionally retrofitted buses that can cost $200,000 and are so large that they have video cameras in the rear to help the drivers back up.

When snowbirds aren't roosting on some government no-man's-land, they're moving about from campground to campground, or parked quietly on a side street in Palm Springs or La Jolla for the night, or visiting friends and relatives from coast to coast. It's easy: They just pull into brother Bob's driveway, run a 110-volt line into his basement, and they're home. Anywhere, so long as it's level. And warm.

Harry Watson, who lives with his wife in a remodeled Trailways Sceni-Cruiser, puts it this way: "The first snowflake that hits me is God's fault—the second's my own." The snowbird's creed.

Slab People are sensitive to the accusation, made publicly by a county supervisor, that they are "freeloaders." On the other hand, they take great delight in locating a deal. "Let's not put it cheapskates," Watson says. "Let's put it, they're very economy-wise and they don't spring for nothing. You can go out here to the swap meet and peddle something, and if it ain't a bargain they ain't buyin'." The snowbird way of life.

> Break 23. This is the Gray Wolf up in number seven. I have an electric trailerjack I'd like to sell. If anybody's interested, I'll be down at the swap meet. . . .
>
> Yeah, go ahead, Lucky Lady. Little Mac and Big Mac wanted me to tell the people that they lost their Pekingese dog this morning, dark brown in color. Its name is Cheetah. It is deaf and partially blind. . . .
>
> I got a single-shot Stevens bolt-action rifle I'd like to sell. Also, I got a whirling red light like on the highway patrol cars. . . .

WHEN THE SLAB-NESTING snowbirds pass in the streets, they call out to each other, "Hi, there!" and "Good morning!" like the happy-go-lucky day hikers on a National Park nature trail. But what would life be, after all, without a few problems, something to chatter about on the radio? Because there are others who live on The Slabs besides docile retirees. It is anybody's land, up for grabs.

Some RVers grouse about the increasing number of younger families scattered among them. A woman on a bicycle declares to a newcomer in a station wagon: "There's no jobs and so they go on welfare—and some of 'em living better than us! Five, six kids—and getting paid for each one of 'em! Why, they're living so good out here they don't want anything else!"

The Mayor, on his rounds with the propane truck, points to two teenage boys who are trying to hitch a ride out of town and observes sourly: "They're not in school and they don't have no work, and all they want to do is raise hell out here. The parents let 'em run in the streets. First thing you know, somebody'll have a bonfire and these kids'll come along and throw bullets right in the middle of the fire! And they'll go off!"

There is some thievery. Occasionally, a generator will vanish in the night or a battery will be lifted. Consequently, Slab City is well armed. "Oh, yes!" the snowbirds exclaim, surprised I should ask. "Of course, everybody carries guns!"

A sheriff's deputy—one of two who patrol The Slabs on a casual basis—discounts the crime element. "Their main thing," he says, "is fighting over which group owns which CB channel." But then he recalls a shooting last year down in The Wash on the less reputable outskirts of Slab City and another incident the year before when an old man was dragged out into the desert, beaten, and buried half alive.

The snowbirds' first line of defense against any sort of emergency is its pair of CB radio networks. Here, from the safety of their own capsules, they can reach out for one another and share a tentative community. "It's exciting!" the woman on the bike tells the one who has just arrived on The Slabs. "You talk to somebody on the CB and wonder what they're like. Then you go out and meet folks and see if they match their handle!"

Every evening at 6 A.M. a throaty woman code-named Double P comes on Channel 23 to emcee a news and announcement program. If a Slab Citizen needs medical attention, the word is relayed via CB to a listener in Niland named Sky Pilot (a minister in real life), who telephones for an ambulance or paramedics. If someone on The Slabs needs to be located in a hurry, a good ol' boy named Rolling Stone will hunt him down with his P.A. system and flashing yellow dome light.

Although, as one gentleman remarked, "We're all characters when we get old," Rolling Stone has a particular flair. He is seventy-six years old, used to do logging and haul wild horses in the Pacific Northwest, and is now so round in the middle that if he were placed on the ground he probably would roll like a stone. He lives in a yesteryear mail truck painted with before and after murals of Mount Saint Helens, and he drives around making announcements through his loudspeaker for a small fee. Whenever one sees Rolling Stone, he is perched on that pedestal seat, wedged into the truck. For him, it seems, the motorized life is not just a style but a crucial adaptation. The speaker on the roof extends his range, gets him out where his legs cannot.

One day, for example, as he sits parked on Main Street he notices a woman on the next slab drawing water from a one-hundred-gallon tank. He snatches up his microphone, and his voice booms out through the stillness: "HEY, MA'AM! THAT WATER BELONGS TO THE MAN NEXT TO YOU!"

She looks up, startled. Shouts back weakly, "I thought he was gone!"

"YOU'RE WRONG!" the voice scolds. "THAT'S NOT THE CASE!" Rolling Stone watches over The Slabs, helps to keep an unofficial justice, enforces common decency, befriends the luckless. The man whose water rights he defended now pulls up in a van—a rickety little guy with one arm. Rolling Stone blares out: "HI, BOB! HOW YA DOIN'?"

Bob shuffles over to the truck. "Still kickin'," he allows. "But not very high."

Rolling Stone asks, "I heard you had trouble with your brakes....Some body might have cut the line, eh?"

"Yep!"

"Oh my God!"

"Cut the line and took my trailer key."

"Lord have mercy!" the big man cries. "I drove back from Julian with no brakes," Bob laments.

"Jiminy, God Almighty! Ain't that awful!"

"Lost my billfold 'long the way."

Rolling Stone reaches for his own wallet. Pulls out two fives. Overhead, swarms of helicopters are beating their blades, flying north over The Slabs on their way to the Chocolate Mountains. The choppers have been passing over all day—big Hueys with supply tanks dangling down from their bellies. They're taking part in maneuvers staged by the Army's Sixth Cavalry Brigade down in Holtville. The word around Slab City is that one hundred snowbirds are parked for the winter on the old Holtville airstrip, and now they're right in the middle of the make-believe battlefield. Those lucky ducks.

IT'S MOVIE NIGHT at the camper's Christian Center. Housed in an office trailer, the center is the only formal gathering place in town, but its activities don't exactly cause traffic jams. Its most popular event is the free Tuesday blood-pressure readings given by a visiting nurse. On Saturday nights the Christian Center shows films, and this week it is *Stagecoach*, the John Wayne classic. The snowbirds sit, rapt, in metal folding chairs as the stagecoach—basically, the original RV—leaves civilization behind and heads into Indian territory. A fellow calls out from the audience: "Sure beats a Toyota!" The woman behind me whispers to her friend: "He was always my favorite, John Wayne. Got a picture of him on the door of my fridge." But let's not kid ourselves: This is a dangerous journey, a dangerous world. The Apaches are all around—and you can bet they're not just out to rip off a Yamaha generator.

Now it is nighttime. The stagecoach passengers have made camp. Clare Trevor wanders away from the fire and John Wayne warns: "Don't go too far, Miss Dallas. Apaches like to sneak up and pick off strays." But he isn't one to mince words. He sidles up to her and proposes: "Look, Miss Dallas, you've got no folks and neither have I....I've got a ranch across the border. It's a nice place. A real nice place. Trees, grass, water. There's a cabin there, half built. A man could live there. But it'd be...lonely." Yes, we understand this dream: a little patch of heaven for a retired gunslinger and his gal. The dialogue is drowned out by a new wave of helicopters beating low over the Christian Center. . whap whap whap whap whap. A woman whispers, "They're circling us now!" In the end, the cavalry rides in to rout the Apaches, and John Wayne takes off for that sunny southern paradise with the girl, who is tougher than she looks.

IN THE SUMMER out on The Slabs, it gets so hot that, at night, Harry Watson says, "My wife wets down a cot and lays on it and then lays a wet towel over her, and that's how she sleeps—kind of soppy." He points to the remnant of all-weather carpet next to his unit and adds, "But I sleep dry. I just curl up on that rug there." It gets so hot that any self-respecting snowbird is long gone to some forest camp in the Cascades. The only people left in Slab City are those dozen or so local households whose sprawling tin and plywood Hoover-villian encampments stand out in grim and comic relief against the sea of snazzy heat-reflective aluminum. The year-rounders are the ones with the junked autos in their yards, the heaps of scrap iron, the unruly dogs, the chickens, the goats, the discarded tires, the children. The ones whom the snowbirds call (as if to set them apart) "squatters." Charles Tye is one of them. In fact, he says, he has lived on this land since 1934—before there even were slabs. His neighbors back then were men like Whistlin' Jack and Blinkin' Jack, Two-Step Shorty, Hood River Blackie, and Stovepipe.

Nowadays, the grizzly-chinned Tye resides on the slab of a former bar-racks right down the street from the Mayor and his wife Lucky Lady. He lives in an eight-by-six-foot camper shell that is part of a much larger compound that includes an old school bus, several shacks and shanties, two outhouses, thirteen people of various generations, and Tye's big, black dog, Nigger. Of his neighbors, Tye opines: "They're ass-holes. Them ain't neighbors. They've got the place ruined. No privacy, no nothin'. Drive down the road...they get in front of you...five, ten miles an hour...." Still, it merely amuses him. "They come down here and we cuss them out," he says. "Then we go up to Oregon and they cuss us out." He shrugs. "It all works out."

Tye understands that there are people in the county government—and clean-nosed neighbors here in Slab City—who would like the permanent settlements wiped out. Recently, a man came up from El Centro to inform Tye that the only buildings allowed were those on wheels. But Tye says that a strange thing happens when those government agents come by. "You get deaf. You don't hear nothin'."

Tye probably has the lowest blood pressure in Slab City (though surely he doesn't have it monitored at the Christian Center). He says of the bureaucrats: "I figure they got plenty of machinery. If they want to tear it down, there ain't no hard feelings. Let 'em tear it down...He motions toward his '60 Chevy. "I got a bed right in the back there...fishin' gear and everything. All I have to do is get in it and go."

Other denizens, too, fly in different circles than the snowbirds. The road into Slab City is lined with that teeming and rapidly spreading form of mobile Western commerce known as the swap meet. Auto, RV, and appliance repairmen offer their services alongside people who sell leatherwork, fresh fruit, and an enormous variety of junk. There's even an H&R Block agent. The air is like a carnival, and in fact, there are some old carny people on the strip, along with country people, unrepentant hippies, and desert rats. Some of them live down in The Wash. Nevertheless, the attitude is roughly the same as the snowbirds'. A swap-meeter named Robus tells me: "I've got a three-wheeler, a Jeep, a motorcycle, a Cadillac, and this bus. I can go anywhere around here. There's so much private space, and what I really love is the six-gun law. Ain't nobody messes with me here. You ain't got no system here. You're your own law here. You do right...or you get buried."

The farther one ventures into the suburbs (as it were) of Slab City, away from the safety of the pack, the more variegated the humanscape becomes. Lanny LaRue lives rent free in one of Patton's old ammunition bunkers on private land west of The Slabs. He lives there with his grandson, his goats, his seventeen French poodles, and his abiding dream of leading a crusade to save the hungry children of the world from starvation. Tears come to LaRue's eyes when he describes the parade he envisions: the huge bell tolling once every two seconds, every time a child dies. Tears trickle down his cheeks when he pictures himself—his white mane flying in the wind—telling the gathered multitudes about redemption and atonement. He explains, he apologizes: "In my later years, I've been very much concerned about humanity."

MEANWHILE, BACK IN the city, a CB jock is asking if anybody knows how to lift up a monochromatic toilet so he can lay down some new carpet. It is a Sunday afternoon in late January. The sun is shining, as usual. It's the same old eighty degrees. A man strolls Main Street in a safari hat. A carryall with Minnesota plates drives past with its horn tootling out the notes to "Glory, Glory, Hallelujah." I am sitting on the vacant slab in the center of town with two boys, Bryan and Tim. They have lived on The Slabs for most of their lives, winter and summer. Bryan, who is eighteen, declares: "Slab City sucks." For excitement, he says, "you stand out in the rain with a bar of soap." The horn is still tootling in the distance: "...He is trampling out the vintage where the grapes of wrath are stored...." The paper in my lap says that Imperial County's unemployment rate is holding steady at thirty-two percent. Bryan and Tim laugh when they admit that they were the ones who tossed the bullets into those people's campfire, for something to do. But the people had gone to bed. And they was just blanks, anyway.

That night the southern sky is ablaze with flares. Slab Man and Slab Woman sit in their folding chairs, watching in wonder. The flares are shooting up from behind the mountains, from Holtville, where the Army is holding its maneuvers.

Slab Man says: "They must be having a night game."

Slab Woman answers: "Well, I suppose so."

The rest of the sky is a perfect half globe of stars. The Slab People know the city folks will not see these stars tonight, even though they're free. The desert air is still—no breeze at all—and blessedly quiet. Not a sound to be heard, except for the consoling chatter of the diesel generator and the far-away percussions of the Sixth Cavalry making America safe for democracy.

VII.
Law and Order

PETER COLLIER AND DAVID HOROWITZ

Getting Away with Murder

W HAT FIRST ATTRACTED Wayne and Joan Pope to the Carousel
Apartments in Concord, nineteen miles northeast of Oakland, was
the sign outside the manager's Office: FOR FAMILIES WITH CHILDREN. They had
looked at other apartments where they had been made to feel that kids were
a liability. Carousel seemed different—not just another stop on the way but a
place where they could settle in. They already had two daughters; a son was
born shortly after they moved in.

Joan Pope tried to involve herself in every aspect of her children's lives.
The rapport among them was so strong that she sometimes felt the family
was a psychic union. Working as a volunteer in the Concord schools, she was
disheartened by the number of children who had none of this closeness, kids
who had the necessities but were otherwise left to fend for themselves.
Michael Garcia was one of them. He and his mother lived in the same
apartment complex as the Popes; he had been in the same sixth-grade class as
their oldest daughter, Pam. As far as Joan could tell, Michael had never really
known his Chicano father. His mother worked full-time, and her parents, an
old-worldish Japanese couple, seemed unable to understand him. What
struck Joan particularly were the stories he wrote and the drawings he made.
The images and words showed an obsession with warfare: bombs exploding,
airplanes mercilessly strafing antlike victims, tanks squashing the life out of
humans caught in their inexorable treads.

Her own children were a world away from the one inhabited by this sad
and brooding boy, and she was glad of it. Blonde and blue eyed, and
unquenchably enthusiastic in the manner of girls her age, Pam Pope
especially seemed on top of things. She did well in school and had many
friends, but what impressed her mother most was that she never tried to
improve her own social standing by scorning pariahs like Michael. When he
knocked on the door one afternoon and asked Pam to come up and help him
with his math, she agreed without hesitation. A premonitory shadow passed
through Joan Pope's mind: Michael was always alone and untended, and, on
the threshold of their thirteenth birthdays (they had been born within days of
each other), he and Pam were both budding into adolescence. But Joan
trusted her daughter to do the right thing and merely reminded her to be

back soon because they were going to an Oakland A's family night game as soon as her father got off work.

Pam hadn't returned by five o'clock. When Joan went to ask where she was, Michael said she had left shortly after arriving. Joan looked all around the building and then returned to the Garcia apartment. By this time Michael's mother was home from work. She said that Michael had become ill and couldn't come to the door. Joan got some teenage friends of Pam's to help with the search. Finally she called the police. While everyone rushed in and out of her living room, she sat down for a moment and collected her thoughts. She caught an image of the building's garbage disposal area. Feeling sick already, she asked one of the teenagers to go down and investigate the green plastic bags under the dumpster.

"And of course that's where they found her," Joan says. "What happened is that when they got to his place, Michael made sexual advances, which Pammy rebuffed. This made him angry, and when she turned to leave he picked up a bicycle chain and strangled her. And he proceeded to rape her. The policeman who investigated told me that there was blood all over the rug. Michael tried to wash the blood, but it wouldn't come clean. Finally he wrapped Pammy in a couple of garbage bags and carried her downstairs to the parking lot. He tried to put her in the dumpster, but he couldn't lift her, so he shoved her underneath."

It was late 1977 when Michael Garcia was placed in the custody of the California Youth Authority. Joan Pope knew that the boy was deeply disturbed; rather than wishing for vengeance she was glad that he would get the long-term attention he obviously needed. For herself, she knew that it would be impossible to put Pam's murder behind her, but she hoped to distance it enough in time to pick up the pieces of the family's life. She was still concentrating on this task in 1980 when she heard that Michael was back in Concord again.

His presence might never have become known if the mother of a high school girl he was dating hadn't become suspicious of him and the unexplained hiatus in his past, begun talking to people at the police department and city hall, and found out about Pam Pope. The newspapers got wind of the story and made it an emotional issue in the community. The judge who had presided over the case said that he was distressed by Michael's release. Police pleaded with the Youth Authority at least to release Garcia in another town.

The fragile truce Jean Pope had declared with her daughter's fate was broken. She now found herself wondering about something she had never before considered—the justice of it all. "I had one question for the Youth Authority," she says. "That question was, why? Why was Michael released?

Why was he kept so short a time? I kept asking, but the Youth Authority never answered. They just said that as far as they were concerned, he was 'rehabilitated.'"

Joan Pope wondered how it was possible for someone who had done what Michael did to have been rehabilitated in so short a time. As she looked into it, however, she found that the handling of the Garcia case was no bureaucratic lapse. It was part of a pattern. While Michael Garcia was in the custody of the Youth Authority, Arnold Magallanes, an eighteen-year-old member of the Northside Gang in Baldwin Park, decided to go for a drive one morning and kill some rivals. Aiming out the window of Magallanes's car, he and two friends shot at a seventeen-year-old youth walking to school. Missing him, they drove to a high school and loosed a volley of gunfire at two students, missing again. Finally they pulled alongside a fourteen-year-old boy, shot him five times, and left him for dead. The Los Angeles County probation department, which had already dealt with Magallanes on a prior offense, asked for "maximum sentencing." Two corrections officers and a psychologist who examined him said that he was so aggressive and sophisticated in his criminality that he ought to go directly to adult prison. Disregarding this advice, the judge in the case made Magallanes a ward of the Youth Authority. The Youth Authority held him for just seven months before putting him back on the streets.

In April 1980, Francis Hernandez age seventeen, was paroled by the Youth Authority after serving six months for burglary. Nine months later he was arrested for committing two brutal sex murders in Long Beach. Darryl Ivory, also seventeen, was released after doing twenty months for auto theft and robbery. During the two weeks he was on parole before being rearrested, he was involved in a series of fourteen holdups, including one in which he killed a paperboy. Eighteen-year-old Donald Ortiz was released by the Youth Authority during the 1980 holiday season and killed a young Whittier man on Christmas Day.

"It's a shameful situation," says Joan Pope. "They say their policies are ment to protect the kids they have to deal with. But they don't care about kids like Michael or they wouldn't treat them—and the rest of—so cynically. The Youth Authority just cares about its own power. The people that run the organization seem to like playing God with children's lives."

THE CHILD SAVERS

CALIFORNIA IS THE youth crime and punishment capital of the nation. On any given day there are more than 8,000 young people in custody here, three times the number in any other state. California employs more than a quarter of all staff involved in youth corrections nationally and spends twenty-three cents of every dollar the county devotes to juvenile offenders. At the apex of this weighty bureaucracy sits the California Youth Authority (CYA, or YA). Agency of last resort for the most serious young criminals the state has produced, the CYA is also the last stop on the tragic path leading from juvenile hall to adult prison and the last chance for the increasingly hard-pressed juvenile justice system to have any credibility whatsoever. It is because the Youth Authority occupies such a crucial position that policies such as these are so shocking:

● Allowing gangs and violence to dominate the atmosphere of its institutions.

● Releasing as "treated" troubled and dangerous young criminals, most of whom have never been forced to deal with their crimes.

● Holding serious offenders for scandalously brief confinements.

● Giving only minimal supervision during parole and frequently obstructing law enforcement agencies that must deal with parolees who commit more crimes.

● Suppressing research and statistics that show the dimensions of its failure to have any effect on the control of juvenile crime in this state.

The Youth Authority today—contemptuous of public safety, monstrously inefficient, an edifice of semantic deceit—is the end product of a long and complex history of youth connection in California, what Joan Pope accurately describes as playing God with children's lives. It is possible to see a piece of this history by going to the small town of Ione and visiting the old Preston School of Industry, commissioned by the legislature in 1889 as part of the state's first big move into the emerging field of juvenile corrections. Told to design a structure that looked as little like a prison as possible, architects drew plans for a huge brick castle of 120 rooms that looked as though it had been plucked out of the Rhine Valley and deposited by whim on a rise in the middle of the Mother Lode. The bricks are crumbling now. The castle hasn't been used for twenty-two years, but it still stands, an eccentric ghost from the bygone era when the juvenile justice system was concerned about wayward kids, orphans, and runaways instead of murderers and sex criminals.

Preston and its companion school in Whittier were part of a movement that had been gaining momentum in the United States since the early nineteenth century, when courts began to hold that the state had a right, indeed a duty, to assume guardianship of children abandoned or abused by their natural parents. *Parens patriae*—as this doctrine was known—was the outgrowth of the Enlightenment belief in the innate innocence of all human beings, especially the young. It became the justification for the development of juvenile courts from which the public, the press, lawyers, and all other participants in the adversary system would be excluded. It also became the justification for child-saving institutions like Preston that would accept wards from juvenile court and divert them from lives of vice and idleness.

In the fifties, the first decade in which juvenile delinquency was acknowledged as a major social problem, the Youth Authority began an ambitious building program that soon gave it four forestry camps, ten schools, and two 300-bed intake clinics (or "reception centers," as they were known in the agency's argot) in the northern and southern parts of the state. At this moment of transition, a modernized "campus" was built at Preston, and the old castle, which had housed thousands of boys in a half century of operation, was scheduled for demolition, a death sentence that was stayed at the last minute when architectural historians proved that the structure was an excellent example of Romanesque revival.

When California's adult prisons seemed to be on the verge of terminal violence in the sixties, the Youth Authority was the only upbeat story in state corrections. Foreign penologists came to visit Preston and the other institutions, as did correctional officers from other states. They applauded the YA as uniquely progressive, one of the few such agencies open to new developments. In 1966, for example, after running its own pilot program on the effects of diversion (then regarded as one of the promising trends in penology), the Youth Authority initiated a probation subsidy program under which it made grants to counties to keep serious offenders in the community under intensive probation supervision rather than shipping them to the YA. Population in the Youth Authority institutions began to drop. Six new schools on the drawing boards for the Stockton and Chino areas were shelved, and three of the existing schools were closed. Juvenile court judges liked the idea of keeping youthful offenders out of institutions where they might be "labeled" as criminals. The counties liked the $4,000 grant they got as a sort of bounty for each delinquent they kept in the community. The YA liked the idea that it was winning the war against juvenile crime.

By the early seventies the strategy had fallen apart. Juvenile courts were putting repeat offenders on repeated probation. The $4,000 that had looked so attractive a few years earlier no longer bought anything like intensive supervision. A system designed to deal primarily with truants, runaways, and incorrigibles—the so-called status offenders—was under assault by a new clientele that committed crimes against people, not just against property or public decency, crimes that challenged received notions about childhood and human nature itself. Michael Garcia was just one of the new clientele. Sixteen-year-old Todd Gjevre murdered his parents for their insurance money. Jay Geha, seventeen, bludgeoned an elderly Moraga woman to death when she questioned him about property he had stolen. Sharon

Wright, fifteen, shot a San Francisco cabbie in the back of the head during a holdup. Jake Trujillo, a seventeen-year-old gang member, killed another young man by ramming him with his car. And for each of these individuals whose offense made news, there were dozens more who remained anonymous case histories inside the Youth Authority.

By the end of the seventies, juvenile crime had become a new ball game, as the Youth Authority knew very well, since places like Preston had become war zones where violent young criminals assaulted staff almost as frequently as they did each other. But to have frankly addressed the changed reality would have been to admit the extent to which the whole system of juvenile justice in California had failed. And so the YA continued to play by the old rules. Administrators still called their wards "kids," although their average age had climbed to over eighteen, and referred to offenses such as murder and rape as "delinquent acts." Institutional jargon still employed phrases like "acting out" and "exhibiting poor impulse control," as if the YA were dealing with children guilty of nothing more than first-degree tantrums. The Youth Authority still claimed to be in the business of "rehabilitation," although its parolees, beneficiaries of a bureaucratic fundamentalism that washed their records clean and made them born-again innocents, recommitted crimes at such high rates that San Quentin, Folsom, and other adult prisons had come to resemble YA alumni organizations.

Throughout 1981, YA administrators made brave attempts to celebrate the agency's fortieth birthday. The California Youth Authority had, in fact, come a long way. It had begun as a three-man board trying to upgrade the quality of youth corrections and had wound up a swollen bureaucracy with more than 4,000 employees, one for every three wards under its supervision, spending $250 million a year. It had begun as a handful of idealists wanting to save the souls of delinquent children and had wound up accounting for dangerous young criminals as units of bed space. Its elaborate, almost theological self-justifications had become so well-known in the law enforcement community that cops and DAs shared the joke that the letters CYA actually stood for "Cover Your Ass."

PREP SCHOOL FOR PRISON

THE PRESTON SCHOOL OF INDUSTRY today is really not a school, nor are its wards particularly industrious. It has the forced cheer of a summer camp for boys who may not want to be there; the unacknowledged prison beneath this disguise keeps showing through. Working staff are armed only with holstered Mace and tear gas, but security men in idling vans materialize as if by magic whenever a group of the institution's 580 wards rotates from one activity to another during the day. The "lodges" in which they live have names in keeping with the bucolic setting, but even they turn out to be part of an ominous code. (Linden is protective custody for homosexuals, informers, child molesters, and others who might get "shanked" by a knife made in an arts and crafts class; Tamarack is Preston's equivalent of solitary, where wards who have committed a serious assault sleep out their days in double-locked cells; Juniper is where they put the dangerous repeat offenders the staffers call "knuckledraggers.") If ambiguity is more deeply engraved on Preston's identity than on other Youth Authority institutions, it is because this is the "big house" for the northern part of the state, handling the older wards and those who have caused trouble elsewhere and been shipped here, the last stop on the route to Soledad, as part of what is known as "bus therapy."

An outsider sees only the symbols of the gangs (blacks wearing blue or red bandannas—"flying the rag," as it is called—to indicate gang affiliation, Chicanos adorning their possessions and sometimes their bodies with the boxy, graffito-like letters and emblems of the placa that tell whose home boy they are). White inmates, who constitute about thirty percent of the YA's prison population, tend to remain aloof from gang activities, but for the majority they are a fact of life. Administrators must juggle the numbers of blacks and Chicanos in the dorms so that the less organized and aggressive black gangs can hold their own. "It's like in the joint," says one ex-con who graduated from Preston to San Quentin. "Gangs are part of the scheme of things. The administration doesn't even try to get rid of them. It just tries to use them to establish a balance, which it can tip any way it wants."

One of the few places exempt from this atmosphere of latent menace is Redwood Lodge, a thirty-five-bed intensive treatment program for wards who might be sent to mental hospitals if they weren't so dangerous. A self-contained therapeutic community within the Preston campus, Redwood has psychologists, social workers, nurses, and counselors working with wards whose days are scheduled hourly from an impressive menu of therapeutic modalities—assertiveness training, shyness group, bioenergetics exercises, interpersonal process recall, and so on. The program is designed for those whom supervising psychiatrist Dan Palmer calls "crazies" and the rest of Preston's population refer to as "dings": the young man who swallowed spoons, toothbrushes, and other objects; the one who rolled himself into his blanket and refused to emerge for food or disposal of body waste; the one who cowered in a corner, afraid to sleep because of the demons ready to inhabit his body. Redwood excludes those whom diagnostic tests identify as relatively sane but "hardened types." Of this group Palmer says, "They are so rigidly set in their criminal ways that even intensive treatment is useless. For them criminality is so intrinsic that their personalities would crumble without it." In all, fewer than five percent of Preston's population receives treatment at Redwood. The rest see a consulting psychiatrist for half an hour a year—when the annual report that may get them paroled is being prepared.

Training and treatment are at the heart of the Youth Authority's mandate, the subjects its administrators stress in their publicity and the reason the agency spends $24,000 a year per ward, almost double the sum allotted for an inmate of an adult prison. But the training received at a place like Preston is of questionable value. Wards move in and out of trade programs according to whim and disciplinary status. Only fifteen percent of all YA parolees find jobs utilizing skills they have learned in the institution, and sixty percent of them experience prolonged unemployment. As for treatment, it is virtually nonexistent.

"We're lucky if the kids in the general population see a counselor privately once every week or two," Preston superintendant James Embree admits. "We'd like to deal more with anger and acting out, but we have such limited resources that this is impossible. To the extent that we do much counseling at all, it is basic survival stuff that might be helpful on the outside—how to rent an apartment, how to use public transportation, how not to react by picking up something and hitting your boss the first time he criticizes you on the job."

A tall, articulate black man who grew up in Harlem and went into corrections work after a stint in the marines and a college basketball career, Embree is aware of the inadequacies of the situation. "I never claim that a guy should be released from Preston because he's 'cured.' I just say that he's gone as far as he can go given what we can offer him. With a lot of the guys who leave here that means practically nowhere. We know that. Some haven't been touched. A few may actually go back out there worse than when they came in. But what can we do? If we were to keep them in YA until they were ready to go out, really ready it wouldn't be possible to build enough institutions in the state to hold them all."

What is true at Preston is true of the Youth Authority generally, although few administrators confront the issues as forthrightly as Embree. The illusion that the young people who go through its institutions have been rehabilitated is central to the Youth Authority's child-saving identity and bureaucratic clout. But it is a hypocrisy that YA staff members find increasingly difficult to live with.

Treatment was the issue that led Doyle Roberts, a superintendent of the Southern Reception Center in Norwalk to quit in frustration after twenty-six years with the Youth Authority. "At any given time they've got four hundred or so guys in YA who've committed murder," Roberts says. "And what are they doing for them? Programming them as if they're delinquent children—just mixing them in with the general population and letting them do their thing. My God, if you have the same program for murderers, if you treat people who've taken a human life the same way you treat people who've taken a car, how can you claim to be doing treatment?"

Treatment is also the issue that led Howard Lee, a psychiatrist who has worked at the Northern Reception Center in Sacramento for sixteen years, to wage a quiet guerrilla war against the system. "I often write in my reports," he says, "that such and such a ward shouldn't be considered for parole until he has at least come to terms with his commitment offense. By this I really don't mean anything fancier than just admitting that he did it. But most of the time even this doesn't happen. The institutions may set up situations where a ward can 'express anger' and all that, but rarely do they bother to demand that he deal with his crime. I keep writing it in my reports—this ward must be made to deal with his commitment offense—in the hope that this sentence will at least be there to haunt somebody later on, after the ward has been released and committed another serious crime."

Bruce Latimer, a parole agent at the Fred C. Nelles School in Whittier, one of the YA institutions for younger offenders, ages fourteen to seventeen, agrees with Lee. When he was a youth counselor he was involved in a case he still feels typifies the Youth Authority's attitude toward the crimes its wards have committed. "We had a young man who had molested six kids. During his stay at Nelles he washed pots and pans very efficiently but didn't do much introspection. We were instructed not to talk to him about his committing offense because he was moody and it might 'upset' him. He was paroled to San Diego without ever being upset. Within a few days he had molested three more little kids."

If it causes many employees to have grave doubts about the efficacy of a stay in a YA facility, the issue of treatment also evokes the Youth Authority administrators' most feverish attempts at rationalization. Theodore Odland, a psychiatrist and chief of the agency's medical services, begins by insisting that the YA does offer treatment—"for those who want it." Aside from the fact that it makes voluntary what is supposed to be mandatory and places the onus on the least responsible party in the correctional transaction, this comment ignores the coercive power of the gangs the Youth Authority allows to establish the rules inside its institutions. As one former ward says, "If you're seen talking to the man too much—'hanging on the leg,' as we call it—you're going to get in trouble with the group."

Odland cites the example of intensive treatment programs, such as the one at Redwood, as evidence that the YA is still "in the forefront of correctional psychology." But, in fact, there are only three of these programs in all of the Youth Authority—about 120 beds for almost 6,000 wards, and despite the sense of élan of many therapists, the results after several years of operation (at an average annual cost of $30,000 per bed) are actually quite modest. "Our preliminary studies show that we do reduce craziness," says Redwood's head psychiatrist, Dan Palmer. "They also suggest that kids who've been through the program tend to move from crimes against people to crimes against property. Beyond that we just don't know."

Odland mentions Proposition 13, the rightward drift of public policy, and the difficulties of dealing with psychological disorders in an environment of incarceration. Finally he shrugs and makes a gesture of impotence that is richly symbolic. "If I can help a situation by worrying about it, I will. If not, why bother? I admit that at first the fact that lots of guys with real problems leave YA without treatment is disturbing. But it's like a medical student who thinks he'll never get over the horror of that first cadaver—you find that you can adjust to anything."

MOVING THE INVENTORY

REHABILITATION IS ONE of the most vexed concepts in penology, experiments to determine its success having yielded only ambiguous results even under the most ideal circumstances. And, as Jim Bascue, Los Angeles deputy district attorney in charge of prosecuting hard-core youth gangs, points out, circumstances are far from ideal in the Youth Authority. "Most of the young people they get in there were never habilitated. Where does the YA, which gives them a lick and a promise, get off making all these claims about rehabilitating them?"

This is not to say that many of the young people who have passed through the YA haven't turned their lives around in dramatic ways. David Pounds has been a parole agent at the Nelles School for fifteen years and during this time has seen many young people restored to themselves. "If a person is ready to make changes in his life, he'll do it. We may be able to help once they make the decision, but there's no way any intervention on our part can force it to happen. The only genuine rehabilitation any of us have ever seen is self-rehabilitation."

Howard Lee agrees. "We in the Youth Authority talk a lot about trans-actional analysis, reality therapy, Gestalt, and all that. But even if a lot more of it took place than actually does, it would be hard for me not to be skeptical. You can't deal overnight with problems it has taken years to create. The fact is that for the kind of people we get in the Youth Authority, there's only one treatment that might work, and that's time."

But time—a context for reevaluation and change—is the one treatment the YA never tries. Even if the daily regimen in YA institutions was not dom-inated by gangs and con games, there is no time for the self-rehabilitation

Pounds, Lee, and others in the Youth Authority know is the only hope for a lasting change in wards' lives. The average length of stay for all forms of homicide is about thirty months, eighteen months for rape, eighteen months for assault, sixteen months for extortion/kidnapping. Even if YA officials pretend not to know that this is a scandal, criminals on the outside see it for what it is. It is common knowledge among law enforcement officials that adult gang members offer young criminals the chance to prove themselves as "shooters" in contract killings, knowing that they will be through with the YA and on parole in not much more time than it would take an adult murder case to get through trial.

As always with the YA, there is an appealing rationale for a questionable policy. "We are dealing here with young and changeable people," says Pearl West, who from 1976 until late 1981 was director of the Youth Authority (she resigned after a confrontation with B.T. Collins, Governor Brown's tough new chief of staff). "We are dealing with them at an absolutely critical moment in their lives. If we keep them in a regimented environment longer than necessary, we withhold from them the decision-making skills one comes by normally in the larger world." In fact, wards are released from YA institutions after brief confinements not because they have been treated or rehabilitated and not because of the dangers of regimented environments but because of the pressure to make space for the ever growing numbers of young criminals being processed by the juvenile justice system. The result is what one employee caustically refers to as "moving the inventory."

This has evolved because of the symbiotic relationship between juvenile court and the YA and the tacit agreement that neither of them will hold the other accountable for what it does. In dealing with a juvenile, a judge does not set a specific sentence but merely puts the ward in the YA's custody with a maximum confinement time (to age twenty-one if the offender is sixteen or younger, to twenty-five if he is older) and the understanding that parole will come whenever there has been "Sufficient progress." It is the indeterminate sentence, discarded in adult corrections but kept in the juvenile system because of the presumption that rehabilitation is taking place. However, the Youth Authority makes the indeterminate sentence into what amounts to a determinate one that is much shorter than an adult would receive for a comparable crime. After leaving juvenile court, a ward is sent to one of the reception centers for thirty days, during which time he is given tests and evaluated. Then he is brought before the Youthful Offender Parole Board. This board (appointed by the governor) then sets a "parole consideration date" based on the average period of time in which the average ward should be able to deal with the particular offense. In theory, the parole consideration date—after twenty-four months, say, for a rape—is merely a target. In fact, although virtually no treatment takes place in the Youth Authority, it becomes the probable limit of the confinement. With "good time" the de facto sentence may be further reduced by a third, putting the ward back on the streets in sixteen months.

Pressure for early release is constant throughout a ward's stay at a YA facility. Doyle Roberts, a superintendent for five years, recalls how the system works: "Let's say you're a supervisor, and you've got wards sleeping in the aisles. You call Sacramento and say, 'Hey, I've got 300 beds here, and I've got 400 kids.' The response comes back loud and clear. 'it's your own damned fault because if you'd recommend early release on some of them you wouldn't have so many around.'"

Bruce Latimer wears a beard and sandals and has won the right to be iconoclastic because he is generally regarded as one of the harder-working parole agents at the Nelles School. He feels that the pressure for early release makes a mockery of the whole system. "If you want to get a kid out early, nothing ever stops you. If you want to hold him until he's ready, you get tremendous grief. If a kid comes in here with a two-year parole considera- tion date and I can't see him getting out in that period of time, I've got to go through tremendous justifications to prove a 'program failure.' And then I'm made to feel that somehow it's my failure. Hell, we had a fourteen-year-old murderer in here who didn't do anything his first year except sit on his bunk and masturbate to newspaper photos of car accidents. The kid was still sadistic and sick, but the administration insisted that he go out on his parole consideration date. It wasn't long before he'd committed an armed robbery."

One of the ways to make more bed space available is to award time cuts. It is possible for wards to earn ten days a month by staying out of trouble and completing the "program" agreed upon in the contract each signs when entering an institution. In some cases it is possible to accumulate time cuts at an even faster rate. At the Youth Training School in Chino, for instance, there is a "super-achiever" program for exemplary wards. Former parole board mem- ber Richard Woolstrum discovered one super-achiever among the case load he had when he came to the board: "It was some kid who was up for second-degree murder. He'd done eighteen months on the super-achiever program, and they'd referred him to parole. Well, I started reading back through the file and saw that he'd been plea bargained down to a second degree. What he'd actually done not only involved murder but rape, sodomy, and dismemberment of the body. I said, 'The hell with this! The guy's not going out.' That was the beginning of my reputation in YA as a Neanderthal."

The effect of all this on the wards is made clear by the opening words of a letter one young gang member wrote home to his brother after his first few days in YA custody: "It's like everybody said it would be—like Dizzneland."

Woolstrum says, "It doesn't take them long to see that being in YA means throwing a football around during the day, playing some pool after dinner, and maybe doing some gang banging after dark, and still getting out on schedule. Not too bad a life, all in all."

It becomes obvious to the young criminals that they are products on a conveyor belt that leads one way: out the YA's door. The agency's cynicism reinforces their own. The serious criminals use their time in YA institutions to run kiddie versions of adult prisoners' con games: extorting money from home from weaker wards, threatening those who go out with their families on day passes with violence if they don't return with dope and other contraband. As parole agent David Pounds says, "The kids do learn something here. They learn the techniques of manipulation and conning they use when they go to the joint later on. Basically that's what we're running here—a prep school for prison."

THE PARADOXES OF CONTROL

LESTER FINSTER IS A LARGE, balding man who works as the YA's supervising parole agent in Santa Rosa. During his twenty-three years with the agency, Finster has seen the average age of the parolee go from under sixteen to over twenty. "The manual says that during the first ninety days you're supposed to see them once a week," he notes. "But with the area and numbers we cover, we're lucky to see them twice a month."

When Finster first became a field agent, parole seemed to have a clear purpose as part of the Youth Authority's end game. Wards who still had available confinement time left from the original determination of their case by juvenile court could be watched closely to see how they performed back on the streets and recommitted to a YA institution at the first sign of backsliding. In recent years it hasn't worked that way.

Marlene Olive is a case in point. The seventeen year old had been convicted with her boyfriend of murdering her adoptive parents and burning their bodies. She was committed to Ventura School for Girls in 1976. Two years later she escaped from a halfway house five days after being transferred there. When police contacted Finster's office for a recent photo of Olive, he was instructed not to cooperate lest he compromise her rights. Olive was recaptured in July 1979. Five months later she was paroled.

Finster's troubles haven't abated. "Not long ago the court sent me a guy who'd been in for attempted murder. Within three or four days of his parole this guy held up some old woman. We had a violation hearing at which this guy threatened to kill me. I fought like hell, and Sacramento finally condescended to send him back to Preston. He was there for two months, and they let him out again. Within forty-eight hours he stabbed a kid to death."

William McCord, supervising parole agent in Oakland, feels that the entire parole operation, which costs the YA upwards of $20 million a year, is ineffective. "The only success we have comes after an individual has made the decision to rehabilitate himself. Then we can be moderately useful by getting him into vocational or training school, buying him tools, paying union dues, that sort of thing. But the rest of it—the visits, the driving around, the checking up—is of little value."

McCord designed an experiment undertaken in 1976 to test parole effectiveness, which he feels turned out to be something like the story of the emperor's new clothes. The idea was to take a number of the wards on parole in the Bay Area and divide them into three groups. One group would remain on regular parole; the second would be provided with parole services only when they voluntarily requested them; the third group would be discharged from parole outright. "The Youth Authority management got nervous and subverted the project," McCord remembers. "But the discharge papers releasing 103 wards had already been signed. It couldn't legally be rescinded, and it gave a unique research opportunity."

The YA's preliminary study found "no systematic differences in the subsequent violational records between 100 wards discharged early and 102 similar wards retained under parole supervision." In a memo commenting on these data, however, YA deputy director George Roberts said he felt "all copies [of the report] should be quickly gathered up and run through the paper shredder." The YA abandoned any further follow-up of what was now a sensitive matter. But Pat Jackson, a sociologist at UC Davis, continued to trace the wards who had been discharged, comparing their progress with that of those continuing to receive parole services. He summarizes the findings of his thesis, *The Paradox of Control:* "The two groups had almost identical rearrest and conviction rates. The difference was that the regular parolees were convicted for crimes that were more serious than those of the group that had no supervision at all."

The final deception of the Youth Authority involves the claim that the majority of its parolees do not commit further crime. Former YA director West claimed that fifty-five percent of her charges had not had their parole revoked two years after their release. "Not too shabby, considering that we are dealing with one hundred percent failures to begin with," she recalls. John Okel, a parole agent in Southern California, responds, "The people up in Sacramento have a very weird idea of what constitutes a 'failure.' If one of our parolees gets arrested and goes to county jail, that's not a failure. A guy who goes to prison in another state, he's not a failure. Hell, I had a guy on my case load who got killed robbing a 7-Eleven store, and that wasn't a failure as far as the YA was concerned."

Feeling that the two-year period on which the fifty-five percent success rate is based was not a sufficient test, YA statistician George Davis took it upon himself to do a five-year follow-up study of 3,000 cases discharged from parole in 1975. Of this number, thirty-four percent were removed from the study because they had committed a crime that landed them in state or federal prison. Of the remaining "successes," only 879 actually had no significant arrest history after five years, which meant that about seventy percent of the original 3,000 had committed crimes again. (This figure is more in line with the perception of true recidivism rates held by most parole officers and parole violations investigators in the field.) The Davis report, which had been distrubuted inside the agency, was recalled as "unauthorized."

SOCIETY'S FAILURES

THE YOUTH AUTHORITY would like people to believe that any criticism of it is reactionary. Charles Kuhl, who was Pearl West's chief deputy director and who has remained in that position, warns ominously, "We must not let society push correctional practices and services back a quarter century or more." And West laments, "The only way we could make a lot of the people out there happy is by taking the kids we've got and shooting them."

The fact is that draconian legislation, such as the bill introduced recently by Assemblyman Gerald Felando (Republican, San Pedro) to allow thirteen and fourteen year olds to be tried and punished as adults, is emerging because Youth Authority policies have abetted and exaggerated natural public fears. Most Californians do not want young criminals shot; they merely want to believe that someone, somewhere, is doing something to protect us from them.

The Youth Authority stands at the end of a long process that begins with child abuse and neglect and goes on to involve arrest and release with warnings, repeated probations, perhaps a stretch of time in a county camp. Rather than exonerating the YA from responsibility for what West and others call "society's failures," however, being the agency of last resort makes its job all the clearer. The young criminals who reach the Youth Authority are self-selected as the most serious threats to law and order, exactly the ones who must be dealt with forcefully if the rest of the juvenile justice system is to have any credibility at all.

The YA spends hundreds of thousands of dollars turning out reports containing what everyone already knows: employment is a key factor in determining success on parole, overcrowding leads to institutional tensions, racial minorities are over-represented in YA institutions. It would be better if these researchers convinced their superiors to heed the literature that shows that a small number of criminals commit an overwhelming majority of all crimes. In one frequently cited study, sociologist Marvin Wolfgang followed a group of 10,000 boys from birth in 1945 to the age of thirty, tabulating their arrests and periodically interviewing them. The chronic offenders—those committing five or more crimes—made up fifteen percent of the group but were responsible for three-quarters of the crimes. All except 627 of them had stopped committing crime by the age of sixteen. By the age of twenty-one this 627 accounted for two-thirds of the violent crimes and almost all the homicides in the entire group.

If small numbers of chronic offenders commit almost all the crimes, it seems also to be true that even their criminality tapers off with age. In a RAND Corporation study completed in 1977, Joan Petersilia conducted in-depth interviews with forty-nine career criminals serving time in California prisons. They admitted committing at least three serious crimes a month as juveniles. While free as adults they had committed only one serious crime every other month.

A criminal justice system that is cost-conscious in terms of public welfare as well as public finance would conclude that, instead of having a harsh system for adults at a time when their aggressiveness is diminishing and a free ride for juveniles at the height of their criminal activity, we should concentrate on the youthful offender who, for whatever reasons in his past life, poses the most serious threat to society. As Los Angeles deputy DA Jim Bascue says, "My unit has a ninety-eight percent conviction rate, and we still can't keep up with our cases. If the sixteen-year-old armed robber or murderer got, say, a six-year mandatory sentence, it would help. When he came back at twenty-two he might not have been rehabilitated, but he would have been out of the way during the peak years, when he's most volatile and dangerous. He might still hold up liquor stores, but they'd be fewer in number. He might still be homicidal, but he'd be less likely to actually commit a murder. It's not much to ask for, but in this business you quickly discover that half a loaf is better than none."

Because it doesn't even offer half a loaf, the Youth Authority presides over a system that does far less to correct offenders than to create victims. The ultimate victims, of course, are those like Joan Pope, who are betrayed first by the loss of a loved one and then by losing their belief in justice, and the rest of us, who find our faith in the young contaminated by fear and suspicion. But the first victims are the "kids" whom the YA and its subsidiaries in the criminal justice business profess to care about so deeply. Instead of mindlessly processing them through programs designed to get them out of custody as quickly and painlessly as possible, it should just stop and listen for a minute to what these kids have to say.

Jill is a fifteen year old who has been on probation since the age of twelve. She was arrested thirteen times and placed on probation repeatedly until she was recently arrested for burglary and sent to a county camp for sixty days. "I think they should have put me in here that first time I got busted," she says. "It would have seemed so bad then. Now it don't seem like too much. I don't like the judge for letting me go so many times. Even this last time they take me to court, my probation officer, he goes, 'Okay, Jill, I'll get them to give you one more chance.' I look at him, and I go, 'No! Now you go on and let me just do my time so I can try to learn how to behave.'"

MICHAEL HARDY

Letter from a Man in Jail

IN RESPONSE TO our conversation on Tuesday, September 3rd, I am presenting some topics that will most certainly come under the title of OVERCROWDING.

Principally, there are two categories that will include all problem areas, which are: Administrative & Social.

Definition: *Administrative-counselling*—case records, staff supervision/custodial care.

Social—interaction between inmates/staff, activities for rehabilitation. The following topics could be expounded:

● *Individual cells for mainline population* house two inmates in an area 6' x 10'. Whereas the mainline population have (2) inmates per cell, men who have committed assaults on other inmates or guards have single-cell status. Single-celling of troublemakers increases the overcrowding on the mainline and has a negative effect on inmates who are doing a lot of time. Long-termers will assault staff/inmates just to get a cell all to themselves!

● *Inmate work force is very small.* Approximately 600 inmates out of a total of 2,994 are now working. There are not enough jobs to supply everyone who wants to work. New inmates are put on a waiting list that lasts for years. Those without financial support from friends have no means of obtaining their necessities.

● *Feeding is a major problem.* Since 1982 there have never been more than two hot meals served daily. Sack lunches have been substituted for the noontime hot meal. During lockdowns feeding days are alternated for hot meals. (Only one hot meal per day.) If your building eats on Mon. Wed. Fri., the following week you will only eat one hot meal on Tuesday & Thursday.

- *Showers* are held approximately once a week because there are only twelve shower stalls for about 620 to 800 men in a building.
- There is no system whereby an inmate can have his *clothes cleaned* or exchanged regularly because the laundry room cannot accommodate the entire population. Inmates have to wash their clothes in a sink because staff has banned plastic buckets for this purpose.
- The *yard for exercise is too small* for the entire population, so workers and non-workers yard has been established. The non-workers come out once a week, and the workers have the weekend. Even with the splitting, gang violence increases because there are so many people in such a small area.
- When the number of *inmate sign-ups for religious services increased,* (non-workers) the administration cancelled all ducats. This ducat system allowed non-workers to sign up for chapel services and be escorted by staff to the chapel. Ducating has now been abolished, and religious freedoms are denied to non-workers on the weekend. If you don't work, you cannot attend services on Saturdays and Sundays.
- The majority of the stabbings occur on *the weight pile,* where men lift weights. It is grossly overcrowded so the guards in the tower cannot see what is going on. Ex: One man was stabbed to death, wrapped up in a blanket, and staff never saw it take place.
- There are *only four telephones* open to the population when they sign up for calls. Months may pass before you can get a phone call.
- The library only has a capacity for twenty-five people!
- *Counsellors cannot meet the needs of the inmates adequately.* They hardly know their caseloads because they don't have time to talk with them. For the past two years this writer has not been permitted to attend his annual screening review due to the violence in the institution. So much time is spent with the troublemakers that the mainline gets overlooked. My reviews have been held in absentia for the past two years!
- *Sick call* is only on Wednesdays for workers, and if you miss it, well, try next week.
- *The education program* only caters to about sixty people, and there is talk of turning this into a housing unit to house more inmates. This means education will be leaving soon.
- Obtaining items from the store is utterly chaotic, considering non-workers have one day to go out of the week. Inmates spend out of their account on a monthly draw basis as high as $110.00. Out of 600-800 people trying to get in line for the store, the canteen can only process ninety of these people during a day.

    All of the above figures will have to be checked for accuracy, but are generally correct.

I have done nothing more than present you with subject matter. I have not tried to attempt to present any of this material for a critical review of grammar, etc., because this letter is only a rough draft.

I hope that I have been of some help to you.

Due to the nature of this letter, please be sure to keep the lines of communication open to acknowledge receipt.

Respectfully submitted,
Michael Hardy

P.S. This writer has chosen to leave out describing much of the violence that goes on here, but has prolific information on this particular subject.

JOHN SACK

God Rest Ye Merry Aaron and John

His neighbors knew him as Stan. He had been a professional boxer, and the sad-looking sagging skin of his eyes still testified to his discomforts once as a California middleweight. On this hot afternoon, he lay sprawled in the white-light flashes of bulbs though not in any boxing ring: in the hall of his simple white stucco home in Oakland's hills. In his hand was a quite inadequate handkerchief, in his chest like a heart operation was a hole three inches wide with little pellets inside. His death and the one close by of Suenette, his lover, evidently owed to a shotgun put to their chests and a few coups de grace from a .32.

In minutes, the cops were descending on Stan's scared neighbors, asking, "What did you see?" Well, there wasn't one but two murderers, the neighbors agreed. A tall black man and a shorter one, the two had arrived in a Gremlin and had entered the modest house as a getaway driver waited outside. An hour later, Stan, another man, and a boy had arrived in a Cadillac and had been ambushed at the front door by the two intruders. "Go ahead and kill me," Stan shouted, according to one ashen neighbor. At that, Stan was bashed with a baseball bat, a billy stick, or a rod, according to various neighbors, the others escaped but Stan was pulled into the house, whereupon, the neighbors said, the sound of firecrackers began and the two men hurried off.

The neighbors weren't in total accord on the murderers' IDs. The taller man had a shirt with a dark floral print, a light floral print or no floral print—he had or hadn't a hat with silver medallions, and he was unknown to

the neighbors except to one who knew him as Mr. Bailey. The man who was
shorter, none of the neighbors remembered except for one who gauged him
as five-foot-six. "Or something like that...."

W AS SOMEONE TELLING lies about Aaron Owens? He had done nothing wrong, but one afternoon when he was out driving his Volvo he was arrested by six trigger-fingered policemen. He was told, "Freeze," he was photographed, fingerprinted, written up as being black, brown-haired, brown-eyed, five-foot-eight and twenty-eight, and was brought to a four-person cell at the county jail. He heard on the PA system, "Lock up," and the cell door closed with a car-crash sound on this astonished man.

His cell had a sink with a cold-water faucet and a toilet without a toilet seat. On the walls like a set of shelves were four steel beds, and Owens sat on the bottom right with a partial distraction, a novel, until the pale gray light went out at ten o'clock, when he slid under the scratchy blanket. In this concrete box, the other three prisoners slept so their feet faced out, so their heads wouldn't be hit by a mop handle, a mop wringer, whatever, in the dim and dangerous night, but Owens slept so his head wouldn't be by the toilet bowl.

At daybreak, the PA system said, "Unlock," the door clattered open and he was taken in handcuffs and leg fetters to a crowded court. A judge with a sheet of long paper droned that he was accused of a felony—to wit, murder—in that on May 13, 1972, he had killed a man and a woman whose first names were Stan and Suenette. The judge, a woman, asked if he wanted a lawyer, and Owens answered, "Yes, ma'am, I do."

He wasn't so worried now. He had an unassailable alibi. The day of that double murder was the day before Mother's Day, and Owens remembered that he was ten miles away at the time with some yellow chrysanthemums for his and his wife's worthy mothers. As the murders occurred—as the shots sounded out, he was wrapping up these chrysanthemums at the florist's, and he was presenting them to the two happy mothers up in another county. His wife, his mother, his wife's mother, his wife's father, and his and her brothers and sisters all could testify to his far remove from the scene of the carnage, and Owens said to some sheriffs now, "I'll get this straightened out."

"We hope so," the sheriffs told him.

OWENS DIDN'T KNOW if the sheriffs meant it. He wondered if they hadn't set him up. Growing up outside of Oakland in the one-story slums of Richmond, he had bothered the law enforcement agencies since he was ten. He wondered now, Was this their revenge?

At ten, Owens had stolen someone's hubcaps as a present for a Mr. Mose.

He was caught, and a few months later he slipped a Velveeta cheese up his corduroy trouser leg as a present for poor old Miss Duckett. "Honey, don't ever do that without asking me," the mortified woman told him, but Owens by twenty had stolen in practically all of Richmond's cluttered stores. At some, he had "dipped" in their registers for their $20 bills as he diverted the counter clerk's eyes to his provocative copy of the *Enquirer*. At others, he had offered a $10 bill for a packet of Chiclets but had refused the $9.80 change, saying, "No, wait, I don't want any $1 bills, here is a one and just give me a five—no, wait," until he had conned the dizzy counter clerk out of a $10 bill and the Chiclets too. "Thank you, sir," Owens had said in a good-humored voice with a warm bugs-bunny smile.

It was little-league crime, but in Richmond the cops didn't like it. Recently, Owens had been secreting speed in some colorful boxes of Kellogg's cornflakes, selling the little round pills for $1 each, and the irate police were onto him. "I'm going to bust your black ass," one eager beaver in Richmond had told him, once swooping down on Owens as he sat eating a hotdog at Doggie Diner. Another day, Owens was at his home hosing the grass when the eager beaver actually tackled him and found a yellow pill in Owens's sock. Owens was soon released in the absence of probable cause, and now the cop shouted every day, "We're gonna get you! We're gonna get...."

But murder? A bum double-murder rap? Whoever wanted a life's imprisonment for a laughter-loving con man? It seemed not a little vindictive, since even the Richmond police knew that Owens never used guns. He went hunting, sure, but he shot at the unprotesting posts and telephone poles as his companions shot at the rabbits telling him, "You little madman! You scarin' the rabbits away!" A most gentle man, Owens couldn't even kill a fish, didn't anyone at the station house or in this jailhouse in Oakland know?

IN JAIL ONE DAY, the sheriff delivered a light brown three-piece suit to Owens's cell. Owens put on a white shirt and a brown striped tie, he put on the $300 suit, and in the breast pocket he put a brown striped handkerchief before he stepped into the ornate elevator down to superior court, a sheriff accompanying him. In the courtroom a courteous bailiff said, "Mr Owens? Would you sit here, please?" and Owens sat down at a handsome wooden table.

To his left was his court-appointed lawyer, a man who was sitting raking his almost vestigial hair. To his farther left was a man name of Bailey, who looked like a linebacker and who was being tried as Owens's accomplice, though the two had just met in this very courthouse, saying, "You must be Bailey," "You must be Owens." To his left, furthermore, was Bailey's corpulent lawyer, to Owens's right was a smooth-looking district attorney, and up front was a judge whose nose had a wart which he wouldn't remove, being a Christian Scientist.

The trial began. At an early recess, the DA strolled over to Owens asking him casually, "How you doing?"

"Fine," Owens answered pleasantly. "You know, I didn't do this crime."

"I know that," the DA nodded. "And that's what Bailey's saying too. He didn't do it, you didn't do it, there's nobody dead, and do I want to buy the bridge to San Francisco?"

Owens laughed. A con man could tell a con man anywhere, and Owens sensed that the DA was just attempting to gain a strategic advantage by fussing up the defendant. Not taken in, Owens smiled at the DA, saying, "You aren't going to convict me."

"I certainly am," the DA said with conviction.

His name was John Taylor. A white, he, too, had grown up in Richmond and Owens was right: *he* was an artful dodger himself. In his youth, he had stolen from the same stores as Owens, nodding to the clerks while climbing over the stiles with a fishing reel or a fishing pole. At last arrested like Owens, he had been driven prophetically to Owens's part of Richmond and had been asked by his worried father, "You want to grow up like these people here?" "No, Dad, I don't," said Taylor, but though he didn't go to reform school but to Berkeley he hadn't changed: he believed in a sort of benevolent con as a DA's modus operandi. In court, as a witness delivered himself, he nodded his head impressed, he raised an eyebrow unconvinced, and, by these understated acts, he introduced all the innocent jurors to a very impressive item of evidence: himself, the honest district attorney.

"Anyone," Taylor would say, "can convict a guy who's guilty. It takes a man with skill to convict an innocent one." But there Taylor overstated himself, for he wasn't at all aware of Owens's innocence. How could he be? He had the best eyewitness, the friend of the murdered man's, the one who drove home with him on May 13, 1972: a black whose name was Brown.

"ALL RIGHT," Taylor said to Brown. "What did Stan do?" "He stuck his key in," Brown answered.

Brown, on the witness stand, was recalling the last five minutes in Stan's curtailed life. Stan was wearing a black leather coat, said Brown. He was approaching his white stucco home at 333 Florence Avenue in Oakland. He put his key in the keyhole, said Brown, it opened and Bailey in black leather gloves and Owens in white cotton garden gloves came out, a .32 pistol in Bailey's hand and a sawed-off shotgun in Owens's. Startled, Stan stepped back and he stumbled on Brown's little two-year-old boy, who was behind him and who began crying as Stan fell down. Apparently rattled, Bailey and Owens shouted at Stan, "Get your black ass in the house," but Stan arose like a champion shouting to Owens, "That shotgun, I'm gonna stick it right up—" At that, Bailey hit Stan repeatedly with a black billy stick, pulling him in as Stan's girlfriend, Suenette, stood in the house sobbing, "I didn't let them in!" "Oh shut up," Bailey told her, according to Brown, and Bailey slapped her as Owens prodded at Brown and his little boy with the shotgun, shouting, "Get in! Get in!" "No, let them go," Bailey said, but Owens said, "No, man, they gotta go," meaning die, all this according to Brown.

A few feet away from the glowering witness there were tears in Owens's eyes. Owens felt that a man who could murder a little toddler was a man beneath contempt. Once, Owens had even gone from drive to reverse, tearing up his transmission when a careless child ran in front of his Oldsmobile on Jenkins Way. He loved little kids: he loved to buy them bright bicycles, to ride them around on motorcycles, to wink at them mischievously with a pair of retractable automobile headlights. Kids called him Uncle Aaron, and Owens had tears because he believed that the spectators in this court might believe he had really said, "No, they gotta go."

"How can this baby harm you?" On the witness stand, Brown was saying he asked that of Owens and Owens explained, "He can talk, can't he?" "No, he can't talk," Brown said and Bailey, standing inside the white stucco home over Stan and Suenette, shouted to Brown, "Oh, get outa here." Brown and Brown junior fled, in the house was a *pop, pop, pop*, and minutes later the Oakland police found the riddled bodies of Stan and Suenette in the splattered home.

"Are you sure," the DA was saying to Brown, "that this man here, Aaron Owens, is the man that had the shotgun on May 13?"

"I'm sure," said Brown.

"Why are you sure?"

"He wanted to kill my two-year-old. I don't think I could forget," said Brown.

In fact, Brown wasn't "really" sure that the man with that shotgun was Owens. Bailey he had known personally, and he had identified him to Oakland's police as the man who was wielding the big black billy stick and the .32. Owens he never had met, but police discovered a telephone call from Bailey's motel room to Owens's home and so had produced an old, curled, black-and-white photo of Owens for Brown's inspection. As fate would have it, Bailey had not placed the telephone call. It was really from Bailey's lover, Loretta, to a friend of hers who'd dropped in coincidentally on Owens's wife, but the police didn't know this and Brown, on looking at Owens's somber photo, said, "That's the man." On second thought, it then seemed to Brown that the mug in that photograph had a darker color, two mutton chops, and two bugs-bunny teeth that he didn't recollect on, the man who once shouted, "No, they gotta go," and Brown at last said to Taylor, the clever DA, "I don't really know...."

"Listen," said Taylor, as he and his star witness sat in Lakeside Park in Oakland. "Didn't you tell the police you'll never forget the man who was going to kill your little boy?"

"Yeah, I guess I did," said Brown.

"So please don't forget it," Taylor told him and bought him a Casper's hotdog with onions, mustard, and relish.

ALL WAS FAIR in a criminal court in Taylor's philosophy. He believed that the police should determine who in their district had or hadn't wasted someone like Stan or Suenette and that after that he should stop at nothing to let that determination stand. The judge, the jurors, the witnesses—he had to exploit them all if the people were to prevail and if Owens or someone wasn't to get away with murder.

Owens the con man had to admire him. "You really smooth, Mr. Taylor," Owens said to his opponent once. "Well, hello, Mrs. Dominici. Well, hello, Mr. Dimicurio," Owens continued, imitating the DA's charm and his careful pronunciation whenever he greeted one of his all-white jurors. "They falling all over you, Mr. Taylor," Owens said.

"Yeah, I think you're in trouble now," Taylor agreed.

One day to Owens's concern, there was a ten-minute recess and Taylor was sitting whispering to the eager beaver from Richmond, the cop who had called to Owens, "We're gonna get you!" The two were glancing at Owens as such quite intimidating words as *Owens, sawed-off,* and *shotgun* seemed to shape themselves on their well-pursed lips. Now, at Owens's home there were indeed a few shotguns, one of them sawed, that he didn't fire at rabbits but at telephone poles, and he was afraid that the cop, knowing somehow, was talking about them to Taylor. Owens's nervous lawyer went up to the two conspirators.

"Shh," Taylor whispered to his apparent informant as Owens's lawyer approached them. "Hi there, Mike," Taylor greeted him.

"What are you two talking about? My client's dirty deeds?" Owens's lawyer laughed.

"No, Mike," Taylor told him. "We aren't talking about him. We just were talking about his sawed-off shotgun. No, no, I'm just kidding you, Mike. His shotgun wasn't sawed off, the officer tells me."

"Heh heh."

"But...," Taylor persisted, "Owens may have sawed it off after the officer saw it, Mike."

"Heh," Owens's lawyer said, and he returned to Owens's table saying, "They know about your gun." The jurors too, he cautioned, would know about it if Owens elected to testify and be cross-examined by Taylor. Hesitant, Owens stared at the two still whispering men, who, in fact, knew nothing at all and were sharing things like "Owens, blah-blah, shotgun, blah-blah-blah," and Owens chose to absent himself from the perilous witness stand—to not report he was miles away with a present of yellow chrysanthemums in those critical minutes of May 13, 1972. Score one for Taylor, who had gone into those dramatics just so the jurors wouldn't be exposed to Owens's alibi. The con man had been outconned.

No matter. There were a dozen earnest witnesses—mothers, fathers, brothers, sisters, kids, and Owens's telephone operator wife—to Owens's far from brutal pursuits that day, and now one after another testified so. By now, Owens was quite intrigued with the sly white district attorney, and he wondered how the DA even hoped to refute all those honest-sounding citizens. Understandably, Owens was fascinated when in the closing arguments the DA confessed that the mothers, et cetera, all were being completely honest. "*But,*" said Taylor, continuing into a most unusual argument as Owens and the jurors listened practically mesmerized, "did you ever go out to the Oakland A's? It's the ninth inning, see, and it's a tie game and Bando hits the ball...."

"No!!!" IT WAS THIRTY minutes later, the jury was out and Owens was up in his cell retelling the closing arguments to his big and burly white cellmate, the leader of the Hell's Angels in Oakland, Sonny Barger. "No," Sonny was laughing in utter incredulity as Owens reported on Taylor's unforeseen baseball game.

"I'm serious," Owens insisted. "He told them, Ladies! Gentlemen! Bando's hit is a grounder and Campaneris, Campy on second base is running, is rounding third, it'll be very close, everyone, it'll be at the plate and Campy *slides.*...And," Owens interrupted himself, "I couldn't believe it, Taylor was laying there on the floor, man, on the floor!"

"No," Sonny laughed as Owens in his white underwear lay on the concrete floor of their cell.

"He was laying there in his four- or five-hundred dollar suit," Owens insisted. "He had his right hand in the air and he's saying the umpire's saying you're out!"

"You're out! No," Sonny roared, tears in his hooded eyes.

"And," Owens continued, "Taylor's saying that in the stands they're saying

Boo! He's safe! He's safe! And they aren't dishonest there, says Taylor. They actually saw him as safe because they all wanted him safe and, ladies, gentlemen says Taylor, the same goes for Owens's family. They really believe they saw him the day before Mother's Day in 1972. Whoo," Owens concluded. "Taylor is outasight, man."

By now, Sonny was doubled up on the right lower bunk. "You're out," he was shouting, his hand stretching up, and he was still shouting it three days later when the jurors returned to the stone-silent court with a guilty verdict for Owens and Bailey. "Hey," Bailey shouted now at the jurors, rearing up in the courtroom like Big Daddy Lipscomb. The bailiffs leapt up, Owens stood up because everyone did, the bailiffs shouted, "Sit down, sit down," and Bailey and Owens did. And sentenced to life imprisonment by the wart-nosed judge, the innocent man was too mortified to look at his sobbing mother when he was escorted off to Folsom Prison.

There, Owens was known as B47824. A con man even in Folsom, he contrived to still be in Jordache jeans, to live in a cell painted pastel blue, to sit inside in a Barcalounger looking at tropical fish, a Sony, and the Oakland A's. He never said die, and, far from calling the case closed, he looked for a court of last resort inside of Folsom's castle walls. "I didn't do it," he said to his nodding psychiatrist. "I was out buying flowers," he said to his grinning therapy group: to one dozen murderers, one participating guard, and the warden's attractive assistant.

A murderer said, "Did you get receipts?"

"No, I paid cash," Owens said.

The warden's attractive assistant said, "Did the florist remember you?"

"No."

The parole people recommended he show remorse. They told him at Folsom, "We need to know that you've had a change of—"

"Gentlemen," Owens protested, "if I come here a hundred thousand times I can't show remorse when I didn't do it."

"You aren't helping yourself," the parole people chided him.

And they were right. In the end, Owens saw there was no other recourse but Owens himself. To exit out of this surreal dream, he saw he first needed to enter it as his favorite fictional hero, Sherlock Holmes. He needed to do by himself what the DA didn't: he had to solve the case from inside of Folsom, somehow, so as to catch the real murderer.

ON SATURDAYS, OWENS'S wife and his two pretty little girls used to come through the metal detector to the grim visitors' room at Folsom. His wife, distraught, had lost her telephone operator's job and was living on $293 monthly welfare. His daughter Evangela was getting in fights with the other fourth graders because of their taunts of "Your daddy in Folsom," and Latonja, his other daughter, was often avoiding this by just skipping school. "You'll never get a respectable job," Owens would warn her. "You'll get a fast-food restaurant job," but Latonja kept getting Fs.

Owens's father died, Owens's mother got ill—but fate was a lot more generous to Taylor. At his office in Oakland, a bit of good fortune occurred that in time would effect metamorphoses on his and also on Owens's lives. A pretty attorney whose name was Joanne and who wore flower-covered ties in the courts became a DA herself, and Taylor one afternoon had to go to her pine-hidden home in Oakland's hills. It was Sunday, and Joanne was asleep underneath a wine-colored quilt in a bed of old antique oak as Taylor encountered her. "Joanne," he whispered, embarrassed, and, not really waking up, Joanne reached up and embraced him as Chopin's waltzes played on her stereo set. "John," Joanne whispered, and Taylor moved in that same afternoon and never moved out.

Until now, his one delight was to win, not predominantly for the sacred sake of Justice but for the thrill of winning itself. But now Joanne was suggesting (in poems, sometimes)—suggesting to him that what really mattered, he had already won.

> *The sight and sound of you*
> *remembered brings me peace in*
> *this gray green morning.*

No longer was Taylor certain that the meaning of life consisted of putting people like Owens in concrete cages. "How to understand it," he wrote to Joanne,

> *Searching, looking, trying,*
> *somehow missing the point*
> *I'm close but it eludes me.*

In time he grew weary of being a DA in Oakland. The parole people at Folsom invited him up to Owens's annual hearings, but Taylor just mailed them a letter saying, "Owens is known as a very dangerous person," and he went skiing at Tahoe instead.

HALFWAY TO TAHOE, at Folsom, a number of whites had been trying to murder the black men and had been using knives and sharpened screwdrivers on Owens. One morning Owens, as upbeat as ever, stepped into the shower singing

> *Beautiful morning*
> *I'd like to go outside today,*

a song by the Rascals. He soaped with Camay and shampooed with Head and Shoulders, improvising

> *I want to go outside tonight,*
> *I want to be with yoooo tonight.*

And singing this, he spied a white convict through the wet lather as the man was swinging a mop wringer down at Owens's head. Ducking down, Owens picked up a scrubbing brush and he knocked off the man's glasses, the man escaping but the old wringer leaving a gash in Owens's back. In his cell, he got alcohol, codeine, and butterfly bandages that a black friend stole from the prison hospital, for Owens couldn't go to the hospital himself. He knew that if he wasn't covert about it, he could be put into solitary lest he attempt to get his revenge.

It was his sixth year in Folsom. Well, at least he was safer here than in San Quentin, by San Francisco. There, a leader of the Black Guerrilla Family was the son of Stan, the murdered man, and Owens might be on his hit list as well as the Aryan Brotherhood's. A man was stabbed every day at San Quentin, but Owens by now had ascertained that he *had* to be at San Quentin to catch the real murderer and so escape from a life of six-by-ten apartments, of fetid dining rooms, of three-in-the-afternoon curfews, and of bloody butterfly bandages. To transfer there, he had practiced a con on the prison people in Sacramento, saying, "My lawyer's closer," "My family's closer," "My mother has arthritis now," but Sacramento had always said no.

One day, though, as Owens recovered from the mop-wringer wound, he happened upon a newspaper column called "And Did You Know?" Did you know there's a sidewalk-spitting fine? Did you know there's a no-hippopotamus law? Did you know, if a warden wants a particular prisoner in his particular prison he can request him? "I'm goin', I'm goin', I'm tunnelin', out," Owens shouted, and he wrote immediately to a friend at San Quentin who literally had the warden's ear: the warden's barber. A rapist en route to the dentist there carried the note to San Quentin.

A few days later, there was an unaccustomed sound in Owens's echoing prison block. It was the click-click-click of high-heeled shoes, and the prisoners whistled or shouted, "Oh, baby," as a pretty brunette in her twenties and in a nice white dress went to Owens's steel cell. "Aaron," she said as Owens looked up from feeding his two or three hundred tropical fish.

"Rosemary!" Owens gasped. It was the warden's attractive assistant from Owens's therapy group. "The papers came from San Quentin. Tomorrow," she told him, "I'll have the warden sign it."

"Thank you!" Owens replied. "Now hurry up out of here, please! You know how people talk!"

A VAN CARRIED HIM to San Quentin and Owens, a con man anywhere, asked for and got Cell 488. One door away was Bailey, the co-defendant at Owens's trial who had since confessed to the murders, showing remorse, and who now found a sudden friend in this prison in Owens. "My crime partner," Bailey called him.

His crime partner, Owens thought. It was Owens's hope at San Quentin to discover the actual partner by worming his name address and any incriminating evidence out of the horse's mouth. Of course, Owens couldn't simply say to Bailey, "Who was the other murderer with you in May 1972?" To rat on a man was abhorrent here, and Owens couldn't get the essential data if Bailey couldn't be somehow conned out of it. Bailey, at six-foot-six and 240, a bully, a real bruiser, a man who possessed a two-foot tire iron in his cell, somewhere, would be the most dangerous game in the con man's career.

Day after day, the two would visit in Bailey's comfortable cell. It had gold wall-to-wall carpeting belonging to Bailey as well as a TV, stereo, and a sofa where the two prisoners sat playing chess. Or playing backgammon as they drank glass after glass of orange wine, a wine made from stolen oranges. Or as they smoked marijuana—or Bailey and Owens would tend to Bailey's own tropical fish. "They actin' kinda funny," Bailey might say as his guppies, like drunken drivers, hit all the boulders in Bailey's tank.

"They got a fungus infection, man," Owens would tell him. "It's known as ic."

"Is it serious?" Bailey would say.

"No, I got some medicine for it."

From time to time, their conversation would touch on their trial in Oakland. And then Owens, playing his queen to his king's rook's five, might say, "You remember the neighbors on Florence Avenue? They testify there was a getaway car."

"Yeah," Bailey would muse while he moved his knight to his king's bishop's three.

"They testify there was a driver, too."

"Yeah, that was Robert. Now back that bitch up," Bailey would say.

"Robert," Owens would murmur with no idea who Robert was, and he would withdraw his queen to his king's rook's four.

Or another day, Owens, while pouring his ic medicine on Bailey's fish, might comment censoriously on Bailey's pinups. "Hey, those are my honeys there," Bailey would growl.

"Well," Owens would say, and Owens would smoothly summon up Bailey's lover in 1972, "Well, whatever happened to ol' Loretta?"

"Aw, she was a greedy broad. She stop by the liquor store two or three times that day," Bailey would say.

"The day all that shit jumped off?"

"Yeah. She was there with Robert," Bailey would say.

"In the car?"

"In the car. How come the water's becoming blue?" Bailey would say.

"It's the medicine for the ic," Owens would tell him.

So did six months go by. In that narrow cell, Owens eventually got Robert's address in Seattle and Loretta's address in Los Angeles in her new career as a pop singer for MGM. It wasn't much, and Owens discerned that he wouldn't ever be Sherlock Holmes if he just operated out of Cell 488. It seemed elementary that he had to get, somehow, an associate somewhere outside of San Quentin.

BY NOW, TAYLOR was about to go into private practice in Tahoe. "John, you've burned out," he was twitted by Bailey's fat lawyer, but John and Joanne had already chosen an office with a wide picture window over the sailboats on Tahoe's lake. In his last week in Oakland, the DA was invited to Owens's annual hearing and he drove over the serpentine bridge to San Quentin. It was closer than Folsom.

Taylor parked, and he walked through the old iron gate like the one to Paris's ancient Bastille. In the small hearing room, he heard the parole people saying to Owens, "We need to know if you've had a change of—"

Owens interrupted them, "You say that year after..."

"Mr. Owens—"

"I've told you, if you want remorse you're never going to get it."

Taylor could not understand it. In his youth in Richmond, he too had been prompted to show remorse when he was arrested once with a bundle of stolen fishing poles. "I'm sorry," Taylor had cried convincingly, though he was just sorry that he had been caught. His crocodile tears had gotten him off, a few could be shed quite effectively now by Owens, Taylor believed.

"I'm tired of this farce every year," Owens said. The hearing ending, the DA approached him to share in a not unpleasant reunion and to ask this impenitent criminal why he didn't fess up. "You know why, Mr. Taylor," Owens smiled.

"I really don't," Taylor said.

"You know I didn't do it."

"I know you *did*," Taylor said. "I prosecuted you."

"But that was to get me off the streets, wasn't it?"

"Absolutely not!" To have to protest what he had assumed was a postulate was a second unprecedented phenomenon to Taylor. Though he had heard hundreds of criminals say, "I didn't do it," this convict was the first to insist that he, Taylor, the honest district attorney, knew he didn't do it. "No, we don't play that way," he protested to Owens. "We play by the rules, remember?"

"You really think I did it!"

"Damn right I do," Taylor said, but he had sudden doubts as he walked out of Owens's hearing room. He wondered how if Owens had done it, Owens had even suspected that the prosecutor didn't know it. At his car, Taylor routinely opened his trunk before driving out to the farthest gate, and he sat contemplating there as the guard closed the trunk after seeing no inmates inside it. His thoughts were on Owens as he drove over the twisting bridge to Richmond, a jungle gym of refineries as in the worst of New Jersey. Like hundreds of Kilroys, the tops of old tires peered from a stagnant bay as Taylor turned onto a freeway before driving up to his pine-hidden home on Merriewood Drive.

Joanne was inside sipping wine as Taylor walked in. She looked at his fur rows, "Is something wrong?"

"Joanne," Taylor slowly told her, "I think that guy may be innocent." Not knowing how to prove it, though, he left for Tahoe three days later.

MEANWHILE, OWENS, IN Bailey's luxurious cell, was stripping the eights, nines, and tens from a deck of playing cards for a cooncan game with Bailey. "Some coons can't," Owens laughed, "and I'm one who can," but Owens had more aspirations than to lay his eleven cards down and say, "Cooncan." At their recent reunion, it was in honest astonishment that he had practically gasped to Taylor, "You really think I did it!" Taylor, he had discovered, had been unaware of his inappropriate innocence and so might be quite receptive to some sudden proof of it. So now, Owens's intentions weren't to say to Bailey,

> *Peter Wheater Straw,*
> *The devil's son-in-law,*
> *Cooncan,*

but much more audaciously to con him into reporting to Taylor who his real accomplices were in 1972.

"Jump, Judy," Bailey was saying, laying a four-card spread on his orange sofa.

"You know," said Owens, drawing a card himself, "we could get a new trial, probably."

"How?" Bailey asked.

"We got new evidence," Owens said. "We got Robert, Loretta, we got the guy they said was me—"

"I'm not gonna rat," Bailey interrupted.

"Be cool. No one can harm that guy," Owens said. "No one can testify against him."

"What about Brown? He testified against you."

"He did," Owens said. "So his credibility's zilch."

"I don't understand."

"He swore it was me. So how can he swear it was someone else? Who would believe him?"

Bailey reflected. "You think there could be a new trial?"

"If you write to Taylor," Owens said.

In the end, it was after another precarious year of cards, chess, sex—in a corner of the visitors' room with one of Owens's visitors—and of sick tropical fish that a letter came to the picture window office in Tahoe and Taylor, overwhelmed, drove to San Quentin to sit in that paneled hearing room and to put his questions to Bailey. Why had Bailey murdered Stan in 1972? "He disrespected me," Bailey said—Stan had recently bullied him and had extorted a TV, a Polaroid, a Mexican piggy bank, and $270. And why had Bailey murdered Suenette, too? "She went for her gun," Bailey said—Suenette had reached for the .38 she carried under her sheath skirt. And who drove the Gremlin getaway car? "Robert and Loretta," Bailey said—Robert lived in Seattle and Loretta lived in the Hollywood Hills. And who was the other murderer? "It was ———," Bailey said, and he named a man who's still living at ease in Oakland in 1985. Owens was right: the man was never arrested, since the district attorney has no witness against him.

"I thank you, Mr. Bailey," Taylor said, and he then checked out of San Quentin to devote himself to Owens's vindication. He got him a lie-detector test. He flew up to Seattle and down to Los Angeles. He got some immunity for Robert and Loretta and listened emotionally as Robert said, "I've heard you've got the wrong guy," as Loretta said, "Oh God, I've wanted to talk about this," and as both informed on the same unworried murderer in Oakland. From the Oakland police, Taylor got the murderer's photograph and Owens's, too, and, his eyes darting from one to the other, displayed the two black-skinned mugs to Joanne, his law partner and lover in Tahoe. "You don't mean they're two different men," she exclaimed, and Taylor answered, "I mean exactly that." And then, again he drove over the serpentine bridge and he showed the men's photographs to the one who was locked in San Quentin. Owens stared at those twins saying, "Man. Is that cold," meaning ain't that the living end.

"I've got some good news," Taylor told him.

"What's that?"

"You're going to get out," Taylor told him.

It was like lifting a sack of cement off Owens's shoulders. Owens dropped to a crouch, holding his fists to his eyes, and he had tears there when he rose slowly, saying, "God God!" The two men embraced and Owens ran to a patio of this prison, screaming for joy.

ONE MONTH LATER, he was still in his cell in San Quentin and Taylor was really beside himself. He had filed a report on Owens concluding, "Owens was wrongly convicted," but no one in any authority cared to know of his own complicity in Owens's three thousand days in Purgatory. The wart-nosed judge said to Taylor, "I think you're being set up," and the new district attorney said, "You're atoning for some thing, apparently." At the court-house's elevator, the lawyer for Bailey said, "I know that Owens is guiltier than hell,"

"How do you know it?" Taylor asked, and he just stared as Bailey's lawyer patted his own fat stomach.

"My guts," Bailey's lawyer explained.

Brown, the eyewitness, the one who put Owens in 488, clearly didn't want him out. "The man I saw was Owens. If not," he said to Taylor apprehensively, "I hope you'll tell him I didn't mean harm." The resistance of just about everyone to the proofs of Owens's innocence inflicted a sense of existential irrelevance on Taylor. He felt like someone in Kafka who, the more he would hammer away, the more the nails would emerge from the wooden board. He now had proof that the other man and not Owens, had multiple telephone calls from Bailey and proof that the Gremlin getaway car was Robert's and proof that Loretta was in it—it mattered not, it actually hurt, it seemed to reinforce everyone's insistence on Owens's imprisonment. At last, Taylor perceived that if Owens was in his cell because of a con job, possibly only a con job could extract him. Taylor called up a district attorney telling him, "I'm going to go to the *Tribune*."

Very soon after that, a van arrived at San Quentin and Owens was hustled into it. The drivers, two sheriffs, took him to Oakland but there their radio ordered them, "Don't take him to Oakland! Drive him around," so the sheriffs took him to Lakeside Park and bought him a strawberry shake for forty-nine cents. Then, "Take him to Santa Rita," the radio said, and the sheriffs took the incredulous man to that former concentration camp and to solitary confinement, telling him, "You aren't a prisoner here." "Hurry up," a sheriff told him at five the following morning, and Owens was brought to a courthouse where he waited half a day before a bailiff said, "Mr. Owens? Please stand over here. Stay seated," the bailiff said as the judge hurried in.

BY NOW, THE wart on the judge's nose was as big as an Imperial prune. It smelled of rotten flesh but the judge wouldn't go to the dermatologist, being a Christian Scientist. Sitting down, the judge said to Owens, "Good morning sir," and then endeavored to demonstrate how any miscarriage of justice here was Owens's fault. He showed to Owens his rap sheet, whose entries commenced in his childhood with the theft of four hubcaps for Mr. Mose. He asked if Owens hadn't at times used aliases like Adrian Owens and Adrian O'Day and if Owens hadn't perhaps used the alias ————, the name of the second murderer. He asked if Owens hadn't in fact been arrested with a sawed-off shotgun shortly after the murders in 1972.

"No," Owens answered, amazed at this interrogation.

"All right, sir. If," the judge with the tumor continued, "if you were wrongly convicted, we can be grateful for having a second chance. I do set the information aside," he said, meaning that he was now dropping the murder charges, and he then asked the bailiff if Owens had any new warrants against him. Owens hadn't, having been out of town for 104 months, and the judge reached over his lofty bench to offer his hand to the speechless defendant.

Owens didn't move. "Go, fool," his mother whispered. "Go shake the man's hand and get out," and Owens like a herpetologist sort of touched it.

"Good luck. You may be excused now," the judge concluded.

At first, Owens thought one of the bailiffs would have to conduct him out. He said, "And good luck to you, sir," eyeing the judge's unwholesome prune. He stood there until, it seemed, a pin dropped somewhere, a spell in the air was lifted and Owens, his hands in the hands of his two now teenage daughters, ran to the inconceivable sunshine on Seventh Street.

The judge died of cancer right after that. Owens's anxious lawyer became a judge in Oakland himself. Owens's wife had an illegitimate son, Latonja dropped out of tenth grade but Evangela graduated. In Tahoe, Taylor got married to his new law partner, and Owens, awaiting divorce, got engaged to a bus driver over in San Francisco. Taylor's new wife became a judge and he and Owens became friends, and the two con men would reminisce of old times together in Oakland. Owens sued California for $10 million, but he collected only $10,000, and he's now working at murder trials for $450 per day. A witness for the defense, he tells the uncertain jurors that he wasn't sentenced to death for two murders in 1972—and providentially not, for his last appeal was denied in November 1975 by the Supreme Court in Washington. So just last month would have been the tenth anniversary of Owens's execution.

RANDALL SULLIVAN

Growing Pains

There seems to be little public sentiment for the commercial marijuana grower. In past years, growers have tried to build a "flower child" image whose activities have done no harm to anyone and, in fact, have brought prosperity to economically depressed communities. The facts are that because of the violence associated with marijuana cultivation and the type of people that basically make up the grower's subculture, the quality of life has diminished where growers have taken a foot hold in the community. —1984 Final Report,
Campaign Against Marijuana Planting

I T WAS EARLY IN THAT first spring, almost five years ago, Tom Hoertkorn recalled, after he bought the riverfront land up on Fox Creek, in the redwoods off Highway 36, downstream from the Carlotta general store, that the neighbors began to stop by the house during the late afternoons, one at a time, "to sort of feel me out, see where I stood on the issue."

The issue on Fox Creek, in southern Humboldt County, was the community's leading industry: marijuana.

It was natural that the neighbors would wonder about Hoertkorn. He looked a little on the suburban side by southern Humboldt standards, a short, slight man who wore L.L. Bean corduroys and an earnest expression, with cleanshaven, snubbed features and fine, limp hair cut meticulously around his ears. Hoertkorn suggested the sort of guy whose idea of stepping out was a glass of wine with dinner on special occasions. He spoke through a vague stammer that was enhanced by soft, almost liquescent brown eyes.

"My answer was that I didn't need the money, but that if the wolf was at the door I wouldn't hesitate to do whatever was necessary for my family," Hoertkorn recalled. "I didn't have any moral objections. As long as my property and my family were respected, what other people did to make their living was none of my business."

The neighbors mulled this over for a month or two and decided Hoertkorn was good people. He and his wife Jan and their two daughters Suzanne and Angela settled into the private property camaraderie of the area, bartering berries for baby-sitting and fertilizer for firewood, chipping in to keep the lane graded, watching the neighbors' gates when they were away from home and figuring out fast who the NO TRESPASSING signs were meant for. By the end of his first year on Fox Creek, Hoertkorn knew the identity of the growers. "Most people try to maintain a low profile, but no one really tries to hide what they're doing. No one's ashamed of it. We have one neighbor, he tells everyone he meets he's a grower. He debates people in public, at the store, at meetings. It's a political thing with him, maybe even religious. But he's a very sincere person, and well respected."

Like everyone in Humboldt County, Hoertkorn had heard the stories of patch pirates, marijuana thieves who rode the back roads four to a Land Rover, brandishing Uzis and depositing homesteaders in shallow graves, of the land-mined plantations patrolled by ravenous dobermans where the carcasses of gut-shot deer and poisoned raccoons were littered among the sinsemilla stalks after the fall harvest. None of the people on Fox Creek, though, had ever experienced any of these things firsthand, and as far as anyone there knew the travesties were taking place exclusively in the pages of big city newspapers.

The pot farmers on Fox Creek were raising families and marijuana side by side. "Mom 'n' Pop growers," Hoertkorn called them, folks with a few acres who put in ten or fifteen or twenty plants in the spring and spent most of their illicit income to install solar panels in their roofs or sink septic tanks in their backyards or truck in gravel for their dirt driveways. Even the people Hoertkorn regarded as "the best-liked family in the area," the Hatchers—"the ones who are always there when somebody's kids are sick or their water line breaks"—supposedly grew a few plants every year to fill in the modest income John Hatcher made as a carpenter.

"I know old-time residents, retired loggers and ranchers, who farm pot to supplement their social security checks," Hoertkorn said. "Rural people are just naturally attuned to doing whatever it takes to maintain their land and their home. Whether you're hurting your neighbors means a lot more up here than whether you're obeying the letter of the law."

It was an attitude Hoertkorn had appreciated from the beginning of his stay in Humboldt County, eighteen years earlier. The somewhat sickly scion of a family that had made a modest fortune investing in shopping centers, he moved north from San Francisco with a plan to stay in Humboldt only as long as it took to finish a biology degree at the state university in Arcata. By the time he got close to graduation, though, Hoertkorn had decided he was never going to leave a place where the world's tallest trees grew down to the waterline of the world's widest ocean. The air was rich there and in summer the sequoias were 200-foot prisms in the sunlight. Like most who remain, Hoertkorn was one of those soggy mystics who cherish even the winters: 100 inches of rain, clouds full of rocks, tidal fogs, six-foot ferns growing out of the moss on fallen logs. It was a country of long silences and a reverential regard for personal privacy. The rugged formations and steep forests of the coastal hills had long prevented large settlements. Before the white man, California Indians spoke more than 100 dialects, a diversification of language unmatched anywhere else in the world, and nowhere more evident than on the North Coast.

The myths perpetuated among the whites who settled this backcountry were of rugged individualism often carried to criminal extremes. Black Bart robbed twenty-eight stagecoaches along what is now Highway 101, and an early matriarch of Eureka society, Kate Robertson Asbill, made her reputation by horsewhipping a lawyer outside the Vance Hotel on Second Street. During Prohibition, Garberville constable Jim Thomas was known to take off two or three days every month to cook up a fresh batch of moonshine. After the World War II timber boom went bust, those loggers who lived on in legend were redheaded Irishmen and blond Swedes reputed to drink all evening, fight all night and fornicate till dawn, when they were up at first light to work another twelve hours in the woods.

During his twenties, Hoertkorn found a place in this pageant of primal man. After dropping out of college he built ferrocement fishing boats in the coastal village of Trinidad, taking to the sea himself when sales were slow. By the time Angela, his youngest, started school, however, Hoertkorn was facing forty and prepared to consider a less backbreaking form of endeavor. In 1980 he bought the land on Fox Creek and evolved into an organic farmer, growing berries under a private label for a frozen foods company. Jan got a job as librarian at Hydesville Elementary School, and there were always checks from the family in San Francisco to see them through lean times. Within a few months on Fox Creek, Hoertkorn came to the conclusion that his neighbors were "divided about 50-50, half growers, half not." It was a peaceful coexistence at the beginning, "but then a couple of years ago things started to change drastically," Hoertkorn said. "There was a different group of people coming in. Not land-oriented like the rest of the people up here, just buck-oriented."

"Los Angeles types," Hoertkorn called them. Instead of ten or fifteen plants, they would put in fifty or one hundred, "raising two or three new buildings on their property, parking big new boats and nice new cars in the driveway, all within a year or two. They flaunt what they have and how they got it. Naturally it upsets the home people. You get jealousy, which is always bad for a community."

All of a sudden, out on Highway 36, Hoertkorn recalled, "you'd see these POT GROWER GO HOME signs. It got uncomfortable."

It got considerably more uncomfortable after 1983, when the California

Bureau of Narcotics Enforcement, the U. S. Drug Enforcement Administration and more than thirty local law enforcement groups put together a paramilitary police force they called the Campaign Against Marijuana Planting. Armed CAMP troops raided in fourteen counties but concentrated on southern Humboldt—"the hot spot," a spokesman for California attorney general John Van de Kamp called it.

For reasons that kept the people on Fox Creek guessing all winter, however, CAMP had overlooked the Carlotta area. Hoertkorn and his neighbors read in the San Francisco papers about "a sky darkened by helicopters," but never saw a single one themselves. "We didn't know what to believe," he said.

By 1984 CAMP had been expanded to include ninety-one agencies working in thirty-seven California counties, but again southern Humboldt drew the big crowds: of the 158,493 plants seized state wide, 65,800 were pulled out of the ground in a forty-mile radius around Garberville. Once more, though, it was all quiet in Carlotta.

"After that, some of the growers around here started getting pretty bold," Hoertkorn said. "They were putting plants right out in the open, easy to see from a plane."

In 1985 the planes finally came—and so did the helicopters. Hoertkorn was working on the water tower at the edge of his property on the afternoon of August 22 when he heard the first one, a red Bell "Huey," come thundering in over the bowed redwoods at about 100 feet, headed straight for his home. Hoertkorn watched the helicopter drop as it made its approach, settling into a hover at about fifty feet, directly over his house. By the time Hoertkorn reached his front door, the windows were rattling and the shelves were spilling books onto the living room floor, where he found Suzanne and Angela, aged fourteen and eleven, crouched in opposite corners, crying hysterically.

The red chopper flew away without landing. A shaken Hoertkorn told his girls it was just a big noise, no damage done. He made phone calls to his neighbors, who could tell him only that CAMP was in the area.

Twenty minutes later, Hoertkorn was making instant coffee in his kitchen when he heard a knock at the door. Outside, two dozen men wearing camouflage uniforms and combat boots were jumping off a convoy of trucks in his front yard, all of them armed, most carrying semiautomatic assault rifles or shotguns. The man who knocked on his door informed Hoertkorn that there was a "felony in progress" next door and that his cooperation would be required. After several moments of incoherence, Hoertkorn gathered himself enough to ask if the men had a warrant to be on his property. They didn't. Hoertkorn pointed out that they had driven into his

driveway through a gate posted with three NO TRESPASSING signs. The uniformed men conferred briefly among themselves, shot Hoertkorn "several
threatening looks" and withdrew to the gate, where they set up a roadblock.

An hour later, Jan made it home through the CAMP roadblock, "madder
than I've ever seen her in eighteen years of marriage," her husband said.
While Hoertkorn tried to explain what had happened, a second helicopter, a
white one, swooped in over his property, dangling a long metal cable. The
helicopter slowed in the air above the five-acre parcel across the lane, then
dropped below the treetops. When it rose in the air again, there was a net
filled with marijuana plants at the end of the cable, and the chopper was
once again over Hoertkorn's property, hovering with the marijuana above
the house—"like they were showing off a trophy," he said. For the rest of the
afternoon, he and Jan stood under the prop wash out by their water tower,
taking out-of-focus photographs.

That night, Jan sat up until sunrise with a sick stomach. Angela, "the
out-door girl" who played in the woods from morning till night, refused to
leave the house for three days. Suzanne became convinced the phone was
tapped and moved it into her little sister's room.

Hoertkorn himself felt only a suffocating rage: "All of the women I've
talked to use words like raped and violate and I think the rest of us feel the
same way. Maybe a city person can't understand this, but our land is like part
of us. We live it and breathe it. People here cultivate a kind of tranquility.
When it's abused we take it real personally."

Within a few weeks Fox Creek was visited by a second, smaller
contingent of narcotics agents, armed not with assault rifles but with papers
from the U.S. attorney's office. Notices of forfeiture were presented to every
landowner on whose property marijuana had been found. This included the
Hatchers, whose five acres were being seized for the alleged cultivation of a
dozen plants.

"They used to tell us in the sixties that marijuana distorts reality," Hoertkorn said, "but in the eighties it's the marijuana laws that distort reality."

When the government was gone, several of Hoertkorn's neighbors
approached him to ask if he blamed them for the trauma of the CAMP raids.
Hoertkorn replied that he was glad it had happened. "My daughters maybe
had seen things like this on television, but I don't think they believed it could
ever be real. Now they know it happens, even in this country. We all know. It
was a good reminder. We're not as free up here as we thought."

*Until the advent of CAMP, marijuana cultivation in many rural
areas of Northern California was a low-risk, high-profit criminal
enterprise. It is difficult to characterize typical marijuana grow-*

ers, but one common thread is their desire to make money through illegal means. —IBID

BY THE TIME she was twenty, Leah Allred* had decided "there was no place I was going to fit in ever." From the honor roll at a high school in Long Beach, where she graduated ten days after the Kent State killings, Leah had matriculated to the English department at Berkeley, where she stopped going to classes during February of her freshman year. "I'd listen to people talk about what they were going to do, become teachers or lawyers or what ever, and it all sounded so...arbitrary," Leah said. After a long summer vacation, Leah enrolled—under pressure from her parents—as a sociology major at Cal State Long Beach. That lasted four weeks. "I was living at home and it was like being back in high school. Also, Long Beach depressed me. It was becoming all six-lane roads and shopping centers." As a last resort, Leah's father, a real estate agent, sent her north to Humboldt State, where she declared for political science but kept falling asleep in class. "It was like I had narcolepsy or something," she recalled. "Every time a lecture would start, I'd nod off."

Though she hated the school, Leah loved the place: "There was this tang in the air and the light was sort of smoky. I felt very robust when I wasn't in class." Afraid to face her father, however, with the news that she'd dropped out of her third school in two years, Leah "faked" her way through the fall semester—"it really wasn't that difficult"—and began working as a waitress in nearby Eureka. "I was trying to save some money, figuring I'd be out on my own pretty soon. Mostly though I was just sort of dreaming, waiting for something to happen." Something finally did; Leah got pregnant. The same day the doctor told her, she decided to have the baby: "I just realized that being a mother was one thing that I had no qualms about." Leah's boyfriend Stuart, a sculptor-writer-dishwasher who had dropped out of school the year before, supported her decision—"but that's about all he supported," she said.

While her belly was still small enough to hide under a sweater, Leah went home for a visit. "I found the whole L.A. area so ugly," she said. "Concrete spreading over everything like some kind of dry lava from a volcano you couldn't see, and the endless straggle to keep up with the people next door, down the street, on the next block, on the other side of the world. Up here [in Humboldt] people were different. The difference was that they liked being different. They valued it. Eccentricity is sort of admired in this area."

The next time Leah got off the bus in Eureka she was five months pregnant and Stuart was waiting at the terminal to tell her he was ready to

---

*The names and identifying details in this section have been changed.

give country living a try. He knew people down near Garberville and took Leah for a visit. "We drove down the Avenue of the Giants," she remembered, "and I just kept saying, 'Yes! Yes! Yes!'"

During the early 1970s the green nooks and remote crannies of southern Humboldt were beginning to fill up with the remnants of the counterculture born miles south and several years earlier in San Francisco. Many of the people Leah met in Garberville had been traveling around the country in buses and vans for months, even years, before deciding that the redwood forests of the Northern California coast were the ideal place to take root. "This area has always attracted a lot of independent spirits, which is maybe another way of saying misfits," Leah observed. "Compared to other places there's very little pressure to conform or perform. People who'd probably be in institutions or on the streets if they stayed in the cities have been able to find homes here."

The explanations are as much economic as environmental. Sparsely populated and largely subdivided into twenty- and forty-acre homesteads, southern Humboldt entered the seventies dependent on government spending, summer tourism and a dwindling logging industry. The result was a buyer's market in which some of the world's lushest landscapes were available at bargain prices. During the early part of the decade it was possible to move into a house on forty acres for as little as $5,000 down and payments of $200 a month. Undeveloped land, which Leah and Stuart had in mind, was even cheaper.

After their daughter Beth was born, the three of them moved into a house in Garberville, sharing the rent with two other tenants. For almost half a year, Leah worked two jobs, as a motel maid and a cocktail waitress, while Stuart got himself hired as a tree planter for a timber company. With the $1,600 they saved, the $500 Leah's father gave her and cash from the sale of Stuart's Volkswagen, they were able to buy a flatbed truck and make a down payment on eighteen acres of steep ravines and brushy second-growth forest in the hills northwest of Garberville, a part of southern Humboldt where locals claim it rains 200 inches some years.

"We thought we'd pretty much live off the land," Leah remembered. "Grow our own food, fill in with food stamps, maybe get summer jobs when the woods were open or the tourists were in town."

Life in the country, however, did not proceed as planned. The first vegetable garden went into the ground too late and was an almost total failure. "Only the cucumbers really came in," Leah recalled. "We practically lived on pickles that winter." The little family called an army tent home until November, well into the rainy season, when Stuart and a friend finished a one-room shack with a sleeping loft that they built mostly out of salvaged wood. "The windows were pieces of plastic nailed to two-by-fours and you got splinters if you walked on the floor in your socks." Leah said. "The wood stove wasn't well vented; more smoke blew out into the room than went up through the roof." The road into the homestead had become a long mud puddle when the rain started to fall, and it stayed that way all winter. Leah and Stuart had to park the truck out by the pavement on Mattole Road and slog three-quarters of a mile on foot to go into town. Stuart had bought the flatbed with the idea of hauling firewood, but that summer he discovered that cutting cords was a lot of work for very little reward. He lasted out the first winter, but couldn't endure the second. One day in January he drove away in the truck and never came back.

Leah stayed on alone with her infant daughter; "Maybe it sounds strange after everything I've been saying, but I loved it here, even at the beginning. For the first time in my life I felt at home. I got lonely sometimes, but I had Beth and she was a lot of company." She went on welfare that winter, using almost half her monthly check to make the land payment and eating off the rest. With the $300 she had hidden in the base of her treadle sewing machine, she bought an old Dodge Dart and drove into Garberville one morning a week to shop. Leah had stopped setting her hair a long time ago; out on the land she stopped bothering even to brush it. She took on a sort of white Rastafarian look, with a thick, tangled, dark blond mane framing a lightly freckled complexion, wide-set brown eyes and cleft chin. The baby fat she had carried into her pregnancy melted away, and for the first time Leah "felt like a woman" as she sashayed through town in the thermal underwear tops, long skirts and leather work boots she wore almost every day. "I really liked the way I looked back then," she remembered, and so did the brawny man with the black-bearded smile Leah met one spring day at the food stamp office.

Mel was a stonemason from Southern California who "smiled a lot but hardly ever said anything." He had discovered that construction work was available for about four months out of every year in the Garberville area, "which was fine with Mel," Leah said. "He was a hard worker, but not a very ambitious person, if that makes sense." Mel moved out on the land with Leah in May and stayed fifteen months. She remembered him fondly: "Mel made a lot of improvements. He finished the floor, put in glass windows for me, vented the stove so it stopped smoking. He built us a new privy and put a little porch on the front. The place looked a lot better after he left than before he came, and so did I."

At the end of his second summer on the land, Mel went off to Oregon to work on a friend's fishing boat. A month later he wrote Leah that he'd decided to stay and urged her to move up. "But I'd found my place," she said, "and I wasn't going to leave it."

It was Mel who planted the first marijuana on Leah's property—"strictly for personal use"—three spindly stalks that grew to about six feet and yielded maybe a quarter of a pound in buds. "It occurred to me right off that there might be some spending money in this," Leah said, "but that was about as far as my thinking got."

Her mind raced ahead the next fall, though, after a neighbor asked if she was interested in some seasonal employment. The man was a witty, middle-aged hippie with a graying ponytail who claimed to have flunked out of Caltech, and Leah was thrilled when he offered her $8 an hour, tax free, to manicure marijuana plants. "He had about thirty-five plants, all at least fifteen feet tall and real bushy," she remembered. "I was amazed that marijuana got that big. He was getting a pound a plant." When the neighbor paid Leah for her two weeks' work, he threw in a small packet of seeds and suggested a couple of volumes on cultivation.

Over the long wet winter Leah discovered that there was an agricultural revolution happening in Humboldt County. Certain homesteaders had begun to experiment with the genetics of marijuana, breeding the tall, slender *Sativa* hemp indigenous to North America with the squat, bushy *Indica* cannabis native to Afghanistan, creating hybrids that retained the best qualities of each. The backcountry botanists had also observed that the flowering female plants were using as much as forty percent of their precious bodily fluids to produce seeds. If all the male plants in a garden were eliminated, the growers found that the unpollinated females—instead of producing seeds—oozed more and more of the sparkly, sticky resin that traps pollen and also contains most of marijuana's psychoactive ingredient, tetrahydrocannabinol, or THC. A new strain of grass was born, called sinsemilla (Spanish for "without seeds"), a plant whose THC content is often greater than that of Colombian marijuana and significantly greater than the Mexican pot many people smoked in the sixties.

During the spring of 1977, Leah started her seeds in Dixie cups, and in May, while Beth solemnly observed, she planted the twelve-inch sprouts in holes filled with chicken manure on a southern slope above the creek that ran along the edge of her property. For five months she watered her garden by hand, carrying a Rubbermaid bucket up the hill "at least ten thousand times," Leah said. "My legs were like iron by September."

Nine plants survived disease, rodents and mold until the October harvest, all of them close to twelve feet tall by then, with a yield of five pounds in processed buds. Through her neighbor, Leah sold the crop for $6,000 in $100 bills. "An untold fortune, as far as I was concerned," Leah remembered. "I was too excited to go out. Beth and I got into bed with the money and just spread it out all over the covers. I couldn't stop laughing."

By the spring of 1978 Leah had sunk a septic tank, installed a flush toilet and put in a sink with running water. That fall she harvested thirteen plants from two separate gardens watered out of plastic Kolaps-A-Tanks. The eight-and-a-half pounds of buds sold for more than $12,000 cash. Leah's first purchase that year was a generator, to which she connected the stereo that had been in cardboard boxes for four years. Later she would add a master bedroom to the back of the house, with greenhouse windows that provided a panoramic view of the hills she had been staring at every morning for two years through a single sheet of smeared glass.

Leah traded in the Dodge for a used Ford pickup and gave herself a shopping spree in San Francisco for Christmas, Beth, who now had the loft to herself, started the first grade with a wardrobe of new clothes.

By the end of 1980 Leah had treated herself to a March vacation in Maui, purchased a Chinese rug for the living room and traded in the Ford pickup for a Renault. She had learned over the course of time that many, maybe most, of her neighbors were also growing marijuana, "but there was no competition among us at all," Leah said. "It felt like there was enough for everybody. Harvest was a time of celebration."

No wonder. In Humboldt County, where the ceaseless hills and rocky soil made farming untenable, marijuana had changed everything. Money made the back-to-the-land movement work. "It was like the sacred herb had saved us," Leah said. "We were going to be able to keep our land without having to pay the price of abject poverty or of doing work that was demeaning or destructive. It just all seemed to form a perfect configuration."

The configuration grew more complicated, however, as the good news spread. In 1977 the *San Francisco Chronicle* published the first story about marijuana money in southern Humboldt, and it was the publicity, in Leah's opinion, that "brought in the bad element." At first it was just more reporters, but then came the cops and robbers. For the first time, narcs became a nuisance, though still nothing to get into a panic over. The raids then usually amounted to a half-dozen deputies aboard a garbage truck, Leah remembered, and you were only at serious risk if you planted a garden that could be seen from the road. Many of the county's big busts were actually hilarious; you'd read about them in the *Redwood Record* under headlines like OFFICER CHASING DRUNK FINDS 200 PLANTS or LAWMEN CHECKING WRECK TURN UP POT. More problematic were the patch pirates. Most were nothing more than "some kid on a Honda with a Hefty bag and a pistol strapped to his leg," as the Record's editor Mike Lee put it, though it could not be denied that an armed nineteen-year-old boy could make a considerable impact on the countryside.

It was probably the summer people, though, the ones who came into the county strictly to do business, who were the real harbingers of doom. Some aging surfer from San Diego would trade in his 280Z for a Toyota truck, drive north in the early spring, plunk a few thousand down on forty acres, promise a big balloon payment in two years, put in a 250-plant garden, clear maybe $125,000 after expenses, winter on the beach, come back to do it again the next summer, then disappear forever. The summer people not only attracted more police, they also attracted more rip-off artists. A market developed for armed guards. An older brother of one of Beth's friends claimed to have earned $4,000 by spending two months sitting up nights with an M-16 in a 600-plant garden near Blocksburg.

"You could see the beginning of a taint on things," Leah said. "In a business where people operate on handshakes and hard cash, you need trust. And people just weren't as trusting."

The advantages of growing, though, still outweighed the disadvantages, Leah thought, and not many people in southern Humboldt were inclined to disagree. Business was booming in Garberville. Within ten years the number of families in the area who were living on welfare plummeted from almost twenty percent of the population to barely three percent. The liquor store was stocking French champagne by the case, and Garberville's big emporium, Murrish's, was displaying Weiss clippers in bushel baskets by the checkout stands. A young entrepreneur from India opened a business called Astral Travel just off Main Street and began booking winter flights to Mexico, Hawaii and the South Pacific. In October of 1982—the same month the paper began carrying a weekly "Bust Barometer"—Mike Lee ran a special piece in italics on the *Record*'s front page. "New, small businesses are popping up all over Southern Humboldt-Northern Mendocino," the story began, and went on to report that thirty-six new establishments had begun ringing up sales during the past year in the Garberville-Redway area (population 1,611) alone. No mention was made of the marijuana industry.

Lee, who came to Garberville in 1977—"looking for a good old country redneck town," he remembered with a wry laugh—had learned responsible journalism the hard way, after one of his early columns linked the influx of $100 bills in town to local "pot farming." "That hit like a nuclear bomb," he recalled. "People were really angry at me. They all said it was going to bring trouble. A lot of the older merchants really didn't want to think about where the money was coming from."

JUST OVER THE county line, Mendocino's longtime agricultural commissioner, Ted Erickson, in 1980 declared marijuana the area's number one cash crop. An infuriated board of supervisors forced Erickson to tear the marijuana page out of every copy of his annual report. When he repeated his remarks for "60 Minutes" early in 1981, Erickson was charged with "erratic behavior" and fired from the job he had held for twenty-eight years.

In Humboldt, the silent majority clearly supported a policy of live and let live, as the county's two most powerful politicians, conservative ten-term congressman Don Clausen and dark-eyed district attorney Bernard DePaoli, discovered after the 1982 elections. During their campaigns, Republicans Clausen and DePaoli had each endorsed raids by state narcotics agents in southern Humboldt. "You better start thinking about changing your life-style," Clausen advised the residents of Garberville, while DePaoli estimated out loud that half the 108,000 people in Humboldt County were "dependent on marijuana for their livelihood, one way or another." In November, both men lost by two-to-one margins. In southern Humboldt alone, the vote had gone fifteen to one against him, DePaoli announced.

Those who wanted to typecast greater Garberville as some vast wooded haven for renegade hippies, however, were missing the place. "When I first came here, there was a definite hip/straight schism," Mike Lee remembered. "But over time the two sides grew together." The mix of crusty old-timers and young seekers from the cities aligned the real and the ideal in a delicate balance. The common values became a love of the land, a yearning for self-sufficiency, contempt for bureaucratic authority and a bedrock belief in the spirit of free enterprise that, as Leah put it, "the Gettys and the Exxons and the rest of Ronald Reagan's friends use to justify corporate takeovers." What emerged was a community that staged athletic events like the Kinetic Sculpture Race and the 5 Bar/5 Beer/5 Kilometer Marathon; with an elec-torate that would vote two-to-one for the nuclear freeze and three-to-one against gun control; where the weekly newspaper would follow up a two-part series, the dangers of dipping (chewing tobacco, that is), with a front-page story on the growing local heroin problem.

For Leah, like a lot of other people in southern Humboldt, 1982 would be both the best and worst of years. She turned her biggest profit ever, $22,000, yet at the same time saw the taint thickening at an alarming rate. That summer the county was crawling with people who had come in to make a fast buck. Up at Island Mountain, agents raided a garden where they arrested three Frenchmen who were in the country on tourist visas. Over in Phillipsville, deputies found thirty opium poppies planted in the middle of a pot Patch. And the rip-offs were becoming more outrageous. A team of uniformed thieves posing as sheriff's deputies "raided" at least a dozen growers. In Redway, sixty-five-year-old Ralph Lewis was attacked by three teenagers who hit him over the head with a nickel-plated bar, and when the police arrived it was the old man they arrested; seven pounds of processed pot had been recovered from Lewis's truck, and another eighty pounds from his home.

A drug rip-off was a "low-risk crime," said Sergeant Floyd Gustin, commander of the sheriff's substation in Garberville, "Ninety-nine percent of the time the victims don't report a robbery involving drugs. I hear about it a couple of days later." He had recently responded to a report of machine-gun fire in Redway, Gustin said, "and the only ones who would tell me anything were the kids going to school on the bus."

That fall, the wire-service stories with Garberville datelines weren't about marijuana and money, but about marijuana and murder. In 1982 Humboldt tied San Francisco for the highest homicide rate in the state. Within a few months that year, five murders—all allegedly "drug related"—were reported in southern Humboldt, more than during the three previous years combined. Bodies were discovered under the Moody Bridge just west of Garberville, in a sleeping bag on the side of the road in Zenia, buried in shallow graves at Blocksburg and Rancho Sequoia. The event that truly gave people pause, though, was the killing of Kathy Davis.

Kathy was a pillar of the community, a dark, delicate woman who had lived in southern Humboldt since 1969. A former Berkeley social worker, she sat on the county grand jury and served as director of the Community Credit Union of Southern Humboldt. She had been a founder of Papa John's organic pizza parlor and a volunteer at the local hospice for the terminally ill. Kathy was also a marijuana grower, working an eleven-acre homestead off Salmon Creek Road. She had gotten into the business because her job as a waitress kept her away from home nights, Kathy said, and she wanted to spend more time with her adopted daughter.

On the night of September 29, 1982, she was in bed reading *The Clan of the Cave Bear* when two men wearing Halloween masks walked through her open breezeway, held a .38 revolver to her head and said they wanted her money, all of it. One of the men was twenty-year-old Rene Palomino, who had manicured marijuana for Kathy's ex-boyfriend; Kathy had once allowed him to sleep at her house for two nights with his wife and baby. The other was Palomino's twenty-eight-year-old uncle, Armando Mendoza. Kathy gave the two men everything she had, $1,000 in $100 bills, but Mendoza insisted there was more. When she told him that was all of it, Mendoza dragged Kathy into the small drying room under the sleeping loft, beat her with the barrel of the .38 until her face was gone, and left the body on the floor amid sixteen pounds of sinsemilla buds.

A neighbor with a motorcycle and a Colt .45 strapped to his leg caught Mendoza just after first light the next morning. Within an hour D.A. DePaoli was on the scene, wearing a Smith and Wesson revolver on his hip and a nine-millimeter automatic tucked into his boot. A highway patrol helicopter flew into the canyon, searching for Palomino as the frantic homesteaders on

Salmon Creek stampeded out into the morning fog to cut down their crops. The helicopter landed in a yard where an American flag thirty-five feet tall was flying. A man armed with an Uzi and a .357 magnum confronted the pilot and was granted instant immunity.

More than 120 of Kathy Davis's neighbors held a wake for her, joining hands around a small pond to sing "Amazing Grace." Kathy's adopted daughter scattered her ashes around an apricot tree. In Eureka, Armando Mendoza pleaded guilty to second-degree murder and was sentenced to sixteen years in Folsom. Rene Palomino was allowed to plead as an accessory after the fact and got a year in county jail.

In Leah's neighborhood, more than a dozen neighbors formed what they called a "security collective": a patrol of two armed growers would be on the road every night between August 15 and the end of harvest.

In 1983 there were no murders at all in southern Humboldt, but this didn't make headlines anywhere except the *Redwood Record*. The news out of Garberville that year was the arrival of CAMP. Warned by the attorney general's office of the planned raids months in advance, Leah and her neighbors took pains to conceal their crops, camouflaging with manzanita and planting closer to the trees. Despite their efforts, at least a half-dozen growers who watered their gardens out of the same creek Leah used got busted. The CAMP troops missed Leah's crop that first year, but the patch pirates finally found it. One morning in September she walked into the largest of her three gardens and found nothing left of the fifteen-foot plants that had been there the day before except six-inch stalks.

Leah was still able to harvest a dozen plants, enough to carry her through the next year, and that winter she was one of the few local growers who suggested that CAMP might have a positive aspect. "I said the raids might drive out the big commercial growers and the rest of the greedy people," she recalled. Leah saw signs of a spiritual resurgence; the popularity of the "soulless" drug cocaine had peaked and passed in the community. "I thought maybe things could go back to the way they'd been before," she said.

The philosophy of positivism was easier to preach than to practice, though, as Leah learned one afternoon in July of the next year. "I drove into town when I heard CAMP was coming," she remembered. "I came home that night and my house had been ransacked; they'd tacked a receipt for eighteen plants on my front door." Leah was never charged with any crime—the gardens were far from her house and there was no physical evidence to prove she had been the grower—but the loss of her entire crop and the watering system seemed punishment enough. "I'd saved a little money, but we had to start getting food stamps again that winter," she said.

The community was having its own economic difficulties. Gil Gilbertson, motel owner and past president of the Garberville-Redway Chamber of Commerce, reluctantly admitted his trade was off twenty-two percent, and "some merchants say they're down twenty-five to thirty percent from the year before," Mike Lee reported.

Leah's economic decline was even steeper: as the CAMP troops moved in for their third season in southern Humboldt, she culled her garden down to just five plants. "I need that much just to survive out here," she said. "Even if I harvest, I'll be back on welfare by next summer."

> *Henry David Thoreau was an advocate of civil disobedience against what an individual might perceive to be an unjust law. Thoreau said, however, that one must be prepared to accept the consequences of their* [sic] *acts of civil disobedience.* —IBID

DON SINOWAY WAS thirty-six years old and on the high side of the way up in 1981 when he retired as a big-city lawyer and moved his family to a homestead near the southern Humboldt hamlet of Miranda, twelve miles up 101 from Garberville.

He rented the office on Avenue of the Giants a year later, he said, only because his law books were molding in the damp air at home. "I figured I might eventually set up a small practice, work maybe two days a week." The first indication that Sinoway's services would be in greater demand came during September of 1982, when state narcotics agents performed a series of "test raids" in the New Harris area of southern Humboldt. "They came in with helicopter attacks, swooping and dive-bombing the countryside, going into homes without warrants," he recalled. "It was the prototype for CAMP." Sinoway drove into the hills east of Garberville for a community meeting. "The people in the area were outraged," he remembered. "They said, This is still America, isn't it?"

Sinoway didn't have an answer, but he was familiar with the question. Back at Georgetown University's law school, his favorite class was Supreme Court Seminar. "We had reserved seats for the oral arguments," he recalled, "and I got to witness firsthand the final rulings of the law of the land. It made quite an impression." After clerking for a federal appeals court judge, Sinoway had gone on to specialize in constitutional law, an unusual choice for an ambitious young attorney, though one that proved profitable when he began handling class-action suits.

He began to grasp what was developing in Humboldt County, Sinoway said. "I could see a whole new area of the law opening up right under my nose. There were obvious issues of the Fourth Amendment where there were no precedents at all. It was tremendously exciting."

The next spring Sinoway called his own meeting: to organize the Civil Liberties Monitoring Project. The group was incorporated in Miranda in June of 1983, at almost the same instant Attorney General Van de Kamp was in Sacramento announcing the cration of CAMP.

"Van de Kamp said they would be using U-2 spy planes and satellites to locate gardens," Sinoway recalled. "He was saying things like they could see shoelaces and license plates. Scare tactics."

In July, Van de Kamp announced that every CAMP trooper would be given three days of special commando training. "We realized then that they would be coming in heavy," Sinoway said. "We contacted NORML [the National Organization for the Reform of Marijuana Laws] and met with their attorneys to discuss a lawsuit against spying on private citizens."

Sinoway and NORML were still talking on August 24, 1983, when CAMP staged its first major raid, hitting the ground at an untamed little mountain village called Denny, just across the line from Humboldt in Trinity County. That night, Sinoway got a phone call. "It was a group of hysterical people all shouting at once," he recalled, saying their town had been taken over by uniformed troops and sealed with roadblocks, that children had been separated from adults and guns were everywhere. Sinoway drove in by the one-lane road off Highway 299 the next day, arriving in Denny about an hour after the last CAMP troopers had gone. "What I heard was just amazing," he remembered. A woman named Pat Parsons said she had awakened to the sound of engines at about seven that morning. She went to the window, Parsons told Sinoway, and saw a convoy of pickup trucks pulling into her pasture. Badly frightened, Parsons pulled on a pair of pants, grabbed her boots and ran barefoot out the back door. As she lay in the dirt under a holly bush, she watched several dozen armed men, most wearing camouflage, climb out of the trucks.

"I had no idea who they were," said Parsons, who six years earlier had fled "crime-ridden" San Francisco for a forty-six-acre ranch on New River. The former microbiologist now worked a gold-mining claim with her husband, raised a few head of cattle and filled in with seasonal employment on a Caltrans highway maintenance crew.

As she made her way through the forest toward a neighbor's house that morning, Parsons said, she had watched a large green helicopter rumble into the valley, skim across the pines and land in her front yard. It was late afternoon before she returned home, Parsons told Sinoway, and the uniformed men were gone. She found the lock on her front gate cut, and the pasture where the helicopter had landed was strewn with marijuana plants, sections of irrigation hose, lunch bags, soft drink cans and candy bar wrappers. The cattle had been let out of their pasture, and her vegetable garden was trampled. At the house, a ladder stood raised to a second-story window. Inside, a picture album lay open on the dining table. Missing were two of Parsons's state unemployment checks, a sheaf of mining claim documents and the small scale she and her husband used to weigh gold.

Another area resident, Judy Rolicheck, told Sinoway the armed troops had blocked her driveway at about eight that morning. Her husband, an employee of the Trinity County Roads Department, had left for work while it was still dark, Rolicheck said, so she stayed inside the cabin with her daughter Deena and fifteen-month-old granddaughter Althea. At about 8:30 she had seen several uniformed men walk up the driveway. "They shouted for us to come out of our cabin with our hands up," Rolicheck recalled. When the women stepped outside, they found the cabin surrounded by more than a dozen men with guns. From the other side of the creek, Rolicheck's doberman, Duchess, began to bark and ran toward the troops. "Deena and I asked to let us get Duchess, who had never bitten anyone in her life, so we could chain her up," Rolicheck said. "The head trooper told us no, to get back on the porch with our hands up, at which time the troopers shot Duchess with a shotgun. She was crying, and Deena asked for someone to put her out of her misery. Another trooper shot her with a rifle, and she died."

Eric Masset told Sinoway that he and his wife were headed into town from their mining claim four miles north of Denny at about 11:30 that morning when they were stopped by "six men with camouflage uniforms with their guns pointed at us." After they were allowed to pass, Masset said, the couple picked up supplies at Ladd's store but found the road home blocked by the highway patrol.

At Hawkins Bar, where other stranded neighbors had gathered, the Massets were told that the Grover Ladd Elementary School was being used by the troops as a staging area and helicopter landing zone. Sue Masset, concerned about her two daughters, aged nine and eleven, drove into town with another woman to pick the girls up, but found the school closed and the area "cordoned off." She parked a few hundred feet away, Sue Masset said, "but as soon as we opened the doors two troopers with guns jumped at us... shouting, "Back in your rig! Back in your rig!" When the two women explained that they were looking for her daughters, Sue Masset said, the CHP troops "told me that the girls had gone by and not to get out of my truck. I drove up and down the road and guns were pointed at me the whole time."

She parked at Ladd's and went ahead on foot toward the roadblock, where she was searched and told she could not pass without giving her name, social security number, eye color, driver's license number and home address. The officials filled out something they called a field interrogation card and said she would need it to enter or leave town.

It was after eight before the Massets, unable to find their daughters, got home through the roadblock that night. As the CAMP troops came from the countryside into town, Eric Masset said, they began to chant, "War on Drugs! War on Drugs!" The Massets did not see their daughters until the next afternoon, when the two girls and several other children were released from the schoolteacher's home where they had been taken under armed escort the day before.

Neither Pat Parsons nor Judy Rolicheck—nor for that matter the Massets—had been charged with any crime, Sinoway discovered. Nor had Denny postmistress Katherine Bauer, who said the CAMP troops had threatened to "open up" on her house when she walked to the end of her driveway to watch them pass. No marijuana had been found on their property, which the CAMP troops had entered without warrants. As the story of the New River raid spread through Northern California, CAMP officials in Sacramento denied any "unprofessional conduct" and reported that more than 1,900 marijuana plants had been seized in the Denny area—mostly out of the national forest—during the two-day "operation."

"It was obvious we were seeing a whole new approach to law enforcement," Sinoway said. "CAMP wasn't just coming in to tear out marijuana gardens, they were staging the military invasion of an entire community. They were saying, basically, that anyone who lives in the same neighborhood as a dope grower, and doesn't report him, faces guilt by association."

As Sinoway gathered affidavits in Denny, CAMP gathered momentum in Humboldt County. By the first week of September, people in the Garberville area were expecting the worst. They had been expecting it for two years, ever since the afternoon in 1981 when then-attorney general George Deukmejian jumped out of the police helicopter Angel II and landed in a blaze of camera lights at the northern Mendocino town of Willits to announce the War on Drugs. Wearing a black cap that bore the emblem of a green marijuana leaf with a red slash through it—the future CAMP insignia—Deukmejian had supervised the arrest of a sixty-seven-year-old grandmother. A year later, he was elected governor.

"I was in a local bar the night before the first CAMP raid, and the rumors were flying," *Record* editor Mike Lee remembered. "Everyone was certain that an armed platoon of the National Guard was camped south of Garberville. People said there was an aircraft carrier off Shelter Cove."

Early the next morning, CAMP spokesman Al King held a press conference in town to describe the threats posed by "booby-trapped gardens" and "terrorist tactics" among the growers. The raid itself was mostly a media event, attended by an ABC network camera crew, a team of French journalists and a correspondent from *National Geographic* who complained that this sort of thing had been a lot more fun in Mexico, where "they met us at the airport with sandwiches and margaritas."

CAMP came in, as it developed, with neither a National Guard platoon nor an aircraft carrier. There were four helicopters and approximately eighty-five men, and the raids in southern Humboldt were simply smaller-scale replays of Denny.

It was October, at the height of harvest, before Sinoway got his Denny affidavits before U.S. District Judge Robert Aguilar. Though "disturbed" by what he read, Aguilar said, he could not issue an injunction against CAMP without evidence of "a continuing and persistent pattern of abuse."

"After that, CAMP basically stalled us for the next year," Sinoway said. "They tried to move the venue to Sacramento. They delayed our discovery. They wouldn't respond to our letters. It took me a month just to get [CAMP attorney] Tom Dove to clarify their break-in policy."

While Sinoway inched his way toward a second hearing, CAMP troops swarmed into southern Humboldt for the summer of 1984 at twice the strength of the year before. Sinoway and his team of volunteers followed in the raiders' wake, collecting the indignant testimony of rural residents of the areas CAMP had hit hardest: a blind grandmother from Rancho Sequoia who said that after she and her guide dog had been chased by the heli-copters, the animal refused to lead her on her own property; a teacher at the state day care center in Briceland who told Sinoway that children frightened off the playground by the helicopters had asked her to lock the doors and windows during flyovers; an elderly man from Alder Point who complained that CAMP troops had torn out his flower garden and cut down his prize Christmas tree to make a helicopter landing zone; the supervisor of the Alder Point/Harris Summer Recreation Program who reported that her field trip party had been threatened with arrest when they arrived at Black Sands Beach on a day CAMP was burning marijuana there; a Blocksburg farmer who said he had been detained by CAMP troopers who wanted to check his hands for callouses.

On October 17, 1984, with the declarations of those five people and more than fifty others before him, Judge Aguilar issued the injunction Sinoway asked for: CAMP troops were prohibited from entering any private property other than open fields without warrants and ordered to keep the helicopters at least 500 feet from any person, structure or vehicle.

"I think one thing the judge's order did, immediately, was convince people here they weren't powerless," Sinoway said. "CAMP seemed to believe that the residents of this area have no rights politically. Any involve-ment in drugs is unpopular, and they figured they could go after the pot growers while it's open season."

With the arrival of CAMP '85, Sinoway, who had planned to work three days a week, was "hardly ever home anymore." The key attorney on what had grown into a $100 million class-action suit against CAMP, Sinoway was also representing many of the growers who had been arrested on criminal charges in the previous summer's raids.

"You know, under the traditional legal definition, there are two classes of crime," he explained. "There's *malum in se*, that which is bad by itself, and *malum prohibitum*, that which is bad because it is prohibited. The second category is always political, economic, social. It changes constantly." According to Sinoway, the national War on Drugs was nothing but "a cover for our failures. People in power want the unemployed steelworker in Dayton whose fifteen-year-old daughter is all sexed up and out of control, whose seventeen-year-old son isn't pulling the kind of grades he needs to become a doctor or lawyer, to believe that marijuana is the root cause of their problem. It's a lot easier than facing the truth."

Whatever Sinoway felt about the drugs, however, he could not deny that it was escalating. In April of 1985, just as the spring planting began in southern Humboldt, the first federal grand jury ever convened north of San Francisco held hearings in Eureka. Frustrated by the refusal of local juries to hand out heavy sentences to growers, federal authorities now sought to use grand juries and new forfeiture laws that allowed for the confiscation of land belonging to pot farmers.

"The stakes are rising," Sinoway said. "The forfeitures are definitely their big weapon." CAMP's strategy now seemed to be choosing only people who had considerable equity in their homes.

Among Sinoway's newest clients were three businesses located in Chicago, Washington state and Oregon—all advertisers in the magazine *High Times*. "The government is trying to force them to provide customer lists," he explained. "Now you're getting into the First Amendment and trade secret privileges. At times you feel like you're involved in some sort of last stand here."

> *One objective of CAMP is to provide a public awareness program on the inherent dangers associated with marijuana cultivation and trafficking.* —IBID

ED DENSON WAS still a relative newcomer to southern Humboldt. He had spent most of his adult life in the Bay Area, managing during the sixties the bands Country Joe and the Fish and Joy of Cooking. Later he ran a music school and eventually created Kicking Mule Records, a mail-order folk label much like one he and guitarist John Fahey had owned years earlier. In 1980, verging on middle age, Denson got divorced and sold his house. That same year, the lease on his warehouse expired. "I realized there was nothing to keep me in San Francisco anymore," he said. "I had a mail-order business that I could run from anywhere in the world."

Denson and his wife-to-be drove up the coast looking at real estate. It was in southern Humboldt that they found "the most for the least": thirty acres of pine and redwood, a log house, a large barn and electricity, adjacent to a paved road, all for $110,000. Their plan was to lead a quiet life, but CAMP was to convince Denson he would have to go a lot farther than 200 miles to find one.

"The helicopters flew over my ranch as many as thirty-five times a week during the summer of 1984," Denson remembered. "They would pass right above my house at treetop height. It brought my business to a stop. I had no illusions about the reality of the situation. I had been in the Free Speech Movement in Berkeley in the early sixties. For the first time in twenty years, though, I felt like doing something, getting involved."

He called the Federal Aviation Administration first, Denson recalled. "The FAA told me, 'That's CAMP and we have no jurisdiction.' I said, 'Who does?' and they didn't know." Furious, Denson sat in his office making long-distance calls through an entire workday. The sheriff's department in Eureka said they had no authority; CAMP was a state operation. In the late afternoon, Denson finally got through to CAMP headquarters in Sacramento. "They said the pilot was not a government employee. They said, 'He's a contract worker and we really can't control what he does.'"

But without the helicopters, explained CAMP deputy commander Bill Ruzzamenti in an interview with Humboldt historian Ray Raphael, "we just couldn't get the job done nearly as effectively. The helicopters have provided us with a sense of superiority that has in fact established a paranoia in the growers' minds and has kept us from getting involved in violence with the growers. It's not perceived as an equal situation where they might conceivably fight and win. When you come in with a helicopter, there's no way they're going to stop and fight; by and large they head for the hills."

So the aerial assaults continued through August into September. Denson lived in Alder Point, near what had formerly been the community's economic mainspring, the Louisiana Pacific lumber mill. Only a few months earlier, the company had closed the mill, and now CAMP was using the abandoned site as its central staging area. The neighbors whose homes had been entered described a pattern of petty harassment: water pipes cut, closets emptied, refrigerators unplugged so food would spoil. Denson remembered that a friend who worked as a professional musician said that during the search of his home CAMP officers had torn the front board off his fiddle—" 'looking for drugs,' they said. We're talking about an irreplaceable antique, a beautiful instrument. I was incensed."

For his part, Ruzzamenti believed the residents of southern Humboldt were aware of a deeply felt shift "back to conservative thinking," as he put it. During the late seventies, a fifteen-year trend toward increased support for the legalization of marijuana had been reversed. Opinion polls showed people headed in the other direction ever since, and by 1985, seventy-three percent of the adults in America were opposed to legalization, said the Gallup organization.

"So what?" said Ed Denson. "I didn't care if people were against marijuana. It would be all right with me if ninety-nine percent of Americans got so upset about marijuana they stopped buying it. What bothered me was that the government had apparently declared war on this area and the people who live here."

After the summer raids of 1984, Denson spent the entire winter brooding: "Nothing had gotten to me like this in a long time. I felt so powerless and violated. The older you get, the more you can let stuff go by. But then something comes along that you can't let go by, and it becomes very important. *Very* important."

Early in the spring of 1985, Denson heard that a group of people calling themselves the Citizens Observation Group was planning to monitor the CAMP raids that summer. The first COG meeting turned out to be the biggest political event in southern Humboldt history, standing-room-only at the Veterans Memorial Hall.

"Everyone wanted to know, 'What can we do?'" Denson's friend Deirdre Ryan (not her real name) remembered. "We didn't think anything. CAMP said we were all growers, but when the question was put, 'Who would vote for legalization?' everybody in the room raised their hands. Big growers, you know, don't want marijuana legalized; it would take the profits out."

COG first decided to go to the county board of supervisors, but "there was nothing there," according to Ryan. "Then we contacted the media. But they all write press releases for the government. Finally, we decided to go out and collect our own evidence firsthand."

The group held a "benefit boogie" in Briceland to raise money, gave each member training in "nonviolent tactics" and began holding regular Wednesday meetings at which were discussed matters such as the philosophical implications of tying pink and yellow ribbons around a video camera microphone so CAMP troopers would not mistake it for a weapon.

Denson became unofficial team leader for the Alder Point area, following the drug raiders with his driver, Frank Cieriorka, who saw political action two decades earlier during a SNCC voter registration drive in Mississippi.

The group saturated southern Humboldt with its "See CAMP, Call COG" leaflets, and "the response was tremendous," said Denson. "When the first convoy came over the hill toward Alder Point, I got seven calls before they reached the mill. I heard when they left town, when they made the top of the hill, every mile of the way."

Going in after the raiders, the first thing you usually saw was "the women and children coming out of wherever CAMP was hitting," Denson said. CAMP set up roadblocks that stopped most of the COG teams far from the scene of a raid, but sometimes the watchdogs got as close as the helicopter landing zone. At Honeydew, a COG team that approached the site of a raid became their own evidence after they were surrounded by ten uniformed men with drawn guns, body searched, photographed and threatened with arrest if they failed to provide ID.

In September of 1985, almost a year after Judge Aguilar's injunction; COG introduced evidence that CAMP was violating it. After arguments from both sides, Aguilar agreed with the people of southern Humboldt that it would be necessary to appoint a court monitor to accompany CAMP on its future forays into the countryside. Minutes after the judge read his order, Bill Ruzzamenti told reporters that CAMP just might not come back to Humboldt County in 1986. "There's too much bureaucracy," he said.

"I guess that means us," said a smiling Ed Denson.

The anger that had set him off the year before was mostly spent. What was left behind was a bemused but cautious scorn for "the other side." After an entire summer in pursuit of CAMP, the emblematic event remained the raid on Rancho Sequoia. Following phone reports that morning, Denson and the Alder Point team were unable to locate CAMP but found the Rancho's residents huddled behind a gate. Just up the road, the COG car stopped when someone spotted a document tied with a red ribbon and wedged in a fence. It was a photocopy of an aerial photograph of the area, which showed two rows of dots in a clearing surrounded by trees. Denson assumed the dots were marijuana plants. Attached to the photocopy was a "substantiating statement" filed by a CAMP officer who said that he had heard there were four "redeye missiles" (heat-seeking rockets used in Vietnam) in the area. "We investigated," Denson recalled, "and it turned out that the CAMP guy had been hanging out undercover in one of the bars here, where he heard several people talking about Red Eyes. It was the name of the local softball team."

VIII.
Arts and Letters

The Best Books, 1976-1986

T HE PAST DECADE of literary life in California has been no less sprawling, contradictory and diverse than the state itself. Major changes have
taken place in publishing, bookselling and writing that reflect shifts in
economics and in reading habits that have occurred statewide since the
mid-seventies. Some literary institutions and traditions have taken root, and
there is an uncomfortable self-consciousness about them. Most strikingly, a
distinctive literary movement has emerged that promises to take on more
significance in the coming years: we are witnessing the rise of California
Realism.

Actually, the movement toward California Realism has been evolving for
more than ten years, but it has only recently taken coherent shape. Very
simply, this is a trend toward the use of extreme or bizarre real events and
characters in the service of fiction. Nothing so new about that. But the
realities of certain areas of California life, when reported in journalistic
detail, provide an unusual setting for fiction. What qualifies California
Realism as a special literary category is the unique social and geographic
environment in which the California Realists are writing. If we designed a set
of uniform editions for these writers using David Hockney's pool paintings
for jackets, you would see what I mean immediately.

The unlikely triumvirate of Joan Didion, Joseph Wambaugh and Herbert
Gold is at the center of this movement, and each—in his or her way—has
strongly influenced a new generation of California writers. John Sacret
Young's debut, *The Weather Tomorrow* is a novel about two blue-collar
losers pawing through the wreckage of their lives in L.A. bars, with ex-wives
and children strewn everywhere. The sex and violence that permeate this
book of course echo Nathanael West and Raymond Chandler, but there is a
resonance of familiar themes which connect with contemporary literature—
Norman Mailer's flawed masterpiece *The Deer Park;* Thomas Sanchez's
Zoot-Suit Murders; the short stories of Ray Bradbury and Harlan Ellison;
Gavin Lambert's *Inside Daisy Glover;* and, most sharply and directly, the
works of Didion and Wambaugh.

T. Coraghessan Boyle's *Budding Prospects* is also in the mode of
California Realism, jumping off from the strange tale of an actual marijuana
farm in Northern California into what Boyle calls a pastoral novel with

tongue in cheek. Although an exercise in various literary approaches, his marvelous collection of short stories, *Greasy Lake and Other Stories,* fits our thesis, too. Rudolph Wurlitzer's *Slow Fade* is a send-up of the Hollywood novel played out against a collage of real and mythological events which define today's movie business norms. Wurlitzer incorporates the sense of "extended tolerance" in California that requires a cool acceptance of not only social and economic differences, but of downright psychotic behavior.

Kem Nunn's *Tapping the Source,* which was nominated for an American Book Award, is a parallel send-up of the Ross MacDonald detective novel, but Nunn reaches into California Realism for a grotesque cast of surfers, bikers and devil worshipers in Manhattan Beach to give a terrifying edge of true-to-life tragedy. And, most recently, Bret Easton Ellis's *Less Than Zero* takes us on a tour of those sixties favorites—sex, drugs and rock 'n' roll—as performed by aimless rich teenagers in Beverly Hills. Sections of it are so clearly influenced by Didion that they might be mistaken for one of her nonfiction reports on the strange cutting edges of California. Ellis is a gifted young stylist whose knowledge of the teen scene and willingness to exploit it to its most shocking extremes places him squarely in the flow of California Realism.

Didion's *Play It as It Lays,* published in 1970, is one of the first easily identifiable works of California Realism. It is a novel that was influenced strongly by the New Journalism. (Tom Wolfe's *Electric Kool-Aid Acid Test* was, of course, an early model.) In the books that have followed, Didion has woven the astonishing personal journalism of *The White Album* (1979) into novels such as *A Book of Common Prayer* and, most recently, *Democracy.* Her husband, John Gregory Dunne, has carved a parallel course in his books *Vegas: A Memoir of a Dark Season, True Confessions* and *Dutch Shea, Jr.* In the latter novel, he used the autopsy report on Eula Love, the black woman who was shot by police officers, a report he read in the process of writing a nonfiction article for this magazine.

Joseph Wambaugh's literary career began in 1971 with a novel so full of realistic detail about the lives of Los policemen that he was almost fired from the force. But *The New Centurions* was nothing compared with what has followed. *The Choirboys, The Glitter Dome, The Black Marble* and *The Delta Star* have each taken progressively more graphic examples of California cop life and used them to examine the private psychological tortures of people who confront life and death situations every day. Wambaugh, like Didion and Gold, has alternated between fiction and nonfiction—and as with the books of those other California Realists, only the fact checkers can tell which is which.

His two most recent books, *Lines and Shadows* and *The Secrets of Harry*

Bright—nonfiction and fiction, respectively—are quintessential California Realism. The John Wayne shoot-outs in the border canyons of San Ysidro appear no more real than the murderous desert chimeras of Palm Springs motorcycle gangs, yet both are California scenes stagelit to show us aspects of the human condition from a special perspective.

Since Herbert Gold arrived in San Francisco in 1960 with the wide-eyed awe of a kid from Cleveland, he has been telling tales of the heart, love stories with a universality which reaches far beyond the Rockies. *He-She, Waiting for Cordelia* and *True Love*, stories which touch us all, are placed in the sharp relief of unusual surroundings. His novels are peopled with San Francisco transvestites, hookers, hippies, drug addicts and rock musicians. In his 1981 collection of essays, *A Walk on the West Side: California on the Brink,* he goes out on a blind date in his middle age and finds some woman assuring him over dinner: "I lubricate normally." In *Swiftie the Magician* he casually offers a metaphor that is pure California Realism: "I believe sadness is my power. It's what I ride. On top of chronic subacute melancholy I spin like a surfer, like my friend Rodney the Closet Queen, who goes out to Malibu and rides the waves, pummeling himself with sun and salt, bleached yellow in the head, humming at the beautiful boys, *Mman, a nice one,* but not making it with anyone; flinging himself on the fiberglass, beating his lambflesh against the polluted Pacific."

The last ten years have given us a shelf full of memorable books with distinctive shared characteristics. Whether or not this perceived coherence of California Realism will continue to develop, only time—and literary history—will tell. Happily, as our writers have begun to carve a regional identity, the climate for publishing, bookselling, and plain old reading has grown increasingly sunny during the decade.

Of course, on the publishing scene, there is no challenge to New York dominance, but California imprints have found expanding prosperity. In 1982 Harcourt Brace Jovanovich became the first publisher in history to migrate from Manhattan to San Diego, thus proving that you can edit in the sunshine. Harper and Row still maintains its editorially independent San Francisco division. North Point Press in Berkeley is succeeding with classy books published in quality editions, best represented by Evan Connell's award-winning *Son of the Morning Star.* Hundreds of small presses such as Ten Speed, Black Sparrow, Capra, Celestial Arts and Chronicle Books continue to demonstrate that *The Whole Earth Catalog* was not an isolated phenomenon. Pinnacle Books came and went; Andrew Hoyem's Arion Press in San Francisco has given a new life to limited edition fine publishing; Jeremy P. Tarcher Inc. sold itself to Houghton Mifflin and bought itself back; the University of California Press has developed into one of the first-rate academic presses in the nation; and Price/Stern/Sloan, which started small, is now a $30 million company.

In 1976 California was regarded as a marginal bookselling market— "surfers and hippies don't read" was the common wisdom along Madison Avenue. Largely due to the rise of three major bookselling chains, California has become the biggest bookselling market in the nation. According to the most recent Department of Commerce city rankings, Los Angeles is the number two market (yes, New York is number one), San Francisco/Oakland is number four, San Jose is number nine and San Diego is number eighteen. For many readers, the concomitant disappearance of beloved independent bookstores throughout the state was not worth the big sales figures. But the pleasures of City Lights in San Francisco, Cody's in Berkeley, John Cole's in La Jolla, Acres of Books in Long Beach, Fahrenheit 451 in Laguna Beach, Rizzoli's in Costa Mesa, Zeitlin and Ver Brugge in West Hollywood, Hunter's in Beverly Hills, Book City in Hollywood and Chatterton's in the Silver Lake area of L.A. are still there, and more valuable to their customers than any discount Crown might offer.

OTHER LITERARY INSTITUTIONS have established themselves in California over the past ten years. The Santa Barbara Writers Conference started as a local weekend entertainment and has become a weeklong conclave that attracts students and major authors from all over. Similar gatherings at Squaw Valley, Loyola Marymount University, and UC San Diego make California a summertime mecca for aspiring writers. The Stanford Publishing Course, which grew out of the Stanford Writing Conference, now rivals the Radcliffe Publishing Procedures Course as an opportunity to survey the basics of publishing. And who could forget the Imitation Hemingway Competition sponsored by Harry's Bar and American Grill in Century City? (In the spirit of city rivalry, the Washington Square Bar and Grill in San Francisco has been threatening to sponsor an Imitation Alice B. Toklas contest this year.)

The dawning of cultural consciousness, if not pride, has manifested itself during the past decade in several publications. Most notably, Kevin Starr published *Inventing the Dream: California Through the Progressive Era*, the second volume in his projected five-volume cultural history of California. His first volume, *Americans and the California Dream, 1850-1915*, dealt primarily with the growth of Northern California, and in this second installment he chronicles the birth of Los Angeles. James D. Hart, editor of *The Oxford Companion to American Literature*, wrote *A Companion to California* for Oxford University Press in 1978, providing a useful reference that will be reissued in an enlarged and updated edition in the next few years. Stoddard Martin offered a scholarly analysis of our literary history in *California*

Writers, which concentrates on Jack London, John Steinbeck, Dashiell Hammett and Raymond Chandler.

There is a sadness to reviewing the past ten years of literary life in California, because we lost so many vital figures in those years: Henry Miller, Ken Millar (better known as Ross MaDonald), William Saroyan, Kenneth Rexroth, *L.A. Times* literary critic Robert Kirsch, Richard Brautigan, Dalton Trumbo, Tommy Thompson, Robert Nathan, Leonard Wibberley and Bernard Wolfe—to name but a few.

As a counterpoint to the roster of the deceased, California also produced some of the best first novels of the past ten years. In addition to those by Young, Boyle, Nunn and Ellis, the surprise sensation of the 1984 American Book Awards was the selection of seventy-four-year-old Harriet Doerr of Pasadena as the winner of the $10,000 prize for the best first work of fiction. Her novel, *Stones for Ibarra*, is an elegantly told story of a middle-aged couple from California who moves to a tiny village in Mexico in the romantic hope of reviving a family-owned, abandoned copper mine. When her husband dies of cancer, Sara Everton comes to grips with her own life in a moving philosophical lesson learned from the simple Mexican people of the town.

California readers have a lot more to talk about—and to read—than they did ten years ago. No doubt in another ten years we'll have a West Coast branch of Elaine's.

KENNETH TURAN

The Best Movies, 1976-86

TEN YEARS AGO, Rocky was a fuzzy idea in Sylvester Stallone's head instead of an overinflated ego monster who refuses to go away. Ten years ago, Francis Coppola was the most promising American director since Orson Welles; now he's just another scrambler trying to recover from four flubs in a row. Ten years ago, precious few outside of their immediate families had heard of Pia Zadora, Bo Derek or Rob Lowe; now it's hard to avoid them. Is this progress? What do you think?

Ever since the Babylonians (or was it the Mayans; would you believe the Hindus?) invented the zero, ten years has been a convenient vantage point, a scenic overlook from which to view the flow of passing time. Yet where the film scene is concerned, it's not a pretty picture. Sure, box-office receipts may be up (except for *Jaws*, all of the ten biggest money-makers were made in the last decade), but a lot of that is due to the ravages of inflation. And when it comes to matters of quality, there is so much wrong with the way Hollywood works it's hard to know where to begin.

The two most obvious trends of the past ten years, the slavish pandering to the teenage audience and the unprecedented VCR/cable explosion, have combined to form a pincer movement the old German high command would envy, crushing the market for serious adult films under their iron heels. It hasn't been a cabal or anything, but given the basic industry mentality of *box office über alles,* it was at the very least an accident waiting to happen.

Like a pair of tentative lovers edging toward a greater passion, Hollywood and the teenage market took a while to fully trust each other. The key, and this may come as a shock to their parents, was the absolute dependability of youth. More and more over the past ten years, executives have come to count on the fact that teens simply must go to the movies. It's a cultural rite, a chance to meet friends, to giggle and flirt and feel free of grown-ups; while adults attempt to exercise discretion, kids go and go again. In an industry where profits are everything, despite the lip service paid to antiquated ideas of quality at Academy Awards time, that's all anybody wants to hear.

Serious audiences, already irritated by long lines, sticky floors, loud-mouthed neighbors, bad projection and ever-increasing admission prices, took refuge in home video and abdicated their theatrical rights. More and more, the phrases "I'll rent the cassette" and "I'll catch it on cable" are heard around town. As a solution, however, this is seriously shortsighted, because if theatrical revenues for adult-themed films decline too far, studios will make even fewer than they do now, and those sitting patiently at home may find a longer wait than anticipated.

Under these circumstances, making a ten-best list for the past ten years may seem like a particularly Pollyannaish maneuver, the equivalent of admiring the snappy shine on the captain's buttons as the *Titanic* slowly sinks beneath the surface. It's not that worthy films weren't made over the past decade, it's that they were, if anything, less representative of the state of the film industry than the usual year-end lists are. On the other hand, just the fact that excellence surfaced at all given the obstacles inherent in the process does provide a glimmer of hope. With that in mind, I began composing an annotated list of ten, but it was not as happy a task as I'd expected. Questions of substance and value began impinging on my mind until I felt like a reluctant juror on the Nobel Prize selection committee. Sure I may have liked a particular film, but was it *important,* were its virtues enduring enough to be listed as one of the best of the decade? Finally, after an excessive amount of rumination, I decided on the following group, listed in roughly chronological order:

Annie Hall, Woody Allen's nervy, self-deprecating humor, usually a very particular taste, here hit a gratifyingly broad chord. Personal as ever, dealing in this case with aspects of his real-life interaction with costar Diane Keaton, Allen treated romance in a way that was funny wise and endearing; it's a film very much of its time yet timeless. The line about a relationship being "like a shark...it has to constantly move forward or it dies," is still a staple of late-night conversations, and the film's theme song, "Seems Like Old Times," continues to bring a tear to those caught unawares.

The *Star Wars* trilogy. What can you say about the most fiscally successful cinematic trio ever made? You could say something nasty, that *Star Wars, The Empire Strikes Back* and *Return of the Jedi,* by incontrovertibly demonstrating the awesome strength of the young adult market, were the beginning of the end for adult films. However, isn't it sweeter to remember the great Saturday matinee joy with which these pictures, especially the first one, were made, to revel in the affectionate, knockabout sensibility that still seems too good to be true? George Lucas remembered what the moviegoing experience was all about, and he enabled the rest of us to catch that same giddy wave.

The Black Stallion. Rooted in magic though movies are, it's the very quality of legerdemain, that sense of wonder, that is hardest for today's films to recapture. So what Carroll Ballard accomplished (with the crucial collaboration of cinematographer Caleb Deschanel and a high-stepping bunch of horses) is memorable not only as a classic family film but also because it evoked the openmouthed awe of fairy tales and legends. I'll always remember, the comment a friend's daughter made when she left the theater. "I don't want to hear any adult talk," she precociously snapped as her parents began the inevitable post-film analysis. "I just want to hold on to that feeling." Isn't that what moviegoing is all about?

Apocalypse Now and *The Deer Hunter.* These films share a slot not only because they both dealt with the Vietnam War but because each in its own way is seriously flawed. Francis Coppola's *Apocalypse* was an NFL highlights of a film, filled with bravura sequences that never managed to coalesce, while Michael Cimino's *Deer Hunter* was overhung with an air of portentiousness that came into fuller flower with the ill-fated *Heaven's Gate.* Still, both films were notable for their willingness to deal with a controversial subject before it was quite fashionable to do so and their attempt— Hollywoodized though it was—to do so with a modicum of emotional honesty.

The Road Warrior trilogy. A sense of cultural inferiority tends to leak from the film establishment, a willingness, even an eagerness, to concede that movies made from critically acclaimed novel's are prima facie the best work the medium is capable of. Which is out-and-out nonsense, as *Mad Max, The Road Warrior* and *Mad Max: Beyond Thunderdome* energetically prove. These are motion pictures that really move, eye-popping extravaganzas that provide an imaginative feast for the unfearing. With the possible exception of Walter Hill, whose early *Warriors* still lacks the respect it deserves, Australian director George Miller has proved to be the very best action director currently in captivity, and this is the footage that proves it.

E.T.: The Extra-Terrestrial. Director Steven Spielberg reportedly never stopped fuming because the motion picture pooh-bahs neglected to grace this with the Best Picture Oscar, but he shouldn't worry: his place in America's consciousness is secure. *E.T.* is the highest grossing film ever, and not even a man of Spielbergs skills can fool all the people all the time. Yet his picture has become such a fixture on the cultural scene that it's possible to devalue its virtues, to forget how seamlessly it joined state-of-the-art technology with old-fashioned heart-tugging warmth and theatrics (courtesy of screenwriter Melissa Mathison). This really is one for the ages.

Tootsie. Surely the most consistently funny film of the last decade, *Tootsie* is an example of the system working at peak efficiency. The natural offspring of *Some Like It Hot,* Tootsie offered a terrific star turn by Dustin Hoffman in drag, highly polished direction from Sydney Pollack, splendid supporting work from Teri Garr, Jessica Lange, Bill Murray and Pollack himself, plus a wicked script half the Writers Guild was rumored to have contributed to. But no matter, this is a project where the auteur theory gets thrown out the window and we just have to sit back and admire the well-oiled machinery of Hollywood collaboration.

Fanny and Alexander. Not Ingmar Bergman's best film, perhaps, but such a grand summation of a singular career that it's impossible to resist. Sumptuously photographed by longtime collaborator Sven Nykvist, this is one man's attempt to cram not only all he's learned about film but all he's felt about life into a single motion picture. Bergman flinches from nothing, not the horror of death nor the juicy vagaries and vulgarity of ordinary reality. Everything is welcome, everything is accepted, everything, in its own way, is loved. No film of his has ever been so warm, so understanding of human foibles. It's not a taste of life we get here but the whole cup, overflowing with the best and merriest of spirits.

Once Upon a Time in America. Sergio Leone's three hour and forty minute version (don't even think about seeing the truncated edition) is truly an epic, attempting much and achieving nearly all of what it attempts. To see it is to be captured by a dream, to be swept away by the assurance, daring and vitality of a great director capable of turning past and future, reality and imagination, into a single dazzling phantasmagoria. So consuming is Leone's virtuosity that not only don't all these hours seem too many, they almost feel too few. In these days of timid filmmakers and pygmy production heads, it's expecially gratifying to see this kind of daring in action.

Brazil. Just when you think all the inventive films have been made, that no one is ever going to do something to surprise the eye and nourish the mind, along comes this brilliant piece of political cinema, funny romantic, horrifying and unforgettable. Director Terry Gilliam has tried, with remarkable success, to work as if the gap between popular and serious cinema didn't exist, and in that hope he has in a sense brought film back to those early true believers who felt the cinema could be the world's first truly mass art form. Well, we can dream, can't we, the Sid Sheinbergs of the world notwithstanding.

Now that the list is complete, much as I admire the films on it, something about it fails to please. It feels a trifle stuffy, filled with sanctioned official choices, and it doesn't seem to have room for a whole flotilla of terrific but smaller-scale foreign films that were both satisfying and eclectic. There were *La Balance* and *Diva* from France, *Das Boot*, *Celeste* and *Taxi Zum Klo* from West Germany, *Pixote* from Brazil, *The Chant of Jimmie Blacksmith* from Australia, *Angi Vera* from Hungary, *The Long Good Friday* from England, *We All Loved Each Other So Much* from Italy, and *Sugar Cane Alley* from Martinique. These aren't just curiosities that critics perversely favor, each was a full-bodied, impressive work that could charm any audience with the nerve to forsake the star system and fend for itself.

Which brings up the other difficulty with that ten-best list: its lack of notice of what I feel is the past decade's most impressive and positive development, and that is the emergence of the American independent film. Not only are directors and writers getting increasingly adept at rounding up nonstudio financing for their films, but an entire distribution network has arisen to see that the films find their way into theaters. Since these independent featutes have not had every ounce of quirky creativity bleached and blanded out of them by fearful executives searching for an increasingly mythical lowest common denominator, they are invariably sharper and more meaningful than their mainstream colleagues. So to go along with my institutional top ten, I decided to compile a shadow top ten, films that were either independently produced or, even if studios had a hand in them, had the blessed spirit of independence about them. Again, in roughly chronological order:

Citizen's Band. Director Jonathan Demme and writer Paul Brickman created this delightfully wacky look at small-town America and the CB craze, ably assisted by star Paul Le Mat and character actor Roberts Blossom as the unpredictable Papa Thermodyne. An ill-advised name change to *Handle with Care* didn't help things at all.

Straight Time. For reasons best known to himself, star Dustin Hoffman took to publicly attacking this film even though it contains one of his most finely drawn performances as an ex-con trying to go straight. A lean, no-nonsense nonsentimental film fluidly directed by Ulu Grosbard.

The Stunt Man. In many ways the most quietly adventurous film of the last decade, directed with exquisite ambiguity by Richard Rush and starring Peter O'Toole and Steve Railsback. *The Stunt Man* is a movie that deceives not only the eye but also the mind and emotions, a joyously dishonest piece of business in which nothing is quite as it seems. Is this a dark picture with touches of wit or a witty film with overtones of darkness? Until the final sequence, it's devilishly hard to tell.

The Return of the Secaucus Seven. By showing that a film made for $60,000 could charm audiences as well as critics, *Return* marked a watershed in the American independent movement. Produced, written, directed and edited by John Sayles, this pre-*Big Chill* look at survivors of the sixties is filled with lively, unforced dialogue that is written, not put together by some committee. And what a pleasure that is.

Chilly Scenes of Winter. First released in 1979 under the atrocious *Head Over Heels* title, Joan Micklin Silver's version of the Ann Beattie novel remains for many people the quintessential protrait of the varieties of modern romance. Mary Beth Hurt and John Heard make you laugh to keep from crying.

Threshold. An unlikely subject—the emotional price open-heart surgery exacts from those who perform it and those who endure it—results in an intense film that makes its points with care and discretion. Richard Pearce directed, and James Salter provided a telling, literate script. This is a film that for once refuses to shortchange or trivialize matters of life and death.

Tender Mercies. A moving celebration of life's often neglected small favors, *Tender Mercies* absolutely resists the temptations of melodrama and hoke. Bruce Beresford directed, and Horton Foote won an Oscar for his deeply felt screenplay, as did Robert Duvall for bringing it to brilliant life.

Choose Me. Director Alan Rudolph's loose, offbeat sensibility comes into its own in a fusion of music, romance and dazzling visual style that manages to be personal as well as accessible. A la ronde-ish meditation on lonely men and women looking for love in all the wrong places, *Choose Me* is as heady and intoxicating as a glass of champagne.

Stranger than Paradise. An avant-garde comedy with a determinedly non-cinematic technique, *Paradise* revealed writer-director Jim Jarmusch to be a man of unique and powerful comic gifts. His gallery of characters, especially "don't bug me" Eva and "I am the winner" Aunt Lotte, are not to be believed.

Heartbreakers. A pair of mid-thirties best friends, played by Peter Coyote and Nick Mancuso, explore their relationships with each other and the women in their lives in contemporary L.A. Wry, sad, funny and true, *Heartbreakers* is directed with a sure touch by Bobby Roth.

Though most regular filmgoers have heard of or seen some of these films, it's unlikely that anyone but a critic has seen them all, which is really the heart of the problem. For what we have here is a failure to communicate between two groups that just might adore each other if only they were introduced. On one side you have a mass adult audience desperate for films they can relate to, feeling continually betrayed by Hollywood but fearful of experimenting with films that lack big names or million-dollar ad campaigns. On the other side are the independent filmmakers, willing to work for peanuts but hungry for audiences to look at what they've done. Forget the glare coming off of Steven Spielberg's halo, it's the possibility that these two forces might somehow find each other that's the real light at the end of the dark tunnel that is the current American film scene. Now that would truly be an ending worthy of Hollywood.

IX.
Future Prospects

On Sophistication

ADOLESCENCE IS IN turmoil these days. I mean, it's been hip to be a preppie and a cowboy and a punk and a rocker, but those are...well, yesterday's meat loaf. Consider how L.A. teens have drained their resources: we've exhausted music, fashions and lifestyles from virtually every era. So...um...what's left?

Are you ready for this? It's hip to be an adult. Now it's not hip to say "hip." It's hip to say "in vogue." What Los Angeles is witnessing is an upsurge of sophistication in its teenagers. No one "hangs out" anymore. Now we meet for tea. It's really happening. L.A. is hosting a confederacy of connoisseurs, all under eighteen.

Now look. I'll admit I've read my teenage romance novels. Said words like "gross." (How insipid.) Oh, those golden days of adolescence. Being a teenager is just not cool anymore. Being a teenager being an adult is. At this moment I shun any magazine but *Marie Claire*, films in my native tongue and food with names anyone can pronounce. In all seriousness, L.A. teens have become fascinated by fine foods, Baroque music, etiquette and Marcel Proust. Westwood is empty now; hot spots are the Music Center and restaurants dishing out nouvelle cuisine. Brunch is just cooler than "grabbing a pizza." (You can grab a pizza from the West Beach Cafe, though.) Affected? Certainly. It's like dressing up when we were six. It's extremely pretentious, but FUN, no less, to spend hours discussing Monet's years at Giverny. The only people offended by this trend are my not-so-enlightened contemporaries.

They DO NOT like my French adjectives. (Mauvais is a sublime one. Ennuyeux is, too, but I don't know how to pronounce it.) My history class cringes whenever I get called on. "Oh, God," they groan as one. "There she goes again with those lame-ass words." My words are not lame-ass, I assure you. Being sophisticated is kind of tedious sometimes, you know?

My sister isn't so hot on my criticism of her cornflakes. I, personally, find that a rather uncultured breakfast.

"Really, Jennifer," I sniff each morning. "Why don't you have a croissant like a normal person?"

"I can't. We're out of peanut butter." Really.

But it's amusing, on the other hand. And it's not only me. Rafi tells me passionately that to make pasta with anything but virgin olive oil is absolutely blasphemous. Chris tells me between puffs of his pipe how he's mad about Chanel's spring collection, but that Kenzo just curdles his cafe au lait.

So it's pretentious. "We just embrace style," Chris assures me coolly when I am tempted to stray from Lauren chintz to the T-shirt scene. "It happens, though, that to some kids culture is imported beer. How boorish." I agree.

The order for up-to-date teens in L.A. is to just "stay on top of it!" You know, seeing the exhibits at MOCA before Calendar does, knowing about films before critics do. Understanding Doonesbury. That vein. It's a blast.... I mean, it's quite exhilarating. Granted it borders on silliness sometimes (like when Chris Liu makes reservations under the name Calandre), but it is what's au courant. Mini Grace Kellys and Jean-Paul Belmondos are arriving at Ma Maison these days to dine. They don't own ghetto-blasters, they didn't see the Jacksons on tour and they can quote Camus. They're the hippest kids in L.A. How about that?

"Well," clucked one woman at L'Orangerie as Chris swept in to spend his paycheck on raspberry tarts instead of a bra for his VW. "Aren't you a little young for a meal like this?"

"Of course," Chris smiled as he pulled out my chair with Amy Vanderbilt finesse. "That's why we're here."

As for me, I still have to finish The Guermantes Way and get back to practicing exclamations of "C'est vrai!"

C'est vrai.